A 1006/2

AESTHETICS AND CRITICISM

by the same author

★

INDIANS OF THE ANDES
THEORY OF BEAUTY

AESTHETICS AND CRITICISM

by

HAROLD OSBORNE

ROUTLEDGE & KEGAN PAUL LTD
London

First published in 1955
by Routledge & Kegan Paul Limited
Broadway House, 68–74 Carter Lane
London, E.C.4
Printed in Great Britain
by T. and A. Constable Ltd.
Hopetoun Street
Edinburgh 7

Rigor of beauty is the quest. But how will you find beauty when it is locked in the mind past all remonstrance.

CONTENTS

INTRODUCTION

ergo fungar vice cotis, acutum
reddere quae ferrum valet exsors ipsa secandi.

'To judge of the poets', said Ben Jonson, 'is only the function of poets.' And in our own day Mr. T. S. Eliot has somewhere remarked that only a person who has written poetry is competent to write about poetic technique. It is an expression of the impatience which the creative artist has always felt for the impertinences of criticism and it is an impatience which has every excuse whenever the critic presumes to dictate rules and regulations to the artist, to lay down for him the aims which he should set before himself in his creative work and the means which he should adopt for the realization of those aims. As the Mexican writer on the theory of literature Señor Alfonso Reyes has very pertinently said,[1] *preceptive* criticism when it bases itself upon psychological grounds is patently futile, stultifies when it would elevate generalizations from past practice into canons for future production and when it masquerades the personal preferences of the critic as binding rules of judgement it is fraudulent.

In this book we shall be concerned not at all with that type of critical writing which professes to instruct the producer of art how to go about his job. Our study will be limited to criticism which is written for and from the point of view of the consumer. And to criticism of this sort, written by men who are not themselves creative, no exception in principle can justly be taken. For whether the artist himself is much or little concerned with the estimation in which his work is held by his public, the public is certainly justified in commenting as consumer upon the artistic wares offered for its consumption. The critic with whom we shall be concerned is one who professes to assess the relative merit of such artistic wares from the point of view of the consumer and one who sets up to instruct the lay public how to use these wares in order to obtain the most value from them.

[1] *El Deslinde: Prolegómenos a la Teoría Literaria* (Mexico, 1944).

It is not only the artist, however, who shows himself touchy about the intrusions of the non-professional into his job. The critics, too, are notoriously impatient of criticism from anyone who is not himself a producer of criticism. Should any critic therefore protest against the presumption of the present writer in setting up to comment upon the work of the critics without himself being a professional writer of criticism, we shall answer by analogy that the critic, too, is a producer of wares for public consumption and that the public is entitled as consumer to assess the value of the wares which the critic makes available to it.

The consumers of criticism fall into two classes. To one class belong all those members of the lay public who, as would-be consumers of the productions of the artists, resort to criticism for instruction in the art of appreciating works of art. To the other class belong the specialized aestheticians, who rely upon the particular judgements of the critics for the *data* upon which to found their generalizations about the nature of artistic excellence. The writer undertakes to examine literary and artistic criticism both in the rôle of the aesthetician who requires to use criticism for his philosophical purposes and as a member of the limited lay public which seeks enrichment and enjoyment through contact with works of art. He does not presume to instruct the practising critics in the exercise of their craft. But he does find it necessary to construct a 'critical philosophy' of criticism in order to demonstrate what things criticism can do and what things it cannot do; he makes bold to display the limiting conditions which the critic must accept if his writing is to be serviceable and he claims freedom to placard certain misconceptions whose prevalence voids much critical writing of relevance and profit. For like others the critic must submit to be judged by the profit that there is in his wares.

It has often been said that everyone who reads literature intelligently, everyone who looks at pictures or listens to music with understanding and enjoyment, is a critic in embryo since every response he makes involves some manifestation of individual preference, some element of comparison and some assessment of merit. According to this view of criticism the professional critic merely makes articulate and renders coherent the germinal criticism which is latent in every appreciative contact with works of art. This is an oversimplification which contains an element of truth. In essence all critical writing is an amplification of one of two elementary types of statement: either the critic says 'I like this' or he says 'this is good'. The two statements mean the same thing only if you assume a particular sort of theory about the nature of artistic excellence; according to other theories of what constitutes artistic excellence they are not identical. When

2

he makes statements of the former class, however much he may elaborate them, the critic, it is obvious, is recording autobiographical facts and not voicing judgements about the work of art which is the ostensible object of his criticism. He may give utterance to settled and proved preferences rather than to casual and wayward whims of fancy: he is still describing his own psychological make-up. He may record preferences which are or have been common to particular groups of men, and he is then writing a history of taste. But when he makes statements of the form 'this is good', he is, ostensibly at any rate, uttering an objective judgement about the work of art. Yet his statement will remain indeterminate and no more than a meaningless conglomeration of words until it is known what he means by 'good' as applied to works of art. A theory of the nature of artistic excellence is implicit in every critical assertion which is other than autobiographical record and until the theory has been made explicit the criticism is without meaning. For it is well known that there are many conflicting views about the nature of artistic excellence, and from this it follows that one man will mean one thing and another man something different when each says that a work of art is good or not good. And until each man has made clear to himself and to others what he means when he applies terms of approbation and disapprobation to works of art, his critical writing will stand meaningless and therefore without profit.

The nature of beauty in that sense in which it defines the proper excellence of works of art is the central problem of philosophical aesthetics and a problem about which few aestheticians and very few critics are at all clear in their own minds. Until the theory of beauty is considerably more advanced, such criticism as is not purely autobiographical is likely, therefore, to remain indeterminate, unmeaning gibberish. And this is the dilemma of criticism which provides the excuse and the justification of the present study.

Chapter I

THE CRAFT OF CRITICISM

A work of art requires an intelligent spectator who must go beyond the pleasure of the eyes to express a judgement and to argue the reasons for what he sees.   LUCIAN

As to criticism and what we are to understand by it the writings of the critics offer us too little counsel or too much. Among critics of most standing and repute there are few who have not at one time or another propounded their own understanding of the 'true' nature and function of criticism, wherein lies the pullulation of a new philosophy. But there is no agreement among them, nor any visible trend towards agreement. The drift is, rather, away from any large congruence, and throughout the body of contemporary criticism one observes a hardening of disintegration into competing cults and rival tripudiary cliques. It is difficult indeed to find inapposite or undeserved the condemnation of Mr. T. S. Eliot, whose own contributions have in the words of Mr. F. O. Mathiessen[1] 'quietly accomplished a revolution' in the field of literary criticism, when he likens the professional critics to 'a Sunday park of contending and contentious orators, who have not even arrived at the articulation of their differences'.[2] And in like vein Sir Herbert Read somewhat less caustically rebukes: 'it is a proper complaint against literary criticism in general that it has reached no agreed definition of its boundaries, and until it does it has no serious claim to be considered as a science'.[3] So it is that upon the discords regnant between critics and critics the critics themselves sufficiently insist. But probing from outside we must reluctantly judge more harshly than they; for the root of the trouble runs deeper than a sound and lively disposition to controversy. Not only do critics dispute about matters fundamental to their craft, about the nature, the purpose and the justification of critical judgements, but there has come into our hands no single work by any one critic which professes an intelligible and consistent doctrine of criticism, and we know of no single critic whose practice is habitually in accordance with the doctrine he has

[1] *The Achievement of T. S. Eliot* (1947).
[2] *The Function of Criticism* (1923).
[3] 'The Nature of Criticism' in *Collected Essays in Literary Criticism* (1951).

5

THE CRAFT OF CRITICISM

professed. Recognizing something of this deficiency, Mr. Orlo Williams attributes it with deprecation to the practical and unphilosophical temper of the English mentality. 'We have had', he says, 'moments of pure philosophy—the moment of Locke, Berkeley and Hume, and the more modern moment of Mr. Bertrand Russell—but we have had no such moment in literary aesthetics. That is to say, we seldom find discussed at serious length the fundamental nature of the judgements upon which criticism rests.'[1] The lack is there. But he is too modest in his insularity. For while English criticsm has never been wholly averse from accepting the guidance of doctrines in vogue on the Continent, there exists no theory of criticism anywhere which can offer a solution of the dilemma in which criticism everywhere still founders. Nor is criticism of music and the visual arts more forward advanced in any degree, more stably anchored upon a proved foundation, than the criticism of literature itself.

The critics are in dispute not only about the methods which are legitimate to the conduct of their craft but about the very functions which criticism exists to fulfil; and amidst the confusion of purposes by which they are variously moved one can detect no sign or symptom of ultimate concurrence in a coherent system of cumulative and progressive knowledge. That this is so is lamentable and indubitable; that it should be so gives no occasion for surprise. For criticism has ever lacked its own philosophy, without which research must continue always inconclusive, having no touchstone of relevance nor any criterion to distinguish failure from success. And until you agree what a man is supposed to be doing you cannot agree whether he has done it well. It will be our concern to show that every formulation of doctrine, every casual remark about the critic's function, indeed every assay of practical criticism, inevitably and inescapably implies theoretical assumptions which belong to the province of aesthetics; and therefore so long as aesthetics remains inchoate, criticism must needs be muddled and confused. The critics are practical men engaged upon an ancient and venerable craft which has grown up spontaneously through the ages, taking to itself accretions of richness from many sources and moulding itself to the pattern of successive epochs. And the practitioner is not usually one to analyse successfully the theoretical foundations of his practice or to formulate sound methodology upon the basis of an elusive philosophy. Although the two impulses, the theoretical and the practical, may sometimes coinhere in one person, their disciplines are distinct and when the critics have from time to time sought to clarify the principles of their craft they have done so as amateurs, using uncriti-

[1] *Contemporary Criticism of Literature* (1924).

cally philosophical assumptions about the nature of artistic excellence and the meaning of appreciation which were neither well grounded nor compatible with each other. Philosophical analysis of the humane studies has lagged far behind the rapid development in methodology achieved by the physical sciences in recent centuries; and aesthetics lags far behind them all.[1] It is because aesthetics has crassly failed that criticism has grown up wayward and jejune, an unlit lamp to the many. Denied the discipline of a serious philosophy, practice still veers directionless as an unruddered ship beneath a night without stars.

The present enquiry is concerned with the nature and functions of criticism. Its intention is factual and empirical, not dogmatic. We shall not presume to dictate to the critics what sorts of things they should be about, what the task of criticism ought to be; but our study will more modestly be to elucidate the aims which the critics themselves profess and the purposes which are apparent in their works. We shall find that profession and performance do not invariably coincide and that in the corpus of critical writing, past and present, there can be discerned not a single unifying purpose but a variety of aims corresponding to a diversity of interests which have not hitherto been adequately differentiated or co-ordinated into a systematic whole. As the enquiry progresses we shall demonstrate that criticism of necessity uses overt or tacit assumptions which belong to the field of aesthetics, assumptions about the nature of art and beauty, about the meaning of appreciation and about the valid criteria for assessing and comparing the individual excellences of works of art. It does not lie within the province of criticism, which is a practical craft, to justify the assumptions which it takes over from aesthetics; but to the extent to which these assumptions are false, irrelevant or contradictory, criticism will result profitless and vain. It will be our concern to clarify the philosophical presuppositions which are inherent in the practice of criticism to-day and to show how and in what ways both the function and the method of criticism must inevitably be determined by the nature of the

---

[1] Mr. Clive Bell opened his once widely read book, *Art* (1914), with the words: 'It is improbable that more nonsense has been written about aesthetics than about anything else: the literature of the subject is not large enough for that. It is certain, however, that about no subject with which I am acquainted has so little been said that is at all to the purpose.' And Mr. Leo Stein, in his *A B C of Aesthetics*, said: 'The principal service of Croce to aesthetics has been to almost wipe out the subject, while leaving the word. This service is considerable, because aesthetics has been on the whole so enticing and so unprofitable that its removal from the field of practical attention was a real boon.' I would exempt from these strictures my own book, *Theory of Beauty* (1952), and very few others.

aesthetic dogmas which it adopts; and in order to do this we shall be committed to an examination of the general relations between aesthetics and criticism. So far as may be we shall avoid prejudging issues which are still open in aesthetics and we shall shun the temptation to foist our own aesthetic convictions upon critics who are indisposed to accept them. But we shall reserve only the right and the duty to castigate with every severity the massive befuddlement and obfuscation which everywhere result from an imperfect analysis of purposes, from wanton confusion among divergent practical aims, from the employment of a method and practice incompatible with theoretical professions and not least from sheer muddled thinking. Unfortunately recent advances in the science of aesthetics and the psychology of appreciation have not been marked by such conspicuous success as might make the time seem opportune for the undertaking we propose. Yet clarity of thought where no clear thought has been and discrimination of purposes where all is aimless may ultimately prove as beneficial to practice as they are laudable in intention, and there remains always some prospect that intellectual lucidity, if we can achieve it, may contribute something to enabling practical criticism gradually to become the 'simple and orderly field of beneficent activity' which it would be and is not.

Before voyaging in a field of enquiry so diffuse it is the more necessary to clarify one's terms. Yet in the case of criticism this is by no means easy to do. A definition sufficiently precise to be useful would arbitrarily exclude at the outset something of what is reputably claimed to be germane to criticism. And a definition sufficiently broad to include everything that is claimed would necessarily fail to exclude related but distinct disciplines which are by common consent held separate from criticism proper. The history of literature and art, archaeological and sociological investigation into the artistic productions of different races and epochs, psychological research into the conscious or unconscious motivations of artistic creation, biologies of artists and writers, scientific analyses of the many different techniques and conventions, important sections of acoustics, optics, semantics, that vast literature of exegesis and attribution which Saintsbury aptly named 'Critical Coscinomancy', even philosophical disquisitions upon the meaning of art and beauty—all these and other studies galore cover roughly and in part the same subject-matter as those works of appreciative commentation or assessment to which the name of criticism is primarily confined. And as they are not differentiated from criticism by a difference of material to be investigated, the distinction that is made must lie in the method and object of their approach to a common subject-matter. Yet it is difficult to exclude any of these kindred studies initially by definition because those works of appreciative commentary which generally go by the name of criticism always incorporate something from all or most of these other branches of study into the body of their structure. You will find no work of criticism anywhere which does not embody some art history, some biological or psychological material, some sociological moralization, some discussion of artistic techniques and conventions, some profession of aesthetic dogma, and much else surprisingly besides, all usually introduced with a suasive purpose in order to convince the reader that the critic's assessments of the works of art he discusses should be his. It is certain at any rate that if one were to exclude all these distinct but related studies from the province of criticism, there would be little indeed of criticism left upon which to discourse. It will therefore be necessary to a full understanding of criticism to elaborate the uses which these various related kinds of writing about literature and the arts can have, and the uses which they can not have, when incorporated into the structure of criticism proper.

Since, then, criticism is differentiated from a number of kindred studies which it partially incorporates into itself not by a difference of subject-matter but, if at all, by a difference of interest and purpose, it is clear that criticism can only be defined in terms of function. We can only agree about a definition which would discriminate criticism from, say, the history of art when we can agree about the true nature and function of criticism. Nor do any summary definitions which have been offered serve to short-circuit this conclusion. If we take Mr. T. S. Eliot's 'the commentation and exposition of works of art by means of written words',[1] we are at once bogged down in controversy over the meanings to be attached to 'commentation' and 'exposition'. Mr. Eliot, for example, will have nothing to do with interpretation. 'There is a large part of critical writing which consists in "interpreting" an author, a work. . . . But it is fairly certain that "interpretation" (I am not touching upon the acrostic element in literature) is only legitimate when it is not interpretation at all, but merely putting the reader in possession of facts which he would otherwise have missed.' Mr. Donald A. Stauffer, on the contrary, in common with many other writers on the nature of criticism, holds that interpretation is one of its main functions. 'Every critic', he says, 'is an individual who proposes to act as an interpreter and a systematizer.' As interpretation, 'the intent of all good criticism is in some way to ameliorate the relations between art and its audience'.[2] The difference here seems to

[1] Op. cit.   [2] Introduction to *The Intent of the Critic* (1941).

reside in the meaning each writer has attached to the word 'interpretation', which neither has troubled clearly to define. For Mr. Eliot says elsewhere in the same essay: 'Criticism must always profess an end in view, which, roughly speaking, appears to be the elucidation of works of art and the correction of taste.' Although there are certainly differences between the ideas of criticism which the two men are concerned to expound, they would seem at any rate to agree at least to the view that it belongs to the proper function of criticism to facilitate in others the appreciation of literature and the arts; the phrases they use, 'correction of taste' and 'to ameliorate the relations between art and its audience', are sufficiently close in a genre of writing given to vagueness and imprecision. Nor from the context of the two essays is it possible to gather what precise difference, if any, is to be attached to Mr. Stauffer's 'interpretation' and Mr. Eliot's 'elucidation'. Yet if we are to understand the critic's views of the function of criticism, such undefined differences of opinion between prominent writers on the subject are clearly important. Or again if we take the broader definition offered in passing by Dr. F. R. Leavis, who says that 'what (literary) criticism undertakes is the profitable discussion of litera-ture',[1] we must put a very special and unusual meaning upon the word 'profitable' in order for this description of criticism to exclude the history of art and various other related types of discussion. The long and short of it is that no agreed definition of criticism is possible until critics have agreed about the function and purpose of criticism. And the first step towards such an agreement would seem to be an attempt to reach a clearer distinction between those differences which are genuinely about the function for which criticism exists and those differences which are about the most appropriate methods of fulfilling a function that is agreed. Confusion between these two sources of difference is still everywhere rife and it seems possible that were this source of confusion cleared away, genuine differences about the critic's true function might become more manageable than they now appear.

The matter is further complicated by the fact that contemporary criti-cism is divided into various schools which mildly or acrimoniously main-tain that criticism as such should approximate more closely than it now does to one or the other of its related disciplines.[2] There are those who,

[1] *Revaluation* (1936), p. 9.
[2] A striking illustration of this tendency to segregation is afforded by a sym-posium entitled *The Intention of the Critic*, which was published in the United States of America in 1941 and to which four prominent literary critics contributed essays setting forth the views of four divergent schools of criticism.

obsessed with the truism that literature and art are—like all other products
of human activity—a natural outcome of social forces, believe that they
can be understood only and completely by regarding them as resultants
of the varying social and economic conditions in which their makers have
lived and worked. There results the *sociological school*, which maintains that
criticism can and should 'explain' individual art products by relating their
manifold forms and styles to changes in the social milieu—a conception of
criticism which, when carried to extremes as was done under the influence
of Taine, causes criticism to become absorbed into sociology.[1] Among
contemporaries, for example, Mr. Edmund Wilson, writing in the sym-
posium referred to, would have criticism retain a broadly historical bias,
though admitting that emotional reaction is the critic's sole 'divining-rod'
to discriminate what is good and what is bad among the works of art he
criticizes. And Lionello Venturi, influenced by the writings of Croce,
argued in his *History of Art Criticism* (Eng. Trans. 1936) for the identity
between art criticism and art history, while in the Preface to his *Modern
Painters* (Eng. Trans. 1947) he wrote: 'An attempt has been made to
identify art-criticism and art-history; that is to say, no judgement has been
expressed which is not at the same time historically justified, and no information imparted whose purpose is not the justification of the judgement. In other terms, history is here understood as the representation of
an activity of the spirit—art—understood as the dialectic between those
historical conditions and the creative imagination of single personalities.'
Then there is the *psychological school*, which aspires to render criticism
more 'scientific' by an increased application of psychological knowledge
to its problems. And this school is itself divided into two groups, one of
which would 'explain' works of art from a complete knowledge of the
psychology of the artist, precisely as the sociological critic 'explains' them
as the products of the environmental conditions and the social climate in
which the artist lives and moves, while the other finds more attractive

[1] The danger is apparent in the following remarks from *The Social History of
Art* by Arnold Hauser (1951). 'One may, indeed one must, be content to establish
a correspondence between the history of style and the history of labour organization; it is idle to enquire which of the two is primary and which secondary.'
(Vol. 1, p. 252.) And: 'The new artistic culture of the Renaissance first appears on
the scene in Italy because this country also has a lead over the West in economic
and social matters, because the revival of economic life starts here, the financial and
transport facilities of the crusades are organized from here, free competition first
develops here, etc., etc.' For obvious reasons the temptation to exaggerate the
sociological element is even stronger in literary criticism than in criticism of the
visual arts.

psychological investigation of the processes of appreciation. Of the former group, Sainte-Beuve was the great idealist, while Mr. I. A. Richards has more recently done valuable spade-work for the latter. Sir Herbert Read, while repudiating the desire to make the psychological method in criticism its only method, has recorded that it has long been his tendency to give to his own literary criticism an increasingly psychological direction.[1] In his essay 'In Defence of Shelley',[2] however, he went further in the dogmatic support of psychological and sociological criticism both, when he wrote: 'The only kind of criticism which is basic, and therefore complementary not only to literary but also to ethical, theological and every other kind of ideological criticism, is ontogenetic criticism, by which I mean criticism which traces the origins of the work of art in the psychology of the individual and in the economic structure of society.' As writers conforming to these schools of thought would have it the duty of criticism to 'explain' the products of art and literature in terms of cause and effect by tracing their origin in accordance with general psychological or sociological laws from the known mentality of their makers or from the pattern of the society and age in which they were made, so there is another and apparently contradictory school which would estimate the value or the excellence of works of art (for writers of this shade of opinion almost invariably identify 'value' and 'excellence' when speaking of literature and art) in terms of their effects. Mr. Middleton Murry, Mr. I. A. Richards, the so-called Neo-Humanists such as Irving Babbitt and Norman Foerster, opposed as they are in many essentials, agree in this with a host of writers difficult to classify, that all in their various ways are interested in the ethical or quasi-ethical influences exerted by works of art and literature upon the individual or society and all in their different terminologies maintain that it is a primary function of criticism to assess and grade works of art in terms of the influences which they exert.[3] In contradistinction to both these main groups there have been many critics of the highest repute, such as Sir Roger Fry, Mr. Clive Bell and among contemporary literary

---

[1] Introduction to *Collected Essays in Literary Criticism* (1951).

[2] 1936.

[3] *Prima facie* the sociological and psychological schools, while attracted by the ideal of a 'scientific' criticism, would seem to fall down on the fact that no sociological or psychological knowledge is yet available, or seems very likely to be discovered, which could explain why one man is a creator of works of art while others appreciate without ability to create, or why one man creates well and another badly. The latter group on the other hand inevitably introduces ethical standards into critical assessment and so ultimately absorbs criticism into the wider sphere of applied morals. But of this more later.

critics Mr. John Crowe Ransom, who, each in his own way, have held that it is the job of criticism to evaluate individual works of art by a specifically 'aesthetic' standard which is applicable in no other sphere.

While these are perhaps in broad outline the most important and vociferous schools to-day, conflict of opinion is by no means limited to the differences among them. English criticism has long been reft by a controversy representing the clash between two opposed attitudes of mind and personality rather than two schools of logical thought, with Mr. Middleton Murry as protagonist on the one side and Mr. T. S. Eliot on the other, the former maintaining that the critic responds to works of art by intuitive reactions broadly moral in character and that he should adjudicate upon them in accordance with these spontaneous intuitions, while Mr. T. S. Eliot is as passionately sure that the critic's work of assessment is more reasoned and deliberate, evaluating the heritage of literature and art in terms of impersonal standards concreted in tradition. There are, too, many deviationists whose importance can by no means be neglected. Mr. W. H. Auden, if I understand him aright, would have the critic a kind of social reformer and educationalist, whose function is to work within his specialized sphere for a progressive catholicization of understanding.[1] Not that the pedagogic conception of the critic's function is by any means novel. In 1897 Mr. J. M. Robertson wrote: 'We are finally led to describe and define criticism in general and in particular as simply a way of teaching, a means of propaganda, a method of trying to persuade other people to think as we do.' It is a view which is in no way alien to the outlook of contemporary critics, though few perhaps espouse it with the zealotism of Auden. Of an opposite temper are the many writers of criticism who aspire to do little more than to record their own preferences and enjoyments in an engaging and seductive way. Such, for instance, was Saintsbury's criticism, which is described by Mr. Edmund Wilson as 'a record of fastidious enjoyment'. And Sir Herbert Read gives his blessing to criticism of this type also when, in the Introduction to his *Collected Essays in Literary Criticism*, he speaks of 'a more indulgent activity which deserves the name of criticism' and describes it as a 'certain exchange of appreciative gestures which is part of the civilised behaviour of a society'. There are others again who prefer to concentrate upon analysis of the formal and technical aspects of art, expounding influences and demonstrating the development of styles and conventions. English literary criticism until Coleridge was often mainly a matter of the application to individual

[1] E.g. the essay 'Criticism in a Mass Society' contributed to *The Intent of the Critic* (1941).

works of sharply defined standards which are to-day recognized to be local and evanescent conventions, and although this method of criticism is now widely repudiated, it still creeps insinuatingly into the practice of much contemporary writing.

Amidst so bewildering variety of theory and practice it is difficult indeed to find a path. And the task is not made easier by the fact that few critics profess their adherence clearly and unambiguously to any one of the main schools of thought which we have logically distinguished, the greater part betraying but a bias and a predilection in two or more directions with an emphasis that varies with each occasion. Unlike the critics themselves, however, it will not be our concern to argue that any one type of writing is alone 'true' criticism or 'deserves the name of criticism', for that is merely to quibble about the use of a name and brings with it no increment of fact or comprehension. Our quest will be to uncover some hidden core of agreement, if such there be, and to expose common and tacit assumptions about the nature of criticism which are rarely articulate but still lurk unrecognized beneath the clamour of controversy. Nor is this pretention so rash as it might seem. For when a writer professes his allegiance to a psychological, an historical, a sociological or any other method of criticism, and more particularly when critics argue together about which of the various methods is the most suitable or profitable in criticism, they must share an implicit idea of the purpose for which criticism exists. Unless a critic possessed such an idea about the function which criticism should fulfil, I am unable to see what motive could induce him to choose one method as more serviceable than another; and I am certain that unless two critics assumed a common and agreed idea about the purpose of criticism, any argument between them as to which method in criticism is the more appropriate or the more useful could be nothing else than the bandying to and fro of empty words. A method can only be useful or appropriate in view of a specific purpose or function. Where there is argument about method there must be assumed agreement about function, and methodological disputes exist aplenty.

In an eclectic Introduction contributed to the symposium mentioned above, Mr. Donald A. Stauffer amid much else of minor importance points to three functions of criticism which seem to me to be as nearly unexceptionable as we are likely to find. The critic, he says, has three rôles: 'as an individual responding to the work of art, as interpreter to an audience, and finally as judge'. In the course of a fairly wide reading in the literature of criticism it has seemed to me that, beneath the disputatious ranting and the twittering, a pretty large proportion of critics have assumed—if sometimes unknowing to themselves—that something of this sort is the purpose for which the critic exists. I propose, therefore, to examine this affirmation in case this, or something like this, should provide the basis for agreement which we must seek.

First, it has certainly become fashionable of late, particularly in the United States, to insist that in order to assess works of art the critic must first appreciate them in direct experience. A typical and lengthily argued instance of this insistence will be found in *The Arts and the Art of Criticism* (1943) by Theodore Meyer Greene.[1] Now this seems to me not only true but a truism, not only empirically evident but analytically self-evident, if my understanding of the nature of a work of art and of the meaning of appreciation is at all correct. I therefore propose to take it for granted in the sequel that a critic is a man who appreciates works of art and that his profitable criticism will always be limited by his capacity for appreciation. Before valuing and before describing the critic must, in the words of Matthew Arnold, 'see the object as in itself it really is'. As Professor John Dewey has put it: 'Since the matter of esthetic criticism is the perception of esthetic objects, natural and artistic criticism is always determined by the quality of first-hand perception; obtuseness in perception can never be made good by any amount of learning, however extensive, nor any command of abstract theory, however correct.'[2]

While it has sometimes been rejected, the view that criticism necessarily involves assessment and evaluation, that it belongs to the very essence of the critic's function to order the products of literature and art into some sort of hierarchy of excellence, is treated as a matter of course by the vast majority of critics. 'The professional art critic's function', says Mr. R. H. Wilenski, 'is solely the assessment of values.'[3] Literary criticism, says Saintsbury, is 'that function of judgement which busies itself with the goodness or badness, the success or ill-success, of literature from the purely literary point of view'.[4] Dr. F. R. Leavis entitles one of his published collections of literary essays *Revaluation*. Sir Herbert Read says of the 'science' of literary criticism that it is 'valuation, by some standard, of the worth of literature'.[5] It would be pointless to multiply quotations; no one who has dipped even casually into the writings of the critics can fail to have realized that the great part assume without question that the critic is

[1] 'Criticism,' he says, agreeing with Mr. Stauffer in part, 'whether lay or professional, has three essential aspects, the re-creative (by this he means what is here and more ordinarily meant by "appreciative"), the historical, and the juridical.'
[2] *Art as Experience* (1934), p. 298.   [3] *The Study of Art* (1934), p. 167.
[4] *A History of Criticism* (1900).   [5] 'The Nature of Criticism.'

a man who is supposed to *judge* the material about which he writes and tell you how good or how bad works of art are in relation to each other.

Repudiation of axiological criticism, criticism which concerns itself with gauging worth and estimating degrees of excellence, has come mainly from those writers who have advocated a narrowly psychological, historical or sociological method in pursuit of a 'scientific' ideal of criticism. Not that it has been entirely limited to these. As early as 1885 Mr. R. G. Moulton rejected valuation in favour of the objective analysis and classification of formal properties in an argument which so great an authority on scientific method as Professor Herbert Dingle has called 'the most convincing plea for scientific criticism that has yet been uttered'.[1] 'There is thus', he says, 'an inductive literary criticism, akin in spirit and methods to the other inductive sciences, and distinct from other branches of criticism, such as the criticism of taste. This inductive criticism will entirely free itself from the judicial spirit and its comparisons of merit, which is found to have been leading criticism during half its history on to false tracks from which it has taken the other half to retrace its steps. On the contrary, inductive criticism will examine literature in the spirit of pure investigation; looking for the laws of art in the practice of artists, and treating art, like the rest of nature, as a thing of continuous development, which may thus be expected to fall, with each author and school, into varieties distinct in kind from one another, and each of which can be fully grasped only when examined with an attitude of mind adapted to the special variety without interference from without.'[2] And more recently also the valuational element in criticism has been repudiated in an 'impressionist' reaction from the dull obtuseness of purblind academic criticism, whose facile devotion to ephemeral stylistic conventions and technical standards blights the capacity for genuine appreciation and encourages that complacent obscurantism which is responsible for the initial ridicule of all that is original and creative in contemporary production. 'Criticism,' said M. Jules Lemaître, 'whatever be its pretensions, can never go beyond defining the impression which, at a given moment, is made on us by a work of art wherein the artist has himself recorded the impression he received from the world at a certain hour.' It is the view of the impressionist school of criticism that the critic, first ridding his mind of all prejudices and arbitrary canons and rules, should make appreciative contact with the work of art before him; then, eschewing judgement and putting aside all temptation to praise or blame, he is to describe the

---

[1] *Science and Literary Criticism* (1949).
[2] *Shakespeare as a Dramatic Artist* (1885).

impression made by the work of art on his own mind in untrammelled appreciation. Something akin to this was attempted experimentally by Mr. Clive Bell in *Enjoying Pictures* (1934), where he describes his method as 'that of expressing as nearly as possible my immediate experience without attempting to generalize or draw inferences'.[1]

There are, then, writers professing themselves critics who would substitute for adjudication upon the merits of works of art research into the presumed psychological or sociological 'laws' in accordance with which works of art come into being, classification of works of art into stylistic types, bare historical recording of what has occurred in the field of artistic production or autobiographical reporting of the effects exercised by works of art upon the critic. All these studies are undoubtedly profitable, directly or indirectly, to anyone who is interested in artistic achievement—including those professing critics who regard the assessment of artistic merit as the culminating point in the critic's job. But profitable though they may be in their various results, I believe that all conceptions of criticism which would rid it of valuation and eliminate from it all adjudication upon comparative worth are not only false but demonstrably false in that they are necessarily inconsistent with themselves. The demonstration does not of course take the form of a logical argument showing that the extrusion of valuation is incompatible with some 'true' meaning of criticism known in advance, for this would be to argue merely about the conventional significance of words; and if anyone cared to write about literature

---

[1] The importance of fixing the critic's own emotional experience in commerce with the object of criticism was very much in the mind of Walter Pater (though he never limited the function of criticism to describing that experience). His characteristic preoccupation comes out clearly in the following passage from the Preface to *The Renaissance*: 'What is this song or picture, this engaging personality presented in life or in a book, *to me*? What effect does it really produce on me? Does it give me pleasure? and if so, what sort of degree of pleasure?' You have only to isolate this and you have impressionistic criticism. With it may be contrasted Arnold's characterization of Clough: 'he possessed these two invaluable literary qualities—a true sense for his object of study, and a single hearted care for it. . . . In the study of art, poetry, or philosophy, he had the most undivided and disinterested love for his object in itself, the greatest aversion to mixing up with it anything accidental or personal.' Here you have in germ the two ideals of descriptive criticism—description of the subjective impressions made by the object on the critic (and so, to the extent that the critic is 'normal', upon all competent observers) and objective. The two ideals are conveniently summed up in Arnold's phrase 'to see the object as in itself it really is' and Pater's retort that in order to see the object as it really is one must first know one's own impression as it really is. Of course, neither Arnold nor Pater in fact eschewed judgement and evaluation in their criticism.

and art without making judgements of merit, and if he cared to call his writing 'criticism', he has as much right to do so as the next man. Rather the attempt to divorce criticism from the element of valuation can be shown to be invalid because no known criticism, not excluding the critical writings of those who have claimed to do so, has succeeded in eliminating valuation and because the very notion of a non-valuing criticism, when its implications are fully understood, will appear both impossible of execution and extravagantly ridiculous to contemplate.

Works of art, that is those things which are commonly recognized as works of art in ordinary speech, belong to a special class of man-made objects which we call artefacts. All works of art are artefacts, but not all artefacts are works of art. There is much writing which is not literature, there exists building which makes no claim to be architecture and not all pictorial products make pretentions to be art. And criticism, whether it be frankly valuational or supposititiously non-valuational, is recognized by all to be concerned only and specifically with literature and art. Now it will be our contention that works of art, 'aesthetic objects' as they are sometimes more formally called, can be discriminated within the wider class of non-aesthetic artefacts only by their possession of some property in virtue of which they are meet objects of aesthetic appreciation and not in any other way. And we shall show, further, that when works of art are judged to be good or bad, better or worse than others, they are so judged in virtue of the same property by which they are distinguished as works of art from non-aesthetic artefacts. When a work of art is judged to be of much or little value, it is being judged to possess the property of being a meet object of aesthetic appreciation in a high or in a slight degree. Thus the recognition of any artefact as a work of art, of any piece of writing as literature, is to make a value-judgement of precisely the same sort as those estimations of comparative worth which a critic makes in arranging works of art into a hierarchy of excellence. Logically, therefore, a critic who repudiated valuation from criticism would be debarred from excluding any artefact from the scope of his research and would be bound to devote himself equally and impartially to shipping invoices and sonnets, to cathedrals and jakes, to the pictures in the National Galleries and the representations of 'wanted' criminals in the police stations. Or at the very least he would, if he were consistent with his own profession, be bound to give equal attention to every artefact which any man had produced in the intention and belief that he was creating a work of art. Needless to say, no critic has practised such catholicity of interest; and if he were to do so, his writing would no longer be recognizably criticism. We all know that there exists a very large number of very bad works of art which we and the critic agree are beneath his attention—local drawing societies and adolescent sonneteers turn them out by the thousand. But their neglect is based upon a tacit and agreed judgement of value. In the selection of an appropriate subject-matter for their study those critics who have professed to exclude valuation from criticism have always implicitly accepted and used the assessments of merit and value which are conventionally agreed among the schools of criticism which they impugn.[1] Not only do they confine their attentions to the narrow class of artefacts which are conventionally recognized as art; in practice they limit themselves no less than the critics who openly advocate valuation to what is recognized to be good or passably good art. It is not unusual and evokes no astonishment to find in works of literary criticism some commentary on the poem by William Wordsworth on Westminster Bridge, which begins:

> *Earth has not anything to show more fair:*

Yet there is no work of criticism anywhere which has devoted a single word to the more pretentious poem written by William McGonagall on London Bridge[2]:

> *As I stood upon London Bridge and viewed the mighty throng*
> *Of thousands of people in cabs and buses rapidly whirling along,*
> *All furiously driving to and fro,*
> *Up one street and down another as quick as they could go.*
>
> *Then I was struck with the discordant sounds of human voices there,*
> *Which seemed to me like wild geese cackling in the air;*
> *And the River Thames is a most beautiful sight,*
> *To see the steamers sailing upon it by day and by night.*

Yet a poem which concludes with such a tribute to the metropolis as the following from a native of a neighbouring country might be thought to have some interest for the sociological critic at least:

> *Oh! mighty City of London, you are wonderful to see,*
> *And thy beauties no doubt fills the tourist's heart with glee,*
> *But during my short stay and while wandering there,*
> *Mr. Spurgeon was the only man I heard speaking proper English I do declare.*

[1] In the selection of artists for discussion in his *Modern Painters* Venturi does not choose those who believed themselves to be greatest or those who had the widest appeal in their day, but those who are assessed most highly by the general consensus of those other art critics who do give themselves to comparative judgements.

[2] I shall perhaps be excused for quoting from my favourite bad poet.

If you are a 'valuing' critic, you may justifiably neglect this and all similar productions as unworthy of consideration. But the poet of Dundee wrote with the conscious and avowed purpose of producing great literature and, in his own opinion at least, he succeeded. 'I bow the knee', he is quoted as saying, 'to Shakespeare, but to no other poet, living or dead!' And, I submit, the complete neglect of a man who makes this sort of claim is tantamount to a value-judgement of the most extreme.

Indeed since bad works of art, i.e. those which are commonly judged to be bad, are much more abundant than good, one would expect that to sociological criticism at least they would be more interesting. The fact that 'objective' critics in practice limit themselves to much the same subject-matter as the 'valuing' critics, although they have no grounds for excluding any artefact from equal consideration, is proof that they implicitly accept the valuations which they profess to reject. And it is on this ground that we shall assume valuation to be integral to the function of criticism as it now exists.

We come now to the interpretative function of criticism, which also is very widely taken for granted among practising critics. To give but one example of an assumption which is pretty well universal, Sir Kenneth Clark writes: 'His (Leonardo da Vinci's) art, and the personality it reveals, is of universal interest, and like all great art should be re-interpreted for each generation.'[1] As has been seen already, 'interpretation' is a moot word; it all depends what you decide to mean by it. Mr. Stauffer does not leave his intention entirely obscure. He compares the critic to a 'lens through which we see'. He draws the inference that we should therefore try to be aware of his particular properties and even goes so far as to claim: 'If the critic is considered as an interpreter of the artist's work to an audience, then ideally, in order to reach an accurate appraisal, the audience should know not only all it can about the work itself, not only all it can about the artist, but also all it can about the critic and his aims.' The conclusion indubitably follows from Mr. Stauffer's conception of interpretation. But that conception is probably erroneous and certainly debateable. One would, if things were so, require critic to interpret critic without end. And within the short span of a single human life a man might well go further by direct contact with the artistic heritage that is open to him, aiding himself by the more reliable researches of the historians, than by entering upon the embattled arena of criticism. For the time being therefore I propose to leave on one side discussion of interpretation and suggest that this function of criticism is, simply, to stimulate and assist, by what-

[1] *Leonardo da Vinci* (1952 edition).

ever means, the appreciation of art and literature by others. Mr Stauffer has the phrase 'to ameliorate the relations between art and its audience'. John Dewey says: 'The function of criticism is the re-education of perception of works of art; it is an auxiliary in the process, a difficult process, of learning to see and hear.'[1] I would suggest, as the sort of neutral phrase we need at present to describe this function of criticism, that we say the critic works to 'stimulate and facilitate the appreciation of works of art by his readers'.

This function of criticism is closely linked to the valuational function, and if you admit the latter I do not think that you can well deny the former. For no critic is content to assess and arrange works of art into a system of comparative excellence without attempting to persuade his readers to accept his arrangement and his hierarchy of judgement. If he were so content, he would simply indulge in appreciation and would not trouble to write criticism, a sufficiently arduous task after all.[2] And the valuation of an aesthetic object, like an ultimate premise in logic, can be accepted either on the basis of authority or from immediate conviction and in no other way. It cannot be demonstrated by argument. So the critic who endeavours to impose his own valuations by authority puts himself in the way of direct appreciation by others and reduces the total enjoyment of art in the world. The only other path open to him is to induce his readers to accept his own valuations by conviction as the result of direct appreciation on their own part. And this he may reasonably do, for no critic would, I think, presume to influence the appreciations of other men unless he were convinced that his own assessments were in some sense better or more correct than their unaided first impressions.

Thus two functions of criticism emerge: the comparative evaluation of works of art and the stimulation and improvement of their appreciation. Though the former may in some sense seem the more fundamental, I am inclined to rate the latter as the more important, at any rate in the vast majority of published criticism. Assessing the relative excellence of works of art is a crude, hit-and-miss affair at best. You can say that one picture or poem is more beautiful—much more beautiful—than another, that one piece of music is very much finer than another; but you cannot say that it

---

[1] *Art as Experience* (1934), p. 324.

[2] We might of course take the view attributed to Dryden that the critic is the artist *manqué* and that, in the words of Mr. Middleton Murry, 'the function of criticism is primarily the function of literature itself, to provide a means of self-expression for the critic'. But even so one presumes that he will rationalize and find some other ancillary purpose in his practice than the sheer indulgence of his need to express himself.

is twice as good or three times as good. And there remains always and inevitably a very wide borderland of doubt. You can say with some assurance that the poetry of Keats is better than that of Longfellow. But to say that Keats is better than Shelley, or Shelley better than Wordsworth, verges on the meaningless unless the assessment is reduced to a number of particular judgements about various aesthetic qualities. Who would dare to dogmatize whether Vermeer or Matisse is the better painter, Brahms or Sibelius the better composer? Mr. T. S. Eliot has said: 'From time to time, every hundred years or so, it is desirable that some critic shall appear to review the past of our literature, and set the poets and the poems in a new order.'[1] With this we may wholly agree. And perhaps every critic of eminence in his craft contributes some tittle of influence towards a constant process of revaluation. But the vast mass of critical literature, while it may and should add to our understanding of, and our ability to appreciate, works of art, contributes very little to the accepted valuations in any age. Nor is it at all necessary that it should. What the critic can give of most value to his readers is a stimulation of interest, a heightening of insight and the education of his ability to make his own appreciative judgements from direct experience; what he can do of most damage is to impose the yardstick of authoritarian pronouncements in the way of direct experience. I cannot do better at this point than quote the words of Professor John Dewey, who went almost too far in the direction I have indicated but who had nevertheless a sounder conception of the uses and the dangers of criticism than many professional critics have displayed. 'Criticism', he says, 'is a search for the properties of the object that may justify the direct reaction. And yet, if the search is sincere and informed, it is not, when it is undertaken, concerned with values but with the objective properties of the object under consideration—if a painting, with its colors, lights, placings, volumes, in their relations to one another. It is a survey. The critic may or may not at the end pronounce definitely upon the total "value" of the object. If he does, his pronouncement will be more intelligent than it would otherwise have been, because his perceptive appreciation is now more instructed. But when he does sum up his judgement of the object, he will, if he is wary, do so in a way that is a summary of the outcome of his objective examination. He will realize that his assertion of "good" or "bad" in this or that degree is something the goodness or badness of which is itself to be tested by other persons in their direct perceptual commerce with the object. His criticism issues as a social document and can be checked by others to whom the same objective material is

[1] *The Use of Poetry and the Use of Criticism* (1933).

22

available. Hence the critic, if he is wise, even in making pronouncements of good and bad, of great and small in value, will lay more emphasis upon the objective traits that sustain his judgement than upon values in the sense of excellent and poor. Then his surveys may be of assistance in the direct experience of others, as a survey of a country is of help to the one who travels through it, while dicta about worth operate to limit personal experience.'[1] We would add that the exceptional critic who brings about some reorganisation in our traditional assessment of our artistic heritage does so not by the authority of his verdicts but by so influencing our sensibility that in our direct commerce with works of art we become aware of new qualities in them and from the new and fuller 'actualisation' which results new relations of comparative excellence directly emerge. Criticism as such stands or falls by its profitableness as an ancillary to direct appreciation.

[1] *Art as Experience* (1934), pp. 308-9.

Chapter II

APOLOGIA FOR AESTHETICS

Critics without the proper philosophical preparation are merely highly impressionable people. JAMES K. FEIBLEMAN

The aesthetic principle is the same in every art; only the material differs. ROBERT SCHUMANN

AESTHETICS is that branch of philosophy whose function is to investigate what is meant to be asserted when we write or talk correctly about beauty. It is concerned logically to elucidate the notion of beauty as the distinguishing feature of works of art and to propound the valid principles which underlie all aesthetic judgements.[1] It is, or should be, a branch of critical philosophy and not a 'normative' study; its object is to increase understanding within its sphere and not to lay down rules for practice. As Bernard Bosanquet has said: 'Aesthetic theory is a branch of philosophy, and exists for the sake of knowledge and not as a guide to practice.'[2] Yet in so far as every practical discipline must benefit from a candid understanding of what it is about, aesthetics has an incidental but a genuine relevance to practice and specifically to the practice of criticism. It is with these practical implications of aesthetics that we are concerned in the present volume.[3]

On the opening page of his *Principles of Literary Criticism* Mr. I. A. Richards made clear his intention to incorporate aesthetics into the job of criticism. 'And the questions which the critic seeks to answer,' he breezily tells us, 'intricate though they are, do not seem to be extraordinarily difficult. What gives the experience of reading a certain poem its value? How is this experience better than another? Why prefer this picture to that? In which ways should we listen to music so as to receive the most valuable moments? Why is one opinion about works of art not as good as

[1] Aesthetics is defined by James Sully (*Encyclopaedia Britannica*, eleventh edition) as: 'a branch of study variously defined as the philosophy or science of the beautiful, of taste, or of the fine arts'.

[2] *The History of Aesthetic* (1892).

[3] The theoretical foundations of aesthetics were discussed in my book *Theory of Beauty* (1952).

another? These are the fundamental questions which criticism is required to answer, together with such preliminary questions—What *is* a picture, a poem, a piece of music? How can experience be compared? What is value?—as may be required in order to approach these questions.' Of these questions some belong to the sphere of metaphysics (What is value?), some to the sphere of ethics (How is this experience better than another?), some to psychology (How can experience be compared?), some to aesthetics. No one of them is proper to criticism as criticism has been commonly understood. We may agree that it is indeed useful that critics should be made alive to the need for philosophical clarification of the ideas and assumptions which they everywhere and necessarily employ in their craft, and because he made articulate the vague persistent repining of criticism for coherent formulation of its principles Mr. Williams has done sound service to the profession. But methodologically it is all wrong to assign the solution of philosophical, ethical and scientific questions to a practical craft. Nor do the results of the experiment which we see suggest that profit is likely to come of this confusion of functions. While it is impossible not to accord some sympathy to any attempt of criticism to undertake on its own account the articulation of the philosophical principles which are presumed in its practice, since aesthetics has notoriously fallen down on its job, yet this confounding of practical and theoretical functions can in our opinion conduce only to added obscurantism. The only fruitful recourse seems still to be to work for a sounder discipline of critical aesthetics, closely linked indeed to practical criticism but not identified with it. It is of course possible and likely that in the exceptional case the same man may be endowed both for the work of practical appreciation and for the theoretical analysis of principles which is aesthetics; if it were not so, neither criticism nor aesthetics could well hope to progress. But it would be too much to expect that in general men trained and gifted in another direction should fortuitously succeed where the philosophers themselves have failed. As one capable literary critic has said: 'Literary criticism and philosophy seem to me to be quite distinct and different kinds of discipline.'[1] We shall, then, treat them as separate. But if any man care to combine the two, the only proviso shall be that he perform efficiently in both.

At one extreme aesthetics merges into metaphysics, and to the extent to which it is metaphysical aesthetics is profitless to practise. It is of no help to the man who aspires to live the good life if you tell him that goodness is action in accordance with the will of God unless you also offer

[1] Dr. F. R. Leavis, *The Common Pursuit* (1952), p. 212.

him an omniscient priest who knows and can interpret God's will for him. So it is of no profit to prove with Schelling that beauty is 'the Infinite presented in finite form', or with Hegel that it is 'the Idea as it shows itself to sense', unless you already have an omniscient critic who can recognize where beauty lies and infallibly detect the degree of beauty inherent in each object that is presented to sense. We do not mean to deny the value and legitimacy of such metaphysical theorization for the metaphysician. But aesthetics has suffered too much from premature speculation about the cosmic significance of beauty before anyone has understood what we mean when we talk about beauty or what criteria we may use to detect it. We shall here be concerned only with the surer if more pedestrian range of critical aesthetics.

The criticism of literature and art stands to this critical philosophy of aesthetics as casuistry stands to ethics. It is the practical application of the theoretical principles which aesthetics exists to illuminate. There can be no single judgement of practical criticism which does not involve latent doctrines of aesthetics.[1] And if your aesthetics is bad, whether it be overt or implied, your criticism cannot well evitate ultimate futility. Yet from another point of view criticism is logically prior to aesthetics. For practical appreciation of the beauties of particular things, and the judgements arising therefrom, are the ultimate and only *data* with which a theoretical study of the general principles of beauty, which is aesthetics, can work. As the student of ethics who seeks to formulate the general principles of moral goodness and obligation must base himself upon concrete verdicts of the moral judgement if his conclusions are to retain any relevance at all to reality, so there can be no valid study of aesthetics apart from concrete acts of appreciation. And philosophic aesthetics may not distort the verdicts of immediate appreciation without vitiating the foundations upon which it rests. In so far, therefore, as criticism embodies and records the concrete experience of men's appreciation of beautiful things, it is autonomous and it alone furnishes the empirical basis necessary to any theoretical study of aesthetics which shall remain rooted in the reality of things and not dissolve in a bright cloud of baseless fancy. Thus the two must venture hand in hand, though distinct. Without criticism aesthetics is nothing; in every judgement of criticism lurks implicit an aesthetic dogma.

But to be useful to aesthetics—or to itself—criticism must become coherent. In so far as criticism involves assessments of comparative worth or excellence, it is obvious that unless the critics all agree to mean the same

[1] The philosophy of art is, in the words of Professor Ducasse, 'the general theory of criticism'. *The Philosophy of Art* (1929), p. 3.

thing, and the right thing, when they formulate judgements about the goodness or badness of works of art, their pronouncements must remain a pudder of anomalous and desultory ejaculations which can have no value for aesthetics until the standards of excellence assumed by each individual critic have been articulated and the various standards by which they judge have been co-ordinated into a systematic unity. Nor is it otherwise with the more modest and pedestrian type of criticism which is description. What then does it describe? If the critic makes the obvious answer that he describes works of art, surely you will retort that a busy man's time were better spent in contact with works of art themselves, even if only in reproduction, than in reading the critic's descriptions. To justify itself, descriptive criticism must claim to be a special kind of description, such description as will be of help to others in appreciation. Descriptive criticism of the visual arts in the past was often written to offer a substitute for seeing the real thing to those of the public who were less fortunate than the writer in being able to study it at first hand. Geoffrey Tillotson very pertinently remarks of such a description written by Ruskin of Botticelli's *Crowning of the Madonna*: 'As well as to indicate his own evaluation of the object, Ruskin intended his description to serve as a second-best for those who lacked the opportunity to see the object itself; and his editors in 1906 noted how much more satisfactory is his description even than the excellent photographic reproduction which by that date they had by them.' But the increase in facilities for travel and mechanical advances in colour-reproduction have now largely cut the ground from under this function of the critic. And if it is to be of help to appreciation, the critic's description must point to features of a work of art which, though integral to a thorough appreciation, would pass unnoticed by the unpractised spectator, *aesthetic* characteristics through neglect of which, though easy for the untrained, appreciation would be emasculated; for criticism that is descriptive is useful only as an aid to appreciation, not as a substitute for it. Yet these aesthetic characteristics are not easily detected and there is no accepted descriptive vocabulary to fit them; so criticism easily swerves to the description of characteristics which works of art share with things which are not works of art, which bad works of art possess in equal measure with those which are good. And such irrelevance may turn the unwary reader's attention away from genuine appreciation to the contemplation of incidentals. The critic can avoid this snare only by knowing what he is doing; only so will he provide pure and relevant *data* for the study of aesthetics, and only so can he be sure of doing his own job efficiently by his readers.

All scientific analysis proceeds under the control of guiding ideas which both determine the nature of the analysis to be undertaken and delimit the field for analysis. A plant will be described in one way by a botanist, in another way by a chemist, in a different way by a dietetist and in still another way perhaps by a horticulturalist. A picture will be analysed in one way by an art historian, in another way by someone interested in the technical processes of its manufacture and in yet another way by a critic. The nature of the analysis to be performed by any science is determined by the whole context of knowledge pursued in each science and to this context every process of analysis must be related. Hence scientific analysis is dependent upon the theoretical furniture of the science for guidance and control. And to this extent at least criticism must and can become scientific, in the sense that its judgements and its descriptions should all be relevant to the purposes which it exists to fulfil. But to be coherent with itself criticism must be controlled within a framework of ideas supplied by aesthetics; otherwise it will remain precarious, chaotic and damaging. If by accident it were successful, there would exist no criteria by which its success could be discriminated from failure. And though there be no consciously articulated body of theoretical principles to guide and direct research, some principles are nevertheless presupposed in every act of analysis; if the theoretical ground has not been formulated and rendered pure from inconsistencies and irrelevances, practical research will incorporate all the inconsistencies and irrelevances of undisciplined popular thought. Criticism cannot be without aesthetics; if it has no sound aesthetic ground, it must work with a bad aesthetics and therefore work badly. Aesthetics to-day is the outcast of philosophy, and criticism is rejected of science. While aesthetics is often confused with the more misguided and myopic meanderings of criticism, the futility of criticism is an inevitable result of the present obnubilation of aesthetics. A different and personal theoretic, a different set of assumptions and a different combination of incompatibles is latent in the practical research of every critic. The physicist, however little he may be addicted to theory, knows by instinct and training that the emotions he experiences towards the objects of his study are irrelevant to his job. Every critic believes that his emotions are relevant and none knows how to make them significant. Aesthetics cannot progress if isolated from criticism, and criticism can hardly gain competence without a sounder basis in aesthetics. Yet if the two go in joint harness, each leaning upon the other, there seems no good reason why the aid which each might give to each should not set both firmly upon the path that leads to progress.

Although to me this adumbration of the relations in which criticism stands to aesthetics seems only plain common sense, it has not universal consent. Not only are there, as we have seen, critics who with Mr. Richards would have criticism work out its own philosophy, incorporating aesthetics into itself, but the greater part is inclined to be restive at what seems to them presumptuous and incompetent dictation from the philosophers, and not a few critics rather ostentatiously repudiate all consideration of theoretical principles from their work. It is an attitude which was anticipated by Pater, who wrote: 'Many attempts have been made by writers on art and poetry to define beauty in the abstract, to express it in the most general terms, to find a universal formula for it. The value of such attempts has most often been in the suggestive and penetrating things said by the way. Such discussions help us very little to enjoy what has been well done in art or poetry, to discriminate between what is more and what is less excellent in them, or to use words like beauty, excellence, art, poetry, with more meaning than they would otherwise have.'[1] But Pater had of course already assumed his own 'universal formula' of beauty—beauty, he was sure, was to be assessed by the degree and quality of the pleasure attending the impression which things made upon him. He was reluctant for his care-free confidence in this formula to be shaken by brutal analyses of logic.

As I believe this demurrer to be based upon a misconception—and as its effect, if well founded, would be to stultify the aim proposed in this book—I am constrained to examine it and, if possible, remove the misunderstanding which gives it currency before proceeding with my own argument. The objection has been formulated most cogently and forcefully by Dr. F. R. Leavis in the course of an essay in which he replies to a complaint of Dr. René Wellek that he did not make more explicit and defend more systematically the assumptions upon which his critical writings in *Revaluation* were based.[2] Dr. Leavis defends his procedure (in part) as follows: 'By the critic of poetry I understand the complete reader: the ideal critic is the ideal reader. . . . The critic—the reader of poetry—is indeed concerned with evaluation, but to figure him as measuring with a norm which he brings up to the object and applies from the outside is to misrepresent the process. The critic's aim is, first, to realize as sensitively and completely as possible this or that which claims his attention, and a certain valuing is implicit in the realizing. As he matures in experience of the new thing he asks, explicitly and implicitly: Where does this come?

[1] Preface to *The Renaissance* (1873).
[2] 'Literary Criticism and Philosophy' in *The Common Pursuit* (1952).

How does it stand in relation to . . .? How relatively important does it seem? And the organization into which it settles as a constituent on becoming "placed" is an organization of similarly "placed" things, things that have found their bearings with regard to one another, and not a theoretical system or a system determined by abstract considerations. No doubt (as I have admitted) a philosophic training might possibly—ideally would—make a critic surer and more penetrating in the perception of significance and relation and in judgement of value. But it is to be noted that the improvement we ask for is of the critic, as critic, and to count on it would be to count on the attainment of an arduous ideal. It would be reasonable to fear—to fear blunting of edge, blurring of focus and muddled misdirection of attention: consequences of queering one discipline with the habits of another. The business of the literary critic is to attain a peculiar completeness of response and to observe a peculiarly strict relevance in developing his response into commentary; he must be on his guard against abstracting improperly from what is in front of him and against any premature or irrelevant generalizing—of it or from it. His first concern is to enter into possession of the given poem (let us say) in its concrete fulness and his constant concern is never to lose his completeness of possession, but rather to increase it. In making value-judgements (and judgements as to significance), implicitly or explicitly, he does so out of that completeness of possession and with that fulness of response. He doesn't ask, How does this accord with these specifications of goodness in poetry?; he aims to make fully conscious and articulate the immediate sense of value that "places" the poem. . . . The cogency I hoped to achieve was to be for other readers of poetry, readers of poetry as such. I hoped, by putting in front of them, in a criticism that should keep as closely to the concrete as possible, my own developed "coherence of response", to get them to agree . . . that the map, the essential order, of English poetry seen as a whole did, when they interrogated their experience, look like that to them also. Ideally I ought perhaps . . . to be able to complete the work with a theoretical statement. But I am sure that the kind of work that I have attempted comes first, and would, for such a theoretical statement to be worth anything, have to be done first. . . . My whole effort was to work in terms of concrete judgements and particular analyses: This—doesn't it? —bears such a relation to that; this kind of thing—don't you find it so?— wears better than that,' etc.

I have quoted from this passage at some length (it is, of course, even more convincing in its entirety) because it expresses a point of view that is typical of much that is best in contemporary criticism, the point of view of a criticism which is professedly and in fact out to encourage and facilitate the appreciation of literature by others rather than to set itself up as an authoritative substitute and antidote for appreciation; and yet it seems to controvert the view which I am writing to recommend. It is necessary therefore to pin-point the differences between us and see what they amount to.

In the words I have quoted four propositions are affirmed with different degrees of iteration. Three, I believe, are largely true and one completely false. It is the intrusion of the false proposition, which seems specious only through its association with the others, that makes the rejection of explicit aesthetic principles from practical criticism at all plausible.

1. It is asserted and re-asserted that the critic is first and foremost one who actualizes[1] a work of art in his own appreciative experience, and that his criticism can have no assurance of profitableness except in so far as he has successfully and completely actualized the object upon which it is directed.

With this statement we naturally have no quarrel. From a theoretical point of view we have seen that it is a truism which needs no emphasis beyond its enunciation, though in critical writing its reiteration may serve the purposes of debate. It is nevertheless to be remembered that appreciation, though necessary, is not enough to make a good critic. Every critic must appreciate; not everyone who appreciates works of art has the qualities of a good critic.

2. It is asserted that there is danger lest the intrusion of theoretical considerations into the act of appreciation may hamper or distort the complete actualization of the work under criticism.

With this also I would agree, at least to the extent that in the actual process and act of appreciation theoretical beliefs and standards must for the most part be held in abeyance. The mechanical application of specific norms to works of art is the fault of academic criticism and seems inevitably to exert an inhibitory influence on the capacity to appreciate anything whatever. Yet in every act of appreciation norms of judgement are latent. Mr. Laurence Binyon has put the point well in the course of an essay upon the artistic ideals of the Chinese. 'To sweep the mind clear of prejudice and preoccupation is an essential condition of apprehending beauty as it really is. As an old Chinese artist complained, "People look at pictures with their ears rather than with their eyes." Not only their conscious criticism, but the impressions they allow themselves to emphasize

[1] The sense in which this word is used is explained on pp. 229 ff.

and single out, imply a theory, however imperfectly articulated. It is important, therefore, that the theory implied should at least be a serviceable one.'[1]

But the danger that theoretical understanding may be put to wrong uses is not sufficient warrant for the rejection of theory. In fact, a theory of art is *latent* in every act of appreciation, however spontaneous and direct. There is no perceptual experience, no conscious life of any sort, which is not selective, and selection involves directing the attention upon certain features, certain relations and groupings, in preference to others. Without such selective direction of attention there would be no awareness at all but only the chaotic confusion of madness. In everyday life attention is directed in accordance with unconscious practical interests; in artistic awareness it is directed by interests of another kind. In the purest act of untheoretical appreciation there lurks a rudimentary and practical notion of what sort of thing that artistic excellence is after which appreciation reaches; and this implicit notion has the makings of an explicit theory and standard of judgement. And what the critic in effect does, what every critic always and necessarily does in holding up his own concrete appreciations as analogues to his readers, is to suggest new and 'right' ways of orientating attention upon the object in appreciation. It is a commonplace of criticism that many people read the words of a poem without becoming aware of the poem, many spectators at an exhibition look at pigmented canvases without seeing the pictures. In advising his readers how to actualize works of art most effectively, how to appreciate them most fully and completely, every critic, implicitly or explicitly, invokes a theory of aesthetic beauty. The extent to which the latent theory becomes overt in exposition is largely a matter of temperament. Some are constitutionally more inclined to rely upon flashes of intuitive perception and the establishment of emotional sympathy, and they are no worse critics for that. Others find benefit from a more logical appeal to the intellect, rationalizing in terms of generalized and intelligible principles. In either case it is the result that counts. The justification of criticism, as a practical craft, is as a propaedeutic to appreciation. And it fulfils this function if by pointing out descriptively or ostensively features of works of art which otherwise might escape the notice of the unpractised observer and so by directing attention upon them it enables him to gain a fuller appreciation of the work—to see more in it, to realize more of it; then by suggesting relations of value among several works of art it invites the reader to test these

[1] *The Flight of the Dragon. An Essay on the Theory and Practice of Art in China and Japan* (1911).

relations in his own experience and to enrich his awareness of each. A critic is to be judged by the success with which he achieves this object; the method by which he does so is subsidiary.

In maintaining, therefore, that aesthetics is necessary to sound criticism we must guard against the misunderstanding of being thought to demand that every critic should be a philosopher or to hold that a grounding in aesthetic theory is a necessary part of every critic's equipment. Adverting to the apparent incongruity between his father's powers of argument and his ignorance of formal logic, Tristram Shandy remarks: 'It was a matter of just wonder with my worthy tutor and two or three fellows of that learned society that a man who knew not so much as the names of his tools should be able to work after that fashion with them.' Familiarity with formal logic is not necessary for a man to reason correctly, and knowledge of grammatical rules neither makes nor is essential to good writing. There may be good criticism without knowledge of aesthetic principles and the critic who assumes theories about the nature of aesthetic excellence implicitly in his judgements is not called upon to justify them. But if only because all the axiological vocabulary of criticism is current in a variety of different—and often contradictory—senses, it is incumbent on the critic to inform his readers what meanings he attaches to his language of praise or blame.

3. It is apparently asserted that the judgement of the comparative worth of any work of art is inherent in the concrete experience by which that work is actualized in appreciation; the critic's value-judgement, it is said, does not involve an assessment of two or more works of art by some standard or norm of excellence but is a direct formulation of an immediate *datum* of experience.

This is patently false. We admit, we have indeed emphatically demanded, that every judgement made by a critic should be directly based upon his own immediate experience of the works of art to which judgement is applied and we have maintained that the worth of a critic's judgements is dependent upon the completeness with which he has actualized the works of art in his own experience. But a judgement is not, and cannot be, the voicing of an immediate experience of appreciation; it is a later, reflective comment upon experience. Whenever two things are compared in judgement they are estimated in relation to some common property or properties which one thing is alleged to possess in greater or equal degree than another. When any one work is judged to be better than another it is always and inescapably judged to have greater value in respect of some property P which it possesses in a greater degree than that other. And all statements that a work of art is good or not good involve such comparison with some implied class of other works of art. And whenever such a judgement is made the property P is assumed to be an essential element in the excellence of works of art, a contributory factor in whatever it is that we mean by beauty. It becomes a norm or standard of criticism.[1] You may not be able to define or describe the property in words; you may be able only to point to it, to indicate it ostensively. But you are still using it as a norm and in effect you are saying: 'In my aesthetic creed there is a property P so related to beauty that anything which possesses P in a greater degree than something else is, other things being equal, more excellent as a work of art, more beautiful, than that other thing.'[2]

How far, then, is it incumbent upon the critic himself to analyse and

[1] Professor Curt John Ducasse rightly says in *The Philosophy of Art* (1929) that: 'All criticism involves reference to some character, the possession of which by the object criticized is regarded by the critic as in some way good, or the lack of it, bad. The object is then examined with regard to that character, and pronounced good or bad in the degree in which it possesses it or lacks it. Such a character so used constitutes a standard of criticism.' This is why the mere reporting of a personal preference for this or that, however firmly rooted it may be, cannot yet be regarded as criticism. As Lionello Venturi wrote in the Introduction to his *History of Art Criticism* (Engl. Trans. 1936): 'A preference in art is always a principle of art criticism. But it is criticism without a universal idea, judgement without a universal pretension; it is a tendency towards criticism, a desire for criticism, a judgement of the senses. It is not yet either art or criticism, it is a process and not a result, it is individual and may belong to a group of individuals. It is not criticism, it is *taste*.' And further: 'Neither a philological work nor an aesthetic theory nor an act of taste fully realizes art criticism. In order that it should be realized, it is necessary that it be centralized in judgement.' Or again: 'What is criticism if not a relationship between a principle of judgement and the intuition of a work of art or of an artistic personality?'

[2] It may be objected that very few of the properties in virtue of which works of art are in fact compared as to beauty can be so generalized into norms of beauty. For example, in the essay from which we have quoted, Dr. Leavis argues that the philosophic symbolism of Blake's poetry is inessential to its poetic excellence but points to the 'direct evocative power' of certain words as an integral element in that excellence. Elsewhere he invites us to admire the poetry of Donne because it reproduces the cadences of normal speech. Yet neither of these qualities could be generalized into a norm of beauty. The words of a revivalist preacher have direct evocative power but are not endowed with great artistic beauty. Neither Dr. Leavis nor any other critic would assert that all poetry should reproduce the cadences of normal speech or that it is excellent as poetry to the extent to which it does so. Yet in these two instances one accepts the rightness of Dr. Leavis's perceptions. The truth of the matter is that neither these nor any other isolable qualities are themselves either constitutive of beauty generally or constitutive of

make explicit the norms of beauty which are implicitly assumed in his every judgement about the relative worth or excellence of works of art? Dr. Leavis argues that this is the job of the philosopher, not of the critic. But in this he is indubitably wrong. For unless the critic defines his norms of judgement clearly and without ambivalence, either by verbal description or ostensively, the judgements which he utters will be strictly devoid of meaning, they will be no more than empty ejaculations. At most the reader can only surmise what meaning was intended in them.[1] Now writing which in its form and structure purports to assert meaningful propositions but is in fact ejaculatory is, I submit, bad writing. It fails in the purpose which it proposes to itself, the communication of meaningful propositions. To demand that the critic shall make his own assumptions clear is therefore simply to demand that he shall write well in his own

the specific beauty of the objects where they are detected. They become elements in the beauty of aesthetic objects only by a relation of congruence in which they stand to the organic whole which is the object in its totality. All such qualities may therefore be at some times important elements in an organic whole which is beautiful and at other times incongruous and therefore antithetical to beauty. It is a common fault of practical criticism that in assessing particular works of art it points to such qualities which in the instance under consideration are essential to its beauty but which are not always or everywhere essential or contributory to beauty; we are thus left with a large number of aesthetic properties which in some cases are indicated as prominent features in the excellence attributed to a work of art but in other cases are absent or even detrimental to excellence. And the result is confusion. Criticism should, ideally, not only indicate features which contribute prominently to the excellence of specific works of art but also indicate how they are contributory in this specific instance (but not in that) by reason of their organic relations to all the other qualities which together constitute the totality of the object.

[1] The point has been made by Professor Stephen C. Pepper: 'A thoroughly competent critic is one who has both intimate experience in the art he is judging and possession of reliable criteria of criticism. He may or may not be conscious of the grounds in which his criteria are supported, just as a man who uses a tool may or may not know how it is manufactured. With the tools of criticism, it seems best for the men who use them to know how they are made and to be able to judge if they are well made. There are too many fake instruments of criticism on the market. Yet many good critics do not seem ever to have examined the tools they use. By the chance of a good tradition or a good teacher they pick up a good investment and get good results. But the greatest critics, I think, have made an effort to examine their tools and have done something that amounted to showing their source of justification in one of the relatively adequate world hypotheses.' *The Basis of Criticism in the Arts* (1946). There is some confusion here. Justification belongs to the aesthetician or to the critic as philosopher. Clarification of premises is incumbent on every critic who would both announce judgements and speak intelligibly.

genre. It is for the philosopher to subject the practical norms assumed by the critic to theoretical analysis, to generalize them and construct them into a coherent and complete theoretical system of aesthetics. But the critic must formulate them if his sentences are to communicate meaning at all; and only so far as his practical norms of judgement are in fact coherent with each other will his judgements be consistent. Until the reader has understood what these judgements are, he can decide neither whether they are consistent with themselves nor whether from his own commerce with the works of art in question he is in agreement with them.

4. Dr. Leavis seems, finally, to wish to assert that the specifically aesthetic qualities in virtue of which works of art are compared and ordered by the critic are ineffable; they can be indicated ostensively but they cannot be analytically described in discursive language. With this we are very largely in agreement and we shall have occasion to discuss the point and its bearings upon criticism more largely later. If this is granted to be the case, however, it renders the critic's task of elucidating his norms of judgement more difficult but certainly not impossible; for what cannot be described can be displayed ostensively. In fact, the bulk of ordinary linguistic discourse depends upon such implied ostensive definition for its effectiveness as communication. When I say 'This object is red', all I am in fact communicating is that my visual experience of colour when I see this object is similar within limits to my visual experience when I see all other objects which I call 'red'. My colour-experience itself in its concrete lived *quale* is private to me and cannot be described or communicated in language. I am in fact indicating ostensively a particular characteristic of my visual experiences and saying: 'Do you not also, when in visual contact with this object, obtain an experience similar to the experience you obtain when you are in visual contact with all those other objects which we both agree in naming "red"?' But the aesthetic qualities of things to which the critic of art wishes to direct the attention of his readers are not such habitual objects of attention that they have been concreted in a single word of the language and cannot be unambiguously indicated by pronouncing a word. Nor can they be indicated by combining words into analytical sentences. Therefore their ostensive indication by pointing to a number of cases of their occurrence is the more necessary if a critic is to write intelligibly to others. Sometimes the possibility even of this ostensive definition is denied on the ground that all works of art are individual and unique; they cannot be classified or compared and by analysing them into constituent properties and attributes which they possess in common

with other works of art you destroy the uniqueness of organic unity in which their beauty resides. In a sense this also is true. And in a sense every moment of lived experience is unique and completely individual. But if you press this truth so far as to deny any profitableness to such aesthetic analysis, you are denying the validity even of ostensive definition of terms and you destroy any possibility of profitable and intelligible critical writing at all.

But more important than this, every critic who goes beyond pure description and ventures an axiological judgement about works of art, saying that this work is good and that one bad, that this is better than that in virtue of this or that characteristic, must at some time have made it clear to his readers what he means by 'good' and 'bad' whenever he applies these words to works of art. For critics do not all or always intend the same thing when they make comparative estimates of the merits of works of art. Some critics sometimes mean, when they pronounce a work of art to be good, that it is an accurate description or representation of something not itself; others mean that it stimulates certain approved emotions in themselves or other men; others mean that its moral and social effects meet with their approval; others mean that it has certain not very clearly defined formal properties in a higher or lower degree. And so on. It is not the task of the critic to *justify* whichever of these meanings he cares to adopt for the word 'good' or its cognates when he applies them to works of art; that is the function of the aesthetician, if anyone. But unless the critic is consistent in the meaning he chooses and unless he has made that meaning lucidly explicit to his readers, his criticism must necessarily remain confused and obscure.

In fact, most criticism as it is now written is, in the strict sense of the word, unintelligible. We may gather that the critic esteems this work of art above that, that he considers this one good and that one bad; but we remain in ignorance of what he intends to mean when he says that any work of art at all is good or bad. Criticism is, to this extent, no more than an autobiographical record of unexplained and unjustified preferences and prejudices. This has often been said, but the reasons why it is so, and the remedies for it, have seldom been exposed.

The clarification for which we appeal might seem to have less practical urgency were the verdicts of the critics uniform and their guidance sure—though its theoretical desirability would not even so be less. But there is not unanimity, nor even basic agreement on a fundamental scheme. It is a commonplace that most artists of outstanding originality and creative power have met lack of appreciation or abuse in their lifetime. We know that Beethoven's latest and finest works seemed to his contemporaries to be the meaningless meanderings of senility aligned with deafness, that Rembrandt's paintings were judged to be 'Gothic and crude' by the autocrats of good taste in France. We know the obloquy which the Post-Impressionist painters were required to face. Even in 1925 Cézanne was described by one American critic as 'commonplace, mediocre and a third-rate painter',[1] in 1934 his work was characterized by another as 'meagre and unfulfilled art',[2] while an English critic of some prominence has published his judgement that when you have seen one of Cézanne's indifferent pictures you have seen them all. We know the indignation which was aroused at the beginning of the century by the new enthusiasm for African sculpture. We remember the bewildered ridicule of 'modern' music—of Stravinsky and Bartók, even of Scriabin and Sibelius—which is now accepted and 'placed'. We remember the controversies aroused by D. H. Lawrence and James Joyce, the repudiation of Eliot, Pound, Auden. This is not a new thing in the history of art criticism and it has generally been the established critics who have led the vociferous opposition to the new.

It may of course be argued that the original and creative artist inevitably makes new demands upon sensibility and that response to these demands impels modification of one's habits of appreciation and consequent revision of all previous judgements of the past. Because we have learnt to see the new we now see in the old favourites what we had not seen in them before. This is of course true and is doubtless why the established critics, who are of all men most apt to become set in their appreciative habits, are inclined to oppose the most virulent resistance to the demand for such intimate personal re-adaptation. But the public not unreasonably looks to its critics, who profess themselves guides to taste and discrimination, to be leaders and not laggards in the march of progress and change. But to leave this question on one side, since it has sometimes been claimed that the critic, as distinct from the reviewer, cannot and should not be expected to assess strictly contemporary production, there is still not anything like that conformity of judgement about the art of the past which the general public who do not read the writings of criticism suppose to exist. Literary criticism has largely demolished the safe and standard scheme established by Arnold, which we still complacently absorb in school. If we read the critics, we can no more accept the old formula of English literature: glorious Shakespeare, glorious Milton, age of prose

---

[1] Royal Cortissoz, *Personalities in Art* (1925).
[2] Thomas Craven, *Modern Art* (1934). Quoted without approval by Sheldon Cheney in *Expressionism in Art* (1948).

(Pope no poet), fairly glorious Wordsworth, Keats poet on a par with Shakespeare. Not only have Eliot and Gerald Manley Hopkins arisen as new post-Arnoldian divinities, but Donne has been canonized as a new divinity from the past. Chaucer has again come into his own. Milton is in the melting-pot; Wordsworth is to find his place; Pope is often a poet; only Shakespeare remains supreme as Johnson made him. You may in fact choose any writer you like, any dozen critics you like, and you will find at least ten different assessments, while the three who rank him more or less level will do so for different reasons. That this is not exaggeration anyone who has read critical writing at all extensively will be aware. Indeed, the only thing on which the critics are apparently to any considerable extent agreed is on what to omit as being beneath their notice; and one sometimes suspects that even this seeming agreement is partly, if not primarily, due to the great concern all critics have to criticize one another's judgements.[1]

I do not want to belabour this topic excessively or to burden it with the evidence of examples, which might be made endless. No one is likely to read this book who is not already thoroughly convinced of the truth of what I say. But my point is that the public is not only unable to find in any one critic assessments based upon intelligible premises so that they are capable of verification by direct appreciative experience of others; it will not even find assessments upon which the body of criticism is itself agreed. Therefore the need for clarification of the grounds of critical judgements is doubly necessary, both in order that critics may themselves sort out their differences among themselves and that they may present to the public a coherent estimate which can be understood and judged.

Some part—perhaps a quite considerable part—of the clatter and clash of divergent critical judgements is no doubt traceable to unacknowledged differences of appreciative capacity, or sensibility, in the critics. For sensibility varies enormously from person to person, not only in degree but in range. As one man can appreciate painting but has no ear for music, so one critic has greater capacity to appreciate a certain type of painting or literature or music than another type, while some other critic will be capable of more fully appreciating the types to which the first is less sensible. From these unrecognized limitations in the degree or range of sensibility many of the conflicts of judgement among the critics derive. Such differences are inevitable and might be made beneficial if they were

---

[1] Dr. Leavis's writings are a particularly good example of this, for all his published writings are concerned with criticizing and setting right the critical judgements of other critics.

brought out into the open and one man's endowments made to complement another's limitations. But they are by no means the whole story. A
very large measure of existing discrepancy in judgement is due to latent
differences in philosophy. Various critics, after appreciating, use various
and conflicting standards for assessing the excellence of the works of art
they have appreciated and so they differ in their estimates of good and bad
because they mean different things when they say 'good' or 'bad'. It is
discrepancies of this latter type which aesthetics should either eliminate
or show clearly to be what they are. And it is this which will be our
concern.

The basic problems of aesthetics can then be reduced to two, and
because it has failed to find a solution of either its contribution to criticism
remains both nugatory and distracting. In their simplest form they are:
What is a work of art? and What is appreciation? But neither question is
as simple as it appears—or as simple as Mr. I. A. Richards, for instance,
would have us surmise.

No man can be sure of writing well if he does not know what it is
about which he writes, and the critic is no superman. Unless he knows
what is and what is not a work of art, by what criterion a work of art is
to be recognized, he has no standard of relevance; he will be at cross-
purposes with himself, like a man who is set to match colours in the dark,
and much of his writing is bound to turn out unprofitable both to criticism
and to aesthetics. It is no less certain that unless he knows what a man
is and is not doing when he appreciates a work of art, and how this
which we call appreciation differs from other states of activity or being,
the judgements and descriptions which the critic derives from his own
appreciative experience will be relevant only by accident and good luck.
His writing will in either case be fortuitous and unreliable. And those who
are to read and judge what he writes will be in the same parlous case of
unpreparedness. Yet if the critics do not know, neither have the philosophers been able to reach agreement. The answers they give when they
deign to tackle these questions are conflicting, and no definition has yet
been advanced by critic or philosopher which is not either palpably inadequate or demonstrably false. The main difference between them is that
whereas the mistakes of the philosophers are patent, those of the critics
lurk more often concealed in their tacit assumptions and their practice.

In the previous chapter we described criticism in the words of Mr.
T. S. Eliot as 'the commentation and exposition of works of art by means
of written words', and we went some way towards amplifying and clarifying this description. But we left undefined the term 'works of art'. With

this, the first of the questions mentioned above, we shall now be concerned.

The traditional method of definition in the philosophy of the humanities is to start with an abstract formulation, conjured out of empty air, which is supposed to delimit the essence or quiddity of the field of phenomena which is to be considered. The concrete manifestations in their varied and living multiplicity are then forced by persuasion or abuse into the Procrustean truckle-bed of this definition until distortion and mutilation can speciously be carried no further; the definition is then quietly cast adrift and forgotten. Of such kind are the definitions of religion, society, philosophy, beauty, which are served up by the pundits. As little profit has ever come from this method, we shall proceed in the opposite way, and starting from what is known and admitted, we shall try gradually to refine common knowledge to such precision as it will admit. The purpose of this book will therefore not be to seek *the* definition of a work of art, but to make explicit and precise the several definitions which have most commonly been tacitly employed in art criticism and to show what sort of criticism is compatible with each sort of definition. From the reactions of critics a clearer conception, and a closer agreement, both on what art is and on what criticism does could be achieved by a rigid and honest application of this method—or if not, there is no method of achieving it.

'Art', said Croce, 'is what everyone knows it is.'[1] Everyone knows indeed in a rough and ready way what is a work of art, and this common fund of knowledge will be our starting-point. We see and admire paintings which hang in public galleries and in the houses of our friends. We see sculptures in our public places and museums. Musical compositions are performed in concert halls and transmitted by wireless into our homes. There are fine buildings in our cities and relics of ancient edifices stud our countryside. Opera, ballet and drama are produced for our edification and delectation in places of entertainment. Our children are taught in school to master the milder works of literature by Shakespeare and Shaw, Kipling and Kingsley. These are the things which we mean when we speak of works on art. There may be a fringe of uncertainty, a borderland of dubiety, so that in particular instances we often find it difficult to make up our own minds or agree with others whether this or that object is 'really' a work of art or not; but the general meaning of the term is sufficiently precise for it to have currency and to be of some service at any rate in

[1] His essay, *The Essence of Aesthetic* (Eng. Trans. 1921), opens with this sentence.

common discourse. This is what we mean by art, what the critic means and what the aesthetician means. This is our starting-point. And from this, without leaving the realm of common knowledge, we may venture a first generalization, that works of art are artefacts, objects constructed in any material by consciously directed human endeavour. It is true that the phrase 'work of art' is sometimes used of natural objects, and in particular we speak of the *beauty*—which is the distinguishing feature of the excellence of works of art[1]—of natural scenes, living beings, etc. But the application of the term 'work of art' to anything other than an artefact is always a half-conscious metaphor and when the word 'beauty' is used of natural objects it has another and a different meaning from that which it bears in the discussion of works of art.

But it is also common knowledge that not all artefacts are works of art. Sewing-machines, coal-scuttles and telecommunication systems are artefacts, but they are not works of art in the sense in which the critics of art or their public use this term. We must therefore find the distinguishing feature which is implied in everyday parlance when we rank together a number of artefacts as diverse as a chorale, a sonnet and a cathedral under the common name 'works of art' and yet exclude the great majority of artefacts from this classification. Every practical man makes such a rough and ready discrimination into art and not-art. Furthermore it is the first duty of every critic to make a selection among the products of literature, painting, music, sculpture, etc., of those which are art and those which only pretend to be so, or it may be do not even pretend. Every critic does this and differs from the layman only in that the critic usually holds that what he personally prefers is art (or, as he would say, 'he finds his pleasure in art'), whereas the layman is more prone to admit that there are some things which may be art although they displease him or he finds them tedious. Such an initial selection is implicit in every work on the history, sociology, psychology or technology of the arts, for they all select among a wide class of presumptive art-objects a much narrower class of 'genuine' art about which to write.

Our question What is a work of art? therefore becomes What are those qualities which all works of art have in common and which other artefacts, including those presumptive works of art which are rejected by the critic, do not possess?

When such a characteristic or group of characteristics has been found and agreed, only then can we begin to say that this or that object is

[1] In *Theory of Beauty* (1952) I defined beauty as 'the proper excellence of a work of art' and gave sufficient reasons for adopting this linguistic convention.

'rightly' called a work of art or to discuss whether any particular artefact is or is not a work of art. Many characteristics have been proposed as the distinguishable feature of works of art in the definitions of beauty which litter the literature of aesthetics and criticism. None of them is intrinsically right or intrinsically wrong; for all that such definitions do is to propose certain habits of language, and linguistic usages are not right or wrong but simply more or less customary, more or less useful and convenient. You can say that the connotation given by a certain writer to the term 'work of art' is not conformable with general usage, but you cannot say that it is wrong. What you must demand, however, is that each one abides consistently in whatever linguistic conventions he decides to adopt and also that he makes quite clear to his readers the conventions he is using. If any writer—critic or aesthetician—points to a certain characteristic of things and says 'this shall be the determining feature by which in my language those artefacts which are to be called "works of art" will be discriminated from those artefacts which are not to be so called', he has given a specific connotation to the term 'work of art' and in his subsequent use of vocabulary he is bound to denote by the term 'work of art' all those things, and only those things, which he admits to possess the characteristic to which he has pointed. If, then, in his subsequent writing he applies the name 'art' to any artefact which he admits to be without this characteristic, or denies that any artefact which has this characteristic is art, his use of language is incoherent, his writing becomes nonsense, and neither we nor he can be sure of the meaning intended by any sentence which he writes.

It is by this standard alone that definitions of beauty should be accepted or rejected and practical criticism is first to be criticized by this standard; for except it conform to the requirements here indicated, it is strictly writing without meaning.

Put thus baldly the matter seems elementary and, I hope, obvious. We have attempted in the interests of clarity to reduce it to its simplest terms, but in practice it is of course more complicated than this. For one thing the characteristics by the possession of which any artefact is named a work of art are the same characteristics in virtue of which, according as they are present in greater or less degree, any work of art is correctly judged to be better or worse than another. For, as Mr. R. G. Collingwood has pertinently said: 'The definition of any kind of thing is also the definition of a good thing of that kind; for a thing that is good in its kind is only a thing which possesses the attributes of that kind.'[1] Thus every critical judgement of comparative worth implicitly assumes a definition of the meaning of

[1] *The Principles of Art* (1938), p. 280.

43

the phrase 'work of art' and every definition of a work of art must contain implicitly in itself all the practical standards which, if the definition is accepted, can correctly be employed to assess the value or excellence of particular works of art in any field. It is logically inevitable that this be so. For suppose a group of attributes AB . . . F such that every artefact which we agree to name a work of art possesses all six of these attributes and no artefact which we do not name a work of art possesses them all. Then it is impossible that any work of art could be better or worse than another *qua* work of art in virtue of the different degrees in which they severally possessed some other attribute H. For by definition H must be an attribute which some works of art do not possess at all (although as works of art they must be allowed some degree of artistic goodness) or an attribute possessed by some artefacts which according to our linguistic convention are not correctly called works of art at all.[1] Thus the definition of what shall constitute a work of art is also, inevitably, a definition of the standards by which works of art shall be compared and assessed. The point is important.

To summarize and recapitulate.—There exists a fairly well-defined class of things, which we call artefacts, consisting of all those things which are produced by consciously directed human endeavour. All those things which anyone calls works of art belong to this class. But the class of things called artefacts is wider than the class of things called works of art; not all artefacts are works of art. That this is so there is nobody to deny. Not all literary products are literature, nor all pictorial products pictorial art. A cheque, a grocer's bill, and a text-book on musical theory are no more classified as works of art than are fashion papers, comics or placards panegyric of patent panaceas. The very function of the word 'art' is to make such a distinction among artefacts, and if it were not intended to make the distinction there would be no occasion to use the word at all. Now denotation implies connotation, and it is the first task of aesthetics to specify the connotation of the term 'work of art' by mentioning the attributes in virtue of which this term is applied to some artefacts and not to others. Even this is not easy to decide, elementary though it may seem,

[1] Logically it is conceivable that there should be a group of attributes ABC . . . P such that ABC are possessed by all artefacts named works of art and by no others, D . . . P are possessed (in addition to ABC) by some works of art but not by others, and are possessed by no artefacts which are not works of art. Then when the comparative excellence of any work of art was assessed it might be meant that it was being judged to possess in addition to ABC more or fewer of the subsidiary attributes D . . . P and in greater or less degree. So far as I know, no critic or aesthetician has ever worked with a theory of this kind.

and most connotations which have been proposed involve a denotation repugnant both to common linguistic usage and to the linguistic habits of the aesthetician or critic by whom they are proposed. For example, it is not possible to define the distinction by saying that non-artistic artefacts shall be those made for use and artistic artefacts shall be those made for enjoyment; it is not possible because on the one hand there are non-useful artefacts (children's toys, spirituous liquors) which nobody wishes to classify as art, while on the other hand a definition which excluded from the realm of art architecture and the Useful Arts in general would certainly be thought extravagant and unpropitious by any critic or art-historian who was called upon to apply it in his practice. The products of architecture are often held to be works of fine artistic merit and some products of the potter's craft are kept in museums and collections of art on account of the beauty which is ascribed to them; a critic who is unwilling to challenge such practices may not use this criterion for discriminating works of art.

Again Professor H. S. Goodhart-Rendel, not intending originality, proposes to discriminate works of fine art as all those artefacts which 'exist primarily to touch men's thoughts and emotions'.[1] To choose but one illustration at random, the newspaper reports of a recent trial of a boy of sixteen for the murder of a policeman were written to touch men's thoughts and emotions and that they succeeded in doing so was evidenced by numerous letters to the press. Yet neither Professor Goodhard-Rendel nor anyone else so far as I know would be prepared to classify these newspaper reports among works of art. The proposed definition is therefore incompetent and could not serve as a practical guide in criticism for discriminating art from non-art.

In fact, there exists no definition which is not open to similar refutation from the writings of criticism, no comprehensible definition which has been consistently applied by anyone. The double conclusion is inevitable, both that some modification is desirable in the practice of critics and that further and more coherent thought must be given to the purpose and implications of this classification into art and not-art, good art and poor art. The necessity for greater precision leaps to the eye when it is considered that besides those artefacts about which there is general agreement whether they should be classified as art or not-art, there exists a fringe where it is notoriously difficult to draw a sharp line between those which are works of art and those which are not. Not only do admitted works of art differ among themselves in excellence, but a large number of artefacts lies uneasily in the borderland of opinion between art and not-art. Most

---

[1] *Fine Art* (1934).

men would agree that the Cathedral at Chartres and the Casa de Moneda at Potosí are excellent works of architectural art, different as they are in almost every particular. Most men would agree that a Victorian tenement and a gasometer are not works of art, that the house designed by Mr. Ruskin is an 'architectural curiosity'[1] rather than a work of art. But how to classify and assess the Empire State Building, the New University Library at Cambridge, the Festival Hall, the Battersea Power Station or Hampstead Garden Suburb? Most practical men would accept upon authority that Shakespeare and Sophocles, Emerson and Eliot and Pound wrote works which should be classified as literary art, whereas the detective fiction, the penny dreadfuls and the romances which they, their children and their wives read for enjoyment are not art. With less assurance they might bow to the verdict of the critics that the best sellers of the day—*The Girl of the Limberlost, The Sorrows of Satan, The Blue Lagoon, The Constant Nymph*, and of a later vintage *Gone with the Wind, Forever Amber, Hatter's Castle*—do not rank as literary art, though they buy them and read them. But what of *Grapes of Wrath*, of which so eminent a critic as Mr. Edmund Wilson says that it marks 'the borderline between work which is definitely superior and work that is definitely bad'? There is in literary art a very broad margin of doubt indeed among critics; and if the layman accepts the judgements of the critics when they are able to pronounce, it is with the proviso that he of course has no inclination for literary art and must be free to find his enjoyment elsewhere. In music, too, there are people who delight in *The Indian Love Lyrics*, the *Warsaw Concerto* or Chopin's *Nocturne Opus 9 No.* 2 performed by a restaurant ensemble, but are bored by Bach and repelled by Bartók.

It is for critic and aesthetician together to determine throughout this region of uncertainty whether doubt and discrepancy are due to unexplained differences in perception of the object from person to person or to the use of different and vague criteria for distinguishing what among artefacts is and what is not a work of art. In some cases, too, the criterion by which it is proposed to discriminate works of art is such that it differentiates a different class of artefacts as works of art for each person. The various definitions of art in terms of pleasure, or emotion, which we shall discuss later, are of this kind. When such a criterion is used, there can be no genuine conflict of opinion whether this or that artefact is a work of art or not; it will be art for this man and not-art for the other, and legitimate argument is confined to discussing the linguistic convenience of using a criterion of this sort. A critic who uses a criterion of this sort is

[1] A. Trystan Edwards, *Good and Bad Manners in Architecture* (1924), p. 138.

bound to recognize that although he may distinguish what is and what is not a work of art for himself, he cannot do so for anyone else. And realizing this, he would, no doubt, ask himself what his job as a critic amounts to.

Finally, when a critic compares several works of art in regard to their value or excellence as works of art, he must use a norm of comparison which is integrated with the criterion by which he has distinguished each of them as a work of art. For if he does not do so, he is in effect employing different and incompatible criteria of what constitutes a work of art.

We must, then, apply three standards to any proposed definition of a work of art. (1) It must be applicable by anyone who adopts it to every object which that person classifies as a work of art. (2) It must not be applicable to any object which a person who adopts it is unwilling to classify as a work of art. (3) It must be applied by anyone who adopts it as his sole criterion for assessing the relative worth of different works of art. These are the canons of consistency by which critical writing should be judged by the aesthetician. (And also of course by the reading public; though the latter will of course also judge the critic by the range and acuteness of his aesthetic sensibility and by the clarity or suasive winsomeness of his literary style.)

Chapter III

ILLUSIONISM

ἡ δὲ μελαίνετ' ὄπισθεν, ἀρηρομένη δὲ ἐῴκει,
χρυσείη περ ἐοῦσα· τὸ δὴ περὶ θαῦμα τέτυκτο.

(And behind the plough the earth is black and looks like ploughed land, although it is wrought of gold; a very marvel of craftsmanship.)

HOMER, *Iliad* XVIII, 548

excudent alii spirantia mollius aera
(credo equidem), vivos ducent de marmore voltus.

VIRGIL, *Aeneid* VI, 847

ONE of the most frequently quoted passages in the literature of aesthetics is a sentence from the first chapter of Aristotle's *Poetics*, which runs: 'Epic poetry, tragedy, comedy, lyric poetry, as also, for the most part, the music of the flute and of the lyre—all these are, in the most general view of them, modes of imitation.'[1] Now this is a very odd statement indeed to modern ears. As Professor Gilbert Murray has frankly said, it 'appears to most English readers almost meaningless and so far as it has any meaning, I believe most of them will think it untrue'.[2] Having made this admission, however, he sets himself to demonstrate that the reason why it sounds strange to us is not because what Aristotle meant to say was strange but because imperfect acquaintance with his linguistic habits causes most people to misapprehend his meaning. In the original Greek there is a play upon the word 'poetry', which is derived from a verb *poiein* meaning 'to make' and is in some senses the antithesis of *mimesis* or 'imitation'. By saying that poetry is imitation Aristotle does not therefore intend to deny what we should now call the 'creative' function of literary art; poetry is 'making', but it is a special kind of making, namely the making of imitations or reproductions of something else. Indeed, when he goes on to tell us that what poetry imitates is 'the characters and emotions of men and how they fare', he is in fact, according to Professor Gilbert Murray, proposing a rather good definition of poetry,

[1] Quotations from the *Poetics* are taken, with some modifications, from the translation of Thomas Twining (1789).

[2] 'Poesis and Mimesis' in *Essays and Addresses* (1921).

48

for he is saying that what poetry does—unlike history, for instance, which 'imitates' real happenings—is to create an imitation world of the imagination. For Professor Gilbert Murray thinks that this exercise of the creative imagination is, precisely, the heart and core of poetry, adducing as an exemplar of the typical poet Ovid, 'a man who seems hardly to have lived at all except in the world of his imagination'.[1] He further argues that the doctrine of poetry as creative imagination is not incompatible with Matthew Arnold's definition of poetry as a criticism of life, since the selective representation of what is not but might be is one of the most potent and effective methods of constructive criticism. And he concludes: 'the conception of Art as mimesis, though rejected by almost all recent critics, has a justification and may even show real profundity of insight. Mimesis is, I suspect, not only an essential element in all art, but also our greatest weapon both for explaining and for understanding the world.'

As a *tour de force* of interpretative ingenuity this essay is quite brilliant. It makes Aristotle speak with the voice of Arnold and Pater and turns the doctrine of mimesis into something it was not and could not have been. But fashionable as this method of exegesis still is, it makes complete nonsense of the historical approach. It is in fact more difficult to empty one's mind of the accumulated complexities of the intervening ages and to recover the initial simplicity and crudity of primitive thinking than to distort the words of the early thinkers by reading into them the inherited perplexities with which we now wrestle. Yet only in this way can the early stages of thought in any discipline retain a bearing upon contemporary problems. The present state of aesthetics is confused enough even when seen historically with a just if jaundiced eye. If you haze over the past with the romanticized fogs of to-day, any value which the past might have for us now will be lost.

When Aristotle wrote, aesthetic thought was still rudimentary. Although the Greeks had achieved great things in most of the fine arts, the aesthetic consciousness was still dormant. Throughout Greek literature up to the time of Aristotle and beyond there is not a word written in appreciation of a work of art for its beauty; such discussions of works of art as there are either mention their costliness and magnificence or their

---

[1] The Professor is unfortunate in his choice of an example. Ovid was a man with an excellent talent for versification and a gift for vivid narrative and was one who took great pleasure in the exercise of these talents. But his 'imaginative world' was not a world of his own creating; it was taken over from the mythology current in his time. Ovid himself was a man singularly devoid of imagination and heavily oppressed by the concrete realities of his situation.

moral effects upon the citizen. Consequently there was this fundamental difference between the early gropings of aesthetic thought as we know it in Plato and Aristotle and the aesthetics of to-day, that for the Greeks the theory of art was not yet coincident with the theory of beauty. Nowadays there is no one to deny that, whatever else we may have to say about it, the function of fine art is to create things of beauty—or at least that works of art are rightly judged to be good as art in so far as they are fraught with beauty; our difficulties arise when we try to clarify what it is we mean by beauty. When the present writer defined beauty as 'the peculiar excellence of works of art', while fully understanding that in common parlance the word retains other and wider connotations as well, he was proposing a linguistic convention common to all or almost all the varieties of aesthetic doctrine now current. But for the Greeks the word 'beauty' had primarily a moral and secondarily an intellectual significance. A character or an action of which you approved was 'beautiful' not merely in a metaphorical sense but in the primary signification of the word. And apart from this 'beauty' was intellectual lucidity or apprehensibility. But art was something different again; its connection with beauty was extrinsic and accidental. Plato's moral condemnation of fine art was also typical of a certain puritanical asceticism inveterate in the Greek temperament—and exaggerated into a local virtue in Sparta—which made them constantly suspicious of the non-useful arts and ever ready to condemn on moral grounds—or to excuse, as in the *Funeral Oration* of Thucydides—that which existed for embellishment and delight rather than to satisfy a utilitarian need. Diogenes Laertius, for example, records that the great Athenian law-giver Solon, who said that the word is the image of the deed, banned the dramatic poet Thespis because 'his untruthfulness was damaging'.[1] And in Aristotle himself the moral preoccupation is ubiquitous.

Aristotle left no treatise on aesthetics and claims no originality for the aesthetic aphorisms which he introduced incidentally into his handbooks of practical criticism. He took over the doctrine of mimesis from his predecessors as part of the stock-in-trade of contemporary critical theory. It was developed most fully by Plato and for Plato, in the words of Professor W. D. Ross, 'art is the attempt to copy reality with literal fidelity and to produce the illusion that your copy *is* reality. And this leads him to condemn art on two grounds. The artist is always pretending to be someone else. If he describes a battle, he is falsely claiming to know how battles should be fought. If he puts words into Achilles' mouth, he is pretending to be Achilles. . . . And secondly, the artist never imitates reality directly;

[1] I, 59.

50

he imitates sensible things, which are but the faint shadows of reality.'[1]
Nor was Plato inventing a new doctrine of aesthetics. In his conversations
with artists reported by Xenophon in the *Memorabilia*[2] Socrates assumed
that it is the function of painting and sculpture to produce imitations or
copies of real things and maintained that it is possible by reproducing
bodily gestures and facial expressions for the artist to imitate or represent
character and emotions. 'Do you not think, then,' he asks the celebrated
painter Parrhasios, 'that people look with more pleasure on paintings in
which beautiful and good and lovely characters are exhibited than those in
which the deformed and evil and detestable are represented?' The language of appreciation attributed to Socrates is thoroughly in the spirit of
an age in which the plastic arts had begun to forsake the rigid if vital
formalism of primitive styles for naturalistic modes of representation and
might have been used almost without change by any writer of the early
Renaissance. It is clear, too, that Socrates was expressing a viewpoint
which, if somewhat advanced in his day, presumed ready acceptance by
his more intelligent interlocutors. It was a doctrine of pure illusionism
combined with a strictly moral criterion of judgement.

Thus Aristotle was not enunciating an original doctrine of art any
more than Plato had done, but was assuming a doctrine generally current
in his day. From the early chapters of the *Poetics* we may gather that he
was attempting a rough and ready classification somewhat analogous to
our distinction between the Fine Arts and the Useful Arts,[3] though without the concept of aesthetic beauty to link the two. For him history is not
fine art. Rhetoric is not art. Empedocles should be called a physicist not a
poet. Architecture is not art, for it makes real buildings and not imitations
like the painter who paints pictures of buildings. Art is distinguished from
craft because the artist produces imitations and the craftsman things for
use. And Aristotle is quite clear about the function of fine art. He assumes,
as Socrates had assumed, that its object is to give pleasure; and this too is
its justification. Man, he tells us, has an innate instinct for imitation which
distinguishes him from the other animals, and therefore all men naturally
derive pleasure from imitation. 'This is evident from what we experience
in viewing the works of imitative art; for in them we contemplate with
pleasure, and with the more pleasure the more exactly they are imitated,
such objects as, if real, we could not see without pain; as the figures of the

---

[1] *Aristotle* (1923), p. 287.   [2] III, x.
[3] Cf. Professor H. S. Goodhart-Rendel, *Fine Art* (1934): 'Thus, Fine Arts are
those that must please and may serve, Useful Arts those that must serve and may
please.'

meanest and most disgusting animals, dead bodies, and the like. And the reason of this is, that to learn is a natural pleasure, not confined to philosophers, but common to all men; with this difference only, that the multitude partake of it in a more transient and compendious manner. Hence the pleasure they receive from a picture: in viewing it they learn, they infer, they discover what every object is; that this, for instance, is such a particular man, etc. For if we suppose the object represented to be something which the spectator had never seen, his pleasure, in that case, will not arise from the imitation, but from the workmanship, the colours, or some such cause.' The only significant advance on the more purely moralistic attitude of Socrates is his recognition of the fact that we may be attracted by the representation of objects which are in themselves repellent. This must not be confused with the later Romantic doctrine that the ugly in nature can be transformed as a constituent of a beautiful work of art. The pleasure of which Aristotle speaks is still the pleasure of recognizing what it is that is represented by a realistically exact copy. There could hardly be a clearer statement of the 'illusionist' theory of art—a photograph would conform most clearly to Aristotle's theory. And it is significant that the pleasure derived from workmanship or colour, when the spectator is unable to recognize the representation because he has no experience of that which is represented, is not regarded as germane to mimetic art.

Aside from this criterion of representational realism Aristotle assesses works of art, as did others of his race and time, in accordance with the naïve form of moralistic theory which judges them by their effects in influencing men to become good or unprofitable citizens. For example, when he says in the *Politics* that music is the most imitative of all the arts and that the similitudes produced by music are the most exact paradigms of their models, such as anger and gentleness, courage and self-control, he is simply enunciating an accepted belief of his day that music written in the various 'modes' is highly effective in stimulating various emotional moods, particularly in adolescents, and so exerts an influence on character. It is as if one were to maintain to-day that young men compelled regularly to listen to military bands, jazz tunes, symphony concerts or *Hymns Ancient and Modern* as part of their University training would be differently affected in disposition and character. We should now regard this as a variety of the naïve emotional theory of art and should not speak of music as 'imitating' emotions because it arouses emotions in the audience. In regard to literature, Aristotle holds that the poet should 'imitate' the probable rather than the actual, and believes that what is intrinsically improbable may in the context given to it by the poet seem more probable than what actually occurred, since 'it is probable that many things should happen contrary to probability'. Therefore 'the poet should prefer impossibilities which appear probable to such things as, though possible, appear improbable'. This is, of course, logically to abandon the naïve realistic theory of mimesis and in the way in which Aristotle speaks one may see the germ of that doctrine of the 'typical' which had so great an influence on later literary theory. In fact, however, Aristotle does not develop a general theory of 'typical truth'. His view that the poet should prefer the probable to the actual seems to be connected on the one hand with his belief that the poet's primary function is to display character and that he should therefore select or invent actions and situations which best illustrate the characters of his personages, preferring imaginary to actual situations if the former are more suited to bring out the characters he is depicting. On the other hand it is connected with an unco-ordinated doctrine that plot should have unity and congruity, so that intrinsically improbable incidents may be essential to the unity of a plot and may thereby acquire greater 'poetic' probability than the events as they actually occurred. It is unfortunate that no attempt is made to connect these independent criteria of criticism into a general aesthetic theory.

Such then was the doctrine of naïve realism which dominated the critical practice of classical antiquity, combined as it was with a strongly ethical tendency in judgement. It was not the only principle of criticism that was current, but it was the only principle which was consciously developed into a coherent dogma. It was, for example, this conception of art which induced Xenocrates[1] to omit mention of all sculpture prior to Polycleitos and to praise the latter because he first 'made his statues rest their weight upon one leg'.[2] The primitives, whom modern taste admires for their superior vigour and vitality of form, were seen only as unnatural, unrepresentational and therefore incompetent. By the same criterion Xenocrates ranked Pythagoras above Myron because he knew how to reproduce hair more realistically and Lysippos above Pythagoras because he could portray the hair of the head and the minute details of veins and sinews with still greater delicacy and exactness. And as late as the second century A.D. Plutarch, controverting the accepted view in his

---

[1] Xenocrates of Sikyon, himself a sculptor, wrote a treatise on sculpture in the first half of the third century B.C. It is known to us only through quotations in the *Natural History* of the elder Pliny.

[2] The first step towards realism was to abandon the stiff unnatural stance of the archaic statues.

day that drawing is more important than colouring in a picture, said: 'Colouring is superior to drawing and produces a more lively impression on the mind, *because it is the source of a greater illusion.*' Thus the aesthetic thought of antiquity hardly advanced beyond the conception of naïve imitative realism—and this was the principle of appreciation which was revised spontaneously at the Renaissance.

It is true that Plato in his later works had suggested that there may be a superior kind of inspired art which is not an imitation of phenomenal nature and therefore an imitation of reality at second remove, but a direct representation of reality itself born of a super-sensible intuition of the realm of Ideas. After distinguishing in the *Timaeus* between the eternal and immutable world of real essences which are known only by reason and the changing and perishable world of sensation, he goes on: 'When the Artificer fastens his gaze upon the eternally unchanging and using it as his model reproduces its essential form and power, then everything must necessarily turn out beautiful; but when he gazes upon what has taken upon itself sensory being, using that as his model, his work has not beauty.' In the *Phaedrus* also Plato distinguished the inspired artist from the skilled imitative craftsman and spoke of inspiration as a kind of divine madness or possession, attributing it to a pre-natal vision of the world of eternal essences. This conception of art as an inspired revelation of ultimate reality appears to have had little or no influence on criticism until it was revived in the mystical doctrines of Neo-Platonism and after a long period of abeyance served as the warranty for the rationalistic and mathematical ideals of beauty which took hold upon the speculative minds of the Renaissance, later to degenerate into the formalism of the Academics. It is a mode of aesthetic mysticism which has been revived in the philosophy of the Romantic movement and again in our own time in the context of the Expressionist theory of art, and it will be discussed in that connection. It is subject in all its forms to the basic weakness of all metaphysical theories of aesthetics: it can neither be verified nor serve as a practical guide to criticism. For since we can only know the forms of ultimate reality as they are revealed or imitated in works of art, we can never know whether works of art do in fact reproduce them, or which works reproduce them with greater fidelity than others.[1]

Throughout the Middle Ages the aesthetic consciousness lay crushed and dormant in all Christendom. The fine arts were allowed to continue on sufferance, tolerated in the service of religion, and religion poisoned the spontaneous delight men take in their beauty. The famous Second

[1] See my *Theory of Beauty* (1952), pp. 59-60.

Council of Nicaea, which settled the Iconoclastic Controversy, decreed: 'It is defined with all certitude and accuracy that just as the figure of the precious and life-giving Cross, so also the venerable and holy images, as well painting and mosaic as of other fit materials, should be set forth in the holy churches of God, in the sacred vessels, and in the vestments and hangings, and in pictures, both in houses and by the wayside, to wit, figures of our Lord God and Saviour Jesus Christ, of our stainless Lady, the Mother of God, of the honourable Angels, of all the Saints and of all pious people. For by so much more frequently as they are seen represented, by so much more readily are men lifted up to the memory of their proto-types, and to a longing after them.' Even St. Gregory the Great recog-nized the utility-value of pictorial art for the indoctrination of the illiterate. 'For what writing is to them that can read, a picture is to them who cannot read, but only look, since in it even the ignorant can see what they should follow.' But in no single decree of the Church is there any mention of artistic beauty or taste, and such idea of beauty as survived its dominant indifference is represented by the opinion of Isidore of Seville that 'beauty is something that one adds to buildings for ornament and richness, as occurs in gilded roofs, in precious marble incrustations, and in coloured paintings'.

The awakening of aesthetic awareness from its long sleep of obscur-antism coincided with the revival of painting at Florence, which is associ-ated with the great genius of the artist Giotto, of whom Boccaccio wrote: 'he was of so excellent a wit that there was nothing in Nature, but that he could with his pen and pencil depict it, so that it seemed not to be a mere likeness but the very thing itself; and the visual sense of men was deceived, taking those things to be real which were only painted'. This sort of appreciative comment is typical of the changing outlook of the dawning Renaissance and could hardly have been written half a century earlier. The new delight in art for its own sake was associated largely, though by no means exclusively, with a new impulse towards naturalism, the con-scious reproduction of nature in art without ulterior motive, and above all the depiction of figures displaying by attitude and gesture the emotions of life. By the end of the fourteenth century Cennino Cennini already knew that the most perfect guide of the artist is, not tradition, but 'the triumphal door of drawing from nature'. The artists practised the observation of nature and studied the technical means of reproducing natural effects with a new seriousness. The appreciative literature of the time is replete with praise of whatever seems so effectively to reproduce its object that it creates the impression of being that object and not a representation of it, and both artists and theorists continually hold up realistic fidelity as the ultimate criterion of artistic excellence. Alberti said in his *Treatise on Painting*: 'The painter's business is to design and paint any given bodies with lines and colours in such a manner that whatever is painted may appear prominent and be as like as possible to those given bodies.' And even Leonardo said: 'That painting is most praiseworthy which has the greatest conformity to the thing imitated.' Vasari was only applying the principles of criticism current in his time when he wrote of Masaccio: 'We then of a truth have the greatest obligation to those masters who, by their labours, first taught us the true path by which to attain the highest summit of perfection; and as touching a good manner in painting, most especially are we indebted to Masaccio, since it was he, who, eager for the acquirement of fame, first attained the clear perception that painting is no other than the close imitation by drawing and colouring simply, of all forms presented by nature, exhibiting them as they are produced by her, and that whosoever shall most perfectly effect this, may be said to have most nearly approached the summit of excellence.' Yet it would be a mistake to read too great a profundity into these theories of art or to ask whether, had they known of the possibility of mechanically exact reproduction by photography, they would have regarded the photograph as the supreme achievement of reproductive art. Critics and connoisseurs, and artists too, were roused to emotional and intellectual fervour by the naturalism of the new style of painting, which in contrast with the formalism of medieval art seemed to live and breathe and, as Filippo Villani put it, 'express actions, such as discoursing, weeping and laughing'. The appreciative response was very similar to that which occurred when the plastic arts took a similar swing towards naturalism in fifth-century Athens. From the point of view of general aesthetic and critical theory this recrudescence of the mimetic theory of art was a mistake, a step in a wrong direction. But it was not a deeply reflective theory. Rather it was a spontaneous tribute to a change in artistic style which had succeeded in making sensibility once more conscious of itself.

In the course of time this spontaneous naturalism was inevitably tinged with a quasi-moralistic flavour and it came to be believed that the value of a work of representative art was a coefficient both of the beauty or nobility of its subject and of the fidelity with which that subject was portrayed. Already Dürer was responsible for the statement: 'And a man is held to have done well if he attain accurately to copy a figure according to life, so that his drawing resemble the figure and is like unto nature. And in particular if the thing copied is beautiful; then is the copy held to be artistic, and, as it deserveth, it is highly praised.' The concept of aesthetic beauty was not yet liberated from that of natural beauty, and since our responses to all natural objects are always and inevitably coloured by quasi-moral considerations such as those embodied in words like 'noble', 'tawdry', 'vulgar', 'sublime', which we use of natural scenes and events, the theory and criticism of visual art took on a moralistic tone quite apart from any direct moralizing influences of the Counter-Reformation. The doctrine that great art is the accurate representation of noble subjects was crystallized in the precepts of *La Gran Maniera*, popularized and made respectable in England by the weighty support of Sir Joshua Reynolds. How enormous were its influence and vitality is evidenced by the fact that even at the beginning of the present century a respected artist of the Royal Academy could open a book of instruction on the theory and practice of painting by taking his text from Sir Joshua Reynolds's notes to Du Fresnoy's *Art of Painting*: 'The study of nature is the beginning and the end of theory. It is in nature only we can find that beauty which is the great object of our search; it can be found nowhere else: we can no more form any idea of beauty superior to nature than we can form an idea of a sixth sense, or any other excellence out of the limits of the human mind.' He then goes on in the manner of his master: 'A mean, poor view of nature may be chosen, and may be painted truly; that is to say, the picture may correspond to the idea of its painter: but however great the painter's accomplishment, it will be a poor picture.'[1]

The naturalistic element in this strange partnership was represented—among much else both good and bad—by Diderot, who maintained fairly consistently in his *Salons* that the fairest way to judge a work of art is to compare it with the original which had been its model in nature and to assess the degree of its similitude. The moralistic element is affirmed with some purity in Ruskin's characteristic assertion that 'the greatest picture is that which conveys to the mind of the spectator the greatest number of the greatest ideas'.

This then is the historical background of the doctrine of illusionism. It was taken for granted that painting copies nature—as of course to some extent it very often does—and it was assumed as self-evident that the better and more exactly it copies, the better it is. No one had perhaps ever held *mimesis* as a complete aesthetic doctrine or applied the principle of representational realism as the one and only standard of criticism. No one perhaps had consciously and rigorously proposed to carry the naturalistic principle to an extreme, even as one principle of criticism among others.

[1] Sir George Clausen, *Aims and Ideals in Art* (1906).

Even Sir Joshua Reynolds in a letter contributed to the *Idler* admitted that it must be qualified. 'Amongst the Painters and writers on Painting', he says, 'there is one maxim universally admitted and continually inculcated. Imitate Nature, is the invariable rule; but I know none who have explained in what manner this rule is to be understood; the consequence of which is, that everyone takes it in the most obvious sense,—that objects are represented naturally, when they have such relief that they appear real. It may appear strange, perhaps, to hear this sense of the rule disputed; but it must be considered, that if the excellency of a Painter consisted only in this kind of imitation, Painting must lose its rank, and be no longer considered as a liberal art, and sister to Poetry; this imitation being merely mechanical, in which the slowest intellect is always sure to succeed best; for the Painter of genius cannot stoop to drudgery, in which the understanding has no part; and what pretence has the Art to claim kindred with Poetry, but by its power over the Imagination? To this power the Painter of genius directs his aim; in this sense he studies Nature, and often arrives at his end, even by being unnatural, in the confined sense of the word.'

In contrast to these earlier, spontaneous and unreflective anticipations, realism first emerged as a fully fledged articulate theory of art in rebellion against the conventional artificialities of the Second Empire and in union with the doctrine of philosophical Positivism. Its apostle was Gustave Courbet, who in consequence of the rejection of his works by the jury at the International Exhibition of 1855 held his own one-man show outside the gates. In an open letter published by the *Courrier de Dimanche* on Christmas Day of 1861, Courbet summarized his views as follows: 'The art of painting should consist solely of the representation of objects visible and tangible to the artist. An epoch can be reproduced only by its own artists, I mean by the artists who have lived in it. . . . I also hold that painting is essentially a *concrete* art and consists only of the representation of things *real* and *existing*. It is a completely physical language which uses for its words all visible objects. An abstract object, one which is invisible, non-existent, is outside the domain of painting[1]. . . . Beauty is in nature and is found in reality under the most diverse forms. Once it is found it belongs to art, or rather to the artist who knows how to see it. Beauty is real and once visible it contains in itself its own artistic expression. And the artist has not the right to amplify that expression. If he trifles with it, he risks denaturing it and so weakening it. Beauty as given by nature is

---

[1] Much of this is directed against the painting of historical and mythological subjects popular in his day. It would, of course, equally serve to condemn most religious art.

superior to all the conventions of the artist.' This realist outlook upon art was made to measure for mid-nineteenth-century Positivism, which assumed the world of reality to be no more than the sum of everything which the scientific observer finds in his experience. It fitted into Comte's doctrine that after the religious and the metaphysical epochs we have reached the positivist stage in human development, in which all explanation is limited to the description of appearances. For Realism eliminates the subjective element from art, and substitutes objective recording for imaginative construction. The duty of the artist, like that of the scientist, is simply to observe and to record by accurate reproduction the reality of nature as seen. In the aesthetic theories of the Positivists art was indeed assigned a social function as well. Courbet had spoken of it as a kind of social documentation; Proudhon[1] maintained that this documentation should take the form of criticism and that by revealing the defects of society as it is the artist should work for its destruction in order that from the ruins of the present the perfect society of the future might more quickly arise. But although the aestheticians with their socialistic ideals injected this element of reformatory zeal into the artist's function in society, they had no quarrel with Courbet's view of the relation of art to nature.

Then in 1863 Courbet was succeeded as the leader of the Realists at the *Salon des Refusés* by Manet, who was both an artist of great individual genius and the founder of that school of painting known as Impressionism. In conception and in its origin Impressionism was a stricter and more rigorous Realism rather than a revolt from Realism. Courbet had said that beauty is a quality *in* nature, a quality which the artist can detect if his perceptive faculties are attuned to it and which when detected he is to reproduce as faithfully as in him lies. But beauty as something distinct and added to the reproducible sensory qualities of things remained a metaphysical shadow. The Impressionists ceased to all intents and purposes to concern themselves with beauty. The word is not used by Pissaro or Seurat and only twice by Signac. Influenced by new discoveries in psychological optics and by the work of Chevreul[2] and Rood[3] on colour perception, they set themselves to understand more exactly what is involved in 'seeing' and to discover more accurate technical methods of reproducing what is seen. They understood with the force of a revelation that although

[1] P. J. Proudhon, *Du principe de l'Art* (1865).
[2] Michel-Eugène Chevreul, *De la loi du contraste simultane des couleurs* (1839).
[3] Ogden Nicolas Rood, *Modern Chromatics with Applications to Art and Industry* (1879).

we may look at the same thing—the same chair or tree or mountain—on innumerable occasions and recognize it for the same, in fact our sense-perceptions never remain constant but vary continually with changes of light and atmospheric conditions. What we see are the illuminated surfaces of objects and the medium by which we see is light. The Impressionists sought therefore to reproduce on canvas not the abstract imaginal horse or building which remains substantially the same from one perceptual occasion to the next but the sense-impression itself, the specific pattern of coloured surface-shapes which is given fleetingly and never recurs the same. It was an aim which Leonardo, Rembrandt and other great artists of the past had set themselves as a practical discipline among others—although their technical solutions had inevitably been different; but it had never before been articulated into a conscious principle of art.

But though more rigorously realistic in its intention than any school of painting hitherto, Impressionism carried within itself the seeds of its own inevitable disintegration. Advancing psychology has taught us that sense-perception as such is essentially selective; there can be no such thing as pure sensation in the sense of absolutely passive reception of impressions from without. All perception, whether or not of recognizable objects, involves the discrimination and patterning of the sensory field in accordance with unconscious interests and purposes. And this truth has nowhere been exemplified so forcefully as in the development of pictorial art and the practical investigations of artists during the hundred years from Manet until to-day. For it soon became apparent that there is no one way of seeing nature objectively, but each person sees in his own way, and no man's way is the one right way of seeing for all. Cézanne, for example, denied that visual sensation is primarily the perception of luminous surfaces of bodies and held that these are only the forms under which we perceive a coherent system of receding planes. Other artists found other principles of selection amidst the manifold richness of perceptual nature. It therefore became obvious that the ideal of the Impressionists was not only a wrong ideal but an inherently impossible ideal. It is not possible to reproduce nature as it appears in immediate sensation; it is possible only to reproduce this or that man's vision of nature. The artist's painting is not, therefore, and cannot be, an exact reproduction of nature but is an expression of the way in which he sees nature. Painting becomes an expression of each artist's personal vision. This was understood practically by the artists if it was not fully comprehended by them from the point of view of theoretical psychology and epistemology. And at the same time as the artists were reaching these practical conclusions, critics too were being influenced to reject Realism by the rapid advances in mechanical means of reproduction. The Romantic belief that art is a supreme expression of human personality was too strong to allow even the most realistic of critics to admit that the finest art—because the most realistic—is the copy of nature produced by such mechanical means as the camera. Art, though still perhaps realistic in some sense, was required to express the personality of an artist, to symbolize or represent a personal and individual outlook upon nature and reality.

The movement which began as a search for profounder Realism has thus itself become one of the most powerful influences in the contemporary reaction against illusionism, a reaction which in its extreme manifestations imposes as complete and uncompromising a prohibition upon *mimesis* as that once imposed upon the children of Abraham for doctrinal reasons; and the intense aesthetic fervour with which the modernistic schools repudiate representation is often reminiscent of the religious implacability which forbad the reproduction of God's creation among the Mohammedans and the Jews. From the pronouncements of contemporary artists you may gather statements as vigorously opposed to the mimetic conception of art as the Renaissance was unreflectively in its support. 'One must not imitate what one wants to create,' said Georges Braque in his aphoristic style. 'One does not imitate appearances; the appearance is the result. To be pure imitation, painting must forget appearance.' And in an address entitled *The New Realism* Fernand Léger paradoxically declared: 'There was never any question in plastic art, in poetry, in music, of representing anything. It is a matter of making something beautiful, moving, or dramatic—this is by no means the same thing.' It has indeed become almost a commonplace of contemporary art that the job of the artist is not to copy the external nature which is 'given' in experience but to create something new for experience. Yet this again is still only one side of the picture. Even the most 'abstract' of artists have affirmed their need to remain in close and continual contact with perceptible nature. 'There is no abstract art,' said Pablo Picasso. 'You must always start with something. Afterwards you can remove all traces of reality. There's no danger then, anyway, because the idea of the object will have left an indelible mark. It is what started the artist off, excited his ideas, and stirred up his emotions. Ideas and emotions will in the end be prisoners in his work.' And Piet Mondrian: 'Abstract art is therefore opposed to a natural representation of things. But it is not opposed to nature, as is generally thought.' This continued dependence of non-representational art on nature constitutes a problem which we shall have to discuss in its place. Does it represent an accident of the psychology of artistic creation or does it indicate some more fundamental realistic element in the nature of artistic beauty as such?

But although the mimetic theory of art is now to all intents and purposes obsolete and its open profession is hardly respectable any longer, it remains none the less strongly entrenched in the popular imagination—what a lovely film, how *like*!—and still wields an appreciable influence upon practical criticism of the arts. Enlightened critics may no longer maintain that imitation is the essence of art or that the excellence of a work of art can be estimated in terms of the fidelity with which it copies something not itself. Realism is not any longer demanded of the artist in advance. We can afford to smile with amused toleration at Ruskin's pronouncement upon the painter Vandevelde: 'I feel utterly hopeless in addressing the admirers of these men, because I do not know what it is in their works which is supposed to be like nature.' Yet with a curious ambivalence, when a work of art, old or new, happens to display Realism —Realism of the right sort—it is seldom that it is not accorded praise by the critics for this reason. Moreover, it is despite everything an undeniable fact that the great majority of the products of visual art and all literary art reproduce or describe experienceable actualities of life and are therefore to some extent realistic; and it is as true as ever it was that the makers of art devote much conscious energy to the accurate observation and accurate rendering of natural effects. It remains as important, therefore, as it ever was to understand the significance of these facts in the nature of artistic activity and their bearing upon relevant criticism of the arts. For when all is said and done the realistic theory of art seems to correspond to something inherently true in mankind's instinctive attitude to artistic products. We do look upon any work of art as an imitation, a pretence, as opposed to the realities of life, which are but the material for art; we do not take the same attitude towards the events in a drama or a novel as we would take towards the same events in real occurrence. We do not react to a picture as we would react to the scene which it portrays; for the picture is *mimesis*. We always know that all art is a kind of make-believe of life. And all this seems to be embodied in the mimetic theory of art.

It is for these reasons that I have gone at some length into the history of the Realistic doctrine, as a background to the enquiry which must now be undertaken. The problems of Realism are now disguised in masks of modernity and are debated in a different form. But they are not yet resolved, and to-day, as always, they demand the most exacting indagation from both the theory and the criticism of artistic production.

Chapter IV

REALISM IN MODERN DRESS
1. ART AS SEMANTIC

'Mr. Brancusi claims that this object represents a bird. If you met such a bird out shooting, would you fire?' United States Customs Official

Even Giotto was once a realist. MAX J. FRIEDLANDER

THEORY of art has moved far from Vasari's simple delight in the *trompe d'œil*, and far from 'l'art humanitaire, l'art laique, l'art de la nature naturelle' of Courbet. Challenging the steadfast belief of the Academy that all beauty inheres ready-made in nature, which the artist may ransack for copy but cannot improve, James McNeill Whistler had vociferated that nature provides no more than the raw materials of beauty, from which the artist must select what he needs for a composition in which beauty will be fully displayed. 'Nature contains the elements, in colour and form, of all pictures, as the keyboard contains the notes of all music. But the artist is born to pick and choose, and group with skill, these elements, and the result may be beautiful—as the musician gathers his notes, and forms his chords, until he brings forth from chaos glorious harmony. To say to the painter, that Nature is to be taken as she is, is to say to the player, that he may sit upon the piano. That Nature is always right, is an assertion, artistically, as untrue, as it is one whose truth is universally taken for granted. Nature is very rarely right, to such an extent even that it might almost be said that Nature is usually wrong; that is to say, the condition of things that shall bring about the perfection and harmony worthy of a picture is rare, and not common at all. . . . Seldom does Nature succeed in producing a picture.'[1] That the artist must select and compose with the raw materials of nature is now universally conceded; and the importance to be attached to exact observation and reproduction of natural effects is generally admitted to be a matter for individual style and technique.

It was the Fauvists who first crystallized into a definite theory the

[1] *The Gentle Art of Making Enemies* (1890).

hardly won knowledge that the artist does not merely select from the elements provided by nature to combine them into a composition of beauty, but in so doing *interprets* nature in such a way that through the work of art which he produced he may express to others an individual vision or emotion of his own. 'What I seek to get above everything', wrote Matisse, 'is expression. . . . The expression is the whole disposition of my picture. . . . It is not possible for me to copy nature servilely, because I am forced to interpret it and to subject it to the spirit of the picture.'[1] Thus art came to be treated as a vehicle for expression, a language of feeling and emotion, a mode for the communication of the ineffable. This is the Expressionist theory of art. Yet only a few years later the early Cubists were emphasizing rather the artist's function as creator—no new doctrine but new in the radical implications which were given to it. In the same year that Whistler published his *The Gentle Art of Making Enemies*, Maurice Denis had made the revolutionary statement: 'It must be recalled that a picture—before it is a picture of a battle-horse, nude woman or some anecdote—is essentially a plane surface covered by colours arranged in a certain order.'[2] Carrying this further, the movement initiated by the Cubists gave prominence to the idea that the prime function of the artist is not to copy nature, nor even to re-assemble the material of nature into a beautiful or expressive composition, but essentially to *create something new*, something which should claim attention and respect in its own right and not by reference to any similarity it might or might not have to anything else whatsoever. 'The painter, careful to create, rejects the natural image as soon as it has served its purpose.'[3]

That this change of outlook had progressed outside purely professional art circles was strikingly evidenced in the thirties by the famous case *Brancusi v. The United States*, in which decision was given in favour of the artist that his bronze *Bird in Flight* was a work of art and therefore entitled to duty-free importation. In this decision Justice Waite referred to an earlier decision (1916) which had relied upon the dictionary definition of a work of sculptural art: 'Sculpture as an art is that branch of the free fine arts which chisels or carves out of stone or other solid material or models in clay or other plastic substance for subsequent reproduction by carving

---

[1] *Notes d'un peintre* (1908).

[2] *Définition de néo-traditionnisme* (published in *Art et Critique*, 1890).

[3] Albert Gleizes and Jean Metzinger, *Du Cubisme* (1912). Compare Gauguin: 'It is said that God put a piece of clay into His hand and created all that you know. The artist, in his turn, if he wishes to create a really divine work, must not imitate nature, but use the elements of nature to create a new element.'

or casting, imitations of natural objects in their true proportions of length, breadth, and thickness, or of length and breadth only.' According to these earlier decisions Brancusi's bronzes would not qualify as a work within the classification of fine art. But Justice Waite recognized that: 'In the meanwhile there has been developing a so-called new school of art, whose exponents attempt to portray abstract ideas rather than to imitate natural objects. Whether or not we are in sympathy with these newer ideas and the schools which represent them, we think the fact of their existence and their influence upon the art world as recognized by the courts must be considered. The object now under consideration is shown to be for purely ornamental purposes, its use being the same as that of any piece of sculpture of the old masters. It is beautiful and symmetrical in outline, and while some difficulty might be encountered in associating it with a bird, it is nevertheless pleasing to look at and highly ornamental.'

Both the Expressionist and the Creative theories of art claimed not so much to introduce a new manner and practice in art as to have discovered and made articulate the universal principle and purpose of all art everywhere. And to-day the man is judged simple-minded or a Philistine who still wants his art to 'hold up a mirror to nature'. Naïve Realism, as we have said, is no longer respectable. Yet the old 'imitation' idea will not so easily be uprooted, but retains much of its former plausibility and in more devious ways still influences the writings and the judgements of many who would openly repudiate it with horror. And it is natural that it should. For it seems to correspond to something fundamental in men's plain common-sense approach to art, something more spontaneous and less complicated than the theories of the theorists; and it cannot, perhaps, be wholly wrong. For whenever you contemplate a work of representational art you know at the back of your mind that it is not real, that it is a pretence, a make-believe, not the real thing but a copy—an imitation. And this background awareness colours all your impulses and attitudes towards it. However intensely you may identify yourself with the vicissitudes of the characters in a novel, you still know somewhere in your mind that it is after all only fiction and not truth, imagination and not the reality. You do not really believe that you could walk through the streets of a Utrillo or make snowballs with the snow which you see. Even when you look at a painting by Miró or Wadsworth which 'represents nothing', you do not really believe that those shapes which are not the shapes of anything else but themselves are really solid, one behind the other, with the rough nap of corundum or the lush smoothness of silk, although you see them so. You do not—even subconsciously—expect to be able to

E
65

touch them and move them. This suppressed awareness of unreality which controls your whole consciousness from beneath is the basis upon which the aesthetic attitude is built. The man who leaps on to the stage to save Desdemona from death, the man whose mouth waters at a Van Dongen or who vicariously delights in the beauties of natural scenery portrayed by Cotman or Girtin, the man who weeps for Little Dorrit, and all the many who enjoy a good cry in the cinema—these have not even begun to put themselves into the frame of mind for which artistic enjoyment is possible.[1] They are reacting as they would react to the real.

Moreover it is this awareness of unreality, this suppressed consciousness of imitation, which alone makes possible that 'voluntary suspension of disbelief' which predisposes you to accept with equanimity in a work of art the most outrageous improbabilities of ordinary life. It is because you know that it is a make-believe that you can accept or even take pleasure in such flagrant flights from the humdrum as Chagall's paintings and the *Arabian Nights*, such unrealities as Botticelli's angels, Poussin's nymphs, or David Garnett's imps. This suspension of disbelief in what you know to be untrue is the fundamental and most elementary demand of the attitude of aesthetic awareness. It is an attitude which seems easy and natural to the human mind from the cradle to the grave. If you have the thankless task of entertaining your neighbour's child, you may perhaps make the mistake of reciting to it in all good faith the old nursery rhyme:

> *Hey diddle, diddle,*
> *The cat and the fiddle,*
> *The cow jumped over the moon.*
> *The little dog laughed to see such sport,*
> *And the dish ran away with the spoon.*

If the child responds with glee, he responds as a child should. But if he is a modern child, the chances are that he will say to you: 'Yah, get away wiv yer. Yer can't fool me. Dog's can't larf and no cow can't jump that far.' If this is what he says, you will not reply 'How right you are, old chap!' You will feel vaguely aggrieved and begin to think that there is something wrong with the child. And there is indeed something wrong. He has failed to adopt the aesthetic attitude. He has shown no capacity for the suspension of disbelief, no pleasure in the world of make-believe.

And these two attitudes—the awareness that you are dealing with a

---

[1] 'The truth is that the spectators are always in their senses, and know, from the first act to the last, that the stage is only a stage, and that the players are only players.' Dr. Johnson, Preface to *The Plays of Shakespeare*.

pretence or an imitation and the suspension of disbelief in the improbable —which are the foundation of every aesthetic act, are obviously but two aspects of one and the same habit of mind.

Neither is the question of Realism yet a purely academic one even for serious literary criticism, but realistic assumptions continue to obtrude often under surprising disguises. In an article entitled *Henry James and the Function of Criticism*, Dr. F. R. Leavis voices his disagreement with those critics who think highly of the late novels of Henry James. He describes *The Ambassadors* as a 'feeble piece of word-spinning', *The Wings of The Dove* as 'fussily vague and intolerably sentimental', and *The Golden Bowl*, though said to be more interesting, is still condemned for its 'total unsatisfactoriness'. And these are not advanced as merely personal impressions and preferences but as objective judgements to which other critics ought to accede. We are given very little indication of the objective grounds on which they are based, but the following remarks are suggestive. 'What we are not reconciled to by any awareness of intentions is the outraging of our moral sense by the handling of the adultery theme—the triangle, or rather quadrilateral, of personal relations. We remain convinced that when an author, whatever symbolism he intends, presents a drama of men and women, he is committed to dealing in terms of men and women, and mustn't ask us to acquiesce in valuations that contradict our profoundest ethical sensibility. If, of course, he can work a revolutionary change in that sensibility, well and good, but who will contend that James's art in those late novels has that power? In *The Golden Bowl* we continue to find our moral sense outraged.'

Now this is not a *moral* condemnation, as for example was the criticism of the late Mr. H. G. Wells when he said that he regarded Henry James as a public menace and an altogether pernicious influence on the youth of the age. Dr. Leavis does not condemn James because he thinks that his influence on morals is bad. He is clear that these novels can work no change in our moral views: indeed, if they could revolutionize morality, Dr. Leavis's artistic condemnation would be mitigated. He condemns them simply because they are out of line with the moral views which Dr. Leavis assumes his readers to share, and he enunciates a general principle of criticism that any work of literature which deals with men and women and which contravenes accepted principles of morality must be bad. This is in effect a condemnation on the basis of inadequate Realism. What the critic says is that he is unprepared to adopt the attitude of make-believe with regard to any artistic presentation of moral views which conflict notably with his own and that he proposes to apply to them the same standards of judgement as he would apply to similar views in the world of actuality. He has failed in the aesthetic attitude or has, rather, consciously refused to adopt the aesthetic attitude upon this matter. Where his morals are concerned he will be a Realist. When such a critic is dealing with literary works of another race and time, he usually takes a different stand. I have not, for example, seen the *Ion* of Euripides condemned because it expresses an attitude towards the practice of exposing unwanted female children which is profoundly shocking to modern morality. Presumably because that attitude was really current morality among that people at the time when the play was written the critics are more easily able to place themselves imaginatively in their minds, to accept the convention as 'make-believe' and withhold aesthetic condemnation. But Mr. Leavis is unwilling to do this with a modern writer whose ethical views are not his own. Ezra Pound has said, 'The Goncourt's preface to *Germinie Lacerteux* is the declaration of the rights of men trying to record "l'histoire morale contemporaine", the history of contemporary moral disposition, the history of the estimation of values in contemporary behaviour'. He calls it 'the most succinct statement of the views of the 19th century realists'. The critic who condemns a work which does something else than this, assumes Realism as his criterion of excellence.

I am not, let it be understood, questioning Dr. Leavis's judgement of Henry James's novels. I think that it is too extreme, exaggerated by the critic's own prejudices against the rather otiose members of society used by James as the material for his novels, and somewhat lacking in appreciation for what Logan Pearsall Smith would have called James's 'fine writing'. But this is beside the point. What I wish to illustrate is that the criticism is based upon realistic premises—the demand to treat a work of art as though it were or should be a replica of actuality. And criticism is very abundant in such treatment. Nor of course are intrusions of Realism confined to matters of morality, although they are apt to be most striking in this field. Each critic tends to have his own limitations to 'make-believe', his particular range of interests where, because they concern him deeply, he is unwilling to accept an aesthetic presentation of views that conflict with what he believes to be the right but will apply to works of literature the same standards as he applies in life. Many critics for example —and Auden is a notable case—insist upon using a realist criterion in respect to political or economic opinions and will not judge any work of literature to be good which assumes to be correct political or economic views in conflict with his own.

But more often—indeed much more often—than this negative criticism for lack of Realism you will find that when a work is judged to be successfully realistic, 'true to life' as it is called, it is praised for that very reason, with the concealed implication for theory that Realism is a norm of excellence to be applied in assessing the merits of literary art. Mr. Sherwood Anderson once complained: 'This confusion of the life of the imagination with the life of reality is a trap into which most of our critics seem to me to fall about a dozen times each year. Do the trick over and over, and in they tumble. "It is life," they say. "Another great artist has been discovered." What never seems to come quite clear is the simple fact that art is art. It is not life. The life of the imagination will always remain separate from the life of reality. It feeds upon the life of reality, but it is not that life—it cannot be.' Yet critics continue to esteem those works of literature which are 'true to life' because they are true to life; and very many writers of literature—including Mr. Anderson—go to great pains to observe the minutiae of men, manners and things in order that they may be able to give greater verisimilitude to their writings.

It is because of this ambivalence in the attitude both of critics and producers of art to-day towards manifestations of Realism that it is still necessary to sort out the truth of the matter. The problem which Realism raises is: In what sense a work of art can, and to what extent it should, be an exact replica of real or possible actuality. And how is the critic to cope with imaginative improbabilities presented in art? With the theorists too the old problems of Realism still walk the stage in modern dress. They are nowadays debated in terms of artistic *symbolism* and artistic *truth*, but they are at bottom the same old problems still. Their presentation has been changed and their contexts widened, but their importance for practical criticism is as great as ever it was. We shall therefore endeavour to elucidate these two preoccupations of modern aesthetics against the background of traditional theory and assumption.

The theory that art is essentially a form of symbolism used in the interests of communication between man and man is usually presented in the context of a general theory of semantics and has achieved some prominence with the new schools of aesthetic writing.[1] It will be further

---

[1] This manner of formulating the problems has exercised such writers as Mrs. Susanne K. Langer, *Philosophy in a New Key* (1941), Mr. Thomas Clark Pollock, *The Nature of Literature* (1942), Mr. John Hospers, *Meaning and Truth in the Arts* (1946), Theodore Meyer Greene, *The Arts and the Art of Criticism* (1943), and lay at the base of much of the work done by Mr. I. A. Richards and his followers. To all these writers I owe much for the help I have derived from their writings in the clarification and formulation of my own ideas.

discussed in the chapter on the Expressionist theory of art; here we shall be concerned primarily with the possibilities of symbolic exactness in the arts and its claim to be an artistic virtue.

In the language of semantics, whenever one thing 'stands for' some other thing in our minds it is said to be a 'sign' of that other thing, and the thing of which it is a sign is called its 'referent' or in some contexts its 'meaning'. The practical interpretation of signs is the basis of all animal intelligence. It is involved in all 'learned' behaviour—and in what the psychologists call 'conditioned reflexes'—and constitutes some ninety per cent of our waking activities. We are continually interpreting our sensations as signs of things, one thing as the sign of another thing, and the gestures and attitudes of our friends as signs of their intentions or desires. If we did not do so, we should cease to live, for all forethought, all purposive activity, presupposes such interpretation. At this stage the interpretative use of experience does not necessarily involve conceptualized thought; it may be, as we say, purely automatic, the result of acquired experience, the body's purposive response to the call of environment without the hesitant interventions of conscious design. The child dreads the mother's frown, the adult automatically stops his car when the signals are red. The automatic interpretation of experience which expresses itself in learned behaviour is the starting-point for all study of semantics.

A *symbol* is distinguished from a sign in that conceptualization is involved in the interpretation of symbols. A symbol does not directly invite overt behaviour appropriate to the presence of its referent but instigates the formation in the mind of a concept, which is its referent. 'Symbols are not proxy for their objects, but are *vehicles for the conception of objects*. To conceive a thing or a situation is not the same thing as to "react towards it" overtly, or to be aware of its presence.'[1]

The use of symbols is the beginning of human intelligence. If you say the word 'meat' to a suitably conditioned dog, it sits up and begs or hunts restlessly around for meat, dripping saliva on to the carpet. If you say the word 'meat' to a man, he answers you: 'What about meat?' For the dog the word 'meat' was a sign; for the man it was a symbol, inducing him to have a conception of meat.[2] This no animal can do.

Symbols are conveniently classified as conventional, semi-conventional

---

[1] Mrs. Susanne K. Langer, *Philosophy in a New Key* (1941). I here follow Mrs. Langer's distinction between 'sign' and 'symbol'. Others have adopted other usages.

[2] Mrs. Langer uses the excellent illustration: 'If I say "Napoleon", you do not bow to the conqueror of Europe as though I had intended to introduce him, but merely think of him.'

and natural. You see an inn-sign displaying an indeterminate animal of benign appearance depicted in crimson pigment and surmounted by the legend THE RED LION. The letters are *conventional* symbols for you, since by quite arbitrary associations instilled into you with pain and grief in the days of your youth they put you in mind of three specific word-sounds, and these word-sounds—also by arbitrary associations—cause you to think of an animal belonging to a specific genus, with surface-colour of a specific colour-group unusual to animals of that genus. The picture, however, is a *natural* symbol; it puts you in mind of whatever it represents because it is *like* what it represents and to the extent to which it is like. If now you motor on from The Red Lion and see beside the road a sign with a zig-zag marking, you are led to expect that the road will shortly make a sharp bend. This is classed as a *semi-conventional* symbol, since the shape of the sign bears a schematic resemblance to its referent and yet you could not be expected to understand its import without having learned the conventions of the highway code. If you respond to this sign automatically and without conscious thought, you have used it as a 'sign' in the semantic sense; if it causes you to think conceptually of a bend in the road, it was behaving for you as a 'symbol'.

Natural symbols 'work' because they bear an intrinsic likeness to their referents. A picture of a horse symbolizes a horse to you because it is *like* a horse—there are certain features of your sensory experience when you look at the picture which are no more dissimilar to your present recollection of any of your sensory experiences when looking at a real horse than those experiences were different from one another on the several occasions when you have seen a real horse. The features of similarity may be relatively few and other features of the picture may be wildly unlike its referent; but unless this degree of similarity exists in *some* features, the picture cannot act as a natural symbol. And when it functions as a natural symbol it may, of course, be more or less specific in its reference. A photograph of the late King refers to one individual only. A child's schematic drawing of a man is a symbol for the general concept 'man', not for any specific man. Or it may be so general that it stands only for the concept 'animal' with no assignable species.[1] It follows from this

[1] There is strong reason to believe that the art of painting pictures has its origin in the habit of making natural symbols of objects which we are accustomed to conceptualize. The art of children and primitive peoples is largely restricted to making isolated symbols of individual things. The slow development of landscape painting in Europe is evidence of the most convincing sort of the difficulty of making a natural symbol of a group of objects which are not habitually thought of as a unity. There is a strong psychological barrier to *seeing* as a whole something

dependence upon sensory likeness that a picture can—in general—be a symbol for one concept only. A word can have one or many referents. The word 'braces' symbolizes one thing in the United Kingdom and another thing in the United States. The word 'horse' symbolizes for me either a quadruped of specific genus or a rack for drying washing.

Semi-conventional symbolism plays a not unimportant function in works of art. Mr. John Hospers refers to an article by Manfred Bukofzer on 'Allegory in Baroque Music'. 'We find in the music of the sixteenth century on almost every occasion when the text reads "descendit de coelis" a descending melody, and when the text reads "ascendit in coelum" a rising melody.' Bach uses an augmented or diminished ninth to symbolize distance or, because of its supposed harshness, the emotions of anger or horror. The trumpet symbolizes the majesty of God, the canon or fugue the rigid law of the Commandments, and so on. Sometimes conventional symbols from daily life are introduced into music with a semi-conventional function, as Tchaikowski's use of the *Marseillaise* and the Russian National Anthem in the *1812 Overture* or the less obvious allegories of Elgar's *Enigma Variations*. (On the other hand, when the music introduces a likeness to natural sounds, such as the interval of the cuckoo's song or the clanging of anvils, it is using natural symbolism.) This 'indirect iconology of sound', as Bukofzer calls it, has its parallel in the flat gilt background which symbolizes eternity in medieval paintings, the halo which marks the saint, the cap-and-bells of the jester, and so forth. Literature too makes very extensive use of allegorization which involves semi-conventional symbolism. Some allegories, such as those specific to pastoral poetry, or epic poetry, are common to a large number of writers, persisting within a particular style of writing through many centuries. Others are specific to a period or group. Some are as it were the private property of a single writer, such as the allegories of Blake or Yeats. The part played by allegory in all the arts provides a special study of great interest and importance, but semi-conventional symbolism as such has little importance for the analysis of the general principles of symbolism with which we are now concerned.

which we are not yet accustomed to *conceiving* as a whole. Thus Mr. Max J. Friedlander says: 'Landscape-painting begins with the artist sharply observing single parts, trees, plants, mountains, and making them true to nature, without being able to give verisimilitude to the whole—the relation of the parts to one another. Landscape appeared as an accumulation, a conglomeration of isolated parts until, in the last phase, the particular segment is approached from some vantage point or other and all the details are arranged according to space-logic.' *Landscape: Portrait: Still-Life* (1949).

Verbal language, in sharp contrast to the 'natural language' of the visual arts, is an almost purely conventional or arbitrary system of symbolism. It works only for the group of human beings who have learned to associate particular modifications of vocal noise with particular concepts; your meaning cannot be understood by a person who 'speaks another language'. The element of natural symbolism, when the sound is qualitatively like the experience to which it refers (called *onomatopoeia* in the vocabulary of literary criticism), which survives in language is very small, though apt to be greater in poetry than in prose. There are of course other languages than verbal language, such as the languages of flag-wagging or Morse, but most of these are 'second grade' symbolic systems, obtaining their significance by a conventional equation with verbal languages. The language of mathematics is a pure first-grade symbolic system, referring to concepts without verbal counterpart. Verbal language may also of course function as 'sign', as particularly in exclamation and exhortation, when vocal noises are employed as signs of affective states or to occasion an appropriate response in others rather than to initiate conceptual thought. In speech the two functions are differentiated by inflexion or intonation of the voice, but in written language it is often very difficult to distinguish them. Indeed, some writers have maintained the somewhat improbable theory that all artistic use of language, 'poetry' in contrast to prose, is essentially a development of 'language as sign'; its purpose is to evoke emotional response rather than to convey conceptual meanings.

In the context of a general theory of semantics it does then seem moderately sensible to say that both literary art and representational visual art are *mimetic*; both communicate experienced situations, real or imaginal, by means of symbols, literature mainly by means of conventional symbols and visual art mainly by natural symbols. Nor does it seem so completely nonsensical as before to say that literature 'imitates' that which it describes. For what a written description of events or things does is to communicate from man to man a conceptual situation by means of conventional symbols. And when we say that visual art 'imitates', what we are really saying is also that by means of visual symbols recognizably similar to visual experiences which we have known in the past it calls up a general concept made up out of all that group of similar experiences. This is what the 'recognition' of a representation means. I am not at all sure that this way of describing the matter is very helpful to an understanding of the artistic situation or that it can add much to what plain unvarnished common sense could tell us. But this may be only because I like things simple. On the other hand it is, as we must show, a way of looking at the matter which easily conduces to an attitude of mind towards many of the most fundamental problems of art and criticism which many people now regard as a completely wrong and a very dangerous one. For as soon as you think of something as a symbol you think of it as an instrument employed in the furtherance of an ulterior purpose—the purpose of communication. Your attention tends in consequence to be directed upon the aim and object of the activity, on that which is communicated, while the instrument of communication sinks to secondary importance. The value of the symbol lies not in itself but in its instrumentality; it is a utility-value. And only in so far as is necessary for the fulfilment of the purpose it serves is attention accustomed to dwell upon it. Now this consequence may be right or may be wrong, but it must be faced. First, then, we will show in more detail how this sort of attitude is bound up with the symbolic conception of art and then we shall discuss its consequences for criticism.

All conceptualization involves abstracting from the living actuality of experience and isolating out of the concrete fulness of the given situation-in-experience certain features or characteristics which are common to other experienced situations. The concept is therefore always an abstraction. It may be more or less general and abstract. A very general concept embraces a very large number of experienced situations; its content is correspondingly void and blank, emptied of the vital vividness of experienced quality. It is as it were an outline without colour. A more particular concept embraces a smaller number of experiences but its content is correspondingly more rich and full. A concept may be thought of as a container for experience. The more it contains, the thinner and more formless is the container; the richer the intrinsic character of the container, the less it will contain. So also the words which are the symbols of concepts vary in generality. The word 'colour' refers to more experiences than the word 'red', but it refers to them less concretely and vividly, distinguishes one from another less exactly. The word 'run' refers to fewer experienceable events than the word 'move', but it is more concrete and specific. Conceptualization and language are therefore methods of classifying experience and are the only means by which experience can be communicated with precision. There is, moreover, considerable evidence that the progress of the capacity to think conceptually has proceeded hand in hand with the development of language as an instrument of communication. But because language and thought are so familiar to us and 'work' so well for the practical purposes of our lives, it is often forgotten that the full concrete quality of lived experience can never be conceptualized or communicated in language; it escapes from the net of classification which is conceptualization. This is especially the case with the affective element in experience. Language has a few very general and clumsy words to indicate a few rough types or groups of emotion, but it is unable to discriminate the innumerable delicate shades of difference in the experienced quality of emotional situations or to symbolize the rich variety of our affective life. Emotions cannot be 'described' except indirectly by referring to the objective situations upon which they are directed or to their overt bodily manifestations. We say 'I felt like swearing' or 'I felt hot beneath the collar', but such phrases—or any which language can offer—serve very indifferently to communicate the delicate nuances which distinguish what we felt on any one such occasion from our feelings on all the other occasions which would be similarly described. There is, I think, no reasonable doubt that the 'language of gesture' is far more effective for the expression of emotion and mood than the language of words. You may often see in the face of some unknown person—it may be a fellow-traveller in the bus or train—some movement of the features, a quirk of the lips or a lift of the eyebrows, which seems to express to you with great exactness a mood, an emotion, a passing attitude, which there exist no words to describe. There exist affective states and attitudes of mind which can be known but cannot be thought. Bodily attitudes may express the subtle variations of emotion—despair, disillusionment, ecstasy, jubilation—with far more vividness and precision than the most elaborate and gifted scientific or poetic description could do. For this reason the visual artist can—if he wishes to do so—communicate mood and emotion more vividly and more subtly than the writer. For even in repose the set of the features and the stance of the body are expressive both of passing mood and of permanent mental characteristics. No poet can convey with the vivid realism of a Leonardo head, Picasso's *Celestine* or his portrait of Miss Gertrude Stein, or a Rembrandt portrait, the permanent habits and dispositions of mind which are conveyed to us by these pictures. Nor can the best of poets give us so vivid or exact an impression of passing moods and emotions as Goya's etchings *The Disasters of the War* or in sculpture Rodin's *Le Penseur*. But neither can any poet convey emotion, mood or character as vividly or as exactly as any inferior artist or good photograph. For the two modes of symbolism have different potentialities and limitations; and it is important to understand what can be done by each, what should not be expected of each.

One should not, either, expect language to be able to represent or express the concrete sensory content of experience, for it cannot do so. Though you use the enriched and specialized vocabularies of the costume expert and the interior decorator, you still cannot indicate the precise *quale* of any colour perception except by putting it into a class along with a million other similar but individually different experiences. With shape the case is still worse; only some few regular geometrical shapes have names or are describable. But the painter can convey visual experience with some fulness and exactness, limited only by the limitations of his pigments. For he can provide a material analogue of any visual experience by means of which others can repeat the experience—within limits—as it was.[1] This is a thing that the writer cannot do, just as the painter cannot represent the sequence or relation of events. The painter can represent the sly, the witty, the comic, the tragic aspect of experience in visual form, presenting what no words can represent. 'Tiepolo and Degas saw wittily and are deliciously sly in execution; but what they perceived was a purely visual comedy pertaining to forms alone, a joke that can be rendered only in line and colour. All the wit of this Degas lies inside the frame; and no word of explanation will help anyone to see it. It is a joke about forms told in forms, and it could be told in no other way.'[2] Other artists have seen tragically, dramatically, serenely, complacently—and have represented what they have seen in shapes with directness and concreteness. And nothing of this can the poet do.

I do not say this in order to decry the powers of the literary artist—on the whole his potentialities of symbolic representation are probably something fuller and more complex than those of the visual artist. I have tried only to illustrate the point that each system of symbolism has its own scope and its own limitations, which you must know in order to understand what sort of thing a product of literary or visual art is, what kind of work it may be doing. It is, for example, commonly affirmed that art represents or somehow expresses and communicates 'ineffable' experience, and a great deal of nonsense is apt to be talked about this. If the word 'ineffable' is used in its strict sense of 'incommunicable by verbal lan-

---

[1] Some artists think in terms of the visual experiences of daily life and are faced with the problem of 'translating' their visual constructs into the more limited medium of pigments. Others think and construct in terms of pigment-colours and have no problem of translation. Their constructs are of course apt to be less direct analogues of 'nature-as-seen'. 'But we may safely say that the paintings of Monet, of Pissaro, of Sisley, would not have been at all what they are, if they had not been conceived in terms of what artists' colourmen had made of oil-paint.' Walter Richard Sickert, *A Free House!* (1947).

[2] Clive Bell, *Enjoying Pictures* (1934).

guage', then a very great deal of experience comes within this category—and of this a great deal can be communicated by the natural symbolism of the visual arts. They can symbolize the sensory *quale* of visual experience, which is ineffable to verbal symbolism; their capacity to symbolize affective experience is limited by the superior expressiveness of the language of gesture over the language of words. There is no great mystery about this. But if what is meant by 'ineffable' is some element in experience which can be conveyed by no system of symbolism, then clearly it cannot be represented by the visual or any other form of art. All that could be meant would be that when he arranges his coloured pigments on canvas in a pictorial structure, or fashions sounds into a musical composition, the artist hopes that on making contact with his work of art his public will experience an emotion similar to an emotion which he experienced when he created it. And when poetry is said to communicate experience 'ineffable' to prose the same sort of thing may legitimately be meant. Language, including poetical language, may serve as a 'sign' to evoke emotions in the hearer; and though the transaction may become very subtle and complex, there is no essential mystery about it. But more than this is often meant by the assertion—and when this point is reached the discussion usually and more appropriately turns on the meaning of artistic 'truth'.

In order for one thing to be a sign or a symbol of another thing for any person it is necessary only that they are so connected in his mind that the one thing can 'stand for' the other. There is nothing in the situation itself to determine which shall be the sign and which the referent; that is dependent upon the degree of interest which each thing has for the person in question. Words usually function as symbols for concepts, but we sometimes have a concept and search our minds for the appropriate word to express it; or we recognize or think of a person and search our minds for his name, which we have forgotten. In such a case the concept or the thought is a 'sign' for the word. Language is a particularly convenient system of symbolism just because the slight vocal noises of which it is composed are so completely uninteresting in themselves. Attention can be focused entirely upon the referent without dwelling at all upon the sign. And when this happens, whenever one experience is a sign or symbol of something else, to the extent to which it is successfully and efficiently functioning as a symbol, we cease to be aware of the experienced quality of the sign. It becomes transparent. We are not conscious of it in experience. As Mrs. Langer has said: 'A symbol which interests us *also* as an object is distracting. It does not convey its meaning without obstruction.

. . . But little noises are ideal conveyors of concepts, for they give us nothing but their meaning. That is the source of the "transparency" of language, on which several scholars have remarked. Vocables in themselves are so worthless that we cease to be aware of their physical presence at all, and become conscious only of their connotations, denotations, or other meanings. Our conceptual activity seems to flow *through* them, rather than merely to accompany them, as it accompanies other experiences that we endow with significance. They fail to impress us as 'experiences' in their own right, unless we have difficulty in using them as words, as we do with a foreign language or a technical jargon until we have mastered it.' This principle of the transparency of the symbol, its tendency to vanish from experience in so far as it succeeds in functioning as a symbol, is of quite outstanding importance for the theory of art.[1] For it often happens that what the artist wants to do is *not* to furnish a set of visual symbols but to create the potentiality of a new and autotelic visual experience which you will savour for its own sake and for what it is. He does not want to cause you to think how pathetic the donkey looks or wonder whether the beautiful lady is married, but to savour and enjoy the colours and shapes of the things he has made for you to see. He does not want you to be reminded of the wonderful appearance of a sunset you once saw, but to look at and delight in the sunset he has made for you. This is certainly the predominant purpose of most plastic artists to-day and may have been a subconscious purpose of most artists in all ages.[2] And for this reason the artist often makes his representations unlike rather than just like the things they represent, in order that the observer may be shocked into looking at them for what they are instead of using them as symbols of something else and so failing to see them. And this is

[1] The poverty in the content of the visual experiences of practical life greatly occupied T. E. Hulme, who by a different path reached a conception of aesthetic experience in some ways analogous to that which we shall adumbrate in chapter IX of this work. 'What I see and hear', he asserted, 'is simply a selection made by my senses to serve as a light for my conduct. My senses and my consciousness give me no more than a practical simplification of reality. In the usual perception I have of reality all the differences useless to man have been suppressed. My perception runs in certain moulds. Things have been classified with a view to the use I can make of them. It is this classification I perceive rather than the real shape of things. I hardly see an object, but merely notice. We only see stock types. We tend to see not *the* table but only *a* table.' *Speculations* (1924).

[2] 'If before a landscape you say "what a lovely picture!" the artist, if he hears you, will be flattered—if however you say "what a lovely place!" he will probably resent it as a damning criticism of his work, although in point of fact he set out to tell us what a lovely place it was.' Roger Fry, *Last Lectures* (1939), p. 13.

the source of much conflict between the artist and his public. The public wants to *use* a portrait as a symbol to put it in mind of its subject; it wants to *use* a landscape in order to stimulate recollections of beautiful scenery and pleasant events associated with it. It does not want to *look at* them as pictures. And to the extent it uses them as symbols it does not see them as pictures. But this is just what the artist does not want. With the artist the symbolic function of his picture is secondary and he does not want it to interfere with the experience of visual contact with the picture he has made. M. Jean-Paul Sartre is one who has understood the possibilities of conflict between symbolic function and the function of art. He points out that anything at all may by convention be given the attributes of a symbol. And he goes on: 'Thus, we talk of the language of flowers. But, if after agreement, white roses signify "fidelity" to me, the fact is that I have stopped seeing them as roses. My attention cuts through them to aim beyond them at this abstract virtue. I forget them. I no longer pay attention to their mossy abundance, to their sweet stagnant odour. I have not even perceived them. That means that I have not behaved like an artist. For the artist, the colour, the bouquet, the tinkling of the spoon on the saucer, are things, in the *highest* degree. He stops at the quality of the sound or the form. He returns to it constantly and is enchanted with it. It is this colour-object that he is going to transfer to his canvas, and the only modification he will make it undergo is that he will transform it into an *imaginary* object. He is therefore as far as can be from considering colours and signs as a *language*. What is valid for the elements of artistic creation is also valid for their combinations. The painter does not want to draw signs on his canvas, he wants to create a thing.'[1]

The writer, on the other hand, deals essentially with meanings. For a word without its meaning is simply a trivial vocal noise insignificant for artistic or any other purpose. Yet it remains true that in artistic or poetic language the word as symbol is less transparent than in the ordinary language of communication. It is still the word-as-meaning—or rather as a complex of meanings—but we are required to attend to it to a greater degree than in prose as a thing in itself; it does not wholly disappear into the meaning of which it acts as a symbol in each context where it is used. This is a point which must exercise considerably the attention of writers who would analyse the qualities of excellence in works of poetic art.

Let us consider now what happens when you look at a picture if you are a Realist about art. We will suppose that you are looking at a portrait of your grandmother which you have commissioned from Sargent at

[1] *What is Literature?* (Eng. Trans. 1950).

great cost. You advance your eyes to within a few inches of it, examine the brush strokes and the canvas showing through the paint, study the oiliness and the stickiness, the gloss and the texture—everything in fact that you can see. But you do not see your grandmother. You are looking at it as at any other real physical object, not as a picture. You are not yet using it as a symbol. Then you retire to an appropriate distance and see your grandmother's likeness. You do not believe that your grandmother is really present in the wall of the room, for you know that it is only a picture, a pretence, an imitation. But what you actually see is in certain aspects as like what you saw on some occasion when you did see her in reality as the various occasions when you really saw her are like one another in your memory. And you want her portrait to be so like her that you and her friends will readily recognize that it is her they are seeing and not an old lady in general. It need not be 'exactly like'. You would probably be gratified rather than offended if it represented her as somewhat more dignified, more noble, than she was accustomed to appear in actuality. But you would object to any untoward or degrading features such as snakes for hair or a wart where no wart was. And the reason for this attitude is that you treat the portrait as a 'utility object'.[1] You use it

[1] I propose to use the term 'utility-object' in a very wide sense to denote any artefact which serves any purpose at all other than or in addition to simply existing as a beautiful object. Thus a portrait may serve to perpetuate the physical appearance of the magnate who commissioned it, a successful play may provide an income for its author and a pleasant pastime for a series of audiences, a portrait of Stalin may serve the purposes of political propaganda, an icon of the Virgin may serve religious propaganda. Whether or not a work of art was made for any purpose other than to be a work of art, whether it in fact serves any other purpose and, if it does, whether it serves that purpose efficiently or inefficiently, is completely irrelevant to its excellence as a work of art. The purpose of the artist is, therefore, an irrelevant consideration in judging works of art, for a great number of excellent works of art have been produced incidentally by artists who had other objects in mind—such as earning a living, arousing a sense of indignation at social inequalities, making people laugh, copying as exactly as possible a selected piece of nature, and so on. In saying that these utility-purposes are irrelevant to the excellence of works of art I am not enunciating a dogma of my own but making a generalization from the facts of critical judgement everywhere. Critics allow that some portraits which admirably serve the purpose of perpetuating the features of the subject are good works of art and others bad; critics rank very high as literary art some writings which have been intended to arouse indignation at this or that abuse and some which have done so; other writing which has had the same intention and equal success is simply communist trash with no literary merit in the eyes of the critic. These are facts of criticism which must be recognized in any theory of art which is not to be completely divorced from the realities of aesthetic judgement.

in order to evoke in your mind a more defined image of your grand-mother on the occasions when you look at it and also in order to manifest to men the honour and respect in which you hold her.

Now suppose you look at such a picture as Rouault's *Espagnole*. What you see is a woman of Spanish type, not a specific woman whom you recognize—though a particular woman may have served as model for the picture. You do not value such a picture because it causes you to think of some woman whom you have known but because you happen to like looking at women of that type. And you hang it on the wall of your room because this is more convenient to do than to arrange for a Spanish-looking woman to be present whenever you happen to want to look at one. You are again using the picture as a utility-object. And the same attitude may determine your liking for a flower-piece, a picture of natural scenery, a Dutch interior. You do not select the picture necessarily because it reminds you of a landscape which you have known and loved, but because you enjoy looking at landscape in general and the landscape which you see when you look at this picture suits your taste in landscape. You are, once more, using the picture as a utility-object. Now the critics are very much in the habit of praising representational pictures for the realism with which they reproduce the appearance of things we see in actuality. Such and such a picture causes you vividly to see the faint luminescence of flesh and almost to feel its palpitating softness, such another reproduces the texture of silk with such accuracy that you might imagine you could feel its rich glossiness with your fingers, another makes you see the hundred subtly graded tones in the shadows of a faintly lighted interior, and still another puts before your eyes the 'fruitiness' of apples and grapes until almost you could eat them.[1] I do not wish to say

[1] 'This head is an extraordinary example of how art can imitate Nature, because here we have all the details painted with great subtlety. The eyes possess that moist lustre which is constantly seen in life, and about them are those livid reds and hair which cannot be rendered without the utmost delicacy. The lids could not be more natural, for the way in which the hairs issue from the skin, here thick and there scanty, and following the pores of the skin. The nose possesses the fine delicate reddish apertures seen in life. The opening of the mouth, with its red ends, and the scarlet cheeks seem not colour but living flesh. To look closely at her throat you might imagine that the pulse was beating.' Vasari on the *Mona Lisa*.

'He excelled in the representation of that type of female beauty which emerges to linger, vaguely floating, in the features of a little girl. There are subtleties, adorable endearments of tone in his painting of the hair, of those fugitive locks, inadequately bound by a ribbon, which disperse into the air like grains of dust, and in his painting of that golden irradiation which crowns the forehead or that tracery

that such praise is wrong. But we should be aware of just what it is the critic is inviting us to praise. It is not, in the first place, the accurate rendering of a known object as in the portrait of your grandmother; you need not previously have seen *that* piece of silk or *that* particular Spanish scene. You are not put in mind of any one definite experience from your past. Nor is it some *new* experience that the artist furnishes, for you must already have seen actual silk, actual flesh in that lighting, in order to

of little blue veins that embroiders the temples. He knew how to express the depth, the veiled flame in a girl's eye; how to render the liquid quality of a glance, to soften its expression, to moisten its glow, how to convey the quivering of emotion or passion in the gentleness of a tear restrained by the eyelashes. He put youth into everything: the nostrils tremble, the full lips are parted by a breath, the mouth strains forward in a vague aspiring movement. Glazes heightened by rouges and ribbings of dry impasto, streaks of light superimposed upon transparent half-tones and bursting vividly upon the insubstantiality beneath, suffice to produce upon canvas all these charming faces, these rose complexions, this white, downy skin, full of life from the blood flowing in its veins and bathed in sunlight, these slender necks, these arched shoulders caressing the eye like a pair of doves, these newly formed breasts veiled by the changeful reflected lights of a gauze *fichu*; these are the felicities of a colourist. . . .' Edmond and Jules de Goncourt on Greuze in *French XVIII Century Painters* (Eng. Trans. 1948).

'The great charm of Wilson's landscapes lies in his atmospheric effects. . . . He was the first to show the English the beauty of their own country.' 'The unique achievement of Constable is that, breaking with the tradition both of Claude and the Dutch, he first went for inspiration direct to nature and painted the English countryside in its unadorned beauty as a worthy subject in itself, complete and perfect.' Eric Underwood, *A Short History of English Painting* (1933).

'In his *bodegones*, from the very first, the separate objects possess an extraordinary illusionism. The surfaces, each glowing with its own individual quality, are more than real. This is accomplished certainly by a wonderful technical facility; but that in its turn can be the result only of a still more wonderful intensity of observation, a uniquely detached interest in the object. The painted surfaces, which seem more tangible, somehow, than the originals, end in contours of absolute decision, related to one another in such a way as to make everything inevitable, as if it could not possibly have been otherwise. . . . The figures have all been studied in the studio, each in a concentrated sidelight; but the sum of them all is an effect of new intensity, an impression of incredible vitality. One feels the heat of their blood under the pressure of the hot sun and of the heady wine. This is the very essence of the immemorial Spanish people and their countryside, parched brown under the sullen blue of the sky. The paint itself is thick and leathery, but Velasquez' power to paint illusions has acquired a still greater versatility. There is a still further degree of tangibility in the porcelain bowl and the wine which it contains, in the filled glass upheld by the satyr, or the empty glass upon the ground, in the steel and the leather, the felt and the cloth, the tanned skins and matted hair and the brilliant eyes which dominate the scene.' Mr. Philip Hendy on Velasquez' *Los Borrachos* in *Spanish Painting* (1946).

know and feel that the representation is exact. It may indeed be the skilled craftsmanship of the artist who can do with pigment so much more than the common run can do—but most of the critics would deny that the merit lies only, or chiefly, in the craftsmanship. The only alternative that is left is that the critic is judging the picture for its utility-function, is pointing out to you how nearly it enables you to obtain by looking at it the same delightful experiences you might obtain in real life by looking at those things which the canvas depicts, but without putting yourself to the trouble of searching for the right adolescent girl in the right pose, of visiting Spain or buying a bunch of flowers. I do not think that many critics would agree that these are their motives for giving the praise they do or that they have taken the trouble to analyse what their motives are. But these are the only motives anyone could think of for praising such pictures because of their Realism.

Some years ago Mr. Edwin Glasgow wrote a book[1] to illustrate the thesis that 'from the earliest times the vast majority of people have tacitly assumed that the artist's business is to hold the mirror up to nature and even, if possible, to deceive the spectator and make him think that he is looking at the real thing when he is only looking at a square foot or two of paint'. Artists, too, started with the ambition to make a replica of things as like what they saw as possible. But finding many difficulties in their way, they gradually modified their ideal and 'baffled realism turned to interpretation'. None the less the enthusiasm for visual appearances, for the 'adventitious superficies of things', remains the chief inspiration of artists—or of the artists in whom Mr. Glasgow is interested, who do not include El Greco, Blake or Stanley Spencer—and true to the tradition of Realism but with richer understanding and better methods, artists are still trying to transfer to canvas this 'lure of visible nature'. Mr. Glasgow quotes the following lines of Wordsworth in illustration of the artist's interest in the colours and forms of nature for their own sake:

> The sounding cataract
> Haunted me like a passion: the tall rock,
> The mountain, and the deep gloomy wood,
> Their colours and their forms, were then to me
> An appetite; a feeling and a love,
> That had no need of a remoter charm,
> By thought supplied, nor any interest
> Unborrowed from the eye.

[1] *The Painter's Eye* (1936).

The last three lines do indeed express the poet's interest in visual experience for its own sake. But what the very great majority of contemporary artists would answer to Mr. Glasgow is that nature—as Whistler said nearly a century ago—does not produce pictures. The artist creates constructs of form and colour to be seen for themselves alone, but they are better, more worthy of being experienced, than the appearances of nature. He does not simply try to repeat what nature gives, to render permanent on canvas what is fleeting in reality. Mr. Glasgow (in so far as he is consistent to his own doctrine of Realism) wants his pictures as utility-objects to substitute for nature, that he may more easily and conveniently enjoy the visual experiences which nature could equally supply. This is *not* the artist's aim—legitimate as it may be as a motive for buying the artist's pictures.

We now come to a more complicated case. Many pictures, as has been said, symbolize by means of facial expression or bodily attitude and gesture the character, moods and emotions which men display in real life. They cannot symbolize more than can be symbolized by the 'language of gesture' in the real world which they copy, because their mode of symbolizing is to provide an image or reproduction of the gesture-symbols from which we infer emotions and character in life. In so far as they represent states and affections of the human mind, pictures are, therefore, secondary symbols; they are natural visual symbols of gesture-symbols. Many pictures are nevertheless praised by critics and others for the vividness and the accuracy with which they manifest the profundities and intensities of human character and emotion. Many of the works of Leonardo, to suggest but one outstanding example, have received intensive praise for just this reason. Other pictures—particularly religious and historical pictures—portray people symbolizing the sorts of emotions which they might have been expected to experience in the situations in which they are depicted. These pictures, too, are often praised for their 'psychological Realism', for the exactness and truth, the passion and profundity, of their emotional expression. But still, however delicate or sublime be the emotions, however subtle and precise the impression of character, in so far as you look at these pictures in order to become aware of the mental characteristics or emotional states which the persons depicted in them display, you are using the pictures as utility-objects. There seems, indeed, to be every justification for doing so. It is more convenient to look at pictures than to go walking the streets and marts in quest of 'types'. You can no longer recall an historical scene in order to experience directly its actuality and you may not have a very vivid imagination to picture to yourself what the people participating in it looked like or what sort of feelings they visibly displayed; and an imaginary scene obviously cannot be recreated for actual experience. Hence a special and useful purpose may be served by such pictures as *Dante et Virgile Traversant le Lac de la Ville Infernale de Dite* and *Le Christ au Jardin des Oliviers* of Eugène Delacroix, by the many Crucifixions, Annunciations, Last Suppers and scenes from the lives of the saints which formed a substantial part of the output of most famous painters in the past, and by the *genre* paintings of such artists as Bruegel, Rembrandt, Rowlandson, Holbein, Daumier, who were themselves interested in the springs of behaviour in the human animal. But in so far as you look at these pictures in order to be put in mind of the emotional situations expressed by the faces and attitudes of the persons they depict, you are using them as imitations of natural symbols and you are failing to see them as things in their own right. You are therefore probably failing to see them as the artist at any rate would want them to be seen. Many artists, indeed, realizing that the depiction of emotional situations tends to distract the observer from seeing the pictures they have made, prefer to eliminate all emotional symbolization from their pictures.[1] Mr. Clive Bell once went so far as to say: 'A painter too feeble to create forms which provoke more than a little aesthetic emotion will try to eke that little out by suggesting the emotions of life. To evoke the emotions of life he must use representation. Thus a man will paint an execution, and fearing to miss with his first barrel of significant form, will try to hit with his second by raising an emotion of fear and pity. But if in the artist an inclination to play upon the emotions of life is often a sign of a flickering inspiration, in the spectator a tendency to seek, behind the form, the emotions of life is a sign of defective sensibility always.'[2] This is extremist. Roger Fry, with more leniency, recognized that the emotional content of a picture may comprise symbolized emotions of life—which he called 'dramatic' or 'psychological' values— and also the actual structure of coloured shapes and forms which is the picture; and this latter he called its 'plastic' values. More attention to the symbolized 'life-emotions' means less attention to the 'plastic' forms by which they are symbolized, and appreciation of a picture which combines

---

[1] 'Further, the associations of ideas which once played an essential part in the artistic effect are now suppressed and, wherever possible, eliminated.' Max. J. Friedlander, *Landscape: Portrait: Still-life* (1949).

[2] *Art* (1923). Mr. Clive Bell makes the common mistake of supposing that by symbolizing people who symbolize emotional states by their attitudes and gestures, pictorial art causes the observer to experience in himself these same emotions.

both often requires the conscious transference of attention from one to the other. The shapes and colours which themselves are the picture may also evoke emotions or affective tendencies in the observer quite apart from any symbolic function which they may have. And full appreciation of a picture may involve adjustment between the emotions evoked by the forms in themselves and the emotions represented by the forms as symbols.

I do not wish to argue that pictures should not be praised for the vividness or the accuracy with which they depict emotional situations; that is for the critic to decide. But the many critics who praise pictures for this reason should realize that they are praising them not as pictures to be looked at for themselves but as a special kind of utility-objects. It may be utterly legitimate for them to serve this purpose of utility-objects, they may have been made for that purpose as many pictures most certainly were; but it should still be understood that this is the motive of the praise that is accorded them. And it must be realized further that a bad picture (one which the critic would condemn as bad on other grounds) or a good photograph would serve this purpose as well as the best picture that has been painted. A good photograph of the right subject would symbolize character or emotion as efficiently as a Leonardo. A photograph of a Crucifixion or a Transfiguration with suitable actors would symbolize the intended emotions as efficiently as the most inspired painting. There is no historical or religious scene which could not be represented by suitable actors suitably grouped; and a photograph of the grouped actors would serve as a picture which would convey to the spectator everything in the emotional situation involved every whit as efficiently as the finest painting ever painted. What the photograph could not give is something we value which resides in the shapes and forms and colours of the picture outside and apart from their efficient functioning as symbols. If we value the painting more than the photograph, it is for reasons other than its symbolic efficacy; it is a value which comes to it only when we begin to look at it *not* as a symbol of persons symbolizing emotions by gesture-language but as an aesthetic structure of shapes and colours. If, too, it is a matter of *evoking* emotion in the spectator—many critics, including Mr. Clive Bell, invariably confuse the symbolization of emotion with the evocation of emotion—then in so far as the 'life-emotions' are concerned a bad picture is as useful as a good one. A portrait of Stalin does not need to be what the critic would judge a good picture in order to evoke the appropriate emotions, and a garish image of the Virgin is as effective for stimulating religious emotions in the faithful as any Madonna by Raphael.

On the other hand some structures of shapes and colours do have a power in themselves to evoke emotions of another sort.

It was in order to distinguish what he regarded as the true function of a picture from these subsidiary utility-functions that Matisse said: 'When I see the frescoes of Giotto at Padua I am not concerned to know what scene from the life of Christ I have before me, but immediately I understand the feeling which it conveys, for it is in the lines, the composition, the colour; and the title only confirms my impression.' But if a picture *does* represent an emotional situation, if it does symbolize figures symbolizing emotion, this fact is certainly germane to its full appreciation by the ordinary unspecialized observer. And if it represents anything at all, even though no emotion is expressed, the mere fact of representation is germane to seeing the structure of colours and shapes which is the picture. For a shape which is recognized as representative, as a natural symbol of some known object, immediately acquires additional insistence and weight in the balanced harmony of visual impressions which is the picture. This fact too must be taken into consideration.

Criticism of the visual arts to-day is, as has been said, curiously half-hearted and inconsistent about the realistic question. No one now *demands* Realism as a condition of a picture's being judged good. No one would any longer dream of writing as Vasari wrote, and even in the daily press you no longer find remarks such as that made by the *Spectator* in 1864: 'A picture at best can only represent faithfully the scene or incident to which it refers, and anyone can judge it who has a good eye and knows the story.' The pictorial products displayed in the service of commercial advertisement have accustomed our eyes to seeing the element of Realism attenuated to the verge of unrecognizability, until the visual symbol may almost cease to work as a symbol at all. In posters advertising electric light bulbs, or somebody's brand of rum or shoe polish, we see with equanimity the human figure distorted into the semblance of some grotesque form of insect life, and in fashion magazines the female body insulted to a prurient schoolboy's dream of breasts and buttocks rampant upon a flat and shapeless plank. It is true that popular reviewers still periodically rant against the distortions of Picasso or Moore, the degeneration of Dali or the mannered modism of Modigliani. But that is because the forms created by these artists are strong and disturbing and compel even the untutored spectator to see them as they are in themselves, impelling and powerful, instead of losing awareness of them in their employment as symbols. And disliking this unaccustomed disturbance of sensibility, the public mistakes its unease for a criticism of inadequate

Realism. In truth neither the critics or the public any longer require Realism in pictorial products artistic or non-artistic.

Yet critics and historians of art continue to lavish praise upon artists living or dead either because in their pictures or sculptures they very realistically symbolize some sensuous experience from common life or because they very exactly represent by visual symbols persons who by attitude, expression or gesture realistically symbolize permanent traits or human character or emotionally disturbed frames of mind. Such praise is not wrong. Pictures serve and are made for many other purposes than simply to exist and be looked at for what they are; they have many utility-functions and for these they are manufactured, multiplied and bought. This is a social fact which critic and theorist must accept. And to praise them for competently fulfilling any of these utility-functions is as legitimate as to praise a spade for being a good spade to dig with. But such praise becomes inconsistent with acquiescence in voluntary abandonment of Realism unless the critic makes it plain that he is in fact commending the picture as a utility-object and not as a work of art, although it may very well be both. When he accords such praise the critic is bound always to make clear to the reader that he is judging the picture for the efficiency with which it fulfils a legitimate utility-function, but one which pictorial products which he would judge to be artistically bad or neutral could equally well fulfil. If the critic does not do this, his readers cannot know what he means or does not mean when he says any picture is good or bad.

Chapter V

REALISM IN MODERN DRESS
2. ART AS TRUTH

Chaucer had a deeper knowledge of life than Shakespeare.

EZRA POUND

Le Beau n'est pas le serviteur du Vrai. LECONTE DE LISLE

In this direction fiction is truer than history, because it goes beyond the evidence. E. M. FORSTER

LITERATURE is a mode of art fashioned and constructed out of conventional symbols whose relation to their referents is not one of natural likeness but an arbitrary consequence of acquired habits of association. The Realism of literature does not consist therefore in the exactness of an intrinsic similarity between symbol and experienced actuality but in some relation of congruity, not at all easy to define, between the conceptual or imaginal referent and extra-literary experience. This relation is usually described by phrases such as 'true to life'—or simply 'true'—and literary Realism is manifested when it is assumed that a work of literature judged to display this relation is excellent as literature on that account. As has been said, Realism is seldom now demanded in advance as a general condition of literary excellence; but when it occurs, or seems to occur, it is apt to be seized upon and praised by the critics as though it were.

The sort of assumption we have in mind is that which is made explicit in the following quotation. 'There is one affirmation, and one affirmation only, that the poet, or the painter, or the sculptor makes all the time. It may be indicated by a gesture of the arm. "There! That is what life looks like when it is seen by the seeing eye."'[1] Again the claim is often made that, although it is not to be judged by the scientist's or the lawyer's

---

[1] R. A. Scott-James, *The Making of Literature* (1928). Those who read German will find in Erich Auerbach's *Mimesis: Dargestellte Wirklichkeit in der abendlandischen Literatur* (1946) a very painstaking survey on literary Realism over a wide field.

standards of truth, literature is nevertheless true in some deeper and more fundamental sense of the word; and the quality of its truth is a measure of its excellence as art. Mr. L. A. Reid quotes the following affirmation by Mr. F. L. Lucas, which I take to be typical. 'Some other forms of art may be merely beautiful; by Tragedy, I think, we imply also something fundamentally true to life. It need not be the whole truth, but it must be true.'[1] We do not propose to multiply quotations in evidence or to go through the writings of the critics with a statistical divining-rod. It is our intention simply to make explicit the kind of attitude in judgement with which we shall be concerned; and no reader can voyage far in the literature of criticism without discovering on his own account how widely prevalent it is.[2] Though most characteristic of literary criticism, this concern with 'truth in life' in some recondite and higher sense obtrudes into criticism of all the arts.

I know no writer who has succeeded in explaining what this truth is which art must have, and a good deal of speculation has grown up around it. Critics are quite clear that it is not the truth of science which consists in correspondence with facts and experimental verifiability; it does not exclude the imaginative and the fictitious. Beyond this nothing is clear. But if you clear away all mystification and emotive obscurantism, it can, it would seem, mean one of two things and only two things.

It may on the one hand mean that representational works of art, being constructs of natural or conventional symbols which communicate experience from man to man, must communicate experiences which correspond more or less closely with some actual or possible experiences other than the experience of making contact with the work of art itself. There may be an implication—as there is in the quotation from Mr. F. L. Lucas—that the experience, actual or possible, to which they correspond should be an experience regarded as important rather than one that is trivial or banal. But with or without this implication the demand for artistic truth, understood in this way, is a demand for Realism in some form or other. And the only other sense in which the demand can have meaning is a mystical sense. Some people hold that the primary purpose of art is not to communicate experience by symbols but to provoke emotions in the observer. Some of these people also believe that all or some affective states involve knowledge of reality which is inaccessible to

[1] L. A. Reid, *A Study in Aesthetics* (1931), quoting from F. L. Lucas, *Tragedy*.
[2] Whenever a critic uses the phrase 'true to life', the discerning reader will presume that he is adopting for the nonce a Realist theory of literary excellence.

conceptual reason. Works of art then become 'true' by provoking affective states which involve this non-conceptual knowledge of reality. And this is in essence the 'mystical' doctrine of artistic truth.

In the present chapter we shall be concerned only with the former meaning and we shall try to assess the validity of the demand for 'realistic truth' in literary art by common-sense methods, taking the verdicts of the critics themselves as our criterion of what is good and bad literary art.

In the first place it is clear that neither factual truth in the sense of historicity nor theoretical or metaphysical truth in the usual meaning of these terms is necessary to a good work of art.[1] You do not judge the *Odyssey* a better—or worse—poem because you believe or do not believe that parts of it were based upon an actual voyage in prehistoric times. You do not judge the *Pharsalia* to be a better poem than the *Aeneid* because it is closer to the events of history. Nor on the other hand do you judge *Robinson Crusoe* any the worse for believing that it was based in part upon the actual experiences of Alexander Selkirk or condemn Doughty's *Arabia Deserta* because the material for it was afforded by his own travels. You do not withhold judgement on the artistic merits of ancient Egyptian, Mesopotamian, Aztec, Indian, Chinese, Peruvian art until the archaeologist can inform you whether or not each work was recording a historical incident. Nor do you value the *De Rerum Natura* any the less highly because you have learned to disbelieve in the physics of Democritus or condemn the *Inferno* because you do not accept the Christian doctrine of hell. The judgements of criticism—and these are not casual or wayward opinions of this or that critic, but the most solid and universal consensus you will find anywhere in critical literature—therefore condemn the view, of which Zola made himself the recognized exponent,[2] that a writer should avoid inventing fictional events and persons, limiting himself to recording suitably selected material from what has actually occurred. Broadly and in the main, though they may waver in particular cases, the critics in practice rank a work of art no better and no worse for its historicity or lack of it. Similarly critics in practice regard it as irrelevant to excellence whether a poem asserts a scientific or metaphysical doctrine or not; and if it does, judgement on the excellence of the poem is not held to be affected by whether the critic believes or disbelieves whatever doctrine the poem asserts. Some critics have denied

[1] I am referring throughout to the general judgements of criticism about the ranking of works of art; not my private opinions.
[2] *The Experimental Novel* (1894).

this on principle, but the evidence of their practical valuations always belies their denial.

Recognizing this broad general truth, critics and theorists have often taken the view that literature need not indeed be true in the sense of being a recognizably accurate account of facts which have actually occurred, but it must at least be plausible. It must recount things that might well have occurred even though we have no reason to believe that just those series of events did in fact occur. They quote in confirmation the dictum which Aristotle applied to epic poetry and tragedy, that 'it is not the poet's province to relate such things as have actually happened, but such things as might have happened'. But this criterion is also refuted by the practical judgements of criticism. Many critics estimate very highly the literary merits of some Greek tragedies and epic poems without believing in classical mythology; a critic does not have to profess himself a follower of Sir Oliver Lodge in order to esteem *The Midsummer Night's Dream*; you do not have to find the events described in *Gulliver's Travels* plausible in real life in order to value it as literature or believe in oriental magic in order to appreciate *The Shaving of Shagpat*. In fact, when we read a work of literature as literature we agree with ourselves to set aside all normal considerations of plausibility and to accept as plausible whatever the author makes to be so. For the time being we adopt his conventions of what might very well happen and put them in the place of those reservations of probability which have been instilled into us by the bitter experience of living. It is, once again, the principle of the 'voluntary suspension of disbelief', which is the basis of all aesthetic appreciation. As Mr. I. A. Richards has said: 'There is a suppressed conditional clause implicit in all poetry. If things were such and such, then . . .' The only criterion of plausibility which you can apply is the criterion of internal consistency: the author must remain faithful to the conventions of plausibility which he himself has imposed, it does not much matter what they are. If he does not impose his own laws of plausibility, then we instinctively assume the canons of practical life. If he imposes laws and is not consistent to them, then our *attitude of assumption* is frustrated and we judge the work to be defective. To invent a very crude illustration of what I mean. —If your heroine, Miss Priscilla Fruncible, is a blonde on page one and a brunette on page ten; if in your first chapter she is a gay and unrepentant ignoramus and with no development of character in between takes to quoting from Shakespeare and Horace in the last chapter; if from a sentimental assignment in the garden she comes directly downstairs to take tea with her aunts—in any moderately realistic novel these are blemishes which would not be excused. For such things do not happen. But in *Alice in the Looking Glass* or in the novels of Thorne Smith almost anything may happen, and you do not apply such canons because different criteria of probability have been successfully imposed by the authors. Things are acceptable in *Jurgen*, in *Trimblerigg*, in *The Flying Inn* or in *Mr. Weston's Good Wine* which would stand out like a sore thumb in *The Forsyte Saga*. You may even delight in the unreality of the conditions which the author creates, provided that they are consistent in the degree and manner of their unreality so that for the time being they seem real. Some 'suspension of disbelief' is essential to making any aesthetic contact; without it you cannot begin to appreciate literature or any representative art. Were it not so, history would be the only fiction, the news-reels the only films and text-books of popular science or white papers recording the results of official investigations would rank as the world's most valuable works of literature. Because it is so, 'internal consistency' and not conformity with the actual is the sole standard of 'aesthetic truth' in literary art.

The practical verdict of criticism is, then, that verisimilitude is not a necessary or contributory condition of excellence in literary art, if you mean by it plausibility according to the ordinary practical standards of what is plausible in daily life. The only condition imposed upon the work of art is inner consistency, and practical plausibility may be violated without limit provided that you have this internal consistency. This, I think, is what Mr. E. M. Forster, for instance, was getting at when, in his *Aspects of the Novel*, he said of Fielding's *Amelia* and Jane Austen's *Emma* that: 'They are real not because they are like ourselves . . . but because they are convincing.'

But if correspondence with real or possible actuality is not a necessary condition of artistic excellence, then most certainly it is not and cannot be of itself an *artistic* virtue, or an aesthetic merit, in those works of literature where it happens to occur.

Nevertheless, critics have been reluctant to jettison the belief that in some sense or other verisimilitude—'truth to life' or 'truth to human nature'—is a merit in some or most literature. So it has been argued that literature need not indeed be either true or plausible in detail but that it should exemplify, even in its implausibilities and loftiest soarings of the imagination, what Dr. Johnson called 'general and transcendental truths'. And for this version, too, Aristotle is adduced in support and the passage from the *Poetics* is quoted where he says: 'Poetry is a more philosophical and a more serious thing than history; for poetry is chiefly conversant about universal truth, history about particular. In what manner, for example, any person of a certain character would speak or act, probably or necessarily—that is universal; and this is the object of poetry. But what Alcibiades did, or what happened to him—this is particular truth.' When he wrote this, Aristotle was thinking mainly about tragedy—which in fifth-century Athens exercised a more important social function than it does to-day—and like most Greeks of his time he inclined to apply an ethical standard to the judgement of works of art, assessing them principally by their influence in making men better or worse citizens. He also held a teleological view of reality which has practically disappeared from contemporary thought. He believed that everything—including human beings—has a 'form' which both makes it what it is and is the goal of perfection towards which it tends. Thus, for him, to display the 'general forms' or 'essences' of human character was to display the perfection towards which human beings aspire as their 'final cause' or metaphysical goal. In the seventeenth and eighteenth centuries this principle of criticism often degenerated into a crude doctrine of 'types'—a hero must be a hero, a villain a villain, a fool foolish and a wise man wise. But there still remained something of the old philosophical attitude which found the general more real, more inspiring and more exciting than the particular. And it was because of this that Dr. Johnson could write: 'The business of the poet is to examine, not the individual, but the species; to remark general properties and large appearances; he does not number the streaks of the tulip, or describe the different shades in the verdure of the forest. He is to exhibit in his portraits of nature such prominent and striking features as recall the original to every mind; and must neglect the minuter discriminations, which one may have remarked, and another have neglected, for those characteristicks which are alike obvious to vigilance and carelessness.'[1] His justification for this rule was—as it was with Aristotle—utilitarian. 'He that writes upon general principles or delivers universal truths may hope often to be read, because his work will be equally useful at all times and in every country.'

Crude and dated as this 'type-theory' seems to this generation, it is far from obsolete. Apart from the greater vagueness in their formulation, there is little to choose between the Johnsonian doctrine and the following professions by the Marxist protagonist of the realist novel, George Lukacs: 'The central category and criterion of realist literature is the type, a peculiar synthesis which organically binds together the general and the particular both in characters and situations.' And: 'the live portrayal of the complete human personality is possible only if the writer

[1] *Rasselas*, Ch. X.

attempts to create types'.[1] This theory of 'typical truth' in literature is not necessarily inconsistent with the view, also of venerable antiquity, that the poet expresses general and universal truths by means of concrete images and instances, in contrast to the philosopher who enunciates general propositions. Sir Philip Sidney held that the poet is superior to the philosopher because he gives a 'perfect picture', whereas the philosopher deals in the abstract only. For the poet 'yieldeth to the powers of the mind an image of that whereof the philosopher bestoweth but a wordish description'.[2] In its most naïve form this theory maintains that it is the function of the poet to teach the lessons of philosophy by means of concrete examples which impress themselves more readily and more vividly upon the mind than general statements. The difference between the poet and the philosopher is conceived as analogous to that between the moral philosopher who enunciates general principles of conduct and the prophet who speaks in parables from which general laws may be derived. Both forms of the theory regard it as the poet's function to utter general and universal truths. Whether the expression of the general truth is more vivid and more exciting when given in the form of a concrete example or when it is stated as an abstract generalization seems to be a matter on which sensibility has altered from age to age.

Both forms of the theory are almost equally repugnant to contemporary criticism. It is, indeed, an article of faith with most critics to-day that poetry must be specific and concrete, that its value resides in the intrinsic quality of the experience which it mediates to the reader. So far from being a parabolic utterance of general truths, they maintain that if any 'genuine' work of literature is paraphrased, the paraphrase inevitably lacks not merely the vividness and persuasiveness of the original but precisely that value in virtue of which the original was ranked as literature. Many critics nowadays deny that the poetry of the eighteenth century is good poetry on the ground that it reflects the mentality of an age which was essentially unpoetical because feeling was dominated by intellect and, in the words of the late Professor A. E. Housman, 'man had ceased to live from the depths of his nature'. There is similarly a waning of interest in the poetry of such men as Juvenal and Persius, the Horace of the *Epistles*

[1] Preface to *Studies in European Realism* (Eng. Trans. 1950). For a typical 'modern' statement we may contrast that of Mr. Edward Sackville-West in an appreciation of M. François Mauriac: 'M. Mauriac, on the other hand, regards his creations, not as figures in a day-dream, nor yet as social or economic pawns, but as individual objects of love.' 'The True Realism: François Mauriac', published in *Inclinations* (1949).

[2] *Apologie for Poetrie* (1595).

and *Satires*, Malherbe, Boileau and Voltaire, which critics in other times have ranked as great. Whether this phenomenon be regarded as a temporary phase in the fashion of taste[1] or as the emergency of a truer perception of what genuine poetry is, in either case one can no longer accept that 'typical truth' is a necessary excellence of literature unless one is prepared to do violence to the dominant voice of contemporary criticism.

Yet the conviction that in some sense or other 'truth' is a merit of great literature persists strongly in our day. Still closer to Johnson in phrase than in spirit, Wordsworth said in the Preface to *Lyrical Ballads* that the object of poetry is 'truth—not individual and local, but general

---

[1] The disposition to condemn eighteenth-century verse as 'unpoetical' stems from Wordsworth and Arnold and finds its most characteristic expression in A. E. Housman's *The Name and Nature of Poetry* (1933). Housman used a frankly emotional criterion of what is poetry and what is not and dubs all verse 'sham poetry' which fails to arouse in him certain carefully described physiological manifestations of emotion. In attempting to justify this egocentric standard of judgement he falls headlong into the 'psychological fallacy', assuming that the sole reason why some verse which purports to be great poetry fails to arouse him to emotion and leaves him cold is that the men who composed it were themselves without the capacity for deep emotion. In an excellent examination of this thesis Professor Frederick A. Pottle has shown not only that there is no reason at all for making such an assumption but that there is every evidence that the poetry of Dr. Johnson and of Pope aroused as much emotion in their contemporaries as the poetry of, say, Blake and Shelley aroused in Professor Housman. What the evidence shows is a 'shift of sensibility'—Housman's 'affective mechanism' was not the same as that of the men of the eighteenth century. And specifically: 'It is abundantly clear that in eighteenth-century sensibility feelings were tied to the general; men were excited by generalizations, not by particulars. Men then felt the imagined norm to be more real, more exciting, more poetical, than any particular example.' In the next chapter we shall show that the emotional theory of artistic excellence cannot provide any universally valid principles of judgement but defines a different classification of 'good' and 'bad' art for every age and individual according as emotional habits differ from age to age and from man to man. Certainly neither this nor any other criterion can reveal the achievement of 'universal truth' as a necessary excellence of all poetry for all men. But neither can it legitimately exclude the general from the province of true poetry. As Professor Pottle well puts it, the men of the eighteenth century did not write as they did 'because they were depraved or because they had false taste'. They did so 'simply and solely because particularizations seemed to them prosaic, while generalizations made their beards bristle and sent tremors up and down their spines'. And he concludes that 'critics ought to realize that what they are really evaluating is their own sensibility—or, if that sounds too much like a paradox, that they are always evaluating in terms of their own sensibility'. (*The Idiom of Poetry*, 1941.) Within the limits of an emotional theory of artistic excellence there is no escape from this conclusion.

and operative'. Newman, reading his own views into the robuster language of Aristotle, claimed that it is the essence of poetry that it 'delineates that perfection which the imagination suggests, and to which as a limit the present system of Divine Providence actually tends. . . . Hence, while it recreates the imagination by the superhuman loveliness of its views, it provides a solace for the mind broken by the disappointments and sufferings of actual life; and becomes, moreover, the utterance of the inward emotions of a right moral feeling, seeking a purity and a truth which this world will not give.'[1] There are, it is true, those who, with Mr. I. A. Richards, deny that truth has any relevance to literary excellence at all because they believe that the sole function of literature is to arouse emotions and stimulate mental attitudes.[2] But to whatever view they incline in theory, the majority of critics continue in practice to praise certain works of literature because they seem profoundly true to human nature, to display a deep insight into the human heart or a wise understanding of man's life and destiny. And it seems likely that, whatever the theorists may say, they will continue to do so. The sort of truth which now seems to be expected of poetry is that which we understand by the word 'wisdom' rather than the general metaphysical truths of philosophy or the factual generalizations of science. Nor does it strike strange or extraordinary when Mr. T. R. Henn begins a book on the poetry of Mr. W. B. Yeats by saying that the quality which he values most in that poetry is 'Wisdom'.[3] In a later chapter we shall hope to show that it cannot be other than a utility-function of poetry to convey wisdom in the sense either of knowledge or understanding. But the word 'wisdom' very often carries a rather vaguely defined meaning identical neither with understanding nor with knowledge but implying rather the settled adoption of certain approved attitudes of mind towards accepted knowledge and facts. Such attitudes of mind may properly be communicated by

[1] *Essay on Poetry* (1829), reprinted in *Essays Critical and Historical* (1871).

[2] In his *Principles of Literary Criticism*, Mr. I. A. Richards made the arresting statement: 'People who say "How true!" at intervals while reading Shakespeare are misusing his work and, comparatively speaking, wasting their time.' It is a statement which caught the imagination of critics and has been repeatedly quoted for refutation or approval. Mr. Empson believes that it was said for effect and that Mr. Richards did not really mean it. Yet if you accept the fundamental thesis that the purpose of poetical language as such is to stimulate emotions and not to make statements which are true or false, it follows that the relevance of any poetical statement to matters of actuality and fact is a matter of indifference—except, perhaps, in so far as the reader's belief or disbelief in its relevance to fact may colour subconsciously his emotional reaction to it.

[3] *The Lonely Tower* (1950).

poetry as poetry—and perhaps can only be communicated in this way. And there seems no good reason why such poetry should not be legitimately said to impart 'wisdom' in this sense.

This is a far stride from Johnson's theory of types. But the practical insight of Dr. Johnson often succeeded in hitting the mark beyond the limitations of his age, and I think that there are few modern critics who—although they might prefer to see it expressed in less matter-of-fact language—would disagree that, if literature and poetry have a utility-function, then Johnson was right when he said 'the only end of writing, is to enable the readers better to enjoy life, or better to endure it'.

There are, however, two serious disadvantages to be overcome by anyone who would employ wisdom—or indeed 'truth' in any sense at all —as a principle of valuation in the practical criticism of the arts. They are both practical rather than theoretical difficulties, for in theory there is of course nothing to prevent any critic using any standard of judgement he likes provided that he is consistent in applying it and ensures that his readers understand what the standard is by which he is judging. The first disadvantage—and I think it is a real one—consists in the radical re-organization of accepted critical assessments which a consistent application of this principle of evaluation would involve. The standard of wisdom— though according with many judgements made by many critics, who value a work for its wisdom when it has it and look for some other excellence in those works that have it not—would, if consistently demanded, lead to assessments completely out of line with the great mass of accepted criticism. For all critics do in fact value highly many poetical compositions which have not by any stretch of the imagination this quality of wisdom or universal truth in any high degree. Some lyrical poems by Herrick and Drayton are commonly judged to be very much better poetry than *The Task*, all critics agree that the *Sonnets from the Portuguese* have greater literary excellence than the *Light of Asia*, *Atalanta in Calydon* than *The Vanity of Human Wishes*. Yet however you define 'wisdom', there is more of it in the latter than the former. To deny this would be equivalent to abandoning your case by so distorting the general language as to make wisdom identical with what is usually meant by lyricism or poetical form. If 'wisdom' retains the accepted, if vague, sense which it has in ordinary speech, and the sense which critics who talk about 'wisdom' commonly attach to it, and if it were consistently employed as a criterion of literary excellence, the consequent reorganization of critical judgement would be stupendous. In particular, lyrical poetry in general and with few exceptions would come to occupy a very much lower place in the hierarchy of literature than in fact it is accorded. Indeed, the proposal to make wisdom a criterion of literary excellence only seems specious at all because it is *not* consistently applied and no critic feels called upon in fact to undertake the radical reorganization of his estimates which its consistent application would require. It is, therefore, evident that critics do not in fact propose to regard wisdom as a necessary condition of literary excellence, but when they talk about it they are talking about a utility-function which works of art may, but need not, fulfil.

Or if, again, you were to erect wisdom into a *sufficient* condition for literary excellence, the results would be still more disastrous to agreed and accepted criticism. There is much sound practical wisdom in the writings of many philosophers in addition to the theoretical wisdom in which they specialize. Aristotle, Erigena, Bacon, Mill were wise men as well as keen logicians. There is much practical wisdom in much sociological and psychological writing, in some political oratory, some sermons, some hortatory and pedagogic writing such as Lord Chesterfield's *Letters*, in ecclesiastical manuals for the Confessional, and so on. Yet some of these writings are not classed as literature at all and the rest are ranked much lower than would be the case if they were assessed in accordance with the wisdom they contain. It would be rash indeed to assert that there is less wisdom in Joseph Butler's *Sermons* than in the poems of Yeats, less in Hobbes and Helvetius than in Arnold and Auden, less in Godwin than in Shelley. Nor do critics in practice make this sort of comparison when they assess literary standing. For in practice they do not regard wisdom either as a necessary or as a sufficient condition of literary excellence—to do so would make nonsense of criticism—but when they praise certain works for wisdom and not others, they are judging that—apart from literary excellence—those works have the additional values of serving one of the manifold utility-purposes which literary or non-literary writing may fulfil.

The second objection to using wisdom as a criterion of judgement is that men's ideas of what wisdom is, of the ultimate truth about the world and human life and destiny, vary much more than their judgements about beauty. If, then, the assessment of literary excellence is to be married to each critic's personal conception of ultimate truth and wisdom, it will indeed be very difficult for any reader to know where he stands. It would be necessary for a critic always to inform his readers whether he was judging a work to be good or bad because of the quality of wisdom contained (or not contained) in it and how far his composite judgements were influenced by his assessment of a poem's wisdom, how far by some other standard of literary excellence. The reader would then require to know just what the critic's idea of wisdom was, his views on life in general, religious, political, social and human. For though the literary critic may be expected to have some expertness in the recognition of aesthetic qualities manifested in literature, the world does not, and is unlikely to, look upon him as an expert guide to human wisdom in general. Unless, therefore, the critic who assesses literature by its truth to life in this sense makes this distinction between the several intentions of his judgements, no reader can ever know what he means when he says a work is good or bad. And if he does make it clear that he is assessing a work on the basis of its wisdom, he must then ensure that his readers are fully cognisant of his own philosophy of life: for if he does not do so, they cannot know what his judgements are saying.

I think that there is only one solution to this critical dilemma and that is to make a distinction between the *excellence* of literary products as works of art (their 'beauty') on the one hand and their *greatness* on the other. The qualities in virtue of which their excellence is assessed will be attributes which they share with other types of art and attributes which only works of art possess. Unless this is accepted, we should be using language only for mystification if we call them works of art at all, using a term which we apply equally to music and painting. Their greatness will be estimated exactly as we might estimate the greatness of a human personality or of writing which we do not want to classify as art, in terms of wisdom, sanity, profundity, balance and so on. It is a distinction which I have already suggested in my book *Theory of Beauty*. It was, of course, anticipated by Pater, though without full understanding of its implications, when he wrote: 'the distinction between great art and good art depends immediately, as regards literature at all events, not on its form, but on the matter. Thackeray's *Esmond*, surely, is greater art than *Vanity Fair*, by the greater dignity of its interests. It is in the quality of the matter it informs or controls, its compass, its variety, its alliance to great ends, or the depth of the note of revolt, or the largeness of the hope in it, that the greatness of literary art depends, as *The Divine Comedy*, *Paradise Lost*, *Les Misérables*, *The English Bible*, are great art. Given the conditions I have tried to explain as constituting good art;—then if it be devoted further to the increase of men's happiness, . . . it will also be great art.'[1] I realize that this is not a distinction very much to the taste of critics and those who appreciate literature in general. It means, as Mr. Graham

[1] *Appreciations with an Essay on Style* (1889).

Hough has said, setting up a double standard.[1] It means assessing on the one hand the structural or aesthetic properties of any work of literature and estimating on the other hand separately and distinctly the quality of the human experience which as raw material the author has structured and organized into his work of art together with the wisdom and truth of the attitudes which he fosters towards that human experience. But to those who find this dichotomy incongruous I would say that I do *not* imply that the response which we or the critic makes to a literary work in direct appreciation must be dual. We strive in appreciation to make contact with it for what it is, to know it and actualize it as completely and as faithfully as possible, without prejudices or preconceptions. And our response to it will, inevitably, be a conglomerate of a very large number of reactions to diverse elements in it, all fused into a unity difficult to disassemble. Our response is derived—and at this no one will cavil—from a multiplicity of sources, from the fusion of a number of particular responses, assessments, annoyances and delights, welded into the organic oneness of living appreciation. The critic, however, is more than an appreciator. It is incumbent upon him as critic to pass his appreciation on to others as an analogue and guide to theirs. And to do this the critic *must* reflect and analyse. He must anatomize his appreciations, disentangle the interwoven strands, trace the elements to their sources and justify each judgement by his aesthetic creed. All understanding involves disintegration of the living unity given in direct experience and criticism is, after all, an attempt to convey understanding. And intellectual distinctions may be proper and necessary to the discipline of criticism which would be merely distracting and destructive in the act of appreciation itself. For criticism is not and cannot be pure appreciation, but is born of reflection upon appreciation.

Therefore it is that criticism must recognize a distinction between literary greatness and literary excellence, if only in the interests of intelligibility and common fairness to the reader. Until it does so, the meaning of a very great deal of critical writing will remain obscure, however limpid be the literary style in which it is presented.[2]

[1] In his friendly review in the *Spectator* (November 22nd, 1952), Mr. Graham Hough describes this distinction as 'very unsatisfactory'. It is. Or at least it is very disconcerting to criticism. But it is the only way out for criticism from the dilemma of faulty communication by which it has so long been dogged.

[2] Mr. Ezra Pound, who has probably appreciated more literature than any of his contemporaries, rarely if ever confuses judgements of greatness with judgements of literary excellence—and his criticism gains in lucidity and authority for it.

Music

It is impossible to terminate this discussion of aesthetic Realism without saying something about the semantic theory of music, for music and architecture are the most serious obstacles in the way of a realistic theory of art. The mimetic doctrine has been developed primarily in connection with the arts of painting and sculpture. To say that literature—even drama—'imitates' life seems to be true in a general sense, for its material is taken from life imaginatively adapted to the needs of art. It is a statement which strikes us as more metaphorical, less straightforwardly sensible, than the statement that a picture which we recognize to be a portrait of the king of Siam 'imitates' the king of Siam; with the help of the theory of semantics, however, the analogy between the mimetic character of literature and the visual arts is rendered plausible. But neither music nor architecture is realistic either in the older or in the modern senses of the word; yet both are commonly classified as arts. If, then, we maintain a realistic theory of art, we are merely being obscurantist in speaking of the 'arts' of music and architecture unless we can show some sense in which they too are realistic. What we are saying in effect is that Realism is a necessary condition for any artefact to be classified as art, but there are important groups of artefacts which we classify as art although they are not realistic.

The sounds from which musical compositions are constructed are not the sounds which normally occur in nature. They are sounds specially manufactured for the purpose of musical art by machines designed solely for this. It is comparatively rarely that they act as symbols for natural sounds or that natural sounds are introduced into musical compositions. There exists of course no natural law, nor even any very rigid human convention, forbidding the reproduction of natural sounds in musical structures. More or less exact mimicry of storm-sounds has long been a popular device of musicians. We may have the clatter of galloping hoofs, as in Haydn's *Creation*, the cries of cuckoo and snipe in Beethoven's *Pastoral Symphony,* the call of the hunter's horn, cowbells and church bells, street cries and shrieks of anguish, the rhythms of spinning wheel or marching men, and a hundred other suggestions from the realm of natural sound. More modern composers have experimented with steam whistles and other mechanically produced industrial noises—even the gramophone record of a nightingale's song in Respighi's *The Pines of Rome*. But all these natural symbols of the sounds of everyday life make up a very small part of any musical composition in which they occur, and it is the general opinion of competent musical critics that they tend to be a distracting element rather than an asset and require extreme artistry to be successfully incorporated into a musical work of art. When they are used they are used as foreign bodies ingeniously contrived to fit in where they do not belong. It is true also, of course, that musical phrases—as anything else at all that can become an object of experience—may by arbitrary association become conventional symbols.[1] Thus the opening notes of Beethoven's *Fifth Symphony* conventionally symbolized hope and confidence in victory during the Second World War instead of 'fate knocking at the door'. Rachmaninoff's *Prelude in C sharp Minor* symbolizes for some people Napoleon's retreat from Moscow and for others the emotions of a man who has been prematurely buried when he awakens to consciousness in the tomb. Some composers name their pieces after natural objects—The Sea, Rain, A Cathedral in the Mist, The Girl with the Flaxen Hair—thus inviting specific associations. But when such associations occur, whether they are guaranteed by the composer or not, they are always external and arbitrary; as has been amply proved, unless the association is suggested by the title or by some rhythmic, melodic or structural similarity of a given piece of music with other pieces which already have a conventional association (lullabies, hunting pieces, etc.), it is only by chance that any two listeners would spontaneously make the same association. Music possesses no language consisting of elements capable of being combined into sentences to communicate opinions or beliefs.

Relying nevertheless on the ancient and persisting tradition that music is the most emotional of the arts, musicologists and aestheticians have often argued that music is a natural language of the emotions, representing by natural symbols of sound that affective element in human experience which is ineffable by the conventional symbolism of spoken language.[2]

---

[1] Garcilaso records that in the music of the Incas: 'Each song [words] had its own tune, known to belong to it, and they could not sing two different songs to the same tune. This was why the gallant, serenading his lady at night on his flute, by the tune he used told her and the whole world of his content or his repining as she granted or refused him her favour. But if they had put two different songs to one tune, it could not have been known which of them the gallant wished to express. Thus in a manner of speaking he talked by means of his flute.' *Comentarios Reales de los Incas*, Bk. II, Ch. XXVI. This passage is important as stating—what the writer has observed—that the emotional significance of the music of the Andean Indians derived from arbitrary convention and not from some instinctive and unexplainable response to the supposed emotional mood of different melodies.

[2] I know of no corresponding attempt to bring architecture within the fold, unless it is by applying to it Schelling's metaphorical formula that architecture is 'static music'.

Wagner, for example, maintained that 'orchestral language' expresses 'precisely what is ineffable in verbal language and what, viewed from the rationalistic standpoint, may therefore be called the *Unspeakable*'. The origin of this notion of music is usually attributed to Schopenhauer, who said that music is a semantic for the irrational element in mental life, which he called the Will. It is a view which has wielded a very strong and a lasting influence both on the philosophy and on the practical criticism of music, while its influence has from time to time reflected upon the practice and appreciation of the other arts. Among modern writers it is developed most seriously by Mr. Colin McAlpin and Mrs. Susanne K. Langer.[1] And so long as men were content to accept without question the vague belief that music is highly emotional it seemed an extremely specious way of explaining what occurs when music is made and appreciated. But since experiment and research have begun to be directed upon the emotional function of music, almost insuperable difficulties have made their appearance. There is a century-old controversy whether the appreciation of music is in truth an emotional act or no, and it seems now to be fairly well established that there are two types of listeners to music, the emotional and the perceptive[2]—though it is still a matter for controversy which way of listening is 'right'. But even more devastating than this, research appears to have proved beyond cavil or question that those people who do, or think they do, listen to music emotionally display no uniformity in the emotions they experience or seem to experience in contact with the same musical composition. The divergences among *undirected* emotional response reported both by experienced critics and by untutored laymen are as heterogene as they numerically can be. And in view of this many of the more serious and responsible musicologists have now abandoned the belief that music can in any true sense of the word communicate emotions. As Paul Moos has said: 'Pure instrumental music is unable to render even the most ordinary feelings, such as love, loyalty, or anger, unambiguously and distinctly, by its own unaided powers.'[3] The proved unconformability of emotional reaction to music

[1] *Hermaia: A Study in Comparative Esthetics* (1915), *Philosophy in a New Key* (1941). See also Carrol C. Pratt, *The Meaning of Music* (1931).

[2] This view is developed by Vernon Lee, for example, in Max Schoen's *The Effects of Music* (1927).

[3] *Die Philosophie der Musik* (1922). Quoted by Mrs. Langer. I do not wish to belabour this point further here. It is a point which with a little care can be verified experimentally by almost anybody and ample evidence has been assembled. A useful summary is available in Max Schoen's *The Effects of Music* (1927) and *The Beautiful in Music* (1928).

is not, as has sometimes been affirmed,[1] a false impression engendered by the poverty of verbal language to discriminate emotion. It is, of course, quite true that no words can describe the delicate and fugitive modulations of feeling which people seem to experience while listening to a symphony. But if language were the sole culprit, there would be no positive disagreement within the limits of language to define. In fact, however, different people report opposite or conflicting emotional reactions to the same music. When one man describes a piece of music as 'gay' and another finds the same piece 'melancholy', one calls it 'heroic' and another 'tender', the differences between them are not due to poverty of the language. Language is adequate to show that they *do* genuinely differ. Gurney has the following example of this—one among incontestably many. 'The great "subject" of the first movement of Schubert's B flat trio represents to me and many the *ne plus ultra* of energy and passion; yet this very movement was described by Schuman as "tender, girlish, confiding".'[2] In fact, if you take the descriptive comments of ten leading musical critics upon a piece of music whose emotional 'content' is not defined by accepted convention, you are pretty sure to get ten incompatible types of emotional response. This is a genuine divergence of experience and not the reflection of linguistic inadequacy.

To meet the difficulty that many of those most competent to judge introspectively have repudiated the belief that appreciation of music is primarily an affective act, or that one can best and most fully enter into awareness of a serious musical composition by weltering in a riot of emotion with the musical sounds as background effects, Mrs. Langer has somewhat modified the accepted theory of music as an 'emotional language'. 'If music has any significance,' she says, 'it is semantic, not symptomatic. Its "meaning" is evidently not that of a stimulus to evoke emotions, nor that of a signal to announce them; if it has an emotional content, it "has" it in the same sense that language "has" its conceptual content—*symbolically*. It is not usually derived *from* affects nor intended *for* them; but we may say, with certain reservations, that it is *about* them. Music is not the cause or cure of feelings, but their *logical expression*. . . .'[3] I am not sure that I understand what this means. But if, as I think, it means that music acts as a symbol to evoke not active emotions but images of emotions, just as language symbolically evokes concepts of emotions, I see no intrinsic impossibility in this. We certainly do

---

[1] This view seems to have been held by Liszt, Riemann and others.
[2] Edmund Gurney, *The Power of Sound* (1880).
[3] Op. cit. (1951 ed.), p. 228.

recollect past emotions, think about emotions and communicate facts and ideas about emotions, without actually experiencing the emotions at the time. We know what it means to say that someone is angry and do not have to experience the anger ourselves; having experienced anger in the past and being able to recollect anger imaginally, we know what we are talking about when we talk about anger. And there is nothing intrinsically impossible in supposing that music should provide a more delicate and exact system for symbolizing the subtleties of affective life than the very crude instrument afforded by verbal language.[1] But the supposition breaks down on facts. For in order to be effective as symbolization music, or any other system of symbols, would have to signify the same thing to everyone—or at any rate to all those people who were able to use it for the purposes of symbolic communication. It would have to be composed of elements, each having the same 'meaning' or referent for all people using that form of symbolization, and capable of being combined into higher complexities of meaning (even though the meaning were non-conceptual and ineffable) simply because the elements were without ambivalence. There has been much experimentation in the last hundred years directed to showing that this is indeed the case with music; but the results of experiment have consistently proved the opposite. There is not introspectible uniformity among men's emotional responses to music.

Mrs. Langer therefore modifies her theory once again. She concludes that music does not symbolize actual emotions but the 'general forms of feeling', what the musicologist von Hoeslin called the patterns of 'tensions and resolutions' which are common to musical compositions and the emotional life, the patterns of their 'rise and decline and intertwining'. 'For', says Mrs. Langer, *what music can actually reflect is only the morphology of feeling*; and it is quite plausible that some sad and happy conditions may have a very similar morphology.' It is a view which has appealed to a number of the more speculative musicologists and has had the tentative blessing of the 'gestalt' psychologists Kurt Koffka and Wolfgang Koehler. And among musicians I think Mr. Roger Sessions was intending to say something like this when he wrote: 'I have tried to point out how intimately our musical impulses are connected with those primitive movements which are among the very conditions of our existence. I have tried to show, too, how vivid is our response to the primitive elements of musical movement. Is not this the key both to the content of music and

[1] We know, for instance, that modulations of the voice in speaking can communicate shades of emotion and feeling which language cannot describe and which cannot be easily conceptualized.

to its extraordinary power? These bars from the Prelude to Tristan do not express for us love or frustration or even longing: but they reproduce for us, both qualitatively and dynamically, certain gestures of the spirit which are to be sure less specifically definable than any of these emotions but which energize them and make them vital to us. So it seems to me that this is the essence of musical expression. "Emotion" is specific, individual and conscious; music goes deeper than this, to the energies which animate our psychic life, and out of these creates a pattern which has an existence, laws and human significance of its own. It reproduces for us the most intimate essence, the tempo and the energy, of our spiritual being; our tranquility and our restlessness, our animation and our discouragement, our vitality and our weakness—all, in fact, of the fine shades of dynamic variation of our inner life. It reproduces those far more specifically than is possible through any other medium of human communication.'

Let us, if we can, be clear about what is claimed in this final form of the theory of musical symbolism. So far as I understand it, it affirms that musical art arouses in competent listeners (or puts them in mind of) not specific and recognizable emotions but dynamic or rhythmic patterns which correspond to the normal rhythms of our emotional life; but it arouses or puts them in mind of these rhythms or patterns in a 'pure' form without specific affective content. I do not know whether this means anything or whether psychology would allow such a possibility[1]; but I am pretty certain that such speculation adds nothing of consequence to what we knew when we started to speculate. What we knew is this. People disagree about the emotions they experience when listening to music and disagree about whether or not they actually experience emotions at all. But music lovers agree that, with or without specific emotions, music exercises upon them a very profound effect which, because it is not linked to conceptual or ideational thinking, seems to be generally affective in character. And they agree very often that this effect of music upon them is among the most cherished and important experiences in their lives. I am, however, entirely unconvinced that the explanation offered for these facts makes any addition of consequence to the facts it professes to explain. It seems to me simply to restate them in vaguer and more ambiguous language. I am willing, however, to confess to obtuseness in this and to grant, for the moment, all that the theory

---

[1] Can the patterns of emotional life be at once as rigid as those of a Bach Fugue and as tenuous as the structure of a Debussy Prelude; as concise as a Mozart Sonata and as diffuse as Delius's Dance Rhapsody?

claims. The point that I wish to make—and it is an important point for the Realist conception of art in general—is that on their own premises those who maintain this theory are wrong in continuing to regard music as a form of symbolism. What they say is that music arouses in us not emotions but affective patterns. But what arouses in me an affective condition of any sort at all is not for me a symbol of that affective condition. It is its cause. It only becomes a symbol if it causes me to form a concept or a mental image of an affective state. That is the definition of a symbol. And if it is to be an effective symbol for communication among men, it must arouse the same concept or image in the minds of all men for whom it is an effective symbol.[1] 'To be the cause of something' is not the same thing as 'to be a symbol of that thing'. If A is the cause of B, it becomes a symbol of B only when a group of people, having noticed the causal relation between A and B, think of B when they see or experience A. A piece of music becomes a symbol of an affective condition for me not by arousing that affective condition in me but only when, through my awareness of the causal nexus between the music and my affective state, the idea or sound of the former gives me an idea of a memory of the latter. Mrs. Langer very carefully draws the distinction between a cause and a symbol in speaking of linguistic symbolism; she is guilty of fundamental illogicality in calling music a mode of symbolism because it stimulates affective patterns in some listeners. She does, indeed, speak of it as an 'unconsummated symbol' and she says that 'music has all the earmarks of a true symbolism, except one: the existence of an *assigned connotation*'. This is, of course, on her own definition of what a symbol is, to admit that music is not symbolism at all.

We must therefore conclude that there is no sense in which music can justly be called realistic. If it is so called, the word will be used in a special sense incompatible with the sense in which it is applied to representational visual art and to literature. Music may be true or false in the mystical sense to be discussed, but it cannot be true or false in a Realist sense. It arouses prized affective states in musical people, but it is not a *symbol* of those states—it is their cause. Music does not, except accidentally and incidentally, *represent* any actuality other than itself, either by natural or by conventional symbolism. We do not call *symbols* those harmonies of colour or constructs of shapes which in painting arouse in us 'aesthetic'

---

[1] It may be, as Mrs. Langer suggests, that the 'morphology' of sadness and the morphology of joy are similar. But there is no evidence that in fact it is so—and it is difficult to imagine how one could go about to secure evidence one way or the other.

emotions apart from anything they represent. To do so would be as illogical as to call a dentist's drill a *symbol* because it causes in me a feeling of trepidation when I am sitting in the dentist's chair. And music is in the same case as abstract visual art or the 'abstract' element in representational visual art. It is essentially without symbolic content. Therefore it follows that if musical productions are to be classified as works of art, Realism or representation is not a necessary condition for an artefact to be a work of art.

General Conclusions

Despite its long history and great plausibility, it appears from the foregoing discussion that in the general opinion of contemporary criticism Realism, in the sense of representing or accurately describing an actuality other than itself, is neither a necessary nor a sufficient requirement for any artefact to be classed as a work of art.

It is not a necessary requirement because there are artefacts, such as musical compositions, architectural structures, decorative and abstract paintings and sculptures, which are *not* representative of anything but themselves and *are* commonly classed as works of art. Nor are those works of art which *are* representative (including the whole of literature) commonly judged to be excellent in accordance with the degree or extent of their Realism. A less realistic product is often judged better than a more realistic product, and of two equally realistic works of art one is often judged to be better than the other.

It is not a sufficient condition because there are many artefacts, such as advertising posters and white papers, which *are* representative or descriptive of actuality other than themselves but are *not* commonly classed as works of art.

Therefore: Any critic who wished to adopt Realism as an aesthetic creed and a practical principle of criticism would have to deny that music, architecture, decorative painting and abstract sculpture are art and recognize that photographs and magazine illustrations, white papers and newspaper reportage, are art.

It follows that critics are inconsistent and confused who commend some works of art for being realistic as though their realism were contributory to their excellence as art.

It is, however, an inescapable fact that many works of art are created and traded for purposes other than to exist as works of art for human appreciation. Some of these purposes are trivial, others are of profound social and personal significance. All these purposes can also be served by things which are not judged to be works of art. The critic may legitimately praise a work of art for efficiently serving any of these extraneous purposes in virtue of its Realism. But when he does so he is not functioning strictly as an artistic or literary critic. He is speaking as a sociologist, a moralist, a psychiatrist or an expert on the uplift of the human soul.

It is therefore incumbent upon a critic, whenever he praises a work of art for Realism, to indicate what subsidiary purpose he is judging it to serve in virtue of the qualities of Realism upon which he directs his readers' attention.

Chapter VI

HIERATIC HEDONISM

id quod visum placet.—ST. THOMAS AQUINAS

DECLAIMING in the fervour of Teutonic Romanticism, Friedrich von Schlegel once said that beauty is 'the pleasant expression of the good', unwittingly anticipating in a phrase what has since turned out to be the main tenor and temper of aesthetic doctrine. For in Schlegel's dictum three assumptions are linked without being reconciled. He asserts that it is a necessary feature of beautiful things to give pleasure, that beauty is a mode of expression, and that some sort of moral criterion is relevant in assessing the degree in which anything at all is beautiful. Latent or explicit these three assumptions are common to most contemporary systems of aesthetics and to almost all critical writing. They are taken for granted by art historians, scientists and laymen, professed by artists and obediently swallowed by their public. They have been made the slogans of new movements in art and in criticism. They have influenced every writer on art and beauty and their unconscious tenacity exceeds the strength of reason to uproot them. Refutation has left their vigour unabated. Though logically they would define different and largely incompatible theories of artistic excellence, even philosophers in their formal treatises have tended to assume them all; and for this reason many writers to whom we shall have occasion to refer can be quoted with almost equal plausibility in favour of two or more distinct theories of beauty. Schlegel's assumptions do not embrace the whole field of aesthetic dogma to-day, but they do account for the greater part of it; and by examining severally their competence and their bearing for criticism we shall have accomplished most of the clearance which remains to be done.

In this chapter we shall discuss the hedonistic and the emotional theories of artistic excellence, which are logically on a par and very similar in most of their practical implications. The *Encyclopaedia Britannica* (11th edition) defines fine art first in terms of pleasure: 'The fine arts are those among the arts of man which spring from his impulse to do or make certain things in certain ways for the sake, first, of a special kind of pleasure, independent of direct utility, which it gives him so to do or to make them, and next for the sake of the kindred pleasure which he derives from witnessing or contemplating them when they are done or made by others.' And then in terms of emotion: 'Fine art is everything which man does or makes in one way rather than another, freely and with premeditation, in order to express or arouse emotion . . . and with results independent of direct utility and capable of affording to many permanent and disinterested delight.' These are the two doctrines of artistic excellence which will now concern us.

Neither theory is, of course, an invention of modern times. They are both explanations which have occurred most naturally to the mind as soon as men have begun to speculate about men's addiction to the arts. Aristotle, as we have seen, assumed that the motive and the justification of indulgence in the fine arts lay in the pleasure that *mimesis* gives; and this has seemed self-evident to most men since his day. Cicero said that the best orator is he who 'both teaches, and delights, and moves the minds of his hearers. To teach them is his duty, to delight them is creditable to him, to move them is indispensable.'[1] Quintilian too thought that it is in its power over the emotions that the life and soul of oratory is to be found. Without this all else is bare and meagre, weak and devoid of charm.[2] What they said of oratory they believed to be true also of poetry and of fine writing in general. And these views have been regulative for nearly two millennia. The treatise of Longinus *On the Sublime*, whose re-discovery late in the seventeenth century acted as an incentive to pullulating aesthetic speculation, maintains that the object of poetry in general is to stir the feelings and passions and to uplift the soul in delight. Thomas Hobbes, with his serious and empirical interest in the affective machinery, influenced the trend of English criticism in Dryden, Dennis, Addison and others to a concern for the psychology of aesthetic effects.[3] Dryden spoke with the voice of his century when he said: 'delight is the chief, if not the only, end of poesy', and that: 'instruction can be admitted but in the second place, for poesy only instructs as it delights. 'Tis true, that to imitate well is a poet's work; but to affect the soul, and excite the

---

[1] *Orator*, i. Compare Horace: 'You will win every vote if you blend what is improving with what pleases, and at once delight and instruct the reader.' *Ars Poetica*.

[2] *Institutio Oratoria*, VI, ii, 7.

[3] 'Hobbes is, in general, inclined to judge a work by its effects rather than by its conformity to traditional standards. He is willing to concede much to the principle of delight.' Clarence DeWitt Thorpe, *The Aesthetic Theory of Thomas Hobbes* (1940).

passions, and, above all, to move admiration (which is the delight of serious plays), a bare imitation will not serve.'[1]

All this is eminently sane and reasonable. Pleasure is accepted as a natural thing and that it is natural for men to like to be pleased. Emotion is a natural thing. And when it is seen that many men derive much enjoyment from works of creative imagination which affect them emotionally, it is natural to want to know as much as possible about how it is done. The psychology of this early criticism may often be elementary and as you read their judgements you may often be aware that their sensibility differed in many ways from ours; but it is difficult to find fault with their fundamental assumptions about why men in fact indulge in the creation and appreciation of the arts. It was the German Stürmer und Dränger[2] with their adolescent enthusiasms, their restricted background and their Teutonic yearning to lift up their souls by the shoe-straps into the infinite, who first shut up aesthetics in the rarefied, hot-house atmosphere from which it is only now beginning to emerge into the freshness of daylight sanity again. They were men who without the gift of mysticism longed to be something more than men. For them their emotions were no longer just emotions but 'those obscure, ineffable impressions that flood our soul'.[3] Pleasure was no longer just pleasure but a 'tumultuous rapture'. The enjoyment which men had often before taken in works of art had never before, it seemed to them, been understood for what it is—a titanic transforming spiritual transport, an inner expansion of the whole being, an immersion in the Absolute. It was Goethe who said that after reading the plays of Shakespeare 'I felt most intensely my being enlarged by an infinity'.[4] Poetry and painting became no longer an embellishment and an enrichment of human life but a manifestation of the divine principle of creative energy which pervades and sustains the universe and ferments the human soul. The poet was exalted to God's deputy on earth; like God, a creator. And the creative force seething and simmering in his breast 'stammers over in poetry, in scrawling lines it hurls on to paper adoration to the Creator, eternal life, all-embracing, inextinguishable feeling of what is and was and is to come'. The artist was made once again into a priest officiating the metaphysical eucharist of the Absolute. 'Who is a poet? A spirit who feels that he can create, and who does

---

[1] *A Defence of an Essay of Dramatic Poesy* (1668).
[2] For a rather different estimation of this movement from our own the reader is referred to Professor Roy Pascal's *The German Sturm und Drang* (1953).
[3] Herder, *Brief wechsel über Ossian.*
[4] *Zum Schäkespears Tag.*

create, and whose creation does not only please himself as his work, but of whose creation all tongues must witness: Truth! Truth! Nature! Nature! We see what we never saw, and hear what we never heard, and yet, what we see and hear is flesh of our flesh and bones of our bones.'[1] Through unrestricted emotional wallowing in the arts men were invited to satisfy their romantic craving to be gods or supermen. Little or nothing that was new in critical doctrine emerged from all this ferment apart from the intrusion of the terminology of metaphysical Idealism for the obfuscation of the language of appreciation. But the whole spirit of approach was changed. Beauty became sacramental, hedonism hieratic. And it is this fervent fevered exaltation that modern aesthetic hedonism has inherited in however diluted and luke-warm a form it may survive.

1. *Aesthetic Hedonism*

Mr. Eric Gill, who was influenced both by the romanticized medieval-ism of William Morris and by the philosophical outlook of the Neo-Thomists, was accustomed to oppugn bitterly the habitual assumption of the world nowadays that it is the function of art to please. 'Art,' he says, 'the word which primarily means skill and thus human skill in doing and making, has, in literary circles and among the upper classes, come to mean only the fine arts, and the fine arts . . . are now exclusively aesthetic; they aim only to give pleasure. Hence, however cultivated we may be and however refined our pleasures, we do not associate the word with holiness, or holiness with art. . . . But art, "high art", the sort we put in museums and picture galleries, has become a pleasure thing; it is put there to amuse. Eat, drink, and be merry for tomorrow we die, and the utmost endeavour of our educators is to see to it that our merriment shall be "high class". If we put a painting of a Madonna in our art gallery, it is not because the painter has succeeded in conveying a specially clear view of her significance, but simply because he has succeeded in making a specially pleasing arrangement of materials. A Raphael Madonna! But it is as a "Raphael" that we honour it and not as a Madonna; for Raphael is, or was until recently, held by the pundits to be particularly good at making pleasing arrangements, and we are no longer concerned with meanings. . . .'

The presupposition that it is the function of the fine arts to give pleasure, that the criterion of their goodness is to be sought in their capacity to please, is so ubiquitous, so insidious, that despite the high

[1] Lavater, *Physiognomische Fragmente.*

seriousness and the earnestness with which engagement in the arts has sometimes been regarded, there is scarcely a writer since Aristotle who has not been guilty of it. Our own day is no exception to this rule. When Mr. Santayana proposed for a definition of beauty 'pleasure regarded as the quality of a thing',[1] he summarized an attitude which has become instinctive to our time—so much so, that the more up-to-date and scientific writers are inclined to be impatient at any divergence from it. Yet the only difference between the assumption as made by Socrates or Aristotle and the same assumption as made by, say, Professor Herbert Dingle[2] is that the latter would probably profess to 'justify' it by psychology whereas Aristotle was unconscious of any need for justification. What, then, does the doctrine come to when you strip away the verbiage and look at it squarely? It comes to this. When you attend a football match or a cinema performance with pleasure and remark 'I enjoyed it immensely', you are merely reporting an event in your own psychological history. But if you should say 'It was a fine game', or 'It was a good film', referring again only to the pleasure you derived from it, you are 'objectifying' your pleasure and by a common linguistic confusion you are speaking of an experience of your own as if it were a quality in the object which caused the experience. All attributions of beauty, so the assertion goes, involve error of this sort. Whenever we speak of anything as beautiful, or judge a work of art to be good, we are hypostatizing the pleasure we derive from its contemplation and making of our own pleasure a quality of that which was its cause. And this pseudo-quality, this shadow cast by pleasurable reaction upon the sources of pleasure, is what we call beauty. Mr. Santayana's theory is, of course, more complicated than this; in fact, he holds a rather special kind of theory of the 'Expressionist' type. The assumption that beauty is hypostatized pleasure, that the only true referent of all attributions of beauty is a subjective experience of pleasure, is, strictly, irrelevant to his theory of art. That he makes it at all is but more evidence of the pertinacity with which this assumption still clings beyond all rhyme or reason.

Yet when one has said that the function of art is to give pleasure, it is still luminously clear that this capacity to give pleasure—enjoyment, gratification, delight, satisfaction, call it what you will—is not a *sufficient* criterion to distinguish works of art from all other artefacts in the vocabu-

---

[1] *The Sense of Beauty* (1896). Signor Perenna's statement that the beautiful is 'that which pleases the mind as objective value' comes to much the same thing. See *Che cos' è il bello?* (1905).

[2] Cp. *Through Science to Philosophy*, p. 29, etc.

lary of any aesthetician or critic now writing, and still less in common parlance. We all recognize many other artefacts besides works of art which give pleasure and which satisfy and delight. A rare stamp gives pleasure to a philatelist, a grocer's bill may give pleasure if its amount is smaller than was expected, a motor-car gratifies for reasons other than delight in its stream-lined design. The strength of the doctrine is indeed proved by its power to survive despite palpable incompetence, by its constant resuscitation despite repeated refutation. It has that strength-in-weakness which enables the disease germ to multiply into an epidemic.

It would of course be silly to deny that many works of art give pleasure, even intense pleasure, to many people. 'The ecstasies of love and art are perhaps remotely akin', says Mr. Clive Bell. 'The happiness of love, as distinct from ecstasy, and the happiness afforded by works of art, as distinct from the ecstasy . . . are, I think, just comparable; to be more exact, *my* happiness in love and *my* happiness in art appear to be so. They are comparable in degree; and in kind they have this in common: both are compounded of a variety of pleasures playing into and heightening each other. . . .'[1] The cult of the arts, the time, the money, the energy, which many people—even if they are a minority—devote to securing for themselves the opportunity to contemplate or to possess works of art, are not wholly due either to snobbery or to a vague belief that through this pursuit they will in some undefined way be spiritually elevated and their souls improved. They do it in part because they like doing it and because they derive more pleasure from this contemplation or possession than from other occupations that are open to them. Yet, with all respect for the self-examinings of Mr. Bell, we must still doubt whether pleasure or delight is the most significant, or indeed a very important, element in our contacts with those works of art which are most commonly ranked most highly. The *Agamemnon* of Aeschylus, *Don Quijote de la Mancha*, *The Canterbury Tales*, *Pan Tadeusz*, *An Essay on Man* are all admitted by competent literary critics to be works of more than average merit; but to describe the impression they make upon me when I read them by saying that they give me pleasure and delight—as one might say of the latest drawing-room comedy at the Palladium—would, I am sure, be not only inadequate but a misleading abuse of language. It is not untrue that I experience pleasure in reading them, but to describe this as their effect upon me is to single out the relatively insignificant for salience. Nor do I know any critic who would disagree with this judgement in his own

[1] *Enjoying Pictures* (1934).

experience.[1] Goya's *Caprichos*, Picasso's *L'aveugle*, the *Carceri d'Invenzione* of Piranesi, Memling's *La Descent de la Croix*, the caricatures of Toulouse-Lautrec, the phantasies of Felicien Rops are all admitted in their very various ways to be not perhaps supremely important but nevertheless outstandingly valuable examples of pictorial art; yet I believe there is not a critic but would admit that to describe his experience of these works of art as an experience of pleasure would be, not untrue, but nugatory. Certainly those who hear the *F major Quartet* of Beethoven, contemplate Picasso's *Guernica*, or the *Gethsemane* of El Greco in the National Gallery, those who read *Oedipus Rex*, *The Duchess of Malfi*, *The Ring and the Book* or the *Pisan Cantos* for reasons other than duty, obtain some sort of satisfaction or pleasure and perhaps a very profound satisfaction from so doing; were it not so, they would not indulge in such strenuous and taxing occupations. But there is a sense, and the same sense, in which every human being performs every willed action because he obtains satisfaction from so doing; this is not peculiar to the appreciation of works of art. And it is certain that pleasure is not the dominating characteristic of the experience sought and obtained from such appreciation—if, that is, the word 'pleasure' is used in the sense it normally bears. And if it is used in an extraordinary sense, its use can only be misleading. The truth is that from Winckelmann to Ruskin it was taken for granted that the contemplation of beautiful things should induce a state of calm and placid mental repose cool and collected as sculptured marble. The mind was to be elevated and the soul refreshed with the sublime in frolic holiness; but padded against serious shock, insulated against scorching exhileration and in every way guarded from fundamental disturbance of its complacency. So far as I know, the only great contemporary artist to adhere to this view is, significantly, Matisse.[2] It is a point of view which has almost completely disappeared among artists and critics and is becoming rarer among those who appreciate the arts. Men generally no longer demand that

---

[1] 'Masterpieces are practically never pleasing. Their effect on us is too striking for the definition of "pleasing" to have any true application. . . . The editor of the Dictionary must have been thinking of comic opera.' A. Ozenfant, *Foundations of Modern Art* (1931). 'The *Mass in D* rarely gives pleasure and the choral finale of the Ninth Symphony causes many people pain.' Frank Howes, *Man, Mind and Music* (1948).

[2] 'What I dream of is an art of balance, of purity and serenity devoid of troubling or depressing subject-matter, an art which might be for every mental worker, be he businessman or writer, like an appeasing influence, like a mental soother, something like a good armchair in which to rest from physical fatigue.' *Notes d'un peintre* (1908). He does less than justice to his own achievement.

'beauty' shall lull and sooothe them into a marmoreal repose. Instead, we now find it commonly affirmed that a great work of art must be arresting and stimulating, perhaps to ennoble but certainly to stir and disturb. In practice it is the quality of the experience which is lived through in appreciative commerce with the aesthetic object, the whole experience in all its aspects, its richness, its uniqueness, its reverberative profundity, and not merely its 'pleasure index', which interests the critics when they assess the worth, importance, significance, beauty or greatness of works of art. As Ogden and Richards put it, the hedonistic theory of beauty provides altogether too jejune a language for the modern critic.[1]

Is pleasure, then, a *necessary* feature of a work of art? It is not, as we have seen, a *sufficient* criterion, since many artefacts give pleasure which we are not prepared to classify as works of art; nor is it a very important feature of our contact with any works of art. Unless it is a necessary condition, without which no artefact would be classified as a work of art, the pleasure theory of beauty is both incompetent and completely irrelevant.

It is of course notorious that men show little conformity in the occasions of their pleasures. One man likes tomatoes and another persimmon. One watches cricket and another the dogs. There is perhaps no artefact ever created which has not afforded some pleasure to someone; and there exists no artefact anywhere, nor ever has been or will be, which has given pleasure to everyone. If, then, pleasure is erected into a necessary condition for any artefact to be classified as a work of art, it becomes a purely atomistic criterion, differentiating not one and the same class for all men but a different class of art-objects for every man. The layman, unlike the critic, is often willing to admit that many artefacts are works of art although he personally derives no pleasure from them. The latest Agatha Christie gives pleasure to many people who are merely puzzled and bored by the poetry of Ezra Pound; yet there are those among them who would be ready to admit that the poems are works of art while the detective novel is not. Their admission is made upon the authority of the critics, whom they accept as experts upon what is and what is not art. But if pleasurability is a necessary attribute of works of art, their admission is wrong. The works of Agatha Christie may well be works of art for her fans; or they may lack some other necessary charcteristics for classification as art. But the poems of Ezra Pound are certainly not works of art for

[1] 'The disadvantage of a pleasure view is that it offers us too restricted a vocabulary. We need fuller terms with which to describe the value of works of art.' *The Foundations of Aesthetics* (1925).

those people who take no pleasure in them, so long as you make pleasure a necessary condition for classifying any artefact as a work of art in your critical vocabulary.

Nor can any man compare the degree or intensity of the pleasures of different people. There is no public measuring-rod for pleasure. And for this reason, as an instrument for recording the relative degrees of beauty inherent in various works of art, as a criterion for assessing and comparing artistic excellence, a thermometer as it were of beauty, pleasurability is purely private and has no validity from man to man. A critic may rank the works of Virginia Woolf above those of Victoria Cross in artistic excellence because he derives more pleasure from the former than the latter, comparing the pleasure-index of several experiences of his own. But what he can never do is to compare the intensity of the pleasure he experiences in reading *The Waves* with the intensity of the pleasure some other man experiences in reading *The Girl of the Limberlost*. He can know that Gene Stratton Porter is an inferior artist *for him*; he cannot know whether the pleasure which many other people have often derived from reading her works was more or less intense than the pleasure he has derived from those works of art which have pleased him most. All attempts to make such comparisons among the pleasures of different people inevitably smuggle in considerations of the quality of the experiences which are found pleasurable or of the qualities of the objects by which the pleasant experiences are stimulated. So far as degree of pleasure is concerned, a man can assess only the pleasantness of his own private experiences.

The hedonistic theory of ethics, in the generalized form known as Utilitarianism, was able to surmount the atomic and private character of pleasure by adopting as its criterion of goodness the principle of the greatest happiness of the greatest number.[1] It was able to do this because ethics is concerned with human behaviour in general and there is no human action which has not some bearing upon the common happiness and welfare. But it is not part of the critic's function, as critic, to compare the happiness he and his like obtain from listening to music or looking at pictures with the satisfaction others derive from attending race meetings, cinemas or churches. And if within the limited sphere which is his concern the critic proposed to assess the excellence of works of art on the majority principle by counting heads, it is certain that most of the works which most critics regard as good would rank very low and those artefacts

[1] Whereas simple hedonistic ethics seemed to be refuted by Jeremy Bentham's *mot*: 'Pushpin is as good as poetry provided it be as pleasant.'

which we call pseudo-art—Academy pictures, restaurant and dance music, popular films, diversion novels—would head the list as the finest and most beautiful of works of art. You see this tendency of course in much popular appreciative writing about the cinema, where box-office success is confused with excellence. In such a case the critic's own judgements would rank as one voice only in a democratic vote and would have no rightness or validity for others; his job would be that of a statistician. There is in fact only one argument consistent with this theory of beauty by which the critic could defend his claim to act as a guide and to direct the appreciation of others. It derives from the fact that certain critics—not all—are conscious in their own history of progressive changes in taste which seem to them to constitute a progress. At one time they took pleasure in the contemplation of pictures by Landseer or Munnings; now they prefer the animal drawings of Thomas Bewick, realistically unreal, or those of Maruyama Okio, or those in the Grotte de Fonte de Gaume at Les Eyzies. At one time they delighted in Mendelssohn's *Songs without Words* or in the more syrupy Gounod. Now they take more pleasure in hearing a Beethoven quartet, a cantata by Cimarosa or an opera by Purcell. Such changes have sometimes come as the result of a somewhat arduous cultivation of taste and it seems to such critics that the pleasures they derive from the works of art which now please them are keener and more intense than the pleasures they formerly experienced. Therefore, they argue, these changes in sensibility constitute a development and a progress, and if others would follow their guidance and submit to the strenuous cultivation of taste which they themselves have undergone, they too would experience pleasures more intense. This argument is by no means negligible. Were there more agreement among critics themselves, and were there any real likelihood that it would ever be verified in the experience of even a respectable minority of the population, it is an argument which might almost carry conviction. It is the only one at the service of critics who agree that it is a necessary function of works of art to give pleasure and who nevertheless wish to make judgements of taste which shall have more than a purely autobiographical interest.

Realizing something of these difficulties and wishing to salvage the hedonistic theory of art, many writers on aesthetics have professed to discriminate a special *type* of pleasure which they say is constitutive, or a criterion, of beauty, distinguishing the sort of pleasure we take in beautiful things from other sorts of pleasure which we derive from other kinds of things. At the birth of modern aesthetics the immediate followers of Kant differentiated aesthetic pleasure from pleasure in general by defining it as disinterested pleasure, pleasure 'free from will and desire'.[1] It was recognized that this definition must include as aesthetic such sensuous pleasures as we derive from the perfume of a flower, the song of the birds, the glory of a sunset; in other words, it identified natural beauty and the beauty of art in principle—a fairly bold thing to do with your initial definition. It must also include such 'disinterested' pleasures as our delight in Chanel No. 5, in the bouquet of a rare wine or in a profound combination at chess. Though nobody knew quite what to do about facts such as these, the theory remained orthodox—as far as any theory can be called orthodox in so controverted a subject—from Schiller until it was reformulated and popularized by Vernon Lee in a book which had a considerable vogue some forty years ago.[2] Pleasure in the beautiful, she maintained, is pleasure derived from the mere contemplation of an object without consideration of its usefulness, its capacity to satisfy our desires or its intellectual interest. Professor Ducasse generalized this further and posited that beauty or aesthetic value is assessed in terms of the immediate pleasantness or unpleasantness of the *feelings obtained in aesthetic contemplation*.[3]

But such salvaging operations are condemned to futility. In the first place every attempt to distinguish the *quality* of the pleasure experienced in contact with works of art from the quality of the pleasures derived from other occupations which men find pleasurable, whether it be the delight of the sadist in witnessing a flogging or the satisfaction of a scientist in discovering a new generalization, is committed to an elementary psychological error. Pleasures differ in degree, but cannot differ in quality or in anything else at all but amount or intensity of pleasurability. We do not experience pleasures, but we have experiences which are pleasant. Pleasure is not an element in experience but a quality *of* experience. It is adjectival not substantial. Try to isolate the pleasure from the pleasant experience and you inevitably fail. For pleasure is not the name of a distinct feeling or emotion with a quality of its own. You can never become conscious of a pleasure, but only of an experience or a mental state or condition which is more or less pleasant—and when the experience is at

---

[1] This idea was made current by Schiller. See also Schlegel: 'Pleasure indeed has a higher zest when spontaneous and self-created; and it rises in value in proportion to its affinity with that perfection of beauty in which moral excellence is allied to external charms. It must be a free spontaneous burst of feeling: *not* the result of certain means applied for the attainment of any particular object; for pleasure thus pursued becomes occupation rather than enjoyment.'

[2] *The Beautiful* (1913).

[3] *The Philosophy of Art* (1929).

all complex it is often very difficult to decide just how pleasurable it is. We do not, in a word, experience pleasure; we have experiences which are pleasant or unpleasant in various degrees.[1] Therefore pleasures cannot be compared except in the degree of their pleasantness; all other differences reside in the experiences which are pleasant, not in the pleasure. And therefore the attempt to institute an order of merit among pleasures on qualitative grounds, to grade the aesthetic pleasures higher in a scale of value than some other pleasures, means introducing a moral or a quasi-moral criterion for the assessment of experiences. It means, in effect, the abandonment of the hedonistic theory for a moral theory of beauty. And this is in effect the surreptitious procedure of much practical criticism, which talks of pleasure but assumes in the background a moral discrimination among pleasant experiences.

The above objection is not valid against theories of the type popularized by Mr. H. R. Marshall, for example, who said that 'beauty is relatively stable, or real, pleasure'.[2] It is of course true that there are some kinds of experiences which can be relied on to be always, or almost always, pleasant for a particular person, whereas other sorts of experience are sometimes pleasant, sometimes unpleasant, according to mood and circumstance. But it is equally true that the experiences we have in contact with recognized works of art are not alone in being a relatively stable source of pleasure, nor indeed are they a source of pleasure at all to all or most people. Yet you will find it very commonly asserted by critics nowadays that they—and all good critics—take much care to discount passing whims and fancies and labour to achieve a settled and reliable habit of reaction so that the judgements in which they formulate their preferences for works of art may constitute a coherent system of tried and stable response. 'The critic', says Mr. Middleton Murry, 'has to make sure that his opinion is his true opinion; he has to safeguard himself against accidental and temporary disturbances of his sensibility. Hence the

---

[1] 'Pleasure seems to be a way in which something happens, rather than an independent happening which can occur by itself in a mind. We have, not pleasures, but experiences of one kind or another, visual auditory, organic, motor, and so forth, which are pleasant.' I. A. Richards, *The Principles of Literary Criticism*, p. 92. Compare Oswald Külpe, *Outlines of Psychology*: 'As a matter of fact, there is no qualitative difference discoverable between the pleasantness of a colour and that of a successfully concluded argument, when careful abstraction is made from the very wide differences in all their attendant circumstances.'

[2] *Aesthetic Principles* (1895). In a different context of ideas Professor Dewey has also said that art is that which occurs 'when activity is productive of an object that affords continuous renewed delight'. *Experience and Nature*.

need for a system of principles, refined out of his more constant reactions, to control momentary enthusiasms and passing disgusts.' 'Of course,' says Dr. Leavis, 'the process of making "fully conscious and articulate" is a process of relating and organizing, and the "immediate sense of value" should, as the critic matures with experience, represent a growing stability of organization (the problem is to combine stability with growth). What, on testing and re-testing and wider experience, turn out to be my more constant preferences, what the relative permanencies in my response, and what structure begins to assert itself in the field of poetry with which I am familiar?'[1] Yet the permanent and settled pleasure-habits of the critic, no less than his more spontaneous and uncontrolled whims of fancy, are purely autobiographical *data*. They can have no validity for anyone who does not share them and there seems no *a priori* reason to expect that they would result more in accordance with the experience of the mass of mankind, or even of the majority of the critic's readers, than his more casual and wayward responses. And, as Mr. Middleton Murry again admits, the critic 'stands or falls by the closer or more remote approximation of his views to the common experience of the small minority which forms conclusions about life and literature'. It has long been assumed, but is still to be proved, that cultivated taste is more uniform, or a surer expression of some universal quality in human nature, than casual likings and aversions. Even if it were, it would be still valid only for those who shared it. The only argument consistent with the hedonistic doctrine of beauty by which the critics can legitimately demand that others pay attention to their judgements is the argument already suggested—that they themselves secure more intense pleasure from those of their responses which are stable and tried and that there is a presumption that their method might also work for others.

Those theories on the other hand which, like that of Professor Ducasse, propose to make the criterion of beauty the pleasantness of a special class of experiences which they call 'aesthetic contemplation'—defining 'aesthetic contemplation' in some way other than 'a pleasurable experience'—should, logically, abandon the hedonistic criterion altogether. What they in effect propose to do is to discriminate the class of objects which they will classify as works of art as the class of all artefacts which

---

[1] Even in the nineteenth century critics knew that you should make up your mind about anything before writing about it. So Pater, quoting Arnold with a difference, says: 'In aesthetic criticism the first step towards seeing one's object as it really is, is to know one's own impression as it really is, to discriminate it, to realize it distinctly.'

are, or are capable of becoming, objects of aesthetic contemplation. This I believe to be the only completely coherent method of defining works of art, though it is by no means easy to describe what you mean by 'aesthetic contemplation' in such a way that it shall include for example Sir Roger Fry's pleasurable contact with a French Impressionist painting and exclude the apparently equal pleasure which another man may experience in looking at a Peter Scott bird-piece or the photograph of a favourite film-star. But the pleasure-principle is otiose to this type of theory, and when you have abandoned it as a principle for distinguishing works of art from not-art, its retention as the principle for assessing the relative excellence of works of art is a strictly illogical concession to critical practice, without any shadow of profit or justification.

We conclude.—Pleasure cannot be a *sufficient* condition of beauty, a *sufficient* criterion for distinguishing works of art. It stands to reason that, if you are to be intelligible, you cannot call some things beautiful because they please you and for no other reason than because they please you, unless you are prepared to call everything that pleases you beautiful in the degree in which it pleases you. And this no critic, or anyone else, is prepared to do. Secondly, if you make pleasure a *necessary*, though not a sufficient, condition of beauty, you must be prepared to name a different class of beautiful things for every person. Nothing is beautiful, or has artistic excellence, for anyone except in so far as it pleases him, and nothing can be named beautiful except with reference to the persons whom it pleases. When the critic—as all critics do—speaks of his own pleasure in a work of art as indicative of its excellence, he is advancing a judgement which is valid for himself only or for other people only in so far as their pleasures happen to coincide with his. Moreover, if you make a pleasure a necessary, though not a sufficient, criterion of beauty, you must still indicate the other, and possibly more important, characteristics which are together sufficient to warrant your calling any artefact a work of art in your vocabulary. And in fact most hedonistically based criticism does in fact combine aesthetic hedonism with aesthetic emotionalism, tacitly assuming that anything is rightly called beautiful if, and in so far as, it is both pleasant and also effective for rousing emotions. Therefore we shall now discuss the second arm of the theory, the theory of aesthetic emotionalism.

2. *Beauty as Emotional Stimulant*

Very similar in its logical structure and its bearings upon criticism is the parallel theory that not pleasure alone but emotion, or pleasant emotion, is the criterion by which works of art are to be recognized and discriminated. Historically the emotional theory of art arose in a reaction against the moralistic influences of the Counter-Reformation on the one hand and against a too formalistic classicism on the other. In vigorous opposition to both moralistic and rationalistic aesthetics it began to be asserted in the seventeenth century that the judgement of artistic excellence is based upon feeling and emotion, the appreciation of beauty is a matter of *sentiment* and not of reason. Thus arose the conception of *taste*, a distinct faculty by which we become aware of the beautiful, a faculty grounded upon emotion and not upon the intellectual judgement through which we achieve scientific knowledge. The basic assumptions of this theory have seldom been more forthrightly asserted than by one of its earliest advocates, the Abbé Dubos, who wrote: 'The first aim of Painting is to move us. A work which moves us greatly, must be excellent on the whole. For the same reason the work which does not move us at all, does not engage us, is worth nothing; and if criticism finds in it nothing to reprove in the way of faults against the rules, it means only that a work may be bad without having faults against the rules, as a work full of faults against the rules may be an excellent work.'[1] And the faculty by which men discriminate whether a work of art is beautiful or not was called Sentiment. It was a point of view which had a profound and lasting influence, and in England particularly a very considerable body of aesthetic and appreciative writing was expressed in terms of sentiment and taste. Taste was analysed and discussed, adopted into the vocabulary of the philosophers and psychologists, assumed as a matter of course by critics. It is still a powerful factor in appreciation and criticism and is often assumed by writers unconscious of what it is exactly they are assuming.[2]

Dubos, who was not an original thinker but usefully mirrors the aesthetic thought of his time, had said that pleasure is our only criterion of beautiful art: 'the greatest painter for us is the one whose works give us the greatest pleasure'. Antoine Coypel, a Director of the French

---

[1] J. B. Dubos, *Reflexions critiques sur la poésie et la peinture* (1719). The quotation is taken from Venturi's *History of Art Criticism* (1936). With this should be compared his words about poetry: 'Je définirais la Poésie des mots comme la création rhythmique de la beauté! Son seul arbitre est le goût. Avec l'Intelligence ou la Conscience elle n'a que des relations collatérals. Elle n'a qu'incidemment des rapports quelconques avec le Devoir ou avec la Vérité!'

[2] 'It is through the emotions', says Professor W. G. Constable, 'that the art historian has to judge whether he is in the presence of a work of art.' *Art History and Connoisseurship* (1938).

Academy, had maintained in opposition to the dogma of classicism that:
'The arts exist to please, and it is dangerous to allow a method to interfere
with sentiments which nature has implanted, to submit taste to rules
which are not always understood, and to set up prejudices which blind
instead of enlightening the mind.'[1] Count Caylus, an enthusiastic amateur
archaelogist in advance of Winckelmann, wrote in a letter of advice to a
student: 'You must at your age follow your own taste, let your sentiment
lay hold of you, and seek to charge your memory with beautiful things,
that is to say, with things that affect you.'[2] Pleasure in the beautiful was
seen to be the outcome of taste, and it was recognized that tastes differ
from man to man according to personal temperament and training, historical epoch and nationality. The autonomy of individual taste manifested
in emotional reaction was none the less vigorously asserted in opposition
to judgement by rule. But at the same time it was firmly believed and
barely questioned that underlying the idiosyncrasies of individual taste
and feeling there exists an universally *right* feeling belonging to human
nature as such and common to all men as men, even though imperfectly
and variously manifested from man to man. Individual variations of taste
were assumed to be individual deviations from the norm and ideal of
right feeling which was valid for all men. There was, therefore, such a
thing as right taste and faulty taste, although the only way of acheiving
right taste was to follow and cultivate your own individual sentiment and
feeling. It was this complacent assumption that sentiment is ideally the
same in all human nature, though varying empirically from man to man,
which led to the belief that feeling can issue in a kind of knowledge, less
precise, less susceptible to coherent organization, but none the less
genuinely knowledge than that which is mediated through reason and
intellect. This knowledge of the aesthetic feelings had as its advocates
Giovanni Battista Vico in Italy,[3] the younger Shaftesbury in England[4]
and Baumgarten in Germany.[5] The last of these, who is considered to be
the founder of aesthetics as a distinct branch of philosophy, maintained
that artistic knowledge, the knowledge of beauty mediated by sentiment,
is less distinct than the knowledge of science but is none the less an active

[1] *Discours prononcez dans les Conférences de l'Académie royale de peinture et de
sculpture* (1721).

[2] Quoted by André Fontaine in *Les Doctrines d'art en France* (1909) and by
Mr. F. P. Chambers in *The History of Taste* (1932).

[3] *Principi di una scienza nuova* (1725).

[4] Anthony Ashley Cooper, third Earl of Shaftesbury, *Characteristics of Men,
Matters, Opinions and Times* (1711-23).

[5] *Aesthetica* (1750).

and genuine mode of knowing objective reality. In the language of the time, feeling and sentiment were 'illuminated'.

But the antinomy between the factual variations of taste and the supposed norm of a good taste which should have universal validity was never solved. The sort of quandary into which men got is shown as late as Hazlitt, who said on one page that 'enthusiasm' is the only conclusive proof of taste, a few pages on that enthusiasm is no proof of taste 'without reason and knowledge', and concluded that not 'mere sensibility' but 'sensibility to real excellence' constitutes good taste. His final advice is to the effect that 'to agree with the greatest number of good judges is to be in the right; and good judges are persons of natural sensibility and acquired knowledge'.[1] Yet we have after all progressed nothing beyond this, although we are to-day less optimistically convinced that cultivated taste is likely to be more uniform than spontaneous untaught reaction and less ready to assume that there is any norm of 'right' feeling inherent in human nature as such towards which individual differences asymptotically approximate. The dilemma confronting emotional criticism to-day is the same as it was then. When a critic to-day says that he considers a picture beautiful he implies that he is not merely recording a fact about his own reactions but that (unless he is mistaken) the picture really is beautiful and other people should consider it beautiful as well. So when two critics disagree about the aesthetic quality of a poem, it is assumed that one of them must be right and the other wrong and that they are not merely stating their personal preferences as autobiographical *data*. In other words, criticism assumes that aesthetic judgements have a universal application and validity. But how can this be if aesthetic judgement is formulated on the basis only of feelings, as was maintained by those who upheld taste and recognized that aesthetic pleasure is a feeling? Shaftesbury sought a way out of the impasse by postulating a special *sense* by which beauty is apprehended with the immediacy of direct acquaintance. He thought that this sense is the same as the moral sense and that both the aesthetically beautiful and the morally good are intuitively discerned by 'an inward eye'. His theory of an aesthetic sense had considerable influence upon eighteenth-century criticism, particularly as it was developed by his follower Francis Hutcheson. 'This superior Power of Perception', said Hutcheson, 'is justly called *a Sense*, because of its Affinity to the other Senses in this, that the Pleasure does not arise from any knowledge of Principles, Proportions, Causes, or of the Usefulness of the Object; but

[1] 'Thoughts on Taste'. See Elizabeth Schneider, *The Aesthetics of William Hazlitt* (1933).

strikes us at first with the Idea of Beauty.'[1] Thus through this idea of an aesthetic sense it was hoped to reconcile the belief that aesthetic appreciation arises from emotional response with the belief in an objective standard of taste, by reference to which particular judgements are right or wrong. Facts, however, were too strong for theory and it has gracefully vanished into the limbo of forgotten things.

The assumption of a universal rightness of feeling had nevertheless a profound influence upon criticism, and what was introduced as a philosophical ideal came not infrequently to be assumed as an empirical fact. This confusion alone could make possible such a statement, for example, as that with which Ruskin defined his method in discussing architectural beauty: 'But since all such enquiries can only be founded on the ordinary understanding of what is meant by the term Beauty, and since they presume that the feeling of mankind on this subject is universal and instinctive, I shall base my present investigation on this assumption; and only asserting that to be beautiful which I believe will be granted me to be so without dispute, I would endeavour shortly to trace the manner in which this element of delight is to be best engrafted upon architectural design. . . .'[2] The modern outlook is directly opposed to all this, and nobody to-day would dare to postulate a universal standard of 'right' feeling. In part the change has been brought about by the psychologists, who have discounted the belief that feeling is in any sense veridical or mediatory of knowledge; so we all now believe that while feelings themselves may be judged right or wrong ethically, no judgements of external facts based upon feeling can be true or false. The psychology of emotion, and in particular the findings of psychoanalysis, have shown that some feelings are more fundamental, more universal, others more variable and superficial; but the relation of feeling to the object of feeling is always arbitrary: it is not a knowledge-relation. But there has been another factor also, perhaps more potent though less frequently recognized, contributing to the change of outlook. In the eighteenth century it was assumed not only that cultivated taste approximated towards an ideal rightness of taste, but that the masses of mankind who were unappreciative of artistic beauty owed this defect to lack of opportunity. The assumption was plausible because interest in the fine arts was at that time more widely diffused than it is to-day among the moneyed and leisured classes, while the proletariat had little opportunity at all to cultivate a taste for the beautiful. But the social revolution of our times, together with the enormously increased opportunities for contact

---

[1] *An Enquiry into the Original of our Ideas of Beauty and Virtue* (1725).
[2] *Seven Lamps of Architecture*, Ch. IV (1849).

with works of art afforded by the gramophone and wireless, the mechanical reproduction of pictures, and so on, has radically changed all this.
And unfortunately for the easy assumption of the Age of Illumination, it
is becoming evident that the generality of men do not gravitate naturally
towards the beautiful but display a spontaneous preference for forms of
spurious and meretricious art which the critics whole-heartedly condemn.
Either, then, the critics' ideas of what is beautiful must be radically revised
or the assumption that there is a natural taste for beauty inherent in
human nature as such must be jettisoned. Both alternatives have had
their advocates. Tolstoi is the most notorious of those who have proposed
to classify as good works of art only those which appealed to the vast
majority of men and were capable of arousing specific emotions in the
masses.[1] And under the influence particularly of certain political creeds,
there has arisen in our own generation the demand for a new art of the
proletariat. Typical of this new outlook are the following words of Diego
Rivera: 'After the Mexican revolution, my revolutionary confrères—
then living in Paris—thought that if they gave modern art of the highest
quality to the masses this art would immediately become popular through
its instant acceptance by the proletariat. I was never able to share this
point of view, because I always knew that the physical senses are susceptible not only to education and development, but to atrophy and
desuetude; and also that the "aesthetic sense" can only be reached through
the physical senses themselves. I had also observed the indubitable fact
that among the proletariat—exploited and oppressed by the bourgoisie—
the workman, ever burdened with his daily labor, could cultivate his
taste only in contact with the worst and the vilest portion of bourgoise
art which reached him in cheap chromes and the illustrated papers. . . .
What is it then that we really need? An art extremely pure, precise, profoundly human, and clarified as to its purpose. An art with revolution as
its subject: because the principal interest in the worker's life has to be
touched first. It is necessary that he find aesthetic satisfaction and the
highest pleasure appareled in the essential interest of his life.' And José
Clemente Orozco ranks mural painting as the highest form of art 'because
it cannot be hidden away for the benefit of a certain privileged few. It is
for the people. It is for ALL.' Both these writers assume that there exists in
the masses of mankind a faculty to appreciate the genuinely (or traditionally) beautiful in art, but that this faculty is latent and suppressed and
must be re-awakened. Others, without the stimulus of revolutionary
fervour, seeing the continued apathy to beauty of populations no longer

---

[1] *What is Art?* (1898).

suppressed and the increasing ugliness and banality of democratic civilization, have abandoned the belief in any natural inclination for the beautiful and regard taste and the love of beauty as a rare gift accorded only to the few. In literary criticism those critics who have come under the influence of Marxist doctrines are divided between the belief that the dominant proletariat would spontaneously enjoy what has traditionally been regarded as good literature provided only that its subject-matter was adapted to their interests, and the belief that traditional notions of beauty must be adapted to what the proletariat does in fact spontaneously enjoy.

The other method of dealing with the prevalence of bad taste is frankly to accept that each man's feelings are ultimate for him, to deny that one man's emotional responses can be regulative for others and in an ultimate access of scepticism to reject all absolute standards of good taste. So after a lifetime of musical criticism Mr. Ernest Newman wrote: 'I find that I can no longer read it—thus, I imagine, coming at last into line with the general public. It is bad enough to have to write the stuff; to read it, except for some definite purpose of the moment, is impossible, for the reason that it tells me nothing about the composer, who is the real object of my interest, but only something about the critic, in whom I am not in the least interested. His view of the composer is merely the result of his own personal reaction, which is a matter of no concern and no value to anyone but himself. . . . There was a time when I too, young and innocent, thought my own reactions to music the only correct ones, and believed that everyone who differed from me to be wrong. Older and wiser now, I do not trouble about these things. The proselytizing spirit is dead within me. I have not the vanity to think that my own mental and emotional constitution should be the norm for the rest of mankind, and, therefore, I can only smile when younger writers, or older writers, who by this time ought to know better, implicitly claim that they are the world's norm. There was a time when I had a half-idea that it was really quite intelligent on the part of Providence to have sent me on earth, for had I not been born the world would never have known the truth as to musical "values". In my boyish simplicity I thought that it was essential that other people should feel as I felt; now I have developed, on this point, a toleration so magnificently comprehensive that it amounts to complete indifference.'[1] There can be no doubt that this attitude of scepticism is the logical outcome of modern psychological teaching about the subjectivity of feeling and emotion. And there can be no doubt that it cuts at the root of all

[1] Quoted from an article in the *Sunday Times* by Professor Ducasse in the Introduction to his *The Philosophy of Art* (1929).

claims to objective validity made for the judgements and assessments of criticism.

In contemporary aesthetics the emotional theory takes two forms. Sometimes emotional response is assumed to be *constitutive* of beauty—when we say that anything is beautiful, is excellent as a work of art, we *mean* that it moves us emotionally; and the more intensely it moves us, the more beautiful it is. Thus all propositions about beauty are really propositions about our emotions towards the objects we call beautiful. The other form taken by the theory looks upon emotion as a symptom or indicator by means of which we become aware of beauty and which we can use as a gauge of the degree in which any object is beautiful, while beauty itself is regarded as some rather mysterious property of the object itself in virtue of which it arouses our emotions towards it. The most specific form of this latter theory is that put forward by Mr. Clive Bell and on occasion by Sir Roger Fry. Beauty, they say, is a formal property of aesthetic objects which has not been well defined but which is for convenience called 'significant form'; this property arouses in suitably sensitized observers a specific emotion which is aroused only by beautiful things and its intensity is in proportion to the degree of beauty in the object by which it is aroused. This peculiar 'aesthetic' emotion therefore serves as a 'detector' by which we are able to become aware of the presence of the beauty which we are unable to analyse. 'The starting-point for all systems of aesthetics must be the personal experience of a peculiar emotion. The objects which provoke this emotion we call works of art. . . . This emotion is called the aesthetic emotion; and if we can discover some quality common and peculiar to all the objects that provoke it, we shall have solved what I take to be the central problem of aesthetics.'[1] In many ways this is logically the most satisfactory of all contemporary theories of art. Unfortunately, although Mr. Clive Bell has claimed that all sensitive people agree that there is a peculiar emotion provoked by works of art and only by works of art, the majority of competent critics as well as psychologists with some experience in appreciation have professed themselves unable introspectively to detect the peculiar emotion of which he speaks. And any theory basing itself upon introspective evidence which is rejected by most of those who are presumably most qualified to judge must remain precarious. In any case Mr. Clive Bell could not possibly affirm more than that he is conscious in himself of a special emotion which he only experiences in contact with objects which he is prepared to classify as works of art; he could not possibly know

---

[1] Mr. Clive Bell, *Art* (1914).

whether or not other people have a similar emotional experience in contact with objects which neither he nor they are prepared to classify as works of art.

The emotional theory of beauty has this advantage over the pleasure theory that it offers to criticism a wider vocabulary and affords the critic almost unlimited licence to describe his own emotional experiences in contact with works of art—if this is what is desired of criticism. But except in the special form given to it by Mr. Clive Bell it is no more sufficient a criterion than pleasure for discriminating works of art; apart at least from the dubious 'aesthetic thrill' every known human emotion aroused by works of art is also aroused by things which are not classified as works of art. It is not possible therefore to discriminate works of art from not-art by their power to evoke emotion. The theory also shares with the hedonistic theory the disadvantage that it discriminates a different class of works of art for every person—no two persons experience exactly the same emotional reactions or react emotionally in precisely the same degree to the same objects. Emotion cannot be regarded as a *sufficient* condition for classifying works of art, since emotions can be efficiently aroused by many things which nobody names art. If it is a *necessary* but not a sufficient condition, we are still not told what other attributes must be associated with it to obtain a sufficient criterion. And if the capacity to evoke emotion is a necessary condition of artistic excellence at all, critical judgement becomes as incurably subjective as it is in the pure hedonistic theory of beauty.

It remains therefore only to investigate what kind of criticism, if any, remains compatible with a hedonistic or an emotional theory of beauty— and that that enquiry is more than academic is evidenced by the fact that there is no critic now writing who does not make the assumption on every few pages that feeling and emotion are, if not constitutive of beauty, at least the criterion and detector by which he becomes aware of beauty and assesses the excellence of the objects he criticises and appreciates.

3. *Bearings of Emotional Hedonism upon Criticism*

I chanced not long ago to overhear one of those curious devices of popular entertainment purveyed by the British Broadcasting Corporation, in which a group of minor political personalities is assembled before the microphone to make impromptu discourse upon a random collection of questions about which they may be expected to know nothing. The question which drew my attention was one about the merits of current literary and dramatic criticism. In answer, I remember, the first speaker opined that there is really little wrong with the critics, but it is up to each member of their public to select from among them that critic whose taste most nearly corresponds with his own. A second speaker, while having little fault to find with this, thought that it is also incumbent on the critic to see that he remains constantly in touch with public taste, since if he were to lose contact with it he would be liable to mislead and disappoint those who were willing to accept his guidance. A third, then, consciously elevating the tone of the discussion, suggested that there might be such a thing as objective criticism, as for example whether a play is technically well constructed or if it is well produced. Startled as I was at first by these radical notions of criticism, it seemed to me upon reflection that they were in fact quite surprisingly sound if you once substituted 'reviewer' for 'critic', as was probably the intention of whoever framed the question. The reviewer, or the 'journalistic critic' as he is sometimes called, is paid to do a specific job and his performance satisfies a public demand: if it did not, he would no longer be paid. His job is to anticipate public taste, to inform his audience in advance whether they will or will not obtain from the books, films, plays, music or pictures which are currently offered for their consumption sufficient reward of entertainment to compensate for the time and money expended upon them. When the *Observer* praises a show you pay your money because you judge that you are likely to enjoy it. If then you are bored and unamused, the reviewer was at fault in your case; he anticipated your reactions wrongly. He was paid to act as your guide, you followed his guidance and you were disappointed and misled. Reviewing fulfils a legitimate social function as a concession to natural human laziness. Very few persons can afford the time and the energy to sample all the novels, the poems, the plays, the music and the films which are made available to them week in and week out. Selection is necessary. And people use the reviewers, as they use the opinions of their friends, to help them select those which are most likely to please them.[1]

---

[1] This—admittedly somewhat arbitrary—statement of the reviewer's function will be seen to accord with the view taken by Mrs. Virginia Woolf in an essay on *Reviewing*, published in *The Captain's Death Bed* (1950). 'The reader asks the reviewer to tell him', she says, 'whether the poem or novel is good or bad in order that he may decide whether to buy it or not.' Somewhat more exact is Mr. Leonard Woolf's reformulation in a Note appended to the same essay: 'the function of the reviewer . . . is to give to readers a description of the book and an estimate of its quality in order that he may know whether or not it is the kind of book which he may want to read'. We agree with Mr. Leonard Woolf in protesting against the view that the reviewer's function is not a useful and a necessary one. And Mrs. Virginia Woolf seems to us petulantly misguided when she claims that

But criticism as it is generally understood claims to be something more than this. Mr. Middleton Murry complains that 'the reviewer is expected to compile a library list for the average unintelligent reader and the critic is compelled by economic necessity to become a reviewer'. The reviewer's work satisfies a fugitive but genuine need and is consciously ephemeral. But criticism makes a more pretentious claim. It affects not merely to predict what the reaction of the public, or of some section of the public, to individual works of art is likely to be, but claims to inform the public what its reaction ought to be. For the critic proposes assessments of works of art which claim to be 'right' in some sense other than by being correct anticipations of probable public response. The critic usually knows very well that his valuations are in fact very unlikely to correspond with the reactions of the generality; he publishes them because he nevertheless believes that they are in some sense more right or better than the untutored judgement. If the reviewer's assessment is falsified by the subsequent response of his readers, the reviewer is wrong. If public response is out of accord with the judgements of the critic, the public is wrong. The reviewer predicts, the critic dictates.

I have consciously exaggerated the difference between the activities of the reviewer and those of the critic in order to bring into prominence a genuine difference of function which is always there.[1] It is true that many critics admit, and some assert, that even the most profound critical judgements are inescapably at the mercy of changing fashions in taste and deprecate any hope of ever reaching finality. Croce indeed went so far as because reviewers disagree, the reviewer has failed in his duty to his public, so that it 'seems a public duty to abolish him'. Political columnists are also known to disagree, nor do we in a democratic land seek to abolish them for that. And as different sections of the public are of a different political colour, so all tastes in books and plays and painting and music are not one taste, and each taste requires its own reviewer to disagree with the rest.

[1] But not always recognized. In an essay entitled 'Criticism in a Mass Society' contributed to the symposium *The Intent of the Critic*, Mr. W. H. Auden writes: 'Not only should the critic realize the necessity of coordinating his esthetic values with values in all other spheres of life, but he has a duty in a democracy to tell the public what they are. If I am to trust a reviewer's judgement upon a book I have not read, I want to know among other things his philosophical beliefs.' The reviewer, yes. But the critic, I submit, whatever else his function may be, is not to provide guidance in respect to works of art which we have not yet known in direct experience. Mrs. Virginia Woolf too, in the essay referred to, gives it as one of the functions of the reviewer to comment to the author on his book. But surely, if you make a distinction between criticism and reviewing at all, it is the critic and not the reviewer who should inform the artist of the measure of success he has achieved. The reviewer speaks to the public as consumers.

to say that all criticism is criticism of criticism—the evaluation of past valuations. There is, too, a somewhat tedious fashion among critics to-day, flogging the obvious, to announce that the critic is but a man among other men and fallible as all men are fallible. 'A critic', says Mr. Donald A. Stauffer, 'is not an ideal critic if he thinks of himself as the impersonal voice of truth.' But these very disclaimers imply an aspiration towards an objectivity of judgement which, although it may never become final any more than philosophy ever achieves unshakeable and ultimate truth, nevertheless remains a valid goal and ideal. Criticism never admits that its assessments are automatically discredited if they are found to be out of line with contemporary majority taste. And it is true of course that on the other hand something more is expected of the reviewers than correct guidance about what works of art we are likely to enjoy. Their public looks to them for a line of commentary and appreciation which will help it to conquer its own inarticulateness and enable it to make intelligent if not original conversation about works of art which it has or has not sampled. It must be admitted too that from predicting taste the reviewer comes to exercise an influence upon it. In a pattern of society where all response is becoming more and more mechanized, once a reviewer has established his position as guide and counsellor his public will often find it less exhausting within limits to experience or pretend to the sort of response which its reviewer advises than to experience and respond spontaneously. Like the fashion expert, the reviewer turns into a creator and moulder of fashion. So it happens that while criticism claims the right to direct appreciation, it is in fact the reviewer and not the critic who wields the greater direct influence on public taste.

Now as the public is interested in what it enjoys and not in what possesses some abstract principle of goodness which it does not understand, there can be no doubt that the hedonistic notion of artistic excellence justifies the job of the reviewer and cuts the ground from under any criticism which would be something other than reviewing. Nor can there be any reasonable doubt that aesthetic hedonism expresses more accurately than any other theory the prevailing temper of the age. Of the many social functions which may be served by works of art, that which stands out as most typical of the age in which we are living is the demand that it should exist to entertain. We work in order to win the right to leisure. We then clamour for entertainment in order to make our leisure tolerable to us. We fear to be unoccupied and we are no longer able to occupy ourselves. Boredom stalks us and we must kill time in order to escape from it. We talk of Culture with a capital, and while its mechanical means have been advanced beyond the powers of our parents to conceive, in our schools and homes and market-places the native capacity for it is being stunted and starved of substance. The wireless brings music into every home, where the power to listen to music is gone.[1] Paintings can now be multiplied by mechanical means; we hang poor reproductions on the walls of our empty rooms and patronize the cinemas while the younger artists are driven to more socially remunerative labours. Everyone is literate and books abound, but few know how to read. The illiterate man's natural gift for appreciation is being stultified by too much literacy badly applied. We have the world's best transport system, nothing to transport and nowhere to deliver.

Why do we read books that are neither informative nor fine? Why is our choice of reading matter what it is? Why do so many persons who in their formative years at a university may be presumed to have acquired some skill in the appreciation of the great literatures of the past read nothing in later life but ephemeral and third-rate mediocrity? Why are our libraries stocked with trash? People no longer care to read great literature because its appreciation requires concentration and effort; without expenditure of effort it is boring. But after a brief period of adolescence we now dislike effort and become incapable of it—effort of all kinds, but particularly mental effort. We bet on the football pools instead of playing football; we buy a gramophone instead of playing an instrument; we rely on Messrs. Boots to purvey us reading matter which shall entertain without taxing. Perhaps we so spread our energies that we have no surplus of energy left for intense enjoyment. Perhaps we become so accustomed to having things done for us in a mechanized age that we lose the habit of doing anything ourselves. Be the cause as it may, in our entertainments it is mental apathy we seek, not the opportunity for exercise of the mind's keenest faculties at highest pitch. We no longer amuse ourselves; we are entertained. The most competent mode of art for this generation is the art of the movie, where in the words of Mrs. Virginia Woolf, 'the brain, agreeably titillated, settles down to watch things happening without bestirring itself to think'.

Why do we read at all? We read to 'pass the time', to *kill time*, because when we 'have nothing better to do' with it the bogey of boredom stalks us. We prefer to go to the cinema or to a mediocre play because, although the physical effort is greater, physical contact with our fellows in crowds

---

[1] 'It is to be noticed that the more people use the wireless the less they listen to it.' Constant Lambert, who in Part Four of his *Music Ho!* has said all that needs to be said about the 'Appalling Popularity of Music'.

gives greater security against the lurking realization of our own solitariness. But failing anything else we read a book in order to keep our attention away from the consciousness of our solitude and be comforted. We ask of a book, then—or of the cinema or theatre—that it shall occupy our attention for a brief period of time, 'take us out of ourselves', help us to destroy the leisure we so prize, while making no demands upon us. And what we ask we get. The modern book—the book as an art form—is written to be read once and returned to the lending library. The magazine illustration has served its purpose when the current number has been thrown aside. Jazz tunes have their day and are done. We see our plays and our films once and are ready for the next. But great works of art not only require great and continued effort of concentration, the active exercise of a skilled perceptive faculty, but invite repeated observation. The more we look at them the more we see in them. They have permanence; we need the ephemeral.

Or perhaps this is not quite all we ask. In order that our attention may be held we need mild stimulation of the emotions to which the drabness of our daily life allows inadequate scope, some inducement for wish-fulfilment that we may imaginatively luxuriate in what life denies us—or at the least the comfort of learning that other lives are no less drab than our own. We ask that our day-dreaming be done for us, project ourselves into the story of a book or film and identify ourselves with the hero. We cultivate a state of semi-waking sleep in which we are not even required to make the effort necessary for day-dreaming on our own. A gentle 'affective massage', an anodyne against the felt monotony of emptiness, a narcotic against lurking boredom—we take our art as we take an aspirin in anticipation of the pain.

It is not for the critic to deplore or to defend all this. The social historian may explain it. It is presumably for the elected representatives of the collective will to remove the underlying causes, if the collective will is for social change. But the critic may and should point out that the art which satisfies the requirements of popularity in modern society can have none of the qualities for which art has been called good in the past.

And this is about all he can do. Apart from this he is limited to the function of the reviewer as we have described it. If he makes his own pleasure or emotions a standard for his judgements and still professes to pronounce objective and normative assessments of artistic excellence, he is committed to a fundamental illogicality from which he can escape only by turning moralizer. For the only ground on which he can set his own emotional responses above those of other men and propose them as a norm is a moral ground. If he does not set up as a moralist and is not content to be a reviewer, or is unqualified for the job, the only recourse left to the hedonistic critic is to become a historian or statistician of taste. But in this capacity he would be illogical to limit himself, as historians have done in the past, to the preferences of connoisseurs; he would have to concern himself equally with the likes and dislikes of all men, treating taste as a social phenomenon and putting what has been called bad taste on a par with good taste.[1]

Alternatively the critic might abandon criticism for autobiography and instead of describing aesthetic objects might write the story of his own emotional experiences in contact with them—though his only justi-fication for writing of his own aesthetic experiences rather than some other man's would be the fact that he knows more about them. And in truth the autobiographical element has come to bulk very large in most writing which passes as criticism. As Mr. Geoffrey Tillotson pertinently remarks of Matthew Arnold's critical methods: 'Instead of telling us any-thing about the eighteenth century, Arnold tells us about his own dislike for parochialism, and about his own wish that his fellows would take to bathing more freely in that boosted Ganges of his, the current of European ideas.'[2] Such writing is unconscious autobiography, not criticism as we have tried to define it. And there is no doubt that the autobiographical element in criticism has steadily increased since Arnold's day. Now auto-biographical criticism may command our attention for one of two reasons, and they are the same reasons which render any other form of auto-biography readable. If we are interested in the critic for some extraneous reason—because he was a personal friend or because he had achieved prominence in politics or religion or any other sphere of life—we may like to read the story of his aesthetic experiences. Or failing that, he may succeed in presenting his personal record in a style sufficiently attractive and seductive to keep us engaged until we find in ourselves an inclination to compare his experiences with our own. But such autobiographical writing in criticism stands or falls by the same criteria as any other essay in autobiography—in this case by the hedonistic standard of whether it effectively entertains. As criticism it can claim no validity and by its very nature it is precluded from objectivity.

It might be argued that although the hedonistic assumption invalidates

[1] Such studies as Mrs. Queenie D. Leavis's *Fiction and the Reading Public* (1932) and Miss Amy Cruse's *The Victorians and their Books* (1930) and *After the Victorians* (1938) make a step in this direction.

[2] *Criticism and the Nineteenth Century* (1951).

valuational criticism, it does not preclude or seriously unsaddle descriptive criticism. There are in fact critics who, while accepting the consequences of hedonism, claim to write objective and profitable *descriptive* criticism. But plausible as this may seem, it is not sound. For to be profitable, descriptive criticism must point to those 'aesthetic' qualities of the object in which its excellence is considered to reside—on the hedonist assumption those properties in which pleasure is taken. But as different men take pleasure in different things and relatively few in works of art, so of those who do contact a work of art with pleasure some like it for one quality and others for another. And the source of each man's pleasure is equally right. All the critic can do, therefore, is to indicate the qualities of the object in which *he* takes pleasure—which are the qualities of its excellence *for him*. And his indications have no validity for others except in so far as others happen to like the same qualities of the object that the critic likes.

It will certainly be objected that the indictment of this chapter is too drastic and it will be pointed out that, although all critics sometimes use the hedonistic principle as their standard of assessment, no critics do so always. They do not confine themselves to it but employ other standards as well. This is in fact the point we are concerned to make. In so far as the critic employs, overtly or by implication, a hedonistic standard of judgement,[1] his criticism is open to the consequences we have endeavoured to display. That must be conceded. But in so far as he also uses other criteria for grading and assessing works of art, he is being illogical and inconsistent with himself whenever he does introduce the hedonistic—or emotional—assumption. And as critics who do use incompatible standards are not notorious for warning the reader of the standard invoked in each of their judgements, every accession of inconsistency comes at the expense of intelligibility. In the interests of better communication our plea is for an increment of consistency.

[1] E.g. 'What is the point at which ordinary pleasures pass over into the specific pleasures derived from each one of the arts? Our judgement about the merits of any given work of art depends to a large extent upon our answer to this question.' Bernhard Berenson, *The Italian Painters of the Renaissance* (1930). 'But in poetry means are vital to the sensuous pleasures which, however faintly, poetry must give us before it can exist.'—'. . . literature means matter of any sort written so as to give the generally cultivated reader not only instruction but immediate pleasure—a pleasure that is notable, however much milder and less sensuous than the immediate pleasure given by poetry.' Geoffrey Tillotson, op. cit., pp. 77 and 197. Mr. Tillotson is among those who accept the subjective consequences of hedonism: 'if we do not welcome it as poetry, poetry for us it cannot be'.

Chapter VII

BEAUTY AS EXPRESSION

Painters paint themselves.   JONATHAN RICHARDSON

No man can walk abroad save on his own shadow.

                                        SIR WALTER RALEIGH

Primum est igitur ut apud nos valeant ea quae valere apud judicem volumus,
afficiamurque antequam afficere conemur.   QUINTILIAN

Art is the only means by which human beings can communicate to each other
the quality and quiddity of their experiences.   SIR ROGER FRY

To think of a work of art as a form of self-expression, a way in which the artist externalizes himself and makes his personality manifest to other men, is in keeping with the psychological temper of our time. It is also one of the more conspicuous features in which contemporary art theory differs from medieval and oriental aesthetics. When Leonardo declared that 'il pittore pinge se stesso' he was speaking both prophetically and in the spirit of his time. But the medieval attitude was voiced by Dante when he said: 'Chi pinge figura, si non può esser lei, non la può porre'; and equally in the scholastic doctrine as expressed in Eckhart's characteristic assertion that 'the painter who has painted a good portrait therein shows his art; it is not himself that it reveals to us'. In an admirably well-conceived essay on *The Theory of Art in Asia* Mr. Ananda K. Coomaraswamy has shown that the aesthetic individualism which has run rampant since the Renaissance was a divergence from the medieval ideal, while the latter accords with the practice and principles of oriental art in general.[1] The modern critic who is interested in going behind the work of art as an object existing for appreciation and in using it as a

[1] *The Transformation of Nature in Art* (1934). 'From the scholastic and Indian point of view, any such reflection of the person of the artist in his work must be regarded as a defect; whereas in later European art, the trace of the artist's individual peculiarities coming to be regarded as a virtue in the art, and flattering the artist's pride, the way to aesthetic exhibitionism and the substitution of the player ("star") for the play were prepared. In the same way the history of artists has replaced the history of art.'

token from which to read the personal idiosyncrasies of the man who made it, is inclining to a conception of artistic excellence which would have seemed grotesque to the medieval or oriental mind.

The conception of art as a mode of expression, as 'the language of feeling and emotion', emerging with the new individualism of the Renaissance, was given a stronger impetus by Goethe, Schiller, Schleiermacher, Schopenhauer, and the poets and philosophers of the German Romantic movement in general, and has been prominent in aesthetic theory ever since. The Romantics were little less than obsessed by the idea of the artist as Genius. Their influence worked to cause a shift of attention away from the work of art as an aesthetic object and from its effects upon the observer, while focusing interest upon the creative process in the mind of the artist. The art-product was valued as the *expression* of the artist's uniqueness, as the means by which he *communicated* his inspired insight into reality, or conveyed his wonderfully delicate or passionately intense emotional responses to the less favoured and gifted of mankind. On this view beauty in a work of art is defined in terms of expression: any work of art is beautiful in accordance with the adequacy with which it communicates the inner life or experience of the Artist and in accordance with the quality of greatness and originality inherent in that experience.

This Romantic attitude to art was taken over into Idealist philosophy and its influence thereby spread and intensified. It was formulated into a coherent aesthetic doctrine, not essentially metaphysical in character, by Eugène Véron, one of the writers who influenced Tolstoi's aesthetic views.[1] Art, said Véron, is essentially a language. The ordinary language of the spoken word originated from the expression of emotions by instinctive natural signs—cries of pleasure or pain, anger or desire, eagerness or disappointment, vocalizations of mood and mental disturbance. But as men matured in the capacity for abstract thought, they began to develop a language of purely conventional signs which served for the communication of facts and ideas. This became the language of 'prose', informative and scientific speech. From a form of natural expression no different in essence from other bodily gestures language became an artificial means of communication. But at the same time the language of mimetic signs for the expression of concrete feelings and emotions was also developed and elaborated, becoming the language of art. Scientific language is communication of thought; art-language is expression of mood. The province of art is, therefore, for Véron, wider than the province of the beautiful.

[1] *L'Esthétique* (1882).

Anything which is expressive of the inner life of its creator is art and to this art beauty is of secondary importance. It is the depicting of emotion, feeling, sentiment, character, that is important. Therefore, Véron says, when a fine work of art is before us it is the genius of the artist and his ability to communicate that we admire rather than the art-product we are contemplating. And in conclusion he declares that the idea which he has endeavoured to recommend in his book is 'sincerity in art, by the spontaneous manifestation of the personal emotion of the artist'. All these ideas, crude as they still are, are important anticipations of what have become to-day among the most influential principles of criticism.

In Germany Expressionism was re-affirmed as a conscious principle of art, particularly in connection with stylistic developments in painting and sculpture, in the present century.[1] Its more philosophic formulation is to be found in the writings of Wilhelm Dilthey,[2] who, although leaning primarily towards the empirical and psychological school of thought, was brought into sympathy with the Romantic conceptions by the influence of Novalis. In England the theoretical outlook of Romanticism was combined with outstanding critical understanding in Coleridge and through Coleridge influenced Mr. I. A. Richards, whose work on literary criticism has had more influence on the present generation than that of any other writer. In philosophical aesthetics also most of the older generation of Idealist writers—Bradley, Bosanquet, Alexander, and even Santayana— were influenced to a greater or less degree by the Romantic conception of art as expression. In Italy the most widely read exponent of an Expressionist view is Benedetto Croce,[3] who since the translation of his works into English by Mr. Douglas Ainslie has found a number of disciples among the younger generation of aestheticians in this country. But Croce uses the word 'expression' in a sense peculiar to himself in which, as he repeatedly emphasizes, it is a synonym of 'intuition'. None of his followers has yet succeeded in making his meaning clear to anyone else, but this has had the advantage that each has been free to interpret him according to his individual taste, and the influence of his writing both upon theory and upon practice has been prodigious. Among philosophical writers in this country, E. F. Carritt, R. G. Collingwood, W. T. Stace and L. A. Reid have all come under his spell. 'What the artist is trying to do', says R. G. Collingwood, 'is to express a given emotion. . . . To express it

---

[1] See Sheldon Cheney, *Expressionism in Art* (1948).

[2] Particularly *Die Einbildungskraft des Dichters. Bausteine für eine Poetik* (1887) and *Die drei Epochen der modernen Ästhetik und ihre heutige Aufgabe* (1892).

[3] 'Expression and beauty are not two concepts but a single concept.'

badly is not one way of expressing it (not, for example, expressing it but not *selon les règles*), it is failing to express it. A bad work of art is an activity in which the agent tries to express a given emotion, but fails.'[1] 'The view of beauty which I shall defend', Mr. L. A. Reid tells us, 'will be that beauty is perfect expressiveness.'[2] In the more popular literature of appreciation and practical criticism the assumption that art and literature are modes of expression, that they are in essence the 'language of feeling and emotion', is hardly less insistent than the hedonistic assumption itself. And the meanings variously given to this doctrine range from a lofty if not very profound mysticism to the banality of the platitudinous *dictum* that 'Art is an expression of life'.[3]

Of literature Professor Lascelles Abercrombie has said: 'the whole purpose of a poet's technique is to make a moment of his experience come to life in other minds than his'.[4] Of the visual arts we have the pronouncement of Barnes and de Mazia that: 'We respond to a work of art, to a picture or symphony, not by doing something, but by participating in the experience of the artist himself, seeing and feeling the world as he saw and felt it.'[5] In music Carl Philipp Emanuel Bach asserted: 'Since a musician cannot otherwise move people, but he be moved himself, so he must necessarily be able to induce in himself all those effects which he would arouse in his auditors; he conveys his feelings to them, and thus most readily moves them to sympathetic emotions.'[6] These are overt statements of a belief that you will find disseminated widely through contemporary criticism of all the arts, assumed by the critics and presumed in their readers. The underlying theory is, in its baldest form, that the artist first lives through a certain experience; he then makes an artefact which in some way embodies that experience; and through appreciative contemplation of this artefact other men are enabled to duplicate in their own minds the experience of the artist. What is conveyed to them is not abstract knowledge *that* the artist had such and such an experience, but an experience of their own as similar as possible to the artist's experience in all its aspects, including its affective and emotional content. And the duplicate experience is mediated in the act of appreciation itself. According to this theory any artefact which successfully communicates experi-

[1] *The Principles of Art* (1938).
[2] *A Study in Aesthetics* (1931).
[3] See, for example, Mrs. Hannah Priebsch Closs, *Art and Life* (1930).
[4] *The Theory of Poetry* (1924).
[5] A. C. Barnes and Violette de Mazia, *The Art of Henri Matisse* (1933).
[6] *Essay on the True Art of Playing Keyboard Instruments* (1753. Eng. Trans. 1949).

ences in this way is to be classified as a work of art and the capacity so to mediate experience to a competent recipient is a necessary and sufficient condition of a work of art. It is a conception of art likely to lead to classifications which will often prove unconformable with traditional ideas of what is beautiful; for there is nothing in the theory itself to stipulate that the experience mediated shall be a pleasant or a desirable one. This result, however, the adherents of the theory are often prepared to accept on the ground that any accession of experience is valuable—though they are inclined to stipulate that the mediated experience should be in some way exceptional, if only that it is unusually intense. Many critics, however, combine the Expressionist theory with a moral criterion, valuing a work of art not merely as an efficient mediator of experience but in terms of the moral worth they attach to the experience it mediates. And by this path they achieve a point of view very similar to those who combine a moral standpoint with a Realist theory of art.

It is this in some ways typically modern theory, that the excellence of art is to be sought in its power to communicate experience and to express personality, which we are to examine in this chapter. Although at first sight lucid and reasonable if not right, it is a theory which has been unusually rich in latent ambiguities and in the interests of coherent criticism we must undertake a rather careful examination of what it asserts. And first we must inspect the meanings which are implicit in the key term 'expression'.

The word 'express' has been used in many different senses, which have been analysed and classified by Santayana, Collingwood, Reid and other competent writers on aesthetics. We shall here, however, find it necessary only to distinguish three broad senses of the word which are directly relevant to the discussion of the Expressionist theory of art.

1. *Self-expression.* There is a sense in which every human activity is an act of self-expression. When you kick the stone against which you have stubbed your toe, when you pursue inoffensive lions on the other side of the globe because the lady you love has married another, when you write a sonnet or choose a new suit—then you are in some sense expressing yourself. It is, however, generally admitted that some actions are more completely expressive of a man's personality than others and that some persons have a stronger impulse to self-expression than others. And it is generally conceded that artists are usually men with a strong inclination to express themselves in a particular way.[1] The term 'self-expression' as

1 'Those who compose because they wish to please others, and have audiences in mind, are not real artists. They are not the kind of men who are driven to say

144

currently used involves two distinct ideas: the satisfaction of a man's impulses to express himself in action and action whereby his character becomes manifest to others. It was in the former sense that Mr. Middleton Murry remarked: 'The function of criticism is, therefore, primarily the function of literature itself, to provide a means of self-expression for the critic.' In the latter sense a work of art is said to express the personality of the artist who made it if you can draw valid inferences from it to the psychological characteristics of the artist.

2. A work of art is sometimes said to express an emotion, a mood or an emotional situation. The language of appreciation is more than usually obscure on this point, but I think that one can distinguish three distinct senses in which this is said.

(a) Just as gesture, bodily attitude, etc., express emotions by being *signs* to other people of emotional situations, so representational art—pictures, sculpture, dance, mime—may express emotion by representing (or imitating) people in the attitudes of such emotional significance. The naturalism which was so desiderated in Greek and Renaissance art was not *merely* a realistically exact copy of some natural object but also and much more the representation of people who by bodily attitude or facial expression seemed to be showing forth emotions.

It is to be observed that when we see a 'natural' sign of an emotion, whether it be in real life or pictured in a work of art, the emotion signified to us is not necessarily or usually experienced by us. What occurs is direct observation that such and such a person is displaying signs of emotion and knowledge by inference that he is experiencing the emotion displayed. We have not direct knowledge by acquaintance of his emotion—although no doubt our inferential knowledge may involve calling up an image or recollection of the emotion in question, whereby we identify it. A great deal of confusion has been caused on this point by the assumption that whenever we become aware of an emotional situation by means of a

something whether or not there exists one person who likes it, even if they themselves dislike it. They are not creators who must open the valves in order to relieve the interior pressure of a creation ready to be born.' But 'Though there is no doubt that every creator creates only to free himself from the high pressure of the urge to create, and though he thus creates in the first place for his own pleasure, every artist who delivers his works to the general public aims, at least unconsciously, to tell his audiences something of value to them. . . . From the lives of truly great men it can be deduced that the urge for creation responds to an instinctive feeling of living only in order to deliver a message to mankind.' Arnold Schoenberg, *Style and Idea* (1950). Others, of course, than those accepted as great by critical opinion have had the feeling and the urge.

work of art our awareness is knowledge by direct acquaintance with the emotion sympathetically stimulated in ourselves. This is not so in artistic situations any more than in real situations.

(*b*) It is a fact, though a little understood fact, that certain constructions of shapes, colours, sounds, words, etc., stimulate emotions in us without being 'signs' of emotions and independently of any representational significance they may have. It would perhaps be truer to say that they evoke powerful but vaguely defined affective states than complete emotional situations. When this is meant, there seems no good reason why we should not say what we mean—that these works of art move us emotionally or stimulate affective conditions in us, avoiding the word 'express'. For when you ask what it is they express, the only answer that can be given is the affective state which they evoke. And to identify the expression of a feeling with the evocation of a feeling can lead only to muddle.

(*c*) When a work of art is said to express an emotion, what is sometimes meant is that it is possible to draw a valid influence from the nature of the work of art to an emotional experience of the artist who conceived it. This usage is equivalent to that which we have noted under 'self-expression'.

3. 'Expression' is used in a third sense to mean that a work of art acts as a symbol of a certain state of mind in the artist who made it in the sense that (*a*) it has served him as a medium of self-expression for that state of mind, and (*b*) it causes any person who appreciates it correctly to know that state of mind by direct acquaintance. Thus when we are writing psychological criticism we make inferences about the artist's state of mind and character from characteristic features of the works of art he has made. But when we appreciate correctly there is formed in our own minds through the medium of the work of art, it is said, a state of mind as like as possible to the state of mind of the artist. In this third usage the two meanings of the word distinguished above are combined. This is the Expressionist theory proper. It maintains, as has been said, that artistic activity is a mode of communication whereby artists, by making works of art embody or externalize certain exceptional states of mind of their own in the works of art they create, render it possible for other men, by contemplating these works of art in the correct way, to obtain for themselves identical or very similar experiences. This is the theory whose claim to provide a valid basis for criticism we are now to examine.

1. Expressionism in the Theory of Literature[1]

In 1923 Mr. C. K. Ogden and Mr. I. A. Richards published *The Meaning of Meaning*, a study in semantics which had important bearings upon the philosophy of criticism. To put a long argument very briefly, they distinguished two habits in the use of language (as Véron had done before them), two distinct functions of language, which they called 'referential' and 'emotive' respectively. Language was said to be used 'referentially' when it makes statements and purveys information which can be verified or disproved by reference to experienced actuality. Language is said to be used 'emotively' when its purpose is to cause other people to have emotions or in order to influence the behaviour of other people through their emotions. Confusion arises because the two forms of language have the same grammatical structure and therefore people often suppose themselves, and are supposed, to be purveying information or making statements about matters of fact when they are really only uttering noises calculated to influence the emotions and behaviour of other people. In particular all metaphysical propositions, all statements involving the words 'value' and 'beauty', for example, are nowadays often said to be emotive; they are not susceptible of verification by reference to actuality and are neither true nor false. Literature too is emotive and not referential: the statements it contains are either pseudo-statements (i.e. unverifiable by their nature and therefore neither true nor false) or else their truth or falsity in the sense of their correspondence or non-correspondence with experienced actuality is irrelevant to the purpose for which they exist. The philosophical implications of this theory of semantics are in line with the views of a school of thought which became

[1] Mr. Thomas Clark Pollock has pointed out that the word 'literature' to refer to writing in general emerged early in the nineteenth century. In 1823 De Quincey made a distinction between 'literature of knowledge' and 'literature of power', and it is only very recently that the word 'literature' without qualification has come to be used with reference to writing which is art as distinct from writing which is not. We still use the word in a double sense. We speak of 'the literature of obstetrics' without meaning to imply that everything well written on this subject is to be classified as art, and we say of a piece of writing which we judge to be artistically bad that it is 'not literature'. For convenience I propose to use the word 'literature' in this book to refer to all writing which is classified as art and only to this. So in my vocabulary a piece of writing which a given critic was unwilling to classify as a work of art would not be literature for him. Writings which are claimed to be art but which a given critic does not recognize to be art would be for him false claimants to literature.

popular in the thirties under the name of Logical Positivism. Thus Rudolph Carnap, who proposed to carry into practice part of the philosophical programme set out by Wittgenstein,[1] wrote: 'many linguistic utterances are analogous to laughing in that they have only an expressive function, no representative function. Examples of this are cries like "Oh, Oh", or, on a higher level, lyrical verses. The aim of a lyrical poem in which occur the words "sunshine" and "clouds" is not to inform us of certain meteorological facts, but to express certain feelings of the poet and to excite similar feelings in us.'[2]

The Meaning of Meaning had concentrated primarily upon the referential or scientific employment of language, and in 1925 Mr. Richards published *The Principles of Literary Criticism*, which undertook a similar analysis of emotive language as this is found in literature. It is a brilliant study, involving of necessity the exposition of general aesthetic theory as well as theory of criticism. Despite a somewhat uneasy partnership between native Romantic fervour and the more arid acidity of Logical Positivism, it has exercised a greater influence upon criticism than any other one book published in the last fifty years.

Mr. Richards works with an Expressionist theory of art. The function of literary art, on his assumption, is to excite valuable attitudes and emotions in the reader. These attitudes and emotions, as they come into being in the mind of the reader, are duplicates of similar attitudes and emotions experienced by the author. Thus literature is a device by means of which duplicates of emotional experiences are transmitted from one man to others. Successful communication demands competence on the part of both author and reader and it belongs to the function of the critic both to assess the competence of authors in providing vehicles for communicating their emotional experiences to others and also to assess the competence of readers to respond to the vehicles of communication which the author provides. The critic, in Mr. Richards's philosophy, is also to assess the *value* of the emotional experiences communicated in specific works of art by an ethical standard, and a considerable portion of the book is written to recommend for this purpose a special ethical theory from which the notion of obligation has been eliminated.[3] 'What is good or valuable', Mr. Richards says, 'is the exercise of impulses and the satisfaction of their appetencies.' Anything is valuable which 'will satisfy an

[1] *Tractatus Logico-Philosophicus* (1922).
[2] *The Logical Syntax of Language* (Engl. Trans. 1935).
[3] 'The two pillars upon which a theory of criticism must rest are an account of value and an account of communication.'

appetency without involving the frustration of some equal or *more important* appetency'. Therefore the most valuable states of mind are 'those which involve the widest and most comprehensive co-ordination of activities and the least curtailment, conflict, starvation and restriction'.[1] The part of criticism which describes the value of the experience mediated by a work of art Mr. Richards calls the 'critical' part, and the part which describes the features of the object by which the valuable experience is mediated he calls the 'technical' part.

A more matter-of-fact statement of the Expressionist theory of literature is to be found in a later book written by Mr. Thomas Clark Pollock.[2] Mr. Pollock criticizes Mr. Richards's classification of the uses of language into 'referential' and 'emotive' and proposes instead a main classification into 'referential' and 'evocative'. The difference between them is, as he competently explains, very much more than the difference of a word. He agrees that when language is used referentially or scientifically it can communicate from man to man only information *about* experience; you can direct another man's attention only to the 'referents' of your words and phrases, which are generalized abstractions from experience. You can cause another man to know that you have an experience of such and such a kind (it may be an experience of ideas or of knowledge about events), but you cannot except by an artistic use of language put into his mind the concrete actuality and uniqueness of your experience. 'The limitations of a referential use of symbols are those inherent in the definition of public discriminability. Briefly, symbols so used are effective for communicating only abstractions from the writer's actual experience, whether these abstractions are a pointing at "objects" or a reference to more generalized "ideas"; and the writer can be sure of communicating only such abstrac-

[1] On Mr. Richards's theory the word 'value' is itself an 'emotive' term. Therefore when he says that any state of mind is valuable he is not really making a verifiable statement about it but is using language calculated to induce in his readers an attitude inclining them to welcome and desire such states of mind. Mr. Richards would no doubt answer that what he is doing in his exposition of 'value' is to define the meaning which this word properly bears in criticism. It remains none the less a matter for bewilderment why literature and the arts are not more assiduously and more generally cultivated, since all men always obviously desire and pursue those experiences which are, in Mr. Richards's terminology, most valuable—as Mr. Richards himself believes can be verified from the observed behaviour of mankind—and the most valuable experiences available to the majority of men are the experiences mediated in the appreciation of works of art. It is the realization of this illogicality which has motivated the modification of Mr. Richards's views in his subsequent writings.

[2] *The Nature of Literature* (1942).

tions as are publicly discriminable.' In other words, when they are using language referentially 'human beings attempt to communicate their awareness of referents abstracted from their actual experiences'. This use of language forms the bulk of everyday speech when we seek to convey information and has been refined and perfected in the language of science and mathematics. But in the language of literature men attempt to communicate not abstractions from their experience but the experience itself. And they do this by bringing into being by means of appropriate words a duplicate of their own experience in the awareness of their readers. Mr. Pollock's theory differs from that of Mr. Richards in maintaining that the experiences which are communicated in literature are not limited to feelings and emotions and attitudes, though they include these; they also include thoughts and ideas and perceptions. They may be either experiences of actuality or imaginative experiences. But the experience, whatever its nature, is, in literature, communicated as concretely as possible, so that there occurs in the mind of the reader not merely knowledge *about* the experience, e.g. an awareness that in such and such circumstances a perception of red was associated in such and such ways with a perception of green and was related to such and such emotions, attitudes or behaviour of the percipient; there occurs as complete and as vivid an analogue or duplicate of the original experience as it is possible to cause. In evocative symbolism 'human beings attempt to communicate, not the abstraction from the experience, but the actual experience itself'.

The critic who erects the Expressionist definition of beauty into a philosophic principle of literary criticism must, therefore, it is evident, draw a sharp distinction between the two purposes to which language is commonly put—between language which is intended to convey information and language which is intended to arouse emotion. A similar difference may be noticed in relation to certain other of the arts. In the Inca civilization for example, when writing was unknown, history was recorded by means of galleries of pictures, and even to-day photographs and drawings are sometimes made and preserved in order to record visual facts rather than for the communication of emotional experiences. Music, too, has sometimes been employed by primitive peoples as a 'language' for imparting information rather than an expression of feeling. But for obvious reasons the distinction bulks more important in literary criticism than in criticism of the other arts.

Language may, however, be employed emotively and still not satisfy the Expressionist definition of what is to be classified as art. The parent or the priest may discourse in order to arouse in some other person a feeling of remorse for an ill deed done, although in his own mind there is no remorse for a deed that was not his. The auctioneer is skilled to arouse in his audience emotions of conviction and desire which he does not share himself. In neither case is there *communication* of an emotion experienced in the mind of the speaker and reproduced in the mind of the hearer. It is, therefore, necessary to make a second differentiation between language on the one hand which expresses and communicates an experienced emotion and on the other hand language which produces emotion not experienced by the speaker. Mr. Pollock proposes on this basis to make a discrimination between 'genuine literature' and 'pseudo-literature'. In genuine literature, i.e. literature as an art-form, the writer 'attempts to express linguistically an experience of his own in such a way that the experience may be communicated to a reader. His purpose is thus *both* to express *and* to evoke a human experience.' But in pseudo-literature (examples are the literature of advertising and politics) 'an author is primarily concerned, not with expressing an experience of his own, but simply with evoking in a reader an experience which the reader desires or which for from reason, usually commercial, the author or a publisher wishes the reader to have. In pseudo-literature, therefore, the author's controlling purposes is to *evoke* an experience linguistically, but not to express his own experience.' This principle of discrimination is closely analogous to what is more usually called 'sincerity', a quality which Mr. I. A. Richards defines as 'the absence of any apparent attempt on the part of the artist to work effects upon the reader which do not work for himself'.[1]

Having made this distinction Mr. Pollock then advances as his criterion of *success* in literature or pseudo-literature the extent to which the writer brings into the minds of competent readers the precise experience which he intended to bring. 'An evocative use of symbols is successful as communication if the series of symbols is adequate to evoke in a properly qualified reader the experience which the writer attempted to express, or, if he wrote pseudo-literature, simply attempted to evoke. In other words, such a use of symbols succeeds if as a result of the writer's effort there exists a series of words through response to which a properly qualified reader may receive the relevant experience.' Like Mr. Richards, his criterion for the *valuation* of literature (its success as communication being granted) is ethical—though his morals are more mundane and he avoids the very peculiar ethical flights in which Mr. Richards indulges. Successful communication being assumed, the critic, says Mr. Pollock, 'will judge the value of an experience evoked by literature in the ways he

[1] *The Principles of Literary Criticism* (1925), p. 271.

judges the values of other experiences. He will, that is, judge the value of a work of literature in the last analysis in relation to (1) his own immediate personal needs for experience, and (2) the general socio-ethical system which he really, as distinct from verbally, accepts, and on the basis of which he makes the actual choices which determine, so far as choices can, the quality of his life. In other words, a critic will normally consider "good" a book which gives him an experience answering the needs of his being at the moment, or which would be judged "good" by the socio-ethical-religious standards by which he really lives.'

Now this is a very astonishing notion of literary criticism. The critic is to judge a piece of writing to be *good* if it gives him an experience which he finds morally approbable. It is *successful* if the writer intended to give him that experience. But if this writer did not so intend, or if he intended to give him some other experience, the critic must judge his writing to be *unsuccessful but good*. If, again, a writer intended to give the reader an experience which the critic finds approbable but did not himself have that particular experience, the critic must judge his writing to be *successful* and *good* but *not genuine literature*. No criticism ever has been or ever will be written in terms of criteria such as these. Yet these criteria are the logical outcome of the dual character of the Expressionist theory, which maintains (*a*) that no artefact is to be classed as a work of art unless by its means an experience in the mind of the artist is reproduced in the mind of the observer, and (*b*) that the critic is to judge a work of art (i) in terms of its success in communicating the artist's experience to the mind of the observer, and (ii) by the value he attaches to the communicated experience. Expressionism is, in fact, a theory about both the *effects* and the *origins* of a work of art. The *theory of origins* says that no artefact shall be classified as a work of art unless the artist intended to produce in others an experience which he had in himself—no genuine work of art can be insincere. The *theory of effects* says that if the experience produced by a work of art in a competent observer is different from the experience which the artist had in himself and intended to reproduce, the work of art is to that extent defective. In practice critics commonly assume that any lack of sincerity on the part of the artist leaves traces on the work of art such that the *value* of the experience it affords a competent observer is diminished. But this is an empirical proposition about the way in which works of art come into being and its verification must be empirical. There is no *logical* impossibility that a gifted but insincere artist should mediate to a competent observer more valuable experiences than a sincere but ungifted artist. Yet empirical verification of the degree of sincerity in any work of art is in most cases impossible. You can only know what the intentions of the artist were, or whether he was trying to communicate an experience of his own, if you ask him and if he answers you truly. Artists who are dead have rarely left satisfactory psychological records, and the difficulties of appealing to living artists, whose motives and intentions are often mixed and their powers of introspective analysis small, are overwhelming. To make the judgement about the genuineness of a work of art dependent upon necessarily incomplete and unreliable knowledge of the artist's motives and psychology puts upon the critic an intolerable burden. And in fact critics who judge of 'sincerity' commonly infer from certain features of a poem *which for other reasons they regard as defects* that the artist was insincere and then condemn the poem for insincerity. The adverse criticism is prior to and logically independent of the imputation of insincerity and the latter is really no more than a hypothetical cause to which the defects are ascribed.

Many critics would no doubt like to believe, owing to an obscure moral bias, that a good work of art is never created by an insincere artist. Mr. Richards is reduced to suggesting that there is 'perhaps' internal evidence of a flaw in the poem if the poet is insincere. It may be so. Empirically it seems likely that insincerity is a cause of at any rate some defects in alleging works of art. But to erect it into a principle of criticism, to use it as a touchstone for assessing the excellence of literature or for discriminating genuine literature from pseudo-literature, is to be both illogical and impractical. It is one of the more pernicious results of the false pre-occupation of modern criticism with psychology. Sincerity is relevant only to the study of the psychology of artistic creation, not to the valuation of works of art.

There are obvious affinities between the Expressionist and the emotional theories of beauty in art. Both postulate a selected class of artefacts to which different people variously respond and both assess their excellence as works of art by the nature of the responses which they evoke. In discussion of the emotional theory we found that it allows no basis for objective or normative criticism because while the manner of men's emotional reactions to works of art differs from one man to another, there exists no standard by which you can say that one man's response is right and another's is wrong. What is needed by the critic who professes to assess works of art in terms of emotional response—his own or that of other men—is some criterion of what is the correct emotional response to any work of art. Having a criterion of this sort, he can then check this or that person's reaction by reference to it and can evaluate the correct emotional response to any work of art by whatever moral standards he chooses to apply. Without it, he may judge that one man's response, as emotional experience, is more valuable than another man's; what he cannot do is to show that any one form of response is more relevant or appropriate to a given work of art than another. He is evaluating the man and not the work of art. But the Expressionist theory alleges to fill this gap and to supply a norm of correct response by reference to the original experience as it occurred in the mind of the artist, which the work of art exists to communicate and to which the actual responses of individual observers asymptotically approximate. Any response to a work of art is, on the Expressionist view, more or less right according as it is a more or less exact reduplication of the emotional experience which occurred in the artist's mind and which was embodied by him in his work of art. The critic's function is that of a guide to other men and his job is to tell them what reaction is right and what reaction is wrong towards any work of art—right or wrong in the sense of approximating more or less closely to the artist's own experience.

In this way Expressionism certainly escapes from the dilemma of subjectivism which renders normative criticism of the arts logically impossible to those who hold a naïve emotional theory of artistic beauty. It escapes the logical dilemma by proposing a standard of correct or appropriate response to any work of art by which the relevance of this or that person's actual response may be tested and assessed without the introduction of ethical values. But the standard proposed is one that is from the nature of the case impossible to apply in practice. The escape of Expressionism, however specious in seeming, is achieved only at the expense of making all normative criticism impossible not theoretically but in fact. There is no conceivable way in which the critic can in practice judge how completely or how closely the actual appreciative response of various persons, including himself, reproduces an experience which was once in the mind of the artist unless he has independent knowledge of that experience. He must either assume that his own response is the nearest possible approximation to the artist's experience and therefore the standard by which the response of all other men are to be assessed—an assumption which is obviously illegitimate as long as the critics disagree among themselves—or he must be accredited with some supernormal insight into the mind of the artist. In face of the actual diversity of emotional responses to any work of art there is no other way in which a critic could justify his claim to decide which of any two appreciative experiences more closely approximates to a past experience in another man's mind.

There is no escape from the critic's dilemma, because it is a cardinal tenet of Expressionism—and indeed of almost all practical criticism of whatever school—that art is a special and unique mode of communication, so that the experiences mediated by works of art can be communicated only by works of art and by no other means. The informative language which we employ in daily commerce with our fellow-men and in which text-books of psychology are written can communicate facts and abstractions about experience but cannot purvey the concrete actuality of experience from man to man as it is claimed that this is done through works of art. Every critic knows that a picture cannot be duplicated in words; it must be seen. A musical composition must be heard. A prose interpretation paraphrasing the 'meaning' of a poem does not explain the poem but destroys it.[1] Nor is anything less claimed of prose writing which is judged as literature. In an excellent study of the Victorian Sage, for example, Mr. John Holloway remarks that 'when the outlooks of most of these sages appear in the bald epitomes of literary histories, they lose their last vestiges of interest. They provoke only bored surprise that anyone could have insisted so eagerly on half-incomprehensible dogmas or trite commonplaces. This suggests that what gave their views life and meaning lay in the actual words of the original, in the sage's own use of language, not in what can survive summarizings of their content.'[2] Poetry and the arts attempt to express that element in human experience which is ineffable, which is not and cannot be expressed through the conventional language of logical and scientific discourse. To translate a work of art into prose statement is to take out of it that which makes it a work of art. To use a word coined by Sydney Dobell, you cannot 'intellectualate' a work of art. And it is another universal and necessary tenet of criticism that the experience of an artist which is embodied and communicated in any given work of art can be communicated only by that work of art. You can point to similarities and analogies among the experiences communicated by various works of art; to do so is part of the method of criticism. But in so doing you are abstracting in order to classify, you are 'intellectualating'; and to that extent you are removing the work of art in its original concreteness from the field of attention and substituting for it generalizations. There is no detracting from the ultimate uniqueness of a work of

---

[1] 'The poem', says Mr. Cleanth Brooks, 'does not properly eventuate in a proposition: we can only *abstract* statements from the poem, and in the process of abstraction we necessarily distort the poem itself.' And: 'most of our difficulties in criticism are mooted in the heresy of paraphrase'. *The Well Wrought Urn* (1949).

[2] *The Victorian Sage* (1953).

art and the experience which it embodies. Now your Expressionist critic may have complete conviction of certitude that he and not the other man has realized in his appreciation of a given work of art the true meaning intended by the artist, that he and he alone has duplicated in his own mind as nearly as makes no difference the experience which the artist had and which he intended to convey. But the disaccord of human emotional response remains an ultimate fact for him as for all other critics and certainly he will sooner or later meet some critic who obtained a different emotional experience from his commerce with the same work of art and who is convinced with equal cretitude that *his* experience is the true duplication. And when this occurs, as it all too frequently does occur, there is only one possible means of deciding between them and that is by appealing to the artist himself—by asking him, if he is alive, or searching his literary remains if he is dead.

But this final court of appeal is in the nature of the case excluded from the bounds of practical possibility. It is excluded because there is no means by which the artist can tell you what his experience was except by pointing to the work of art he has made. He cannot tell you in ordinary prose language because experience cannot be communicated in ordinary prose language—if it could, there would (on the Expressionist theory of beauty) be no point or purpose in going to the trouble of creating works of art when the object they serve could be fulfilled so much more easily by informatory prose. And the precise experience which is embodied in any specific work of art can be 'told' by pointing to that particular work of art and no other. You may read a prose account of what took place when a poet was 'inspired' to write a given poem—a narrative of the circumstances in which Keats wrote *On First Looking into Chapman's Homer*, or a psychological analysis of what happened in the mind of Coleridge when he wrote *Kubla Khan*, or Poe's account of how he composed *The Raven*; the artist himself may describe for you all that he knows by introspection about his states of mind during the making of a picture, a musical composition or a ballet in which you are interested; but such prose accounts, however detailed and complete, do not convey to you anything of the concrete experience which, it is said, you duplicate in your own mind when you have correct commerce with the work of art. There is no conceivable way in which the experience communicated by an artist in a work of art can be 'told' by any one person to any other person except by pointing silently to that work of art in which the experience is embodied. Furthermore the critic and the appreciator, not being creative artists, cannot communicate to each other or to the artist the experiences which they severally obtain from commerce with the same work of art except in the 'referential' language of prose discourse. By that means they may indicate differences in response provided that such differences are sufficiently crass and voluminous to be brought within the meshes of referential prose; they cannot show that there is agreement about the subtle qualities of response which make the transaction artistic.

The Expressionist theory, therefore, in getting around the logical dilemma of naïve emotionalism which makes objectively valid criticism impossible, imposes on criticism a condition which makes it essentially impossible in practice. This is not a logical quibble, but a genuine inconsequentiality inherent in the Expressionist theory as such. It is, of course, usually concealed with more or less care and success, but the following blatant example of its occurrence is typical of the Expressionist theory as such. Mr. Stauffer has written a book to explain what poetry is and how its distinguishing features are to be described.[1] His first chapter is headed: 'Poetry is Exact'. And he defines exactness as the property of 'reproducing (or being capable of reproducing) in another man's mind, fully and faithfully, what is in the creator's consciousness when he is thinking primarily as an individual, as a person'. The test of exactness (and of the right to be classified as poetry) therefore involves a comparison between the state of consciousness produced by a poem in a reader and the state of consciousness which the artist translated from his own mind into the poem. In order to be compared, these two states of consciousness must be made to occur side by side in some one person's mind. But the only means by which this can be done is, by the very assumptions on which the Expressionist theory rests, the poem itself. And the poem quite obviously can produce in the mind of any reader only the state of consciousness which it does produce; it cannot produce also side by side with it another state of consciousness (the artist's) for comparison with it. Nor, as has been said, is there any other possible or conceivable means by which the artist's state of mind can be put into another person's consciousness for comparison with his own reactions to the poem. The criterion that is proposed is, therefore, an impossible standard for practical criticism.

What after all is the critic supposed to do? He must first of all decide whether a given work of art is a competent medium for communicating the experience which the artist intended it to communicate, although he has no independent means of knowing what that experience is. He must be able to decide how far his own experienced response and the responses of others severally duplicate the experience of the artist of which he has

[1] *The Theory of Poetry* (1946).

157

no independent knowledge; and he must do this although other critics and appreciators are even less competent than the artist to communicate to him the nature of their experienced response. He must then *value* the unknown experience in so far as it is duplicated in the unknown responses of other people and finally pass judgement on the work of art (*a*) as a successful vehicle of communication (technical criticism) and (*b*) as a conveyor of ethically approved experience. The business is still more complicated as we realize that when we say that the artist *intends* to communicate an experience of his own in his work of art we are speaking in a Pickwickian sense. Works of art are created for all the multifarious motives which move men to action—for glory or for gain, from passing whim or from inner compulsion, to win admiration or to influence the thoughts and actions of other men. As Mr. I. A. Richards is driven to admit, an artist is rather seldom consciously aware that he has in mind an experience which he 'intends' to communicate to other men in his work of art and few artists work with a conscious intention of communicating anything at all. The only discernible common element in the introspectible purposes of creative artists is a desire and determination to get the work of art 'right'. Hence criticism undertakes to decide whether and to what extent ineffable and intrinsically indescribable experiences of his own and of other people in contact with works of art are exact duplicates of ineffable and intrinsically indescribable experiences which the artists were unaware that they purposed to communicate to others through the medium of their art. It is not altogether surprising that on this basis agreement among critics is so slow to arrive.

The Expressionist theory of beauty cannot be proved and cannot be disproved. It postulates a correspondence between experiences which cannot be compared and precisely because they cannot be compared no one is in a position to say that this correspondence does not—sometimes—occur. But equally no one can say when it does and when it does not occur. It is as though you were to assert that every Lord Chancellor bears an invisible resemblance to a certain 'clean old gentleman' in *Iolanthe* and challenge the world to prove you wrong. It may be thought likely that some people when in appreciative contact with works of art sometimes enjoy states of mind and emotion to some extent similar to some of the emotional states which occurred in the mind of the artist who made those works of art. The existence of such similarities can neither be proved nor disproved. But if they exist, it is still certain that a critic can never know when they exist or the extent and degree of similarity on any occasion.

Expressionism cannot be proved to be wrong any more than it can be proved right by the empirical facts of psychology; yet the factual evidence available does at any rate tend to show that it does not seem very likely to be right. For those who apply expressionist principles in practical criticism must assume things about the mental conditions of artistic creation and aesthetic appreciation which are pretty clearly at variance with the little psychological knowledge that we possess about these activities. And although psychology cannot refute a theory of this sort, it can and does show it to lead to very strange and improbable consequences and it will not lead us afield from the general purpose of this study to survey the psychological evidence briefly from this point of view.

1.1 *The Psychology of Inspiration*

We know a fair amount about the psychology of artistic creation, though it is essential to remember that the accounts of this experience recorded by literary artists and others can rarely be treated as pure introspective *data* but are more often than not coloured by the aesthetic ideas of their age. There are, it seems, two moments in the creation of a work of art: the moment of creation proper, when the idea of the work of art is born into the mind of the artist; and the moment of fashioning, when the idea in the mind of the artist is worked up into a communicable and enduring form. The creative moment—often referred to as 'inspiration'— may be sudden or protracted; it may wholly precede the fashioning or be partly coincidental with it. Some artists invent as they work, and in these creative types the idea only becomes conscious as it is worked up into concrete form; in others it seems to leap fully into consciousness and the fashioning of the work of art consists in giving appropriate 'body' to an idea already fully fledged in the mind. The difference appears to be a matter of individual psychology. The two moments are analytically distinct rather than completely separable in practice.

The moment of creation proper is never completely introspectable. Some artists have gone very far in tracing the sources of their ideas, the associations they had, and so on; but there always remains a residue which is not introspectable and it is this residue which is the essence of artistry. In other words, it is not possible by introspective means to reduce the process of artistic creation to logical rule and formula. The ideas which are born into the mind of the artist and worked up into his work of art are not, it seems, emotions to be 'embodied' in the form of art but elements of artistic material itself—musical phrases and themes, lines and verses of poetry, ideas of plot or character, concrete elements of pictorial composition, and so on. They often appear in very odd ways. They may come suddenly and unexpectedly while the artist is engaged in other occupations—often ideas for one work come while the artist is engaged upon another—they often occur in the somnambulistic state between sleeping and waking, sometimes in sleep itself. It is characteristic that they seem to come from 'outside' and with a strong sense of compulsion, so that the artist has the sensation of being obsessed by that which he has brought to birth. The sense of possession, the feeling of being used as a mouthpiece of some power other than himself, is common to creative artists and mystics alike. The work which is being created seems to acquire a reality and a personality of its own, to develop independently of the conscious will of the artist. It does not seem to be the creature of his own brain but the product of an alien influence which the artist does not fully understand.[1] The moment of creation is also characteristically accompanied by more or less intense excitement, by an inrush of life and energy with perceptual and imaginative faculties raised to fever pitch and a strong and specific emotional tone.[2] The degree of excitement is as a general rule greater in proportion as the ideas are born suddenly and fully articulate into consciousness, less intense in cases where the idea emerges slowly and gradually, changing, maturing and developing in the course of a sustained act of composition.

[1] Keats said that some of the things he wrote 'struck him with astonishment and seemed rather the production of another person than his own'. George Eliot told J. W. Cross 'that, in all that she considered her best writing, there was a "not herself" which took possession of her, and that she felt her own personality to be merely the instrument through which this spirit, as it were, was acting.' Thackeray says in *The Round-about-Papers*: 'I have been surprised at the observations made by some of my characters. It seems as if an occult Power was moving my pen.' Elgar described himself as the 'all but unconscious medium' by which his works came into being. These and other references in this section I owe to Miss Rosamond E. M. Harding's *An Anatomy of Inspiration* (1948). The reports of creative artists are too widely disseminated among different times and temperaments and too similar in their general tone for it to be plausible to suppose that they are a result of a particular theory imposed on the artist of what inspiration ought to be like.

[2] Miss Harding quotes Tchaikowski's statements in a letter to Frau von Meck. 'It would be vain to try to put into words that immeasurable sense of bliss which comes over me directly a new idea awakens in me and begins to assume a definite form. I forget everything and begin to behave like a madman. Everything within me starts pulsing and quivering; hardly have I begun the sketch ere one thought follows another. . . . If that condition of mind and soul, which we call *inspiration*, lasted long without intermission, no artist could survive it.' 'The mind in creation', says Shelley in his *Defence of Poetry*, 'is as a fading coal, which some invisible influence, like an inconstant wind, awakens to transitory brightness.'

All these symptoms of inspiration—the emotional excitement when it occurs, the feeling of compulsion and the sense of obsession, the suddenness and unexpectedness with which ideas obtrude into a mind otherwise engaged and the air of strangeness which they often bear—are typical of what modern psychology diagnoses as upwellings of material from the subconscious into the conscious mind. They are not peculiar to the psychology of artistic creation but can be paralleled in other fields of life. Moreover, they occur without empirical difference equally to poor or indifferent artists and to good artists (i.e. those artists who, on the Expressionist theory, successfully create artefacts which mediate valuable experiences to competent observers). Indeed one of the most disconcerting outcomes of such collections of introspective evidence as that assembled by Miss Harding is the fact that all the characteristic phenomena of inspiration are described in indistinguishable terms by good and bad artists alike. Nor has the most penetrating psychological investigation succeeded in detecting any general differences between the mental processes which accompany the creation of a masterpiece and the inspirations of a third-rate botcher. In any case the special emotional features which often characterize the moment of artistic creation—the feeling of compulsion, the fevered excitement, the sense of heightened lucidity and so on—are specific to the conditions of creation and are not communicated to, or reproduced in, the mind of the observer when he appreciates a work of art. The 'ideas' which are born of inspiration are, as has been said, concrete elements of artistic material—sequences and phrases of musical sound, rhythmic verbal images, passages of pictorial compositions, snatches of conversation, general ideas of plot or structure, and so on. When these are worked up with other material into a finished work of art, the resultant creation is indeed communicated and shared by artist and observer, in the sense that the artist arranges that a competent observer shall hear the same set of musical sounds or see the same arrangement of colours and shapes as he heard or saw when he invented them. But this much is true whether the work of art is good or bad, and it is certainly something more than this that is meant by Expressionist critics when they speak of the communication of experience through the medium of works of art.

What the Expressionists seem to wish to assert is, rather, that the artist first experiences a specific 'life-emotion' (an emotion which is not peculiar to the creation or appreciation of art but which might be experienced by a non-creative person in the ordinary transactions of living); he then 'embodies' this emotion in a musical composition, a picture or a poem, which may or may not realistically symbolize the life-object upon which the artist's emotion was directed; and finally, in appreciation the observer reproduces in his own mind the life-emotion which the artist embodied in his work. This theory is perhaps most plausible when it is applied to short lyrical poems of the kind which Wordsworth called 'effusions' and which often do seem to be constructed around some central emotional mood. In a love-lyric, for example, the poet's feelings of affection for his mistress may form part of the subject-matter or theme of his poem in the same way as the physical body of his mistress might become part of the theme of an artist's picture. But even when an emotion of his own enters into the poet's theme and is an integral part of the material from which his poem is constructed, it is seldom if ever that the poet composes in the full fervour of the emotion. Poetry, in Wordsworth's words, 'takes its origin from emotion recollected in tranquility'. In his Preface to *The American*, Henry James says that it is difficult to write of places when under too immediate an impression, since 'The image has had for the most part to be dim if the reflexion was to be, as is proper for a reflexion, both sharp and quiet.' Goethe roundly declared that: 'So long as the poet gives utterance merely to his subjective feelings, he has no right to the title.' Mr. T. S. Eliot has said in *The Sacred Wood* that: 'Poetry is not a turning loose of emotion but an escape from emotion.' And Richard Strauss has recorded: 'I work very coldly, without agitation, without emotion even. One must be completely master of oneself to organize that changing, moving, flowing chess-board; orchestration. The mind which composed *Tristan* must have been as cool as marble.' So far from expressing a personal affective experience of the artist, a certain impersonality and 'distance' seems to be essential to successful composition. 'Does not all art come', says W. B. Yeats, 'when a nature, that never ceases to judge itself, exhausts personal emotion in action or desire so completely that something impersonal, something that has nothing to do with action or desire, suddenly starts into its place, something which is as unforeseen, as completely organized, even as unique, as the images that pass before the mind between sleeping and waking.'[1]

At the very least we must recognize that there are different types of creative psychology. If some have created in the heat and turmoil of emotion and have purposed to communicate their emotion to others by 'introducing' it in the work of art they were creating, there have been others—and among them many who are judged to be supreme—who have sought to achieve an attitude of impersonality and objectivity towards subjective emotional disturbances and whose conscious ambition

[1] *Autobiography* (1926), p. 409.

has been as far removed as it well could be from the Expressionist ideal of transferring an emotional state from themselves to the minds of others. Nor can it be legitimately argued that because an emotion once experienced by the writer forms part of the subject-matter of some literary art, the purpose of such art is to re-create the same emotion in the reader or that the excellence of any work of art is to be measured by the success with which it reproduces in others the emotions of the artist. Indeed, even in the case of those works of art whose subject-matter includes representations of emotional experiences of the artist, the assumption that they were made and exist primarily for the purposes of stimulating similar emotional experiences in others seems to be highly dubious and to involve a misunderstanding of the nature of appreciation, which we must now examine.

I. 2. *The Psychology of Appreciation*

The doctrine that correct appreciation consists in a sensitive reception of communicated emotion is implied in the venerable belief that the good artist must 'move' his audience, and if he fails to do so, he has failed as an artist—to which is usually added that in order to move others the artist must either experience in his own person the emotions he wishes to arouse in them or at any rate he must be very clever at simulating such emotions. So Aristotle said: 'In composing, the poet should even, as much as possible, be an actor; for, by natural sympathy, they are most persuasive and affecting who are under the influence of actual passion. We share the agitation of those who appear to be truly agitated—the anger of those who appear to be truly angry.'[1]

But more exact investigation of what actually happens in the process of competent appreciative contacts with works of art has carried us a considerable distance beyond such naïve formulations. It is, in the first place, now evident beyond cavil or question that artistic transactions involve a duality of emotional causation. There is a class of emotions experienced during appreciation—those called 'aesthetic emotions'—which have their source in the abstract or formal properties of works of art—in arrangements of colours and shapes, structures of musical sound, rhythms of the dance, and so on—apart from anything which they may

[1] *Poetics*. Compare Horace, *De Arte Poetica*, 99-103.

> *non satis est pulchra esse poemata; dulcia sunto*
> *et quocumque volent animum auditoris agunto.*
> *ut ridentibus adrident, ita flentibus adflent*
> *humani voltus. si vis me flere, dolendum est*
> *primum ipsi tibi.*

symbolically represent other than themselves. There are other emotions
—called 'life emotions'—which are embodied in a work of art by means
of realistic symbolism, by verbal descriptions, by the miming of actors or
by the natural symbolism of representational painting. The 'aesthetic'
emotions are aroused in the observer directly as an immediate response to
the formal qualities of visual or aural sensations and, more obscurely, by
response to the formal and structural qualities of verbal symbols. In music
and the non-representational arts in general these are the only emotions
which are or can be aroused. The 'life' emotions on the other hand are
not directly aroused but are presented imaginally and are reproduced in
the observer, if they are reproduced at all, by the reflex action of 'natural
sympathy'. When you contemplate a Mother and Child, whether it be a
Russian ikon of Our Lady of Tenderness, a miniature of the Virgin of
Copacabana, a Raphael or a Memling, you are aware of an emotion of
maternal tenderness mingled with divine reverence symbolized by the
attitude and expression of the female figure. You do not necessarily or
usually 'have' this emotion yourself. You are aware of it imaginally. And
the same thing is true of literature. When you read Coleridge's lines

> *Fear at my heart, as at a cup,*
> *The lifeblood seemed to sip,*

you are conscious imaginally of the fear which he describes, but you do
not experience that intensity or quality of fear in yourself. The lines draw
their 'powerfully emotive force'—to quote Mr. C. Day Lewis—from
'the association of "cup" with "fear" and "lifeblood", the trivial with the
tremendous'. Their poetic quality, their excellence as poetry, resides in a
structural property of the verbal symbolism.

The Realist theory of beauty holds, as we have seen, that a work of
art is good if a symbolized emotional situation is presented in such a way
that the observer is made aware of the presented emotions as exactly and
as completely as possible. The naïve form of the Expressionist theory
holds that it is good if the symbolized emotions are presented in such a
way that the observer is not only aware of them but experiences them as
accurately and as vividly as possible in himself. The rather more subtle
form of the theory popularized by Mr. C. K. Ogden and Mr. I. A.
Richards holds that a good work of art is one which arouses in the
observer a complicated pattern of balanced emotions such that as many
emotions as possible have play without conflicting with each other. In
fact, however, the extent to which a 'presented' emotion is actually
experienced by 'natural sympathy' varies enormously with different types

of temperament. And this is true equally whether it is presented in artistic form, by non-artistic symbolization such as a newspaper report, or in real life by observation. Indeed both in artistic and in real situations when we are moved to emotion we usually experience not the emotion which is presented to us but a *compensatory* emotion—pity when we are made aware of a person experiencing great anguish, horror when we contemplate a person moved by delight in cruelty, and so on. It is probably true that in many readers the emotions presented in short lyrical poems which are constructed around a fairly unified mood are to some extent 'felt' as well as 'imaged'. But in drama, for example, the case is different. When various characters display various and often opposed emotions at the same time, to suppose that the audience know these emotions by directly experiencing them passes the limits of the ridiculous. In our contact with the arts we become aware of presented emotions in precisely the same way that we become aware of them in real life—it is not a purely abstract and theoretical knowledge, but neither is it knowledge by direct acquaintance with the emotions in ourselves. We know them imaginally. It is not true that works of art differ from real situations in that they arouse the represented emotions more vividly in the observer. Artistic situations differ from real situations or non-artistically presented situations as in newspaper reports *only* in that the former arouse in us also direct 'aesthetic' emotions. Indeed, there is a tendency in all the arts except perhaps literature to banish or limit the presentation of 'life' emotions because it is thought that their stimulation in the observer by the reflex action of 'natural sympathy' is damaging and obstructive to appreciation.[1]

It is from an obscure realization of these facts that many have seen in music the most perfect form of art and the model to which the other arts should aspire.[2] For in representational painting and literature there is a duality of emotional content. The represented emotions of life inevitably to some extent affect the emotional disposition of the observer, either by

[1] The change in aesthetic outlook which has come with fuller understanding may be estimated by comparing with the words of Carl Philipp Emanuel Bach quoted above the following statement by Busoni: 'Just as the artist, if he is to move his audience, must never be moved himself—lest he lose, at that moment, his mastery over the material—so the auditor who wants to get the full operatic effect must never regard it as real, if his artistic appreciation is not to be degraded to mere human sympathy.'

[2] See, for example, Pater's well-known statement in the Preface to *The Renaissance*: 'All art aspires to the condition of music.' So too Dryden's: 'poetry is articulate music', and Carlyle's: 'See deep enough and you see musically; the heart of Nature being everywhere music, if you can only reach it.'

a reflective evocation of a mild counterpart of the represented emotions or by stimulating 'compensatory' emotions of pity, etc. Alongside and in addition to this, 'aesthetic' emotions are aroused by the formal patterns of colours and shapes, the structures of word-symbols, etc. And although in the act of appreciation your emotional response may seem to be unitary and undifferentiated, reflectively it is seen to be attributable to these two separate sources. Moreover, as Sir Roger Fry repeatedly emphasized, there may be experienced duality or even conflict between the 'life' emotions which are sympathetically induced and the 'aesthetic' emotions which are directly evoked in the observer. But in instrumental music there is no represented emotional content, no element of 'life' emotion; there is only the 'aesthetic' emotion directly aroused in you by the pattern and structure of musical sound which *is* the music. For this reason emotional response to music is said to be 'purer' than emotional response to representational art. This, I think, is what is intended by the analogy often drawn by artists between abstract painting or sculpture and music. And this is the sort of thing that was in the minds of the French symbolist poets who maintained that a poem, with a minimum of represented meaning, should evoke a unique emotional mood which it alone is capable of evoking.

Empirical investigation of the 'aesthetic' emotions is a task of the utmost difficulty because no language possesses a vocabulary to describe them. They have been studied most fully in connection with music—which has traditionally been regarded as the most emotional of the arts—but even here the results are woefully meagre. Yet two conclusions have emerged: (1) there is far less uniformity among the emotional reactions of competent listeners than had been assumed; and (2) listeners fall into two main types, the emotional and the perceptive, which differ both in the degree of experienced emotion and in the importance which they attach to it. Although there has been much embittered argument between the two types, it has not proved possible to establish that the one type or the other is more competent to judge correctly the excellence of musical compositions.

The factual study of emotional response to music began with Eduard Hanslick, the opponent of Wagner, who in 1854 published his *Vom Musikalisch-Schönen*,[1] in which he vigorously oppugned the current Romantic conception of music as a 'language of feeling and emotion'. Relying upon observable discrepancies among reported emotional reactions to music, he maintained that the relation between musical sound

[1] Engl. Trans. *The Beautiful in Music* (1891).

and affective response is accidental and not natural or inevitable. 'There is no *causal nexus* between a musical composition and the feelings it may excite, as the latter vary with our experience and impressibility. The present generation often wonder how their forefathers could possibly imagine that just *this* arrangement of sounds adequately represented just *this* feeling.' Hanslick's views were propagated in England by Edmund Gurney, and a growing volume of detailed research has revealed that emotional response is much more wayward than even he supposed; different persons of the same race and generation will react differently to the same composition in ways which do not seem to be explainable simply by temperament or impressionability. The better type of musical criticism to-day shows itself increasingly impatient of description in emotional terms and is turning more and more to structural and technical analysis.

Hanslick also made the penetrating observation that: 'With the technically uninitiated "the feelings" play a predominent part, while, in the case of the trained musician, they are quite in the background.' Modern research has revealed that people who claim to appreciate music fall into two main groups, which Vernon Lee called the 'emotional' or 'associative' type and the 'purely musical' type respectively.[1] Those who belong to the former type expect of music a 'message' consisting of more or less well-defined emotional affects, associated imagery and sometimes even a 'story'. The latter claimed that 'whenever they found music completely satisfying, any other meaning, anything like visual images or emotional suggestions, was excluded or reduced to utter unimportance'. It is popularly assumed that the opposite of the 'emotional' type of appreciator is the 'reflective' or 'intellectual' type, that those who do not respond emotionally to aesthetic stimuli are engaged in theoretical analysis or in some sort of discursive ratiocination. This is a mistake. Those who while listening to a piece of music or looking at a picture analyse it theoretically are not appreciating it as a work of art. But the alternative is not emotional wallowing. The complementary type to the emotional is not the reflective but the *perceptive*. There are people whose whole energies at a concert are concentrated upon *perceiving*, upon attaining complete aural awareness of the music which is being played. And these people often find emotion of any sort distracting and mental imagery or day-dreaming impertinent. There is the same general division of types among those who

[1] 'The Varieties of Musical Experience' (*The North American Review*, vol. 207). See Max Schoen, *The Beautiful in Music* (1928), and also Professor James L. Mansell, *The Psychology of Music* (1937).

appreciate literature or painting. There are people who, when occupied in appreciating a picture, turn their whole attention to visualizing the picture before them, striving to actualize in a single comprehensive perception every play of colours, every contained relation of forms; there are others who must always have half their attention or more free to indulge and savour the emotions which stir them.

The contrast between these two appreciative types is not absolute. Those who appreciate perceptively almost always experience *some* emotion or affective disturbance. And it is obvious that a person who is moved emotionally must to some extent have perceived that by which he is stirred. The difference between them lies in the fact that for the former temperament emotion is a distraction from the main purpose of appreciation, while for the latter the essence of appreciation lies in the savouring of emotion. What has not been observed—or if it has been observed, its implications have not been realized—is that emotionality is in inverse proportion to perception. Any increase of concentration on perceiving must necessarily be at the expense of emotion, and increase in emotion means diminution of perceptive attention. M. Jean-Paul Sartre has observed that when you are fully concentrated on reading a book, wholly engrossed in it, your reading is not accompanied by mental images. Imagery and association begin when and as concentration lapses and some part of your attention is freed to wander from the book into day-dream. The same thing is true of emotion. While the whole mind is concentrated upon the object and attention is fully engrossed with becoming more and more fully aware of it, when even the normal background awareness of self wanes and recedes, then there is no room for awareness of emotion. For emotion to be present to consciousness some part of the mind must be abstracted from the object and free to savour it. Every increment of emotion in the act of appreciation must necessarily be at the expense of perceptive awareness. You cannot cultivate at the same time to the fullest extent both awareness of your own emotions and perceptive awareness of the object by which they are excited. For the one awareness interferes with the other. There is insufficient warranty for claiming that emotional appreciation is false, although it is difficult to understand how it can be a sound guide to judgement in face of the startling discrepancies in the quality of emotion experienced by different persons of the emotional type to the same aesthetic object. There is far less warranty for claiming that appreciation is in essence emotional or that it is 'right' or 'wrong' according to the nature and quality of the emotions you experience.

It is unnecessary to underline how damaging this analysis of appreciation must be to an Expressionist theory of criticism. In so far as a representational work of art symbolizes 'life' emotions, that theory entices the critic into the elementary fallacy of supposing that emotional situations symbolized either in words or in pictures are communicated to the observer by being excited in him—that they are felt rather than perceived. This is false. And even if that fallacy is avoided, the fact that 'life' emotions are communicated to awareness neither differently nor more vividly through works of art than by non-aesthetic modes of symbolization makes nonsense of an Expressionist theory of judgement. On the other hand the 'aesthetic' emotions are neither symbolized nor represented, but *are* directly excited in the observer. Yet there is no empirical uniformity in emotional response to aesthetic structures and different people differ widely in the importance they assign to having such responses at all in appreciation. Without such uniformity Expressionist criticism can be in no better case than criticism which bases itself on the naïve emotional theory of art. Artists also have given very contrary accounts of the importance of emotions in their mental states during creation and there can be no possible ground for supposing that one man's emotional response in appreciation is a more exact reproduction than another's either in quality or in degree of intensity of the emotional state of the artist's mind. The Expressionist critic is in fact in no better case than the emotional critic who, with Professor Housman, judges poetry by the bristling of his beard and the tremors of his spine. Nor in face of these facts is there much justification left for maintaining that the essence of the aesthetic transaction lies in the communication of an emotion from the mind of the artist to the mind of the observer.

Although these facts are becoming more generally known, Expressionism remains a potent influence in aesthetics and much practical criticism continues to be written on Expressionist assumptions. Expressionist critics manage in the main to cloak the logical fallacies implicit in their theory, and to give a specious semblance of plausibility to their criticism, by wilfully inviting confusion between the element of communication and the element of valuation. In this theory a work of art is *successful* in so far as by its means an emotional experience is effectively transferred from the mind of the artist to other men.[1] Its *value* is the value of the transferred

---

[1] 'Communication, we shall say, takes place when one mind so acts upon its environment that another mind is influenced, and in that other mind an experience occurs which is like the experience in the first mind, and is caused in part by that experience.' I. A. Richards.

experience. What the Expressionist critics all tend to assume is that the experiences conveyed from man to man by successful works of art are necessarily or in fact highly valuable experiences, a sort of experience which only artists achieve directly and other people only at second-hand through the mediation of works of art. 'Poetry', said Shelley, 'is the record of the best and happiest moments of the happiest and best minds.' And Mr. I. A. Richards adds his authority to the view. 'In the arts', he declares, 'we find the record in the only form in which these things can be recorded of the experiences which have seemed worth having to the most sensitive and discriminating persons. Through the obscure perception of this fact the poet has been regarded as a seer and the artist as a priest, suffering from usurpation.' Now we are not concerned to deny, but would vigorously affirm, that the appreciation of beautiful works of art is among the most valuable experiences of which the human mind is capable. But this value is *not* explainable by the Expressionist assumptions. There is *a priori* no reason at all why vicious, vapid or banal experiences should not be communicated by successful works of art every whit as vividly, as completely and as exactly as supremely valued experiences. There is no warranty in the Expressionist conception of aesthetic commerce between man and man for the assumption that to be *successful* a work of art must be valuable.[1] It has been made to seem specious only by the perpetuation of a false picture of the artist, which has probably done more than any other single error to encourage muddled thinking about the nature and the function of art and its criticism.

The artist, we are told, is a man capable of more valuable experiences

---

[1] Professor Frederick A. Pottle is one of the very few critics who has admitted this. 'We must explicitly separate the critical judgement into two judgements: the aesthetic and the moral, or, as Tolstoi said, into "judgement of art considered apart from subject matter" and "judgement according to subject matter". Poetry is good in the aesthetic sense (is good as art) when it is expressive and infectious; when the poet, contemplating an experience, has succeeded in finding verbal equivalents for it which enable another person to build an experience in *his* mind which is (as we suppose) recognizable like the artist's in quality, and not too much inferior to it in intensity. *That the experience of the artist may be vicious makes no difference in the first judgement.* [Our italics.] Goodness or usefulness is no part of the basic definition of art. And if you are talking about poetry as something to be distinguished from other things, expressiveness is of much greater importance than goodness. A group of words may be expressive and moral, in which case it is poetry, and poetry of a particularly valuable kind; or it may be moral but not expressive, in which case, though it may be admirable morally, it is not poetry at all. Moral profundity may add value to what is expressive, but it cannot in any way make up for expressive weakness.' *The Idiom of Poetry* (1941).

in life than the ordinary mortal, and it is these exceptionally valuable experiences which he chooses to embody in his works of art and communicate to others; therefore in the appreciation of works of art the standard of men's experiences is raised and we achieve such valuable experiences as by our own unaided efforts we could not attain. The artist is a superior man. The critic—although presumably less superior than the artist—is a man of exceptionally fine susceptibilities and better organized than the rest of us to reproduce in himself the valuable emotional experience of the artist. He also has more practice than many of his readers in making appropriate contacts with works of art. He is therefore able to act as a guide to other men and to direct their responses. He is a guide primarily because he is a superior man himself. 'The expert in matters of taste', Mr. I. A. Richards is driven to confess, 'is in an awkward position when he differs from the majority. He is forced to say in effect, "I am better than you. My taste is more refined, my nature more cultured, you will do well to become more like me than you are." ' Yet it is difficult to restrain one's impatience at the implied or blatant assumption of superiority for the emotional habits of the critic which permeates much of contemporary criticism, which is indeed imposed upon it by the Expressionist theory. A man's emotions are, one would think, his own and are ultimate for him.[1] Apart from the great difficulty of comparing emotions in different people, there is no sense in telling a man that another man's emotional habits are better than his, for he cannot copy them. He will either develop a sense of inferiority or he will think you a snob.

But more serious than the amusing or irritating arrogance of the critics is the inevitable tendency of this theory to perpetuate the false deification of the artist-genius. In the past the artist has been a workman. There was a time when the sculptor was not a different being from the stonemason or the architect from the builder. He was simply a better craftsman than the average. From the early Renaissance onwards it came gradually to be realized that craftsmanship is not enough; the artist must possess a certain creative faculty as well. Yet, as Mr. F. P. Chambers has very justly said, 'not until the Romantic age was art regarded as a unique, almost sacred, activity of the human soul and irrevocably alienated from the "knowing powers" '.[2] It was Hegel who said: 'The awakening of every kind of emotion in us, the drawing of our soul through every content of life, the realization of all the movements of the soul-life — this is pre-eminently

[1] Santayana more logically says: 'It is unmeaning to say that what is beautiful to one man ought to be beautiful to another.' *The Sense of Beauty* (1896).

[2] *The History of Taste* (1932).

regarded as the peculiar and transcendent power of artistic creation.' 'The artist', said Baudelaire, 'depends upon nobody but himself. He promises to the centuries to come nothing but his own works; he guarantees nobody but himself. He dies without children. He has been his own king, his priest, his God.' Thus the artist was reverenced as the great individualist, superior to all rules and conventions, expressing in his art the inspiration that is in him. The conception of the artist as uninhibited, as eccentric, as bohemian, as vagabond, but always as the mediator to others of strange but valuable emotional reactions to life, has been popularized by the novelists and lived by the artists. 'If', says Mr. I. A. Richards, 'the artist's organization is such as to allow him a fuller life than the average, with less unnecessary interference between the component impulses, then plainly we should do well to be more like him, if we can and so far as we can.'

The truth is that artists are men as other men, neither better nor worse and certainly not ensamples to all. Artists have been liars, knaves and fools, drunkards and heroes, braggarts and saints, bohemians, businessmen and conventional middle-class bourgeois like Johann Sebastian Bach. Some artists have worked by inspiration, others by rule and method. A large proportion have had a strong impulse towards 'self-expression' in the particular art to which they were inclined. There have been others who have been lazy and who could only be tempted to work by strong inducements; but when they did work, their output was admitted to be good. It is easy to overestimate the importance and universality of this impulse to artistic self-expression, since owing to the economic structure of society it is inherently unlikely that many men will survive as artists unless their impulse to be artists is in fact very strong. What the artist has in common with the competent critic and the connoisseur is exceptional sensitivity and acuity in one or more perceptive faculties. A painter has more than ordinary sensitivity to configurations of colours and shapes. A poet has exceptional sensitivity to the significance of words, logical and evocative; he may be insensitive to music or painting. Neither painter nor poet is necessarily a 'good man' in any of the usually accepted meanings of the phrase. A musician is unusually sensitive to the configurative patterns of musical sounds; he may be insensitive to the values of words—as is indeed evidenced by the librettos of many operas. This limitation of sensitivity is equally apparent in the critic and the connoisseur. We do not expect a man to be a connoisseur of literature because he is a critic of sculpture or a lover of music because he collects ceramics. Nor do any of these limited gifts of sensibility involve general goodness or even a more than ordinarily balanced personality. 'Artists', Mr. T. S. Eliot has told us, 'are not only often insensitive to other arts than those which they practice, but sometimes have very bad manners or meagre intellectual gifts.'[1]

The only *difference* between the artist and the appreciator—that which makes him an artist—is that he has the capacity to invent new configurations in sounds, colours, words, or whatever be the medium he uses. Stravinski has a story of difficulties at the French Customs because he would describe himself as an 'inventor of music', whereas his passport described him as a 'composer'. This is the essence of the matter. The artist is an inventor, and in this and only this he differs from all those men who are not artists. The Romantics were responsible for fixing in the public mind the association between the capacity to produce works of art and that quality we call genius. If you define genius, as was done for example by Ravaisson and Gerard, as the capacity to create, the identification is sound.[2] But as it is more commonly understood, the word 'genius' stands for an intelligible and valid character-type in the science of characterology or the classification of types of personality. In this sense some artists have been geniuses, very many have not. And there have been many geniuses who either had no capacity or impulse to create artistically or who produced works of art that were bad. If ever a man had all the characteristics of that 'genius which is allied to madness' it was Haydon; and Haydon was a very bad painter believing himself to be a very good one.

It is this false notion which is perpetuated by the Expressionist theory and is largely responsible for obscuring the true nature of the artist's activity. To say that we should all endeavour to become as like artists as we can is stupid and impracticable. Sensitivity can to a point be cultivated; but the artist is not necessarily more sensitive than the competent critic or

---

[1] *Notes towards the Definition of Culture.* 'I see little evidence in musical biography that music leads to good behaviour or makes saints of its practitioners. Our Victorian grandfathers, who thought a lot about moral problems, were always puzzled by artists who played and sang like angels but were foul in speech, loose in living and unpleasant as persons. Wagner, who enriched the world, was always robbing his neighbours of their wives as well as their cash. Even Beethoven, who walked with God, cheated his publishers.' Mr. Frank Howes, *Man, Mind and Music* (1948).

[2] 'C'est dans l'invention que sont voir surtout cette force et cette grandeur d'esprit auxquelles on donne de nos jours le nom de *génie*. Le génie de l'aveu de tous consiste surtout à inventer, à créer.' *Philosophie en France*, p. 245. 'Genius', says Gerard, 'is confounded not only by the vulgar, but even sometimes by judicious writers, with capacity. Nothing however is more evident than that they are totally distinct. . . . Genius is properly the faculty of invention; by means of which a man is qualified for making new discoveries in science or for producing original works of art.' *An Essay on Genius* (1774).

connoisseur. And the power to create or invent things worthy of the attention of other men appears to be an inherent gift which cannot be secured by trying for it unless you are lucky or unlucky enough to be born with it in you. Let us be content to know the artist as an inventor and leave it at that. Recognition may ultimately serve him in better stead than incense.

2. *The Bearing of the Expressionist Theory on Criticism*

On this not much more remains to be said. It is clear that the Expressionist critic *must*, if he is to be at all logical, distinguish in his critical judgements between the *excellence* of any work of art as a work of art and its *value* (the distinction which we previously suggested as essential to Realistic criticism to-day). He judges the *excellence* of a work of art by its success in exciting in other men an emotional experience which previously occurred in the artist. And, as we have seen, all such judgements are necessarily nugatory. The critic may judge whether a work of art succeeds in exciting emotion in him (emotional criticism) or he may judge whether, if it is representational, it conveys to his mind an emotional situation clearly and distinctly (Realistic criticism). He cannot judge whether it succeeds in exciting in him an emotion recognizably the same as an emotion once experienced by the artist, because he has no means other than the work of art itself of knowing concretely what the artist's emotions were. With regard to the *value* of a work of art the critic judges by his own moral standards the worth of the experience which the work of art excites in a hypothetically perfect appreciator, but in fact in himself. It is emotional criticism combined with moral assessment.

Expressionism is a bad theory of art because it is unverifiable both in general and in the particular and because it affords no workable criteria for practical criticism. No aesthetician or critic can ever prove that anyone has or has not duplicated in his own experience the experience of the artist, which is said to be embodied in and communicated by his work of art. He cannot begin to prove or disprove it, because the artist (if he is alive) can—as the Expressionist must be the first to insist—only describe his experience by pointing to his work of art, while the critic—not being an artist—cannot describe *his* experience at all. Nor can any critic even begin to prove that his experience in contact with any work of art is more 'right' (i.e. more like the artist's experience) than that of another critic who, from the adjectives he uses, seems to have a pretty different emotional reaction to the same work of art. Critics can compare their *valuations* of works of art. But as these are valuations of experiences in themselves incomparable, such comparisons are clearly worthless. Two critics might give widely different moral assessments of very similar experiences or very similar moral assessments of widely different emotional experiences with no possibility of letting their readers into the secret.

The first task of coherent Expressionist criticism must clearly be to endeavour more exactly to communicate to each other and to the reader the nature of each man's emotional response. And there exists, at the opposite pole from the ephemerality of journalistic criticism, a body of critical writing which seems germane to Expressionism from this point of view. We refer to those works of criticism which are valued and endure for what they are in themselves, as minor works of literary art in their own right, rather than for the presumed correctness or acuity of their critical content. The main purpose of such criticism is to communicate to others the critic's experience in contact with a work of art by stimulating through his words a similar experience in others. Writing of this sort is itself literary art in intention; as the poet in his poem tries (on the Expressionist assumption) to excite in others an emotion which he experienced in life, so the critic in his criticism tries to excite in others an emotion which he experienced in reading the poem. Such works of criticism imply valuations and often facilitate appreciation; but they are assessed primarily on their own merits as literature. Examples of this type of criticism are: Keats's *On First Looking into Chapman's Homer*, Wordsworth's *Scorn not the Sonnet: Critic you have frown'd* and *Milton! thou shouldst be living at this hour*, Blake's *Milton*, Andrew Lang's *The Odyssey*, Browning's *Andrea del Sarto* and *A Toccata of Galuppi's*, Swinburne's *Ave atque Vale* and many another. Different standards are used in judging Francis Thompson's essay *Shelley* and a study such as *The Nascent Mind of Shelley* by A. M. P. Hughes. Parody and satire too tend to communicate directly to the reader attitudes of mind towards another work of art, whereas 'prose' criticism merely conveys judgements *about* it. Fine or paltry, works of artistic criticism are primarily assessed on their intrinsic merits as literary art and only secondarily for their critical content. A great deal of critical writing lies somewhere between the extremes of unpretentious 'prose' composition and fine art. It is assigned a position as minor literary art and classed in the category of *belles-lettres*. Most of the leading critics of literature in the past have been poets and essayists as well as critics. Many of those who have influenced the literature and taste of their day—men like Spenser, Dryden, Johnson, Coleridge, Hazlitt, Arnold, Pater, Eliot, Pound, Auden, Empson—have been originators of literary works outside the field of criticism. And some of these have made their critical writing literary in various degrees. Much the same is true of French, and to some degree of German and Spanish, literary criticism. And even writers who have not ventured outside the field of literary criticism have sometimes aspired to a certain elegance and distinction of writing which is not always found in those who write about scientific matters. One sometimes indeed meets the complaint that owing to the suasive eloquence of his style such and such a critic has wielded an influence disproportionate to the exactness or the profundity of his views in criticism.[1] All this is common ground and undisputed. It does indicate, however, that a critic, to the extent to which he is also himself creative, may be able to communicate to others the impression he receives in appreciation of the works of other artists. He will do so by creating a new work of art, the subject-matter, content or inspiration of which will be his own recollected experience in commerce with other works of art. Nor is it necessary that the critic's work of art should be literary art. The Chinese used often to 'express' in a poem their impressions of a picture; but as often they would express in a picture the impression made upon them by a poem.[2] Songs have been written from the inspiration of poems and poems from the inspiration afforded by music. Music and dance have always been very closely associated and the visual art of décor is inspired by the existence of drama.

There is no good reason why all these forms of art or near-art should not be ranked as criticism in the widest sense. Indeed, in so far as criticism involves putting others in exact knowledge of the critic's experience of a work of art, it can only be done in the form of art. It is criticism without objective validity, but it may fulfil the secondary function of criticism to enhance and stimulate appreciation in others. It will not conform exactly with the principles of Expressionism, since one work of art can never embody or communicate the precise experience embodied in another. But it does seem to be a type, and the only type, of criticism to which Expression might with some latitude lend itself. It can, of course, lay no claim to objectivity in judgement.

[1] 'Take away the object and there remain all the splendours of Pater', says Geoffrey Tillotson.

[2] The Chinese have a proverb: 'A picture is a voiceless poem, a poem is a vocal picture.' One might compare with this the *mot* of the Greek lyric poet Simonides: 'Poetry is a speaking picture,' of which Ben Jonson declared: 'It was excellently said.'

Chapter VIII

TRANSCENDENTALISM

And I know not if, save in this, such a gift is allowed to man,
That out of three sounds he frame, not a fourth sound, but a star.
ROBERT BROWNING

L'art des peintres nouveaux prend l'univers infini comme idéal.
GUILLAUME APOLLINAIRE

I T is possible to imagine a form of the Expressionist theory which would take no account of the element of moral valuation that bulks so largely in most expositions of that theory. If you believe that any increment of experience, any addition to normal human experience in scope or in intensity, is a thing to be desired in and for itself, irrespective of whether the added experience is good or bad by ordinary moral standards, then you will regard any work of art as a good work of art if it leads to an increase of human experience of any sort. Although they have seldom been elaborated into formal aesthetic doctrine, assumptions of this sort play a great part in much practical criticism where works of art are praised and approved because they are thought to broaden or intensify human experience and not only when the experience they convey is thought to be morally good. Common to all such criticism is the assumption that works of art can and sometimes do mediate new experience to those who enjoy them in appreciation. It is an assumption which is very difficult to assess because there are some senses in which it is certainly true and others in which it is as certainly false, while the critics are rarely explicit enough for it to be possible to know whether they are making it in a true or in a false sense.

First, it is quite obviously true that whenever anyone enters into awareness of any work of art he enjoys an experience which is unique to that work of art and that he could not have precisely that experience in any other way. Any combination of musical sounds that is not derivative provides an aural experience which is not provided by any other combination of sounds. Any arrangement of coloured surfaces affords a visual experience different from the visual experience afforded by any other such arrangement. A work of art therefore presents the opportunity for new experience simply by existing as a potential object of awareness which differs in some way from all other objects of awareness. If the theory is asserted in this sense, it is true, innocuous and unrevolutionary. It is valid equally of good works of art and of bad, providing no criterion by which to distinguish between them. But it is often asserted in senses different from this, and more important.

It is indeed very often claimed in books of criticism that a good work of art amplifies and extends human experience not merely by existing as an addition to all other possible objects of awareness but because through appreciation of the work of art the observer achieves an awareness of the world outside himself differing in kind, content or intensity from any experience which he would normally, or could possibly, obtain except through the medium of that work of art. In the one case the critic assumes that the artist is a man who experiences the world more richly, more vividly, more delicately or more profoundly than the ordinary run of men and that by means of his art he enables others to participate in the richness, vividness, delicacy or profundity of his own experience of the world. Thus by appreciating the work of art the ordinary man attains, as it were by proxy and at second-hand, a richer and finer experience of this world than would otherwise be his. But in other cases what is meant to be asserted is that in the proper appreciation of some works of art men obtain experiences not of novel aspects of the actual world but experiences involving direct acquaintance with a mysterious and transcendental universe of ultimate reality of which the actual world is but a manifestation and a mirage. 'The poet', said Pierre Reverdy, 'is in a difficult and often dangerous position, at the intersection of two planes having a cruelly sharp edge: the plane of dreams and the plane of reality. A prisoner of appearance, cramped in the narrow confines of this world—which is, moreover, a purely imaginary one—with which the common run of people are content, the poet clears the obstacle it constitutes in order to reach the absolute and the real; there his spirit moves freely.'[1] The artist, said Baudelaire, is a man tormented by 'la soif insatiable de tout ce qui est au delà' and his work brings to others experience of a 'paradis révélé' on this earth.[2]

Theories of the former type must be classed as a special sort of Expressionist doctrine. Those of the latter type are known as 'Revelatory' and include all interpretations of aesthetic experience as a mode of mystical insight into the world beyond. Both types of theory involve assumptions about the possibility of mediating new experience through works of art which require more careful examination than they have usually received.

[1] *Le Gant de crin* (1926). [2] *L'Art romantique* (1899).

1. *Art as the Extension of Experience*

Musical sounds are not sounds which normally occur in everyday life. Musical compositions do not represent or symbolize anything other than themselves. They neither mediate nor suggest any experiences apart from those aural occurrences which *are* the compositions. Therefore, whether or not music may mediate mystical awareness of a supernatural reality, it cannot expand men's experience of the actual world except by adding to it the aural experiences which are the music itself.

The case of painting is analogous, though less obviously so. A painting may, perhaps, make us see purples and greens in shadows which we had supposed to be black or grey and may thus enhance our sensitivity to the colours of landscape. What such a painting does in fact, however, is simply to offer us visual experiences of purple and green surfaces in a specific pattern. If these visual experiences are interesting or pleasing in themselves, or if they are novel in their representational context, they may indirectly influence our visual habits and encourage us when next we look at shadowed forest to see purples and greens where before we had been accustomed to assume greys and blacks. Pictorial artists have in fact exercised a very profound influence on men's visual habits, and paintings can and do suggest new ways of attending to the external appearances of the actual world. In this way they 'condition' our aptitudes for awareness and by inducing us to cultivate sensivity to aspects of the visual world which we had habitually neglected they indirectly increase our capacity for visual experience. But directly all that any picture can do is to offer the visual experience of the specific arrangement of pigmented surfaces which is the picture. Pictorial art can encourage attitudes of mind to visual experience which lead to new and richer experiences of the actual world; but the only new experience which it can give directly is the visual experience of which it is itself the object.

The case of literature is, as usual, more complex. Perhaps the clearest exposition of the view that the excellence of literature is to be judged by its capacity to extend or enrich men's experience of the actual is that of Mr. Eastman[1]—although it is a view which, as has been said, is very widely

[1] *The Literary Mind: Its Place in an Age of Science* (1931). With the peculiarly feminine malice of which he is a master Mr. Empson has written of this theory: 'Max Eastman . . . attacked nearly everyone else for teaching that poetry ought to teach truths and attacked Professor Richards for thinking that, though not concerned with truth, it ought to convey valuable Attitudes. Max Eastman himself thought that it ought to communicate experience, good or bad (because everyone

prevalent in the practical criticism of our day. According to Mr. Eastman, what poetry does is to 'convey the quality of experience', to communicate the experienced sensory essence of perceptual or emotional states, what he calls the 'tang' or 'feel' of experience. 'Poetry', he says, '*is* the attempt to make words suggest the given-in-experience.' Much the same thing had been said earlier by Mr. T. E. Hulme, a thinker of a very different calibre.[1] Hulme pointed out that in practical life men use their sensory awarenesses of external actuality primarily as signs for action—and a sensation which is used as a 'sign' loses its own intrinsic quality, becomes 'transparent' and is dead to awareness. We attend to its practical meaning and are no more aware of it as it is. We label and docket our experiences according to their practical significance and in doing so know them no longer in experience. We see 'not individual things but stock types'. Therefore 'between nature and ourselves, even between ourselves and our own consciousness, there is a veil, a veil that is dense with the ordinary man, transparent for the artist and the poet'. The facts are indisputable. It is a commonplace of psychology that perceptual—and to a large extent emotional—experience is constantly adapted by us to the practical purposes and necessities of life and that by this adaptation its very character as experience changes and is deadened. We attend to its significance instead of luxuriating in it as it is. Our attention is abstracted from it to what it signifies. But the poet and the artist, it is claimed, are men emancipated from these strong practical habits of mind, men who retain the pristine freshness of experience, who attend to the sensuous and affective qualities of experience as it is experienced and who by communicating the results of this different orientation of attention enable other men to enjoy experience more fully and increase their capacity for it. 'The artist picks out of reality something which we, owing to a certain hardening of our normal perceptions, have been unable to see for ourselves,' says Hulme. So too Mr. Eastman says of the poet: 'to make us clearly, or intensely, or richly, or vividly conscious of this quality (of experience) is the whole of his effort. It is an effort, as Miss Edith Sitwell very accurately affirms, to *heighten consciousness*.' And we, the reading public, 'slake our own thirst for experience in their poems'. Others have spoken in the same vein. Thus Professor Lascelles Abercrombie has said that poetry 'consists in conveying experience itself, undiminished in any vital character, out of the poet's mind into ours'.[2] And

likes to have plenty of experience); and the effect on him so far as he ventured into literary criticism, it seemed clear to me, was to make him prefer very trivial poems.' *The Structure of Complex Words* (1951).

[1] *Speculations* (1924).   [2] *The Theory of Poetry* (1924).

Professor Dewey tells us that the purpose of aesthetic art is 'the enhancement of direct experience itself'.[1] You can hardly pick up a book of practical criticism written about those poets whose work seems conformable to this idea which does not speak of the poet's exceptional capacity for realizing and then imparting to others the sensuous or affective qualities of experience and the consequent effect of his poetry in heightening this capacity in his readers and broadening or deepening the more meagre and jejune content of their conscious life.

Two separate and distinct claims are in fact made by this theory of poetry. The first is that poetry—or at any rate some poetry—conveys to the reader with great vividness and exactness the intrinsic *quale* of the poet's perceptual or emotional experience, its actual sensory qualities of colour, shape, sound, texture, etc., or its affective 'feel'. The other is the claim that such poetry heightens and intensifies other men's capacity to become aware of the sensuous nature of experience in general. The first of these claims is false; and since much criticism commends some poetry for doing this and condemns other poetry for not doing it, it may be thought to be of tolerably high importance to literary criticism that its falsity should be made patent. A poem may induce in the reader an attitude of mind encouraging him to pay more attention than was habitual with him in his day-to-day practical life to the sensed core and feel of experience, dwelling in awareness upon its subtle and changing qualities, and to set a higher value than before upon this kind of 'heightening and enrichment' of consciousness. This poetry can do. What it cannot do is to convey the concrete lived *quale* of one man's experience into the mind of another man, except of course the awareness of the sensuous qualities of the poetic words as vocal noises. When it is said that the poet is a man with a capacity for exceptionally vivid experience who by his verbal constructions conveys 'new' items of experience to other men, something more is claimed for verbal communication than words can achieve. What the poet can communicate by direct inducement is an *attitude of mind* and nothing more. This is a matter so vital to literary criticism and so little understood that it must be illustrated beyond the bare assertion.

There can, I think, be no doubt that language used artistically as it is used in poetry can suggest and evoke attitudes of mind with very great delicacy, subtlety and precision in a well-conditioned reader: attitudes of belief, acceptance, doubt, expectancy, amused toleration, indignant or ironic repudiation, reverence or amusement—attitudes more numerous

[1] *Art as Experience* (1934).

and more finely discriminated than can be *described* in the discursive language of psychology. Take, for example, the following lines:

> *Fuir, là-bas fuir, je sens que des oiseaux sont ivres.*
> *Mais ô mon cœur entends le chant des matelots.*

Of these lines Jean-Paul Sartre has written: 'This "but" which rises like a monolith at the threshold of the sentence does not tie the second line to the preceding one. It colours it with a certain reserved nuance, with "private associations" which penetrate it completely. In the same way, certain poems begin with "and".' This conjunction no longer indicates to the mind an operation which is to be carried out; it extends throughout the paragraph to give it the absolute quality of a *sequel*. For the poet the sentence has a tonality, a taste; by means of it he tastes for their own sake the irritating flavours of objection, of reserve, of disjunction.'[1] In more prosaic language and more systematically Mr. Empson has contributed to the analysis of this function of literary language to convey *attitudes* in his book *The Structure of Complex Words*. In this respect there is of course no absolute distinction between the language of poetry and the language of prose. A book of science or of philosophy is written in language calculated to induce in the reader an attitude of *acceptance* towards the statements it contains; the language of the political orator is designed to induce an attitude of enthusiastic agreement, and so on.[2] Poetry differs only in that it is concerned with eliciting more subtly discriminated and more precise attitudes than the language of prose. Poetry aspires to perfect this function of language as philosophy aspires to perfect the function of language to communicate subtle and precise intellectual positions without ambivalence.

But that poetic language can convey or communicate the felt sensory *quale* of the poet's experience to any greater extent than the language of prose is not the case, though it may seem to do so. T. E. Hulme refers to two lines of Keats:

> *And she forgot the blue above the trees . . .*

and

> *The hill is ruffed with trees.*

---

1 *What is Literature?* (Eng. Trans. 1950).
2 Without writing poetry Mr. I. A. Richards suggests the attitude that every intelligent person of this generation must see the patent truth of what he says. Mr. F. R. Leavis endeavours for an attitude of indignation that there should be any so crass to disagree. And so on.

Now certainly these lines seem to convey a more vivid visual impression than had Keats written 'sky' for 'blue' or 'clothed' instead of 'ruffed'. What happens is, in fact, this: By his verbal description the poet (as the writer of prose) induces the reader to recollect a past experience of his own similar to that which is being described—or, more usually, to *imagine* an experience by forming in his mind a sort of composite photograph built out of a number of more or less similar recollections from his own past experiences—and by a particular conjunction of words induces him to concentrate his attention upon certain sensory aspects of this recollected or imagined experience. In recollected experience one can and often does attend to aspects which in the moment of experience were so little prominent to consciousness that it may seem as if one were recovering in recollection things which were unnoticed at the time. Every man and every psychologist knows that in the moment of actual experience you may be unaware of the greater part of the sensory content of your experience (when a speeding car bears down upon you you do not consciously notice its colour or its shape); yet when the experience is recalled in memory you are able to recover many more concrete aspects than at the time of experience you seemed to take in. It is this that the poet encourages you to do, taking advantage of the potentialities of recollection. And a part of his method—in the case of Keats at any rate—is as follows. The reader's mind is first suitably conditioned to complacence by his adoption of the aesthetic attitude, which may be enhanced by the quasi-hypnagogic character of word-sounds and imagery. Then when his attention is channelled and calmed by a certain luscious softness of rhythmic sound, it is suddenly surprised to alertness by some unexpected conjunction of words. And the shock of slight incongruity works precisely to direct attention upon that sensory content of experience which is often disregarded when perceptions are used as signs in the practical conduct of life. When he writes: 'To what green altar, O mysterious priest', or 'Her wine was dew of the wild white rose', it is certain that Keats induces us to attend particularly to the *colour* of the objects he mentions. In the one case the effect on attention is produced by the initial *unexpectedness* of the adjective 'green' applied to an altar, and in the other by the slight inversion of word order. The same effect would not have been produced had he written 'white wild rose'. But it is just as certain that the poet is unable to communicate the qualitative essence of these colour experiences more exactly or more vividly than the writer of prose—and certainly less accurately than the painter, who can present us for direct visual experience the exact shades of green in the altar, the delicate gradations of white and pink and yellow in the wild rose.

Even were the poet to use the whole range of colour vocabulary invented by the interior decorator or the fashion designer, he would still be far and away behind the painter were he to try to communicate directly the intrinsic *quale* of colour experience. Words cannot do it. They can only influence attention to dwell upon this aspect of what has already been experienced.

Attention may be directed to the form-properties of visual experience by similar techniques. In the lines

> *Stems thronging all around between the swell*
> *Of turf and slanting branches:*

the effect on attention is produced by the slight unusualness of the words 'thronging' and 'swell' in this context. But the words would not impart the concrete shape-quality of the experience to anyone who could not draw up from his memory an impression of a forest glade and the arched shapes of branches with their definite curved contours sharply contrasting with the chaotic formlessness of the undergrowth. The reader pictures these forms for himself because he has already seen them (or others analogous to them), though he may not consciously have attended to the *formal* properties of shape in what he saw.

Poetry may also work the same effect by other means—by comparisons, metaphors, imagery—but the principle is always the same. The poet can only influence you by suggestion to reconstruct from your own stored recollections that which he wishes to present and with the emphasis which he desires. It is in his control of emphasis that he differs from the writer of prose. The method which we have tried to illustrate from the poetry of Keats is one of the more subtle of the poet's devices. It is more efficient than the use of 'poetic diction' as in 'faint damask mouth' or 'vermeil rimm'd' daisies. And it is far more efficient than any attempt at direct description, as when Keats wrote:

> *The colours all inflam'd throughout her train,*
> *She writh'd about, convuls'd with scarlet pain:*
> *A deep volcanian yellow took the place*
> *Of all her milder-mooned body's grace;*
> *And, as the lava ravishes the mead,*
> *Spoilt all her silver mail, and golden brede;*
> *Made gloom of all her frecklings, streaks and bars,*
> *Eclips'd her crescents, and lick'd up her stars:*

So that, in moments few, she was undrest
Of all her sapphires, greens and amethyst,
And rubious-argent:[1]

Even the contained metaphor and the luscious verbosity does not compensate the basic weakness of such a passage and we can only feel how much more effectively a painter might have conveyed the visual experience which Keats is vainly struggling to communicate. He is attempting something which lies outside the confines of language. Mr. Ezra Pound was talking good sense when he advised the would-be poet: 'Don't be descriptive; remember that the painter can describe a landscape much better than you can, and that he has to know a deal more about it. When Shakespeare talks of the "Dawn in russet mantle clad" he presents something which the painter does not present. There is in this line of his nothing that one can call description; he presents.'[2] The 'new' experience conveyed by this line, as by Keats when he is successful, is the experience of the poetry itself, the experience involved in becoming aware of the fused meanings symbolized in the words which are the poem. It does not offer some hitherto unrealized perceptive or ideational experience of the colours or the habits of the dawn. That could be done as well by the writer of prose.

It is frequently asserted in books of criticism that Keats was a man with an exceptionally developed faculty for sensory experience. And this may very well have been so; I certainly would not be held to deny that it was so. But of this I am certain, that as an inference from his poetry it is quite unwarranted. The indications of attention to colour, form and texture in his poems are no more than would be expected as a matter of course from every third-rate pictorial artist, and the exactness with which the qualities are indicated is—necessarily—inferior. Sensuous awareness bulks more largely in the poetry of Keats than, for example, in the poetry of Matthew Arnold. But even the most sensorily alert poet, even were he also a great pictorial artist, could not by words extend the scope of our visual experi-

---

[1] The following lines in contrast call up a vivid presentation of a situation of movement:

> *The specled serpent straight*
> *Comes trailing out in waving linkes and knottie rolles of scales*
> *And bending into branchie boughts his bodie forth he hales.*
> *And lifting up above the wast himself unto the skie*
> *He overlooketh all the wood;*
>
> From Arthur Golding's *Metamorphoses*.

[2] 'A Stray Document', published in *Make It New* (1934).

ences in any other way than by encouraging us to pay more attention to them. Keats directs our attention to the whiteness of the wild rose; the painter may set before us in visual analogue the exact concreteness of its colour and shape. The poet can convey to us no more of the concrete quality of experience than each man is able to conjure up out of his own recollections. The painter *can* do this. He can set before us in direct analogue subtle relations of shades and hues, forms and visible textures which we had *not* noticed before and could not possibly recollect on our own or as the result of verbal directions. I do not think that it is a very important part of his function to do this, but do it he can and the poet cannot. And the same thing holds good of emotional experience. The poet can speak of anger, love, jealousy, hate, but he cannot 'convey' to us more of the affective feel of any emotional situation than each reader is able to delve up from his own emotional past and construct ideationally from composite recollections. The painter cannot depict emotion directly in analogue. But in so far as gestures and attitudes of the body and facial expression are more exactly indicative of fine-spun emotional tone than are verbal symbols, the artist can convey the subtleties of emotion more precisely than the poet—though again it is no very important part of his function to do so. What the poet *can* do is to evoke with great precision very finely discriminated attitudes of mind towards presented situations or series of events. He can enhance our capacity for experience by inducing a state of mind which causes us to set a higher value upon this or that aspect of experience and to cultivate what latent capacity for it we possess. And this influencing of attitude of the mind is perhaps ultimately of far greater importance than the supposed communication of concrete experience that is new.

When it is asserted, therefore, that the artist opens up new avenues of sensation or increases the ordinary man's capacity for experience, great care must be taken to utter and to understand such statements in the right way. The artist certainly increases our opportunity for experience by creating a new object for experience, something which, as a specific construct of shapes and colours, of verbalized meanings or of musical sounds, we have never experienced before. And this he does whether he is a bad artist or a good one. The painter can alter and sharpen our habits of visual attention, guiding us to see and enjoy patterns of colours and shapes in the actual world which would otherwise have passed unnoticed. The poet can convey no new sensory or emotional experience. The most he can do is to induce us to recollect more vividly aspects of our own past experience to which we paid slight attention at the time and produce in us a disposition to give fuller attention to such aspects in the future. No one can give a blind man the experience of seeing or a colour-blind man the experience of colour discrimination. Nor can any man communicate to another types of emotional experience with which the latter is unfamiliar. A man who has never been in love may read all the love poetry in the world and still he will not know what it feels like to be in love. Or to take a more plausible example: a man who has never known 'mystical' religious emotions may read the books of the mystics and the analytical descriptions of the psychologists until he can give from hearsay a correct and complete referential account of the phenomena of mysticism—but it will all be 'meaningless' to him, empty words without concrete significance. And such a man may read all the mystical poetry that is written and he will still remain as innocent of mystical emotion as before. What poetry can do is to give us a new *attitude* to the experience we know. It can persuade us to adopt a 'favouring' attitude towards awareness of the sensory content of experience or towards the affective content of mystical or other experience and to cultivate what latent aptitude we have for it. It cannot put into our minds concrete experience or the aptitude for experience which was not there already. In the Epilogue to a book of critical essays Mr. Stephen Spender has said: 'Poetry is a language which can communicate simply and directly experiences that are not directly communicable in ordinary language. A single poem by Wilfred Owen communicates, immediately and convincingly, experiences that the reader may never have shared, and which certainly are not communicated, although they may be imagined by inferring them, in any other book about the War.'[1] Now when we turn to the essay on Wilfred Owen we find that in fact Mr. Spender does not intend by the word 'experience' what that word would most naturally suggest to the reader—the experience, for example, of being blown into a shell-hole with its attendant emotions of agony, suspense, resignation, despair; he intends what we have described as an *attitude*—and in the case of Owen the specific attitude of pitying solicitude for soldiers and miners. And the poems convey a new experience only in the sense that just that subtle blend of passive pity and sensitive love in just that intensity has not before characterized the mental attitudes of their readers towards those two particular objects of experience jointly. The distinction between inducing a new attitude of mind towards the (actual of potential) objects of experience and conveying new experience is one which it would advantage criticism to recognize.

I suspect that when poets are commended for *wisdom* by the critics

[1] *The Destructive Element* (1935).

something of this kind is usually meant. There is more wisdom, more truth and originality of thought in the writings of the philosophers and mystics than in the poets. A poet may indeed set forth or assume metaphysical or scientific doctrines, though it is no essential part of his function as poet to do so. If he is concerned with the doctrines of philosophy and science at all, as poet he is concerned with the attitudes of mind we take up towards them. But poetry may induce in us new attitudes towards the old problems of human life and destiny, new attitudes towards the metaphysical doctrines that have been invented to solve them, and this often seems to be the ultimate practical wisdom—as perhaps it is. Where the scientific writer of discursive prose can only say: 'You ought to take up such and such an attitude towards the problems of life and death and social obligations', or 'Such and such an attitude is in fact taken up by this or that class of people', the literary artist can arouse the attitude itself temporarily in our minds as we read his words and so give us the awareness in experience of what it is like to adopt that attitude, which we may or may not make permanently our own. He can, moreover, achieve much greater precision in the attitudes he induces than the very crude indications of the writer of prose. Yet even this faculty is not unique to poetry or literary art. It is an extension and a perfecting of that function of language to influence mental attitudes which is employed more bluntly in daily discourse, more energetically by the orator or the auctioneer, more crudely by the scientific or philosophical writer. It is a legitimate function of poetry but not, let it be said, the essence of what poetry is.

Many critics nowadays find the essence of poetry to lie in the fusing of many hitherto disconnected and disparate items of experience within the compass of one verbal metaphor or poetic image. It is a view which has become orthodox with critics of many different schools and one which deserves very serious consideration. But it is not to be confused with the naïve supposition that poetry imparts 'new' experience of the world, for the newness and the uniqueness of the poetic metaphor consist in the experiencing of that fused constellation of verbalized meanings which *is* the metaphor—or the poem—itself. The content of the experience is the poem itself.

2. *Art as a Revelation of the Transcendent*

The belief that all truly great art lifts men out of the mundane world of appearances and reveals to them a transcendental realm of absolute truth has had a long and distinguished history and has influenced on occasion many writers and artists besides those who have accorded to it their regular or reasoned assent. It is a belief which is readily grafted on to other aesthetic theories and it is usually propounded in highly impassioned language verging upon incoherence, so that it is by no means easy to formulate for unimpassioned enquiry just what it is that is believed or claimed. It seems wise therefore, before attempting to reduce the theory to coherent propositions, if we give a few of the more characteristic and less obscure statements of those who have maintained it.

Of music, Schopenhauer said: 'The composer reveals the inmost essence of the world and utters the most profound wisdom in a language which his reason does not understand.' Arnold Schoenberg, who is considered one of the more cerebral of modern composers, nevertheless admits: 'My personal feeling is that music conveys a prophetic message revealing a higher form of life towards which mankind evolves.'[1] With his unabashed robustness Matthew Arnold stated that: 'The grand power of poetry is its interpretative power, by which I mean, not a power of drawing out in black and white an explanation of the mystery of the universe, but the power of so dealing with things as to awaken in us a wonderfully full, new and intimate sense of them, and of our relations with them. When this sense is awakened in us, as to objects without us, we feel ourselves to be in contact with the essential nature of those objects, to be no longer bewildered and oppressed by them, but to have their secret and to be in harmony with them; and this feeling calms and satisfies us as no other can.' And irrespective of whether this feeling that we 'possess the real nature of things' is illusive or not, he thinks that 'to waken it in us is one of the highest powers of poetry'.[2] And speaking of the 'aesthetic thrill' derived from works of plastic art, Mr. Clive Bell said: 'Call it by what name you will, the thing that I am talking about is that which is behind the appearance of all things—that which gives to all things their individual significance, the thing in itself, the ultimate reality. And if a more or less unconscious apprehension of this latent reality of material things be, indeed, the cause of that strange emotion, the passion to express which is the inspiration of many artists, it seems reasonable to suppose that those who, unaided by material objects, experience the same emotion have come by another road to the same country.'[3]

All these are characteristic statements of the Revelatory theory of art. What that theory maintains, so far as I understand it, is somewhat as follows. All or some artists on occasion are able to apprehend the essential

[1] *Style and Idea* (Eng. Trans. 1951).
[2] 'Maurice de Guérin' in *Essays in Criticism (First Series)* (1865).
[3] *Art* (1914).

reality concealed behind the appearance of things by means of an emotion or feeling directed towards the appearances. The artist's emotion is a form of non-conceptual knowledge, involving direct intuitional awareness of the essence, but a knowledge which cannot be understood by logical reason or expressed in the language of concepts. It is this emotion, and the knowledge-by-acquaintance that it carries with it, which is embodied by the artist in his work of art and thus conveyed to the observer, who in the act of appreciation shares the artist's direct apprehension of ultimate reality. The artist stands in an affective state towards some natural object (or towards the cosmos as a whole) and in and through this affective state acquires non-conceptual knowledge of ideal reality. It is this affective state, together with the awareness of essence which is inherent in it, that the artist communicates to others by means of his art. The theory has obvious affinities with mysticism and is often expressed in language bordering upon the language of mysticism.

The Revelatory theory of art traces back to Plato's Doctrine of Ideas. Plato, as has been said, thought that the only true reality is the reality of abstract concepts, which he called Forms or Ideas. The Platonic Idea was something like the universal or the class concept, but was yet fundamentally opposed to an abstraction since Plato believed that it was concrete and real, not constructed in the mind by abstraction from sensory experience but existing prior to experience and known in immediate acquaintance by rational intuition. He thought that the objects of sensory experience and of scientific knowledge are only imperfectly and derivatively real in so far as they imperfectly approximate to, or 'imitate', the Ideas and so partake something of their nature. Such reality as they possess devolves upon them from the reality of the Ideas which partially and imperfectly inhere in them. For this reason Plato rejected the works of artists, such as the poems of Homer and the productions of the great painters and sculptors of his day, because as reproductions of sensory reality they were mere 'imitations of imitations' and twice removed from reality. But Plato was himself too great a natural artist to follow through this theory consistently. And so he also suggested that there is a kind of 'inspired' art, which copies not sensory appearances but the ultimate reality of the Ideas themselves and which derives from a celestial, pre-natal vision of the Ideas by the soul of the artist. This latter notion appealed to men's imaginations and was never forgotten, for it seemed to give a theoretical framework by which to explain and justify the realities of mystical experience. It was revived by the Gnostics, and again by the Neo-Platonists in the third century A.D. Indirectly it has influenced many modern expressions of the theory. Thus Max Beckmann said in almost Platonic language: 'What I want to show in my work is the idea which hides itself behind the so-called reality. I am seeking for the bridge from the visible to the invisible.' And Franz Mark: 'Only to-day can art be metaphysical and it will continue to be so. . . . We will no longer paint a forest or a horse as we please or as they seem to us, but *as they really are*.' Even Giorgio de Chirico, an artist of a very different type, speaks in a similar strain: 'Everything has two aspects; the current aspect, which we see nearly always and which ordinary men see, and the ghostly and metaphysical aspect, which only rare individuals may see in moments of clairvoyance and metaphysical abstraction. A work of art must narrate something that does not appear within its outline. The objects and figures represented in it must likewise poetically tell you something that is far away from them and also of what their shapes materially hide from us.'

Therefore there is always involved in a Revelatory conception of art the implication that the work of art is doing something more than nature, or is doing the same thing better. It brings us into closer and more direct contact with that supernatural world which is the aspiration of the mystic and the visionary, the world of real essences which the natural world of sense perception imperfectly mirrors and ever hides. It is not a copy of nature but a truer copy than nature of that which nature copies. 'Still the arts are not to be slighted on the ground that they create by imitation of natural objects', Plotinus tells us. 'We must recognize that the arts give no bare reproduction of the things seen but go beyond to the Ideas from which Nature itself derives, and, furthermore, that many of their creations are original. They make good where Nature is defective, having the vision of beauty in themselves.'[1] Schopenhauer too thought that the artist attains awareness of the essence of things by an act of mystic absorption which he called 'pure perception'. The artist 'understands the half-uttered speech of Nature and articulates clearly what she only stammered forth'. He 're-produces that beauty of form which in a thousand attempts Nature failed to produce' and 'presents it to Nature, saying, as it were, to her "that is what you wanted to say". And whoever is able to judge replies, "Yes, that is it".' This is, admittedly, a somewhat crude distortion of the theory at its best. But it does represent, however grotesquely, the fundamental belief that the work of art reveals something of which the natural world is a very imperfect image or symbol and reveals it more truly and more luminously than inartistic nature.

English poetry in particular has been deeply coloured by the belief

[1] *Enneads*, IV, 73.

that the natural world is but a shadow and reflection of a higher reality beyond and that the things which we know through the senses are symbols by whose means we can penetrate to an imitation of the divine nature behind.

> The meanes therefore which unto us is lent
> Him to behold, is on his workes to looke,
> Which he hath made in beauty excellent . . .[1]

And Coleridge wrote:

> All that meets the bodily sense I deem
> Symbolic, one mighty alphabet
> To infant minds; and we in this low world
> Placed with our backs to bright reality,
> That we might learn with young unwounded ken
> The substance from the shadow.[2]

Through the writings of the Cambridge Platonists what was already a poetic commonplace was given form and substance for the theory of literature, often somewhat incongruously welded with the Aristotelian doctrine of the universal in the sense of the type. Norris of Bemerton stated the position of the Cambridge Platonists as follows: 'By the ideal state of things I mean that state of them which is necessary, permanent, and immutable, not only antecedent and pre-existing to this, but also exemplary and representative of it.' It was this ideal state of things, particularly in its aspect of exemplary, which poetry was to reveal. 'A Poet', said John Dennis, 'is not so much to consult Nature in any particular Person, which is but a Copy, and an imperfect copy of universal Nature; he is to examine that Universal Nature, which is always perfect, and to consult the Original Ideas of things, which in a Sovereign manner are beautiful.'[3] It was therefore held to be the function of the poet to pierce behind the veil of natural seeming and through the powers of inspiration and creative imagination to reveal a profounder and truer picture of that ultimate reality in which true beauty resides. And in essence, despite the very different language in which it is expressed, this view of poetry is not very different from the Revelatory theory as it is maintained very widely to-day, although modern writers tend to lay more emphasis upon the important rôle of affective states, or of the unconscious mind, both in the

[1] Spenser, An Hymne of Heavenly Beautie.
[2] Destiny of Nations.
[3] Remarks on Prince Arthur (1696).

poet and in the reader, in mediating non-conceptual awareness of reality, and give more prominence, too, to the mediation of an intuition of the order and harmony in the pattern of true reality behind the changing and chaotic manifold of existing things. Often, too, the evocation of a quasi-mystical feeling of identification with the real order or rhythm of the cosmos is held to be the function, or one of the functions, of poetry and art.

A very able exposition of a modern form of Revelatory theory of poetry is to be found in the Clark Lectures of Mr. Cecil Day Lewis.[1] Put very briefly, the gist of Mr. Lewis's argument is that the inspiration and the raw material of every genuine poem consists of an intuition or a system of intuitions—which he calls the poet's 'state of grace'—into some aspect of the essential reality which is cloaked by the matter-of-fact world in which we ordinarily live. The vehicle by which this intuition is communicated is the 'poetic image' or the metaphor in its widest sense. And being communicated it induces affectively in the reader that non-conceptual awareness of ultimate reality which the poet enjoyed. Mr. Lewis endeavours to rationalize the theory in part by means of a Leibnitzian doctrine of relations, whereby every smallest thing in the universe mirrors in itself to some extent the whole universe. 'Relationship being in the very nature of metaphor, if we believe that the universe is a body wherein all men and all things are "members of one another", we must allow metaphor to give a "partial intuition of the whole world". Every poetic image, I would affirm, by clearly revealing a tiny portion of this body, suggests its infinite extension.' It is the poet's task to communicate, not by logic but by feeling, the conviction of this unity of all things. 'The poet's task, too, is to recognize the pattern wherever he sees it, and to build his perceptions into a poetic form which by its urgency and coherence will persuade us of their truth.' The truths of poetry are not verifiable but carry immediate conviction by their 'emotional logic'. And their convincingness is based ultimately on the mystical feeling of unity and oneness with the universe. 'The poetic image is the human mind claiming kinship with everything that lives or has lived, and making good its claim.' Mr. Lewis believes that the poetic image originates from the subconscious mind and favours Jung's theory of the 'collective unconscious' to explain the psychological mechanism of the poet's power, to communicate emotion from man to man. But the theory stands or falls apart from its psychological framework. In essence it contends that poetry conveys from poet to reader an immediate conviction, which reason and

[1] *The Poetic Image* (1947).

logic can neither justify nor shake, in the ultimate harmony behind the apparent chaos of the visible world and that this conviction is associated with an emotional feeling of oneness with the reality of things.

A separate tributary to the main current of transcendental aesthetics demands special mention owing to the important bearing which it had upon several of the most characteristic artistic movements of the present century. The rationalistic and realistic temper of the French mind has always tended to look askance at the illogicalities of unpruned fancy and curb the wings of imagination, excluding whatever lies outside the tangible world of positive experience as no more than morbid delusion and foolishness. French classicism was not a fruitful soil for the 'magic visions of introspective mysticism', for the abnormal, the fantastic or the occult. Yet in contrast with the main stream a small number of French poets have been passionately set on attaining by aesthetic means a non-rational insight into transcendental reality, and it is their influence which has become predominant in French art to-day. Gérard de Nerval, Charles Baudelaire, Arthur Rimbaud, Stéphane Mallarmé, Isidore Ducasse, and others like them, are the true precursors of such men as Alfred Jarry, Guillaume Apollinaire, Max Jacob, Jean Cocteau, André Breton and Paul Éluard, who have been recognized as leaders in the new aesthetic doctrines which have inspired much contemporary production. 'The theories of Baudelaire', says Georges Lemaitre, 'stand as a signpost at the very threshold of the present era.'[1]

Gérard de Nerval lived in the narrow borderland between sanity and mental aberration where the line between hallucination and reality is evanescent and under the influence of visionary exaltation wrote works of imaginative beauty which exercise a strange and potent appeal. Baudelaire, feeling himself disappointed and thwarted by the world of the senses, and the victim of chronic melancholia, believed that the artist's concern must be to attain a mystical insight into supraterrestrial reality beyond the world of sensation. He thought that natural objects are symbols of the supernatural world and that understanding consists in the intuition by a sort of mystic vision of the true relation between the elements of the natural world and the transcendental reality of which they are symbols. In ordinary life this connection is obscured because we habitually link our impressions in logical or conventional sequences which bear no relation to their true spiritual significance. It is the task of the artist therefore to break through this hard crust of conventional banality which is the humdrum world and penetrate to the reality beyond. This he can do because the

[1] *From Cubism to Surrealism in French Literature* (Cambridge, Mass. 1941).

same sublime forms of ideal reality are represented by a number of apparently disconnected symbols in the world of appearance: a colour, an odour, an emotion, an event, a musical aria, may all possess the same symbolic significance and may therefore be interchanged without disturbing the fundamental harmony that lies at the heart of things. Realizing intuitively this 'correspondence' of the symbols, the artist dissociates them and re-combines them in a new way, systematically substituting one symbol for another, in violation of logic and common sense. Thus he destroys the inert forms of drab reality as most men know it and by releasing the mind from the constraint of customary associations alerts it for the revelation of the sublime essence latent in the symbol. He brings a dead world to life and by the vivifying fire of his art reveals the cosmic glory hidden within the humdrum.

Rimbaud, who was deeply influenced by Baudelaire and a greater poet than he, also believed that the poet must pierce through the devitalized banality of the conventional world to the true reality behind by means of a quasi-mystical intuition. 'Je dis qu'il faut être VOYANT, se faire VOYANT.'[1] Like Baudelaire, he thought that the poet achieves this by isolating and transposing the elements of common experience to give them a new life and freshness to reveal the Unknown. Poetry for him was not an expression of emotion or a description of actuality; it was an instrument of visionary enlightenment. But Rimbaud went beyond Baudelaire in developing the thesis that in order to achieve the mystic vision the poet must violently disturb the normal equilibrium of the senses, forcing them to a paroxysm of excess transcending their normal powers. Stéphane Mallarmé was without the intense personal mysticism of Baudelaire and Rimbaud and concentrated on the *word* as something which has symbolic value and evocative power in itself. 'His life was dedicated to the sufficiency and the life of the word.'[2] Whatever assessment the critics accord to his poetic contribution, it was undoubtedly responsible for an important development in poetic theory. For the poem came to be regarded no longer simply as an instrument by which the poet communicated an experience of mystical revelation to other men, but was itself the source of the mystical experience and the revelation to poet and reader alike. Charles Morice, whose critical writing was considered by the younger Symbolists to be a faithful transcription of their creed, said: 'L'Art n'est pas que le révélateur de l'Infini, il est au poète un moyen même d'y pénétrer.

---

[1] Lettre à Paul Demeny, 15 mai 1871. *Lettres de la vie litteraire d'Arthur Rimbaud* (Paris, Nouvelle Revue Française, 1931).

[2] Wallace Fowlie, *Mallarmé* (1953), p. 232.

Il y va plus profond qu'aucune philosophie.'[1] Baudelaire had called art 'sorcellerie évocatoire'. The late Symbolists thought that the poet does not first attain a mystical insight into transcendental reality through some sensory or emotional event in his non-creative life and then communicate that mystical experience to others by embodying it in poetry, but that the mystical experience of the poet and of his readers was the experience of entering into consciousness of the arrangement of words which is the poem. There seems to me no doubt that this was the idea towards which Mallarmé was striving, and it is an idea which has never been completely absent from criticism since. Its theoretical importance is obvious as we have seen that poetical language cannot communicate *new* experience from one man to another, whether that new experience be mystical or not, but a poem always exists as a new object of experience and the experience of becoming aware of any poem is a new experience. What is claimed is that in the case of all genuine poetry the new experience of becoming aware of the poem is in itself revelatory.[2]

The first decade of the present century was characterized by a weakening of positivistic rationalism. The Other World of mystical revelation or non-rational intuition seemed no longer remote and cut off from this world but to interpenetrate the universe of science and common sense. Bergson had raised intuition, a non-rational faculty of the mind, to the status of metaphysical insight superior to cold reason. The belief that while science strives to impose a rational order upon the chaotic manifold of sense-impressions which constitute the visible world, the artist seeks a higher, alogical order of reality, became no longer presumptuous but almost respectable. Among artists the conviction grew that only through escape from the conventional is it possible to achieve knowledge of the authentic. This conviction manifested itself in two phases: on the one hand in a violent attack upon conventional morality, accepted beliefs and traditional art-forms; and on the other hand in exaltation of imagination uncontrolled by reason, in the search for new modes of direct intuition into ultimate reality and in the ascription of new importance to the subconscious mind as the source of imaginative and intuitive vision of truth.

The greatest impetus to this modern tendency, both in literature and in the plastic arts, was given by the fruitful friendship between Pablo Picasso and Guillaume Apollinaire. Baudelaire's principle of the dislocation and recombination of the elements of visual experience in the search for the essential reality behind appearances was adopted under the influence

[1] Charles Morice, *La Littérature de tout à l'heure* (1889).
[2] 'The Poet is he who inspires more than he who is inspired.' Paul Éluard.

of Apollinaire as a self-conscious system by the group of painters who
came to be known as Cubists. 'At the bottom of the Cubist movement',
says Georges Lemaitre, 'was an eager and fervent desire to penetrate
beneath the motley exterior of material appearances and to grasp something of the fundamental substance of reality.' And he goes on: 'The
Cubists never attempted to give an accurate representation of any object
whatsoever; but by means of equivalents and analogies they endeavoured
to impart a spiritual vibration suggestive of the most intimate and secret
characteristic of nature. So when they contended, before a nonplussed or
derisive public, that their incomprehensible pictures were truer to reality
than those of the more conventional artists, they were in a way undoubtedly right; but they referred to a reality different from that which
we apprehend through our senses, a reality that can be perceived only by
intuitive vision and which therefore appears to the common people as
chimerical and fabulous.'[1] Partly by the accident of the influence of Negro
sculpture, and to some extent through the influence of Cézanne, the
Cubists thought that they could penetrate to the real essence behind the
appearances of things by reducing them to geometrical forms as well as
by the dislocation and recombination of their parts. The Expressionist
schools of painters, leaning rather towards theosophical ideas, sought to
achieve the same thing by different means. Their belief has been described
by Mr. Sheldon Cheney as follows: 'An intensely abstract work of art,
affording an enjoyment that may border upon rapture, links with the
mystic's search for personal identification with the rhythm at the heart of
the universe, with the consciousness of dynamic order and harmonious
progression of the cosmos, beyond time and space. . . . Knowing something of the mystic's conception of the structure and meaning of all that
is, we find our faculties better able to identify, and enjoy, the echo of
universal-eternal architecture in creative art. The habit of apprehending
the infinite in the finite is the aim of seeing through to the picture's

[1] Not all Cubists adopted this as their conscious philosophy. Thus in *Du
Cubisme* Gleizes and Metzinger wrote: 'There is nothing real outside us; there is
nothing real but the coincidence of a sensation and an individual mental direction.
It is not our intention to cast in doubt the existence of objects which affect our
senses; but there is reasonable certitude only in regard to the image which these
call forth in our mind.' In 1945 Piet Mondrian wrote: 'Gradually I became aware
that Cubism did not accept the logical consequences of its own discoveries, it was
not developing abstraction towards its ultimate goal, the expression of pure reality.
I felt that this reality can only be established through *pure* plastics. In its essential
expression pure plastics is unconditioned by subjective feeling and conception.'
Plastic Art and Pure Plastic Art (New York).

abstract core. Art here becomes a sensuous means to revelation of cosmic order.'[1]

The Surrealist movement was distinguished by the greater emphasis it set upon the unconscious sources of artistic inspiration, by its open adoption of the principles and techniques of analytical psychology and by a virulent and abusive crusade for the complete emancipation of the subconscious impulses from the shackling constraint of reason and convention even to the point of idolizing automatism and dream. 'In my opinion', wrote Georges Hugnet, 'it is desirable that Surrealism, in its poetic activity, should give the fullest scope to dream activity and automatism, as it did in the beginning.'

The movement was originated by André Breton and Phillipe Soutault in consequence of the interest aroused in them by certain automatic and trance writings of their own, and it came officially into existence with the publication of Breton's *Manifeste du Surréalisme* in 1924. The name 'Surréalisme' was chosen for it instead of 'Supernaturalisme' as a compliment to Guillaume Apollinaire, who had written in 1917 a play with the title *Les Mamelles de Tirésias—drame Surréaliste*. The aim of the movement at its inception was to apprehend, and to display through artistic production, a higher, supramundane reality which lies concealed behind the screen of the commonplace; and its most characteristic doctrine consisted in the belief that this aim can only be achieved by the complete liberation of the subconscious mind from the shackles of intelligence and reason. The aim was often obscured, and the movement itself was brought into justifiable disrepute, by the ostentatious preference of many of its adherents for incoherence and absurdity not only in their artistic output but also in their explanations of the motives which dominated their work. In a world only too ready to be duped by novelty in any form, but the more outrageous the better, there were few of the Surrealists who did not succumb to the temptation to court easy notoriety by displaying facile and meretricious work. Yet for all its extravagance and muddle, such value as it had—and some characteristic and almost first-rate production was undoubtedly inspired by Surrealist doctrines and methods—lay in the belief that through the free play of the uncontrolled subconscious it is possible to achieve an insight into that 'over-reality' which had been the goal of the Cubists and their predecessors. In the words of Georges Lemaitre, 'they concentrated their efforts upon the quest of a trans-

[1] *Expressionism in Art* (1948). Wassily Kandinsky, a theosophist and the outstanding artist of the group, presented a reasoned exposition of their beliefs in *The Art of Spiritual Harmony* (Eng. Trans. 1914).

cendental Surreality, persuaded that its sublime radiance would eventually illumine and regenerate the soul of desperate humanity'. Surrealism has had its day and is now a curiosity of the past. What it did show was that the methods of artistic production which favour the unchecked and un-censored activity of subconscious imagery and association have in some cases enabled the production of works of admitted artistic merit but have not helped men without creative gifts to produce works of an aesthetic merit at all.

In one respect, however, the Surrealists—or some of them—carried aesthetic theory further than those who had gone before, holding not merely that the artist seeks a higher reality behind appearances but that he *creates* the higher reality by fusing together fancy and fact into something new. The child, they believed, lives in a magic world of imagination, in which, as in the world of dreams, visible and tangible things acquire a second reality without losing their concrete substance. The little boy 'playing pirates' on the kitchen table is fully aware that he is seated on a table of deal and is at the same time completely transported into the realm of fancy, where the table is the deck of a ship surrounded by ocean billows. Yet the imaginative world of the child requires material objects on which to feed; the little girl needs the doll which she knows is not alive in order to pretend that it lives. Traditional education of the child isolates the practical and utilitarian aspects of experience so that the world of fancy is divorced from the world of fact. The practical and common-sense world becomes 'real' and imagination 'unreal'. The aim of Surreal-ism is not to find a reality over and above the reality of the common-sense world, leaving that world unchanged, but it is to reconcile what education has divorced, to unite once again fantasy and fact, the world of dream with the world of conventional actuality. Yet it is not a pure return to infantilism that is advocated. Once the reconciliation has been achieved, the dormant powers of the subconscious, paralysed and atrophied by wrong educational influences, are to be cultivated to new vigour and strength so that through them it will be possible again to achieve 'an intense and intimate communion between the human personality and the essence of the universe.' The exposition is not completely coherent because the doctrines of Surrealism are not merely incoherent but take pride in their incoherence.

3. I have set out this Revelatory theory of beauty at some length because it is exceptionally recalcitrant to close definition and difficult to pin down by narrow formulae and phrases. Yet it is far commoner than most

people are apt to suppose. Many artists, many critics and very many people who write and speak about artistic matters quite unknowingly take their stand on this theory although they would be surprised and shocked to be told that they believe in transcendental revelation and are mystics at heart. Everyone who speaks of 'poetic truth' or 'artistic truth' is in fact presupposing a transcendental theory of aesthetics and assuming that art has a revelatory function; for truth which is believed to be valid but incapable of logical proof and insusceptible of ordinary scientific verification is either not truth at all or is necessarily a truth of revelation. And those who believe in a poetic truth which is other than intellectual truth and scientific truth are, whether they like it or not, advocates of a mystical doctrine of aesthetic transcendentalism.

From a formal point of view the Revelatory theory of art presupposes Expressionism in some form, adding to Expressionism another term as Expressionism adds another term to naïve Emotionalism. The three types of theory may be represented diagrammatically as follows:

1. *Naïve Emotionalism*

$$W - - - - - - - - Se$$

W = Work of art

Se = Emotion aroused in spectator

The excellence of the work of art is assessed by either (1) the agreeableness, or (2) the intensity, of the emotion aroused by it in the spectator.

2. *Expressionism*

$$AE - - - - - - - - WEe - - - - - - - - Se$$

Ae = Emotion experienced by the artist

WEe = Work of art embodying the artist's emotion

Se = Duplicate of the artist's emotion aroused in the spectator

The *success* of a work of art is judged in terms of the similarity between AE and Se.

The *value* of the work of art is judged in terms of the moral rating accorded to the duplicated emotion Ee.

3. *Transcendentalism*

There are, as we have seen, two formally distinct types of transcendental theory, which we will call Traditional Transcendentalism and Refined Transcendentalism, respectively.

Traditional Transcendentalism as it is usually advocated is represented diagrammatically as follows:

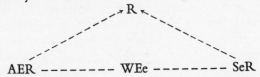

R=Real essence

AER=Artist's emotion which mediates knowledge-by-acquaintance of R

WEe=Work of art embodying the artist's emotion

SeR=Duplicate of the artist's emotion in the spectator, mediating to the spectator knowledge-by-acquaintance of R

The excellence of any work of art is judged by the extent to which the spectator achieves—or feels that he achieves—a revelation of ultimate Reality through contemplation of the work of art.

Refined Transcendentalism is represented as follows:

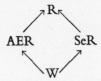

AER=The work of art arouses in the artist an emotion which mediates to him knowledge-by-acquaintance of ultimate Reality

SeR=The work of art arouses in the spectator a similar emotion which mediates to him also knowledge-by-acquaintance of ultimate Reality

The excellence of the work of art is judged by the extent to which the artist or the spectator achieves—or feels that he achieves—a revelation of ultimate Reality through contemplation of the work of art.

The Revelatory theory of art offers a perfectly valid and coherent criterion of criticism: the critic will value any work of art in the measure in which its contemplation causes him to experience an emotion which seems to involve intuitive insight into the true essence of the reality behind the appearances of things. It is perforce a purely subjective criterion.

What evokes such an emotion in one critic may not evoke it in another; and there may be professing critics who experience such emotions not at all. Indeed the problem of communication—in poetry the related problem of lucidity and obscurity—has come to bulk more largely in modern literature and art than ever in the past. For that which to the artist and his admirers may seem to convey a sublime intuition of the supraterrestrial world and an emotional apprehension of absolute truth may, and often does, appear to the generality of people an incomprehensibility or a joke. Many people possess little talent for mystical experience and little inclination to develop such latent talent as they possess. If a man finds a work of art ridiculous which you find revelatory, you may urge him to contemplate it more earnestly, to rid his mind of prejudice and preconception, but you cannot argue with him; if he still finds it ridiculous, for him it is ridiculous and not a source of revelation. For this reason it was one of the aims of Surrealism by giving free rein to the subconscious and eliminating rational control from the creation of works of art to produce an art whose imagery and associations would appeal directly and forcibly to those hidden layers of the mind which are common to all men and thus goad them by violence from apathy to insight. Whether the attempt succeeds or not can only be decided by reference to individual reactions.

The critic may, if he so decides, claim that revelatory power is a necessary condition of works of art: if he says this, he will call no artefact a work of art unless it arouses in him an emotion which seems to involve apprehension of ultimate reality. He may decide to claim that revelatory power is a necessary and a sufficient condition of works of art: if he says this, he will call every artefact a work of art which arouses this emotion in him, even although it possesses none of the other characteristics which have traditionally been thought to constitute artistic excellence. Again he may claim that a good work of art need not necessarily be revelatory but those works of art which are revelatory have a value above and additional to those which are not. In this case he will have to recognize that revelatory power has no bearing upon the *excellence* of a work of art as a work of art, but is contributory to its total *value*. None of these positions is right or wrong and there can be no dispute about them; for the critic is merely defining the critical terminology he proposes to use. If, however, having taken up one of these positions he then makes assessments on other and incompatible grounds, his criticism will be inconsistent with itself and bad. But if he takes up any of these positions, he must recognize that his judgements based upon them will be valid for himself alone and for such people as happen to respond in the same way as he does. If any person does not experience a feeling of revelation on contemplating a putative work of art, that object will be for that person a non-artistic artefact whatever the critic's response to it may be.

Whether this belief that some aesthetic, as some mystical, experiences bestow immediate awareness of a superior reality is true, false or meaningless, is a metaphysical question which makes no matter for criticism. Although you were to show that philosophically the very notion of transcendental reality is illegitimate, or that non-conceptual knowledge of that reality through emotional intuition is impossible, it would not in any way invalidate Revelatory criticism of the arts. For the critic must judge the relative excellence of particular works of art by the *strength* or the *voluminousness* of the Revelatory conviction which each one occasions in him; he is not concerned with the *truth* of such conviction in general. He is in fact a judge of whether works of art evoke a specific emotion, and the degree in which they severally arouse it. If he concerns himself with the truth of the revelation, he is a philosopher and not a critic of art. Most critics to-day, for example, put a low value on the 'Gothic' novels of Mrs. Radcliffe, 'Monk' Lewis, Maturin, Charles Brockden Brown, and on such writing as *In Tune with the Infinite*. But they do so—or should do so—not because they believe that their views of the supernatural are philosophically or scientifically wrong, but because they fail to carry conviction. If they set a higher value upon Edgar Allan Poe or upon much poetry which has no obvious connection with a supernatural sphere, it is because (if they are Revelatory critics) from contact with this poetry they obtain an experience which carries with it a strong conviction of insight beyond the normal mundane connection of things to a higher order and harmony of reality. People who have enjoyed this experience, whether mystical or aesthetic in origin, are unanimous in asserting that the conviction it carries cannot be increased or destroyed by intellectual reasoning or by scientific confirmation or refutation; for it is an immediate emotional conviction which is more emphatic than the emotional force of logical proof or scientific verification. Mr. Cecil Day Lewis puts the matter very clearly when he writes: 'there are such things as unverifiable truths and it is the unverifiable element in poetry which carries the conviction of truth. Certainly, we may take the image, "Brightness falls from the air, Queens have died young and fair"; and we may get the historians to confirm that the second line is historically accurate, and the meteorologists to assure us that when the sun sets it does in fact get dark; and all this verification will not make the image one degree more convincing to us. Between "Brightness falls from the air" and "Queens have died young and fair" there is a rational void. But a spark leaps to fill the gap, and the spark does not expire but glows on, so that the sadness of evening and the sadness of untimely death illuminate each other reciprocally, a light which is extended beyond them and reaches out some way over the human situation all round.'

Yet despite its essential irrelevance to practical criticism there has been a great deal of controversy about the supposed revelatory function of art—conducted often under the mistaken supposition on both sides that if the genuineness of the revelation were disproved, Revelatory criticism would thereby be invalidated. It would carry us too far from the purpose of this book to enter into a metaphysical discussion of the theoretical foundations of aesthetic or mystical revelation; the philosophical arguments are the same in both cases. It may, however, be of interest to explain that from the philosophical standpoint the summary rejection of the Revelatory claim, when it is made for *some* works of art and *some* appreciators of art, has not been substantiated and may have little more to recommend it than illogical prejudice. But, as the brothers Goncourt said: 'Lorsque l'incrédulité devient une foi, elle est moins raisonnable qu'une religion.'

It is a sufficiently generally recognized circumstance that some men do upon occasion enjoy a rather special kind of experience, experiences of a semi-hypnogenic and quasi-revelatory character among which those states of mind commonly known as 'mystical' are included, in which the normal awareness of individual selfhood is partially in abeyance and the subject of experience seems to be placed in direct cognitive contact with a supernal reality. The well-known 'metaphysical revelation' induced in some people by certain drugs is an instance of this type of experience[1] and some aesthetic experiences at any rate belong to the same category. When such experiences are described it is often said that in them the self was identified with the higher reality of the Absolute, merged in the totality of existence or absorbed into the being of God, according to the categories with which the subject is accustomed to think. It is also claimed

---

[1] In an essay entitled *Gas* (1929), Mrs. Virginia Woolf described her recollected sensations under an anaesthetic at the dentist's in the following way: 'We become aware of something that we could never see in the other world; something that we have been sent in search of. All the old certainties become smudged and dispersed, because in comparison with this they are unimportant, like old garments crumpled up and dropped in a heap, because one needs to be naked, for this chase, this pursuit, all our most cherished beliefs and certainties and loves become like that. Scudding under a low dark sky we fly on the trail of this truth by which, if we could grasp it, we should be for ever illuminated.'

that the experience involves immediate knowledge (i.e. knowledge not mediated by inferential reasoning) of ultimate truths of reality and being, although these truths cannot be formulated in public language or subsequently translated into concepts comprehensible to the experient. At best they can be expressed by means of rough and inadequate analogues in the form of images and metaphors. Such experiences are apt to carry a strong and peculiar affective tone, and so powerful is the conviction that the revelation of truth is genuine that there are few people who have once had it and who do not persist in believing that they had received a direct vision of ultimate Truth. Experience of this sort has been greatly esteemed and sought after in most of the religions of the world and has been the inspiration of some systems of philosophy, such as those of (probably) Parmenides, Spinoza and McTaggart, which are among the most sustained and successful achievements of constructive logic that the mind of man has produced. Persons who have particularly cultivated such experience and have displayed a special talent for it are called 'mystics'.

There is no doubt that some artists—not all—have enjoyed the capacity for experience of this kind, either rudimentary or advanced, and have known moments in which they have believed that the essential nature of reality as a whole, or of some part of reality, was revealed to them in immediate awareness. Nor is there any doubt that some artists have endeavoured to embody the experience in works of art so that through contemplation of the work of art the experience itself might be repeated in themselves and in others. And there can be no doubt that some men when contemplating certain works of art have seemed to themselves to enjoy either a mystical experience—presumably similar to that which the artist enjoyed—or, if not the full experience itself, at least the sense of revelation which was an adjunct of the experience. This is the element of undoubted truth in the Revelatory theory of art—this, with the fact that some works of art, particularly works of literary art, tend to foster and enhance the attitude of mind which regards such a sense of revelation as supremely worth while.

The content of the revelation, the truth that is revealed whether in mystical or in aesthetic experience, remains ineffable; even the experient is unable to grasp it intellectually in his own mind. And for this reason many people deny that there is any content of truth in such experiences. They deny that any knowledge of reality is mediated through appreciation of a work of art and claim that the recipient of a putatively revelatory experience simply obtains a feeling which reverberates massively upon his whole conscious state and produces in him an illusion of knowledge where no knowledge is. This feeling, they say, is the sort of affective reaction which you get when the truth of some scientific or philosophical position bursts upon you with illuminating clarity and the sense of intellectual lucidity is accompanied by an emotional attitude of urgent acceptance and complete conviction; but in the case of aesthetic (and mystical) experience it is an empty feeling without the objective content of any truth-proposition to which such attitudes ordinarily refer. Mr. I. A. Richards, whose views I take myself to be expressing, calls such states of conviction 'objectless beliefs', and holds that so-called aesthetic revelation is a sense and feeling of revelation where nothing is revealed.

It is an issue upon which argument is doomed to futility. When the subject of experience adheres to the conviction that he has enjoyed a genuine revelation and not an empty belief about nothing, he is asked by the sceptic to state what the knowledge was which was revealed to him and in which he believes. He replies, of course, that his revelation is ineffable and cannot be stated, but only experienced. And his reply is logical, because if indeed he had such knowledge as he claims to have, he could not state it as he is asked to do. If you decide to mean by 'knowledge' only rational belief in verifiable propositions which can be conceptualized and communicated linguistically, then whatever is thought to be revealed by works of art—by some works of art to some people—is not knowledge. But neither is it ever claimed to be this sort of knowledge. And if you start to discuss what is and what is not rightly called knowledge, you soon find that you are merely comparing linguistic habits and remind yourself with urgency that there is no right or wrong in linguistics but only custom or convenience.

There *is* a point at issue nevertheless, and it can best be indicated by asking: Is there such a thing as knowledge-by-acquaintance, and if so, what are its varieties and scope? That there is knowledge-by-acquaintance is certain. We are directly acquainted with the sensory core of every perceptual situation, whether it be external or internal perception, and without this direct acquaintance we could have no conceptualized knowledge of anything whatever. But the moment of direct acquaintance can itself neither be conceptualized nor verbalized. We are directly acquainted also with the proposition in which we believe, or whose truth we discuss after our interlocutor has painfully dinned it into our head. If we were not directly acquainted with it, we could not discuss its truth. Whether there is knowledge-by-acquaintance with any metaphysical reality is far from certain, although very many men have believed that they had such acquaintance in direct awareness. And what aesthetic

Transcendentalism claims—let us be clear about this—is that some men enjoy a form of knowledge which is direct awareness of metaphysical reality, comparable to the awareness of material reality which we attain in sense perception, and that this knowledge is mediated through an emotion aroused in them by the contemplation of certain works of art. You cannot shake their claim by denying that there is such a thing as knowledge by direct acquaintance or by denying that it is rightly called knowledge. You can only do so by showing either that there is no direct acquaintance with metaphysical reality or that this particular variety of experience to which they point, i.e. aesthetic experience, is not in fact knowledge by direct acquaintance with metaphysical reality. It may be possible to prove one or the other of these things: he is a rash man indeed who would assert that anything, however unlikely, can never be proved. But if it is possible, I do not know how it could be done. On the other hand it seems at least as difficult to imagine any method by which a proof could ever be adduced of the contention that aesthetic appreciation *is*, always or sometimes, a mode of awareness of a higher reality behind the immediate appearances which constitute the aesthetic object. It has indeed proved singularly difficult even to construct a coherent and plausible philosophy on the assumption that this is so without rigorous proof that it is so.

There are two systems of philosophy in vogue which allege to provide a foundation for the claim of aesthetic Transcendentalism that the appreciation of beautiful things mediates mystical knowledge of ideal reality.

The first is the scholastic theory of St. Thomas Aquinas as re-interpreted by Neo-Thomists such as Jacques Maritain[1] and Thomas Gilby.[2] St. Thomas thought that the enjoyment of beauty is a mode of awareness in which the immediate knowledge of sense-perception is transfused by reason but without losing its sensuous character. This union of the sensuous and the rational he believed to be possible because sense-perception is itself a 'cognoscitive' faculty not wholly distinct from reason but, as he says, 'a kind of reason'. The apprehension of beauty is non-conceptual knowledge, and if it is conceptualized, it ceases to be direct intuition, the aesthetic joy vanishes and with it the awareness of beauty. What is apprehended in aesthetic awareness as distinct from ordinary sense-perception is the 'inner splendour' of an object, by which St. Thomas may have meant something not very different from what modern upholders of Transcendentalism have meant by the 'essence' or the 'hidden reality'

[1] *Art and Scholasticism* (Eng. Trans. 1930).   [2] *Poetic Experience* (1935).

of things. St. Thomas took over the classical doctrine that beauty consists of 'due proportion' and also accepted a belief very prevalent in the Middle Ages that all knowledge involves some sort of identification between knower and known. He therefore thought that we are able to apprehend beauty through the senses because the organs of sense, being partly rational, themselves partake of the formal 'right proportion' in which beauty consists. The theory of St. Thomas is difficult to understand without re-interpretation because it is expressed in categories which are foreign and strange to our present habits of thought and—unlike the writing of Ekhart, for example—it does not seem to be based on more than a superficial understanding of aesthetic experience. Unfortunately modern expositions are even more difficult to understand than the original writings of St. Thomas. Jacques Maritain, the most widely read of the Neo-Thomists, says, for example, of aesthetic knowledge, which he calls poetic knowledge: 'I believe it to consist in a knowledge by means of *affective* connaturality with reality as *non-conceptualizable*, because awakening to themselves the creative depths of the *subject*.' He distinguishes it from mystical experience proper (i.e. religious mysticism) on the ground that 'that which is typically *grasped* or *apprehended* in this (poetic) experience is not the absolute but rather the intercommunion of things with the subjectivity they reveal to itself, in the spiritual flux from which existence derives'.[1] I am unable to believe that anyone who finds St. Thomas hard to understand will gain enlightenment from language of this sort. A somewhat similar approach in a different philosophical context may be intended by the able critical writer Signor Leone Vivante, who thinks that by sense-perception we chiefly make contact with the creative principle of indeterminacy which is creativity of the spirit in the universe.[2] I am, however, again unable to understand the language in which his philosophy is couched.

The second philosophical system which might lend support to a transcendentalist conception of beauty is the modern form of Neo-Platonism of which Ralph Waldo Emerson was a notable exponent.[3] Emerson taught that all genuine art is the outcome of inspiration. Inspiration he conceived as a mode of mystical experience in which the artist is a purely passive vessel of the divine afflatus; ideas flow into the mind of Genius from a source beyond himself, from the Over-Soul, the soul of the

[1] *Redeeming the Time* (Eng. Trans. 1943). [2] *English Poetry* (Eng. Trans. 1950).
[3] In the following exposition I am indebted to the interpretation of Emerson's ideas by Vivian C. Hopkinson in *Spires of Form: A Study of Emerson's Aesthetic Theory* (1951).

'All'. The artist is also a man who is peculiarly sensitive to sense-impressions, a man with 'solar eyes' which pierce the dark like meteors. Artistic sensibility is the capacity to interpret sense-impressions as symbols to the imagination and to read the spiritual significance of natural objects; by doing this the artist puts himself in tune with ideal reality. 'The birth of perception throws the artist on the party of the Eternal. This is the ichor of the gods, pulsing already in our veins, and converting us into powers. For this eye, once opened, does not shut.' This process is possible because natural objects are a symbol of the Ideal and in their forms flows the spirit of the Eternal. Nature is a trope, and by identifying himself with it the artist can rise through it to the Ideal beyond. The spirit of ultimate reality is inherent in the forms of natural apprehension, and by becoming one with the natural forms the artist is at one with the Infinite. 'He converts the solid globe of the land the sea the sun the animals into symbols of thought; he makes the outward creation subordinate and merely a convenient alphabet to express thoughts and emotions.' The creation of a work of art—the 'ultimation of thought into things'—is the artist's expression of his new vision and the objectification of his inspiration. As his inspiration comes to him from the divine soul of the cosmos, so in his work of art he communicates to other and less-favoured men something of the vision which has been vouchsafed him. Emerson compares the creator to an aqueduct whose water comes from the heavens and seeps down by force of gravity to the level of the receiver. Thus the great man, the artist, is one 'standing on God' and the small man one standing on the great man.

I have stated this theory largely in Emerson's own language because like many metaphysical theories of its kind it is also a work of art in the sense that when the language is changed into a series of bald propositions it seems to lose not only much of its convincingness but most of its meaning. It requires you to believe that there exists an Ideal reality behind appearances, that the Ideal is spirit having kinship with the human spirit, that it inheres in the forms of all natural things or is mirrored by them and that it is apprehended as inhering in natural things by mystical experience of which aesthetic awareness is a mode. If you believe this, fine art is revelatory of the Ideal in a special sense, although everything that exists is also revelatory to the mind attuned and sensitized to the spirit's radiation. Like all metaphysical theories this doctrine has no contribution to make to practical criticism. The Revelatory critic must still assess each individual work of art according to the conviction of revelation which it produces in him. A general metaphysical doctrine can be combined as well with any principle of practical criticism. Emerson, for example, although he was one of the first of modern writers to speak of 'organic form' as a distinguishing characteristic of works of art, held that works of art derive their organic form from their likeness to natural objects, which also have organic form for those who can see. He therefore used the term in a sense almost exactly the opposite to that which it bears in modern criticism, where it expresses a property of organization by which beautiful works of art are distinguished and set apart from the natural objects which are their subject-matter.

The real impetus to the opposition against aesthetic Transcendentalism comes, however, less from metaphysical convictions than from the wish to repudiate any suggestion that feeling and emotion can ever issue in knowledge. For the claim to possess knowledge by feeling (or by intuition which is emotional in character) seems to conflict with that rigid differentiation of mental elements into cognition, feeling and conation which was inherited from the old faculty psychology and still passes with most people other than practising psychologists as a scientific ultimate. Perception is always thought of as a reaching out to make contact with a (real or apparent) world outside ourselves. By thought we order and systematize the *data* provided by perception into a coherent scheme of practical knowledge, verifiable by further perceptual experience. Feeling is our peculiar personal and entirely private mode of experiencing and involves no 'reaching out' beyond our own minds. But from feeling arises conation, which again is a different mode of reaching out into the external world, the mode of action, which may issue in a practical knowledge but does not involve knowledge of the intellect. Feeling is thus cut off completely from anything objective to ourselves and is thought of as an ineffable agitation with a specific tonality or flavour, an infinitely changeable colouring to all consciousness, but shut up hermetically within the awareness of each subject as he experiences it. Basically the psychologists regard the modalities of feeling as nothing more than our awareness of somatic changes and conditions. Feeling is pure inertness and innerness. Therefore, in classical psychology, the relation of feeling to the supposed object of feeling is always assumed to be accidental, casual and individual. It is not, and cannot be, a mode of cognition. The claim that aesthetic feeling constitutes apprehension of a reality outside the consciousness of the subject cuts across this traditional trichotomy of mental faculties and is therefore treated with scant ceremony by those who regard that trichotomy as the last word in scientific knowledge of mental processes.

The repudiation of transcendental revelation, whether on this or any other ground has, as we have seen, no tendency to invalidate or disturb transcendental criticism of the arts. The critic is concerned only with the sense of revelation mediated to some people by some works of art, not with its metaphysical validity. But the same motive lies at the root of the nowadays very common denial of objectivity to aesthetic properties in general, and this would seem to offer a convenient occasion to deal with that denial. For this, on the contrary, has a very intimate bearing upon practical criticism of all schools.

There is a large number of rather recondite properties which we seem to detect in some objects and not in others, but on the whole in aesthetic objects more frequently and to a greater degree than in non-aesthetic objects; examples are those properties which are referred to by the words 'gracefulness', 'profundity', 'sublimity', 'balance', 'stress', 'texture', 'peripheral or radial rhythm', and even vaguer terms such as 'construction', 'style', 'atmosphere' used with limiting adjectives. These are what we shall call 'aesthetic properties'. Now it is characteristic of the perception of such properties that many people often seem to themselves to detect them, when they do become aware of them, through a feeling or an emotion rather than by cool and passionless perception. And for this reason we are asked to believe that they are not properties of the objects we perceive but reflections of our own emotional response to those objects; to believe that when we say any aesthetic object is well or ill constructed, that it is dramatic or insipid, that it has or has not rhythmic symmetry, we are not describing anything that we have perceived in the object but are talking simply and solely about our own emotions as we contemplate the object.[1] There is no reason at all for supposing that this is

[1] 'We are accustomed to say that a picture is beautiful, instead of saying that it causes an experience in us which is valuable in certain ways. . . . Even among those who have escaped from this delusion and are well aware that we continually talk as though things possess qualities, when what we ought to say is that they cause effects in us of one kind or another, the fallacy of "projecting" the effect and making it a quality of its cause tends to recur. . . . Such terms as "construction", "form", "balance", "composition", "design", "unity", "expression", for all the arts; as "depth", "movement", "texture", "solidity", in the criticism of painting; as "rhythm", "stress", "plot", "character" in literary criticism; as "harmony", "atmosphere", "development", in music, are instances. . . . Whether we are discussing music, poetry, painting, sculpture or architecture, we are forced to speak as though certain physical objects—vibrations of strings and of columns of air, marks printed on paper, canvasses and pigments, masses of marble, fabrics of freestone, are what we are talking about. And yet the remarks we make as critics do not apply to such objects but to states of mind, to experiences. . . . If anyone

really the case except for the assumption we have mentioned that feeling and emotion can never be cognitive, and in contesting it we shall limit ourselves to revealing the invalidity of that assumption. If, however, we maintain in opposition that aesthetic properties are objective qualities of the objects of perception, we are not proposing to embark on an epistemological argument or to suggest that philosophical Realism or Subjective Idealism make the slightest difference to practical criticism of the arts. It is a matter of the purest indifference to criticism whether perceptual properties are objective as the philosophical Realists say they are or whether as the Subjective Idealists have it they are subjective and mind-created. What is important to criticism is to show that those recondite perceptual properties which we call 'aesthetic' are objective in precisely the same sense that primary and secondary sense-qualities of shape, size, colour, etc., are objective. They are perceived in the object and are not reflections of our emotions mirrored upon the object.

'Feeling' is possibly the most overworked and loosely defined word in the whole vocabulary of popular psychology. James Ward[1] distinguished five meanings which it commonly bears in unscientific language: (1) the sensation of touch; (2) an organic sensation such as feeling hungry; (3) an emotion, as when we say that we feel angry or jealous; (4) any subjective state, as when we say that we feel certain; (5) the sensation of pleasure or pain. Touch is, of course, a sensation just as hearing and sight are sensations. Organic sensations such as feeling hungry are also modes of sensory awareness, often strongly associated with conative impulses and pleasure-

says that "The May Queen" is sentimental, it is not difficult to agree that he is referring to a state of mind. But if he declares that the masses in a Giotto exactly balance one another, this is less apparent, and if he goes on to discuss time in music, plot in drama, the fact that he is all the while talking about mental happenings becomes concealed.' I. A. Richards, *Principles of Literary Criticism*. Mr. Richards here and in general confuses the undoubted fact that a work of art is always actualized as a perceptual situation in some person's mind with the inconsequent and incorrect supposition that aesthetic qualities are reflections of emotional states. We are not concerned to maintain that aesthetic qualities or that the 'primary' qualities of colour and shape are or are not objective properties of things outside the mind. That is a matter for epistemology. But we are concerned to maintain that they are as objective, objective in the same sense, as the primary qualities. The balance of masses in a Giotto is as objective, as much 'given' in the perceptual situation we call 'seeing a Giotto', as are the pigment colours and the shapes of which we become aware in the same perceptual situation. They are *not* reflections or projections of our emotions. Beyond the epistemological muddle, Mr. Richards nowhere gives any positive facts to support his very curious beliefs.

[1] *Psychological Principles* (1918).

pain tone. Emotions are complex mental states involving organic sensation, conative impulses and pleasure-pain affect. Emotions and attitudes of mind, such as the attitude of feeling certain, usually but not always have an objective situation as 'referent'; when they do not, they approximate closely to the more diffused modes of organic sensation. It is only in the last meaning of the word, pleasure-pain affect, that psychologists are concerned to assert that feeling is purely subjective. And in this strictest sense of the word there is no one who would dream of denying that it is subjective; for, as we have said earlier, pleasantness and unpleasantness are not separate modes of experience or isolable elements in experience but are qualities of experience or ways in which we are conscious of experience.

Everyone, however, uses 'feeling' in a much more general sense than this and even psychologists struggle with the inadequacies of language to express the subtle nuances and the shades and tones of feeling. It is necessary therefore to be careful that the *obvious* subjectivity of feeling in the strictest psychological sense of pleasure-pain affect does not unwarrantably lead one to assume that it is subjective in all the senses in which the word is used. If anyone asserts that aesthetic qualities are reflections of feeling in the sense of pleasure-pain affect, he reduces all descriptive aesthetic criticism to one of two assertions: my awareness of this object is pleasant in such and such a degree or my awareness of it is unpleasant in such and such a degree. It doesn't matter if the critic says that it is harmonious, rhythmical, balanced, graceful, sensitive, superficial, delicate or crude; he is saying no more than that its contemplation is pleasant or unpleasant to him in a specific degree. If anyone seriously believes this, we do not propose to argue with him. But if this implication is refused, then 'feeling' is being used in another, vaguer sense which must be examined. Aesthetic feelings in general are emotions in which the normal impulse to action is recessive and therefore the element of organic sensation which is present in all conscious emotion is unusually strong. Realizing this, you are no longer entitled to say: 'this is a matter of feeling and therefore it is subjective'. It becomes necessary to distinguish between objective or veridical sensations, which put us into awareness of the 'objective' qualities of the things in the world about us, and 'subjective' or somatic sensations, which merely make us aware of, or enable us to draw inferences about, states of our own bodily organism. And to draw a sharp line between the two types of sensation is by no means an easy thing to do.

What those people allege who maintain that the so-called aesthetic properties are subjective is something like this.—By sight and hearing we become aware of objective conditions in our environment, of colours, shapes and sounds. We also become aware of a number of simple objective qualities which characterize these conditions. We see that a shape is round, that an orange colour is 'between' a red and a yellow, that one blue patch is 'deeper' in the saturation scale than another; we hear that one musical interval is greater than another, that the timbre of a violin is more like the timbre of a viola than a flute. These are objective awarenesses. But when we think we are aware of the more complex objective properties which we call 'aesthetic', we are not, it is alleged, really aware of anything objective at all but of emotional states and their accompanying somatic sensations which are induced in us by our awareness of the simpler objective qualities which we see or hear. When we say that a certain arrangement of shapes is 'balanced' or 'harmonious', we are not really describing any property of the arrangement of shapes which we see but are aware of a feeling of balance or harmony among the conative impulses and organic sensations which our visual perception causes in us. Now this is an extremely curious assertion to make—how curious it is seldom realized—and I can see not the slightest reason to believe that it is true. Let us suppose that when I see a penny as round I really am aware of an objective property of roundess in the object of my perception. If this is admitted, there is no logical reason for denying that when I see another shape as slender, lissom, obese, squat, tapering and so forth, I am also aware of a property in the object of my perception which is objective in precisely the same sense. When I see an arrangement of abstract shapes as balanced —shapes which have no representative symbolism—there is no reason at all to believe that what I am really aware of is a balance among a set of hypothetical conative impulses and organic sensations which these shapes cause in me. There is no possible means by which the alleged conations and organic sensations among which a balance is alleged to be felt can be brought to the level of conscious awareness and the assertion that they exist and that the balance of shape which we seem to see is really a balance among unconscious conations is purely gratuitous.

Language is of course very poor in words with which to describe the more complex qualities of visual and aural percepts and if we wish to speak about more than the simplest qualities of which we become aware in perception, we must very soon have recourse to figurative language. Thus we describe a melody as rippling or dancing, a shape as heavy or soaring, not because we think that the shape really soars or that the melody dances but because we have no non-metaphorical words with which to describe the qualities of which we are aware. It is still more difficult to find language in which to communicate our perceptions of the more complex over-all structural qualities of which we are from time to time aware in more complicated groups of shapes or sets of sounds such as pictures or musical compositions. We say that pictorial structures are ill-balanced, harmonious, rhythmic, baroque, and so on, conscious that our words are woefully inadequate to describe the qualities which occupy our attention. But to say that objective awareness in perception ceases where language becomes inadequate to describe it is pure obscurantism and seems clearly contradicted by experienced fact. It is the sort of belief which could only have gained currency in an age habituated to accept the truth of many apparent paradoxes if only they are uttered in the name of science. It is no more likely that when I describe a shape or a melody as 'soaring' I am describing a subconscious impulse to fly than it is likely that when I describe a penny as round I am referring to an unconscious tendency in myself to walk in circles. Indeed there can be little serious doubt that many persons when using frankly emotional language about aesthetic objects are in fact using this language metaphorically and do not mean to refer to their emotions but to indicate perceptual qualities which they do not know how otherwise to describe. Often when people say that a melody is gay or melancholy they do not intend to tell you that they experienced a gay or a melancholy mood when they heard the melody; they are trying to point linguistically to a complex perceptual over-all property of the melody which was as objective in their perception of it as the difference in timbre between two instruments. When they say that a set of coloured shapes is harmonious they do not intend to tell you that they feel an emotion of harmony among latent conative impulses but to indicate an over-all perceptual quality of the set which is as objective to perception as the difference between orpiment and ultramarine.

The one smatch of plausibility in the asseverations of those who would make all aesthetic qualities into reflections of feeling derives from the fact that in our awareness of them perception often seems to merge into emotion. But this phenomenon is not peculiar to aesthetic awareness; it is a sort of thing which is apt to occur whenever we strain perceptive awareness to its limits. It is a fact admitted in all text-books of psychology that there are regions where perception merges into emotion. When a particularly delicate perceptual discrimination is demanded, as in the matching of shades of colour in costume designing or in the tuning of a violin string, the last fine sensation of difference or congruence is experienced as an emotion. In such cases the emotion or feeling is admitted to bring objective awareness of the same sort which we attribute to visual or aural perception. The same phenomenon is even more apparent in the more complicated cases where an artist, for instance, is required to compare pigment colours with natural colours in the three colour-variables of hue, saturation and brilliance. There is no absolute demarcation in experience between sensation and emotion. Moreover, in all aesthetic contemplation feeling and perception seem to be to some extent interchangeable. We have already noticed that there are some critics who tend to appreciate perceptibly, finding the intrusion of emotion disturbing rather than helpful, while there are others who appreciate rather by emotion. And in general emotional affect and perceptual alertness are in inverse proportion to each other, while there is no ground for asserting that the man who appreciates emotionally realizes the object better or worse than the man who appreciates perceptively. But you cannot draw a hard and fast line and say: 'this emotion was the indirect consequence of a perception aided by association and memory, but this other emotion was purely perceptive'. Still less can you say that when you *seem* to be perceiving complex aesthetic properties you are really experiencing emotion below the level of conscious awareness; that is to insinuate nonsense under the motley of science. And it is no less contrary to fact to deny that an objective awareness may ever be experienced as an emotion.

It may, therefore, be accepted that the aesthetic properties with which descriptive criticism is mainly concerned are objective to the perceptual situations in which works of art are actualized for appreciation and also that our awareness of them may in some cases be experienced partly or wholly as a feeling rather than a sensation. This is a conclusion of vital importance for criticism and should not be left in doubt.

The greatest single advance in practical criticism to-day may be expected to come about through the invention of an agreed vocabulary for communication of observations about complex aesthetic properties; and nothing stands more solidly in the way of this advance than the mistaken belief that it is good science or good philosophy to regard all such properties as illegal objectifications of subliminal emotions. Whether feeling can mediate similar direct awareness, genuinely objective in character, of a transcendental or ideal reality is another matter and one which introduces metaphysical questions concerning the validity of mystical knowledge in general. It is a subject outside the scope of this study and it is not relevant or important for criticism, which need concern itself only with the *convincingness* of individual works of art. This only need be said, that the claim of Transcendental Aesthetics, though possibly false, cannot be proved to be false by the argument that the alleged transcendental knowledge of aesthetics is mediated through feeling and feeling is by its nature a subjective state of the organism which gives no objective awareness. As has been seen, this conception of feeling originated in error and is psychologically outmoded.

To Dr. Carl Jung we owe a now popular division of personality types into the introverted and the extraverted. The distinction is described as follows by a contemporary psychiatrist: 'Introversion consists in concern with subjective experience, with the person's own mental processes and the world of his own thoughts and fancies; extraversion implies by contrast predominant interest in objective experience, in the external world of appearances and outside reality. Introversion has been compared to introspection, but it means very much more than that. The introvert is not simply withdrawn or self-absorbed, not merely preoccupied with himself; on the contrary he is concerned with the meaning below the surface of things, with the nature of reality rather than with its visible and possibly superficial appearance.'[1] The aesthetic theories which we have discussed in previous chapters belong in the broad outline to the type of the extravert. Realism regards it as the function of the artist to make reproductions of the external appearances of things, because he and his critics are keenly interested in appearances. Emotionalism holds that it is his function to influence actively other men's emotions. Expressionism also holds that the primary function of the artist is to influence the emotions of other people by reproducing his own emotions in them, although it could admit that he may influence them towards emotional experiences characteristic of the introverted type. But the concern with exercising a practical influence on the emotions of other people is in itself a characteristic of the extravert and Expressionism therefore belongs to the extraverted type. Transcendentalism on the other hand belongs to the type of the introvert. Its primary concern is to achieve awareness of the true nature of reality underlying the superficial appearances of things and the influencing of other people, or the communication of that awareness to other people, is secondary. It seems unlikely that the truth of the matter rests exclusively either with the extraverted or the introverted type of aesthetics.

[1] David Stafford-Clerk, *Psychiatry To-day* (1952).

Chapter IX

BEAUTY IN CONFIGURATION

Demander à une œuvre d'art qu'elle serve à quelque chose c'est avoir à peu près les idées de cet homme qui avait fait du naufrage de la Méduse un tableau à l'orloge et mis l'heure dans la voile.

EDMOND and JULES DE GONCOURT

Every Poem must necessarily be a perfect Unity, but why Homer's is peculiarly so, I cannot tell; he has told the story of Bellerophon and omitted the Judgement of Paris, which is not only a part, but a principal part, of Homer's subject.

But when a Work has Unity, it is as much in a Part as in the Whole: the Torso is as much a Unity as the Laocoon.

WILLIAM BLAKE

The spirit of the forms is one.—ÉLIE FAURE

WITHIN the last half-century a new conviction and confidence in the autonomy and high dignity of artistic production has taken hold of the minds of that small minority of men who are still moved by loveliness and beauty. They have seen that a work of art in its essence is not a means for the communication of experience from man to man but a newly created thing which exists primarily to be experienced for what it is in itself. Every work of art is an invention. It is autotelic. It is not made to be a duplicate of anything else in nature but to be something finer and better than nature gives us to experience. Art is not an expression of life but an addition to life and life's enrichment. This is a haughty, arrogant conception, but perhaps the only one which could continue to vindicate for artistic achievement the high importance in man's scheme of things that has traditionally been claimed on its behalf. In aesthetic theory it involves the repudiation of Realism along with Emotionalism and Hedonism, including the insidious doctrine of Expressionism. While it is not inconsistent with the Transcendentalist claim, it does not necessarily involve it and can stand alone. It will have art subservient to no functional purposes, neither representing nor expressing nor pleasuring. This new attitude is apparent in the words of Edward Wadsworth, who wrote in *Unit One*: 'A picture is no longer a window out of which one sees an attractive little bit of nature; nor is it a means of demonstrating the personal sentiments of the artist; it is itself, it is an object; a new unity expanding the idea of the term "beauty".' And with a different motivation, expounding the New Thomist aesthetics of M. Jacques Maritain, Eric Gill had already said: 'We are so very much aware of the personality of the man who paints on canvas representations or abstractions of landscape that many writers and critics suppose that the very being of art simply is self-expression, and that the criterion by which to judge it is the moral character, noble or otherwise, thus expressed. This is a great error. . . . What makes a work of art valuable is not the personality impressed upon it, but its essential goodness as a thing made. . . . Beauty is the criterion.'[1]

Once you stand firmly in this belief that it has nothing to do with the excellence of a work of art whether it represents, expresses or arouses emotions, it is no very great step to that etiolated preciousness of the old-fashioned 'aesthetes', who thought that the pure beauty of art is sullied and contaminated if it should serve any incidental purpose of usefulness. And indeed many of the moderns have fallen into this error of the nineties. The attitude which was succinctly expressed by Théophile Gautier in the sentence from the Preface to *Mademoiselle de Maupin*: 'Il n'y a de vraiment beau que ce qui ne peut servir à rien,' crops up again in André Gide's: 'L'œuvre d'art doit trouver en soi sa suffisance, sa fin et sa raison parfaite,' and in many another statement of contemporary critics and theorists. It is important therefore to realize that there is no logical connection between these two views. It is as silly to argue that because usefulness is irrelevant to artistic excellence, therefore a work of art is less good as a work of art if it is useful, as to argue that because a work of art is not created in order to make the fortunes of the art-dealers, therefore it is more beautiful if it is given away than if it is sold for a high price. We have no inclination for the vapid doctrine of 'art for art's sake' and it is not an implication of the theory which we shall expound in this chapter. What we shall be concerned with is a theory about the quality of artistic excellence, the quality in virtue of which any object is judged to be or not to be a work of art and to be more or less excellent as a work of art. This theory necessarily treats as irrelevant to artistic excellence all traits which works of art have in common with things which are not regarded as works of art and all attributes which are possessed by some but not by all the things which are regarded as works of art. It does not deny that works of art may serve many purposes, do serve many purposes, other than that of existing to be experienced in appreciation; but it disregards such purposes

[1] 'The Criterion in Art' (1928), published in *Art-Nonsense and Other Essays* (1929).

as irrelevant to artistic excellence, since they are obviously served by other things than works of art and not all the things which are classed as works of art do in fact serve such purposes. It is therefore a theory about one quality only of works of art—the quality in virtue of which they are classified and assessed as works of art. It does not deny that works of art have other qualities also and that these other qualities may often enhance their total human and social value. A work of art may serve as a solace in disillusionment or as a substitute for religion, and men may prize it for this and judge that as a solace or a substitute it is very excellent. But this is not the same thing as to prize it as a work of art; there are many other forms of solace, and all men who suffer disillusionment do not turn to art for their comfort and cure. We do not deny the personal and social values of art. But we shall try to keep clear the *logical* point that when you are judging about artistic excellence you are not judging about something else and when you are judging about something else you are not judging about artistic excellence. If we insist upon separating in principle the utility-functions of art from its own proper excellence, we are doing no more than the scientist who does not identify the application of scientific knowledge to industry with the disinterested pursuit of scientific truth. Less we can hardly do. For if art is allowed to exist at all as a distinct category of man-made things, it must have some quality of excellence peculiarly and specifically its own. We must then perforce go along with Charles Lalo when he says: 'Il faut bien que l'art existe quelque peu *pour lui-même* avant et afin d'exister *pour autre chose*, sous peine de n'exister pas du tout.'[1] Or at the least we must follow Henri Focillon's precept: 'Pour en poursuivre l'étude, il serait nécessaire de l'isoler provisoirement.'[2]

The property whose claim to be the essence of artistic excellence will now be considered is variously described as 'form', 'structure' or 'configuration'. And although nobody has yet succeeded in making very clear what it is, it is much more obvious what it is not. As often happens in the early stages of a new exfoliation of expanding consciousness, the unessential has tended to be regarded as improper; and the peculiar logicality of the French mentality in particular has inclined them to condemn everything utilitarian as detracting from the proud purity of uncontaminated 'form'. It is an attitude which is apparent in the pronouncement of Maurice Denis that: 'Toutes les qualités de représentation et de sensibilité sont exclues de l'œuvre d'art.' It is a change of attitude not confined to theory. It has gone hand in hand with revolutionary changes in the manner of making works of art, most prominently in the arts of painting

[1] *L'Art loin de la Vie* (1939).   [2] *Vie des Formes* (1947).

and sculpture. The artist who paints or sculpts in the 'modern' style will often go to great trouble to eliminate from his work all recognizable resemblance to natural objects; or if traces of resemblance are allowed to remain, they are no more than residual intimations in a totality where the pattern created in the artist's brain takes pride of place. The pictures of the modern artist are not anecdotal and he no longer reproduces figures which express emotions by their attitudes and gestures. If he uses the human figure at all, he rather ostentatiously banishes from his reproduction both sensuous appeal and emotional symbolism. The Still-Life is the type of modern painting *par excellence*, is indeed in a sense the only *genre* of which the modern style permits. For the human figure is reduced to an element of Still-Life and the emotional associations of landscape are negatived to the emotionally neutral condition of the casual group of insignificant objects from which the Still-Life is constructed.[1] That which is represented, if a painting represents at all, strives to be as far as possible without emotional significance or sensuous appeal of its own, which might distract the attention of the observer away from the qualities or emotion of the form-pattern which the artist has created. Even in the Still-Life the modern artist no longer attempts to represent realistically the sensuous properties of the objects which he portrays—the delicate sheen of silk, the bloom of flowers, the soft translucence of flesh. The only sensuous appeal that is left is the sensuous quality of the artist's own materials, the pigment, the marble or the bronze.

Nor are the shapes of the artist's subject to be realistically portrayed, or their colours; they are subordinated to, become simply raw material for, the formal pattern which the artist creates. Three methods of subordination are practised. Sometimes the shapes of an object may be progressively shorn of inessentials and pruned of everything that is otiose to the artist's conception until a new 'abstract' shape is born, which seems to be the

---

[1] In a somewhat different context Roger Fry said of the modern Still-Life: '. . . it is in the Still-Life that we frequently catch the purest self-revelation of the artist. In any other subject humanity intervenes. It is almost impossible that other men should not influence the artist by their prejudices and partisanship. If the artist rebels against these, the act of rebellion is itself a deformation of his idea. If he disregards them and frees himself from all the commonplaces of sentiment, the effort still leaves traces on his design. But the Still-Life excludes all these questions and guards the picture itself from the misconstructions of those whose contact with art is confined to its effect as representation. In Still-Life the ideas and emotions associated with the objects represented are, for the most part, so utterly commonplace and insignificant that neither the artist nor the spectator need consider them.' *Characteristics of French Art* (1932).

essential core of its form. This was the method of Brancusi, perhaps the greatest sculptor of modern time. Thus, as the American judge pronounced, his *Bird in Flight* 'has neither head nor feet nor feathers portrayed'. This is the method of abstraction proper, which has also been employed in the field of colour to some degree by Gauguin, more surely by Matisse, occasionally by André Derain and most perfectly by Paul Klee. A quite different method is that of building up from the observed shapes of a randomly assembled group of objects a new over-all shape-pattern invented by the artist. When this is done, the objects represented in the picture may remain recognizable and 'like' to various degrees, but the degree of their likeness is determined solely by the requirements of the artist's over-all pattern-conception. What they may not do is retain an individual significance or appeal deriving from their retained resemblance as reproductions and distracting from the sole importance of the total picture-pattern. Georges Braque is the most consistent performer in this method and Juan Gris perhaps the most talented. It is the method favoured by Ozenfant and Paul Nash and a host of others. Fernand Léger's paintings are usually 'impure' in this method, since their subject-matter retains an emotional reference to the factory or drawing-shop. The third method, finally, is that of constructing a work of art from what are sometimes wrongly called 'geometrical' shapes, building as it were *ab initio*. Artists who work in this style neither build up out of nor abstract from the observed shapes of natural objects, but favour the method of uninhibited creation. The influence of 'actuality' in paintings and sculpture of this type is no more than the generalized sum of the artist's whole visual experience in life. This is the method adopted by such artists as Piet Mondrian, Naum Gabo, Antoine Pevsner, Ben Nicholson, Barbara Hepworth in some of her work and—less purely—by Alexander Calder.[1]

When artists of this 'modern' school compare the visual arts with music, as they are wont to do, they are thinking of music as an 'architecture of sound' or in the sense of Combarieu's definition: 'La musique est l'art de penser avec des sons sans concepts.' They are not thinking of it in the way assumed, for example, by Bernhard Berenson when he wrote of the Venetian painters: 'Their colouring not only gives direct pleasure to the eye, but acts like music upon the moods, stimulating thought and

[1] 'The shapes we are creating are not abstract, they are absolute. They are released from any already existing thing in nature and their content lies in themselves.' Naum Gabo in *Circle* (1937). Mr. Willard Huntington Wright (S. S. Van Dine) has said in *Modern Painting* (1915): 'So long as painting deals with objective nature it is impure art, for recognizability precludes the highest aesthetic emotion.'

memory in much the same way as a work by a great composer.' Berenson has put his finger on what the modern artist strives to *avoid*. If they regard music as the ideal and the paradigm of art universally, it is because they think of musical compositions as structures of sound which exist only to be heard with no content of representation or associated emotion to distract from the perception of the structure and the aesthetic emotion provoked by its form. So they would make paintings and sculptures which are pure constructs of visual forms, existing solely to be perceived and free from all distractions of representational content or communicated emotions. Such works would, certainly, 'express' the personality of the artist in the sense that every highly premeditated activity is an expression of man's personality. But their function is not to express personality; it is to exist and to be experienced in and for themselves.

Both artists and critics have long known that the special characteristic of creative activity in the arts lies in *enforming*, imposing form upon an inchoate material. Johann Joachim Winckelmann realized that the central problem of art, its creation and its criticism, is the problem of form—and by 'form' he meant, not as Boileau had meant, composition in obedience to known rules, but something more intimate and vital, form as the expression of the 'true character of the soul'.[1] Goethe and the Romantics in general also understood that the artist is concerned with the creation of form. But Winckelmann was sensitive only to one limited mode and style of form—the particular harmoniousness of representational form which is to be found in the sculpture of late classical antiquity, whose superficial symmetry induced in him the tranquil and collected delight which was long thought to be the sole and certain indication of beauty. He did not distinguish between the form created by the artist and the form resident in the natural object which was the artist's model, and he would have been completely nonplussed by Gaudier Brzeska's statement that the sculpture of the Greek 'was derivative, his feeling for form secondary. The absence of direct energy lasted for a thousand years.' The Romantics in their turn thought of form as the outward manifestation of the soul and spirit of men of genius or as the revelation of transcendental reality; and though they talked of form, they thought of emotional vehiculation. The detailed study of objective form as such is traced back to Johann Friedrich Herbart (1776-1841), who, albeit with false aesthetic assumptions, tried by the methods of experimental psychology to demonstrate beauty of form in abstraction from the sentimental content of works

[1] 'Complete beauty appears only in the face of those whose mind is serene and exempt of all agitation.'

of art. His follower Robert Zimmermann[1] developed what was in effect an elementary phenomenology of form in opposition to the emotional 'empathy' of Robert Vischer[2] and the study of style in terms of form gradually became a guiding principle in a new school of art history. It received fresh impetus from the work of Wilhelm Worringer[3] on the Gothic and from Conrad Fiedler,[4] another disciple of Herbart, who originated the theory of 'pure visibility', maintaining that art is a special mode of knowledge as visibility and that the history of art is the history of the development and progress of this knowledge. In this century art historians have become more and more interested in studying the characteristic changes of visual forms as such, tracing parallels between the stages of growth from primitive to mature, from mature to decadent, among widely diverse peoples and ages and cultures. Henri Focillon in France[5] and Heinrich Woelfflin in Germany[6] believed that the evolution of artistic form has its own laws and 'dialectic', independent of any symbolic, iconographic or expressive function of the impressed forms. It is in the character of the forms that the style of a period lies and the style of any individual artist within his period. And it was believed that style in form changes from one generation to another by irresistible laws of development, independent of social conditions and individual taste. It was a new way of treating the history of art which has had a very strong influence even beyond those who belonged to the formalist school proper. In England Roger Fry became firmly convinced of the absolute value of

[1] *Allgemeine Aesthetik als Formwissenschaft* (1865).

[2] *Drei Schriften zum ästhetischen Formproblem* (1872-90).

[3] *Formprobleme der Gotik* (1920); Eng. Trans. *Form in Gothic* (1927).

[4] *Schriften üeber Kunst* (1913-14).

[5] 'Toujours nous serons tentés de chercher à la forme un autre sens qu'elle-même et de confondre la notion de forme avec celle de l'image, qui implique la représentation d'un objet, et surtout avec celle de signe. Le signe signifie, alors que la forme *se* signifie. Et du jour où le signe acquiert une valeur formelle éminente, cette dernière agit avec force sur la valeur du signe comme tel, elle peut le vider ou le dévier, le diriger vers une vie nouvelle.' And: 'Nous ne disons pas que la forme est l'allégorie ou le symbole du sentiment, mais son activité propre; elle agit le sentiment.' *Vie des Formes* (1947).

[6] 'Es gibt der Kunst eine innere Entwicklung der Form. So verdienstlich die Bemühungen sind, den wie aussetzenden Formwandel mit den wechselnden Bedingungen der Umwelt in Beziehung zu bringen und so gewiss der menschliche Charakter eines Künstlers und die geistig-gesellschaftliche Struktur eines Zeitalters unentbehrlich sind zur Erklärung der Physiognomie des Kunstwerks, so darf man doch nicht übersehen, dass die Kunst, oder sagen wir besser, die bildnerische Formphantasie nach ihren allgemeinsten Möglichkeiten auch ihr eigenes Leben und ihr eigene Entwicklung hat.' *Gedanken zur Kunstgeschichte* (1940).

abstract form-properties independent of sentiment, feeling or representation, although he believed (at any rate in his earlier works) that formal relations in painting tend to the realization of the one visual quality of volume. Even Émile Mâle, an enthusiastic student of iconographic significance in medieval art, wrote in the Preface to his *Art religieux de la fin du moyen âge en France*: 'Je reconnais sans difficulté que l'étude des formes offrirait presque autant d'intérêt que l'étude des idées directrices. Au fond la moindre ligne est d'essence spirituelle; le jet d'une draperie, le contour qui cerne une figure, le jeu des lumières et des ombres peuvent nous révéler la sensibilité d'une époque tout aussi clairement que le sujet d'un tableau.' Élie Faure, though in many ways opposed in principle to the configuration doctrine of beauty, nevertheless held that the changing styles and manners which characteristically represent changes of social and cultural conditions are expressed in a characteristic evolution of stylistic forms.[1] Even general criticism of the visual arts has changed radically in tone under the influence of the growing interest in form. Thus a recent criticism of Vermeer calls attention rather to structural properties in his work than to representational skill or to the sentimental significance of what is represented. 'We have learnt to appreciate to the full the effectiveness of his composition, with its audacious rhythm of line and extraordinary monumental power, even within the small compass which he favours.'[2]

This sort of writing may not tell much, and may show obvious symptoms of developing a new jargon of obfuscation, but at least it tells something about the picture *as a picture*.

Thus the theory that beauty is a coefficient of formal structure is not limited to the new modes of production practised by the modern revolutionaries, but is held to be valid of all art everywhere. It is valid in the sense that the advocates of the theory are prepared to classify any artefact as a work of art if it has the right sort of structure and to deny that any artefact is art unless it has the right structure; they are prepared to assess the excellence of any work of art in terms of its formal structure, not in terms of its representational realism, the emotions it evokes or the pleasure it gives. They point out—what is unquestionably true—that many less realistic pictures are valued by the majority of critics above many pictures that are more realistic; and they claim that the basis of judgement is not

---

[1] In his *Évolution des genres dans l'histoire de la littérature* (1890), Ferdinand Brunetière endeavoured to display the history of literary forms as a kind of 'evolution of species' proceeding by their own inherent laws of development.

[2] Tancred Borenius, Introduction to *Dutch Indoor Subjects* (1946).

the degree of realism but quality of structure. They admit that a good picture will give more pleasure than a bad one to a man who knows how to look at it rightly; but the merit of the picture consists, in their view, not in its capacity to serve men's pleasure but in its capacity to be looked at. They deny that a picture is good because it arouses emotions of association (symbolized emotions), whether these are communicated from the mind of the artist or not, and they set little value upon incidental titillation of the senses.

The theory is undoubtedly important to criticism and is less obviously out of gear with the spontaneous practice of criticism and appreciation than the other theories which we have considered. Its main drawback is an inability to define the quality of formal structure in virtue of which some configurations are judged to be good and others bad. Mr. Clive Bell said many years ago that the investigation of 'significant form' was the central problem of aesthetics,[1] and—if this theory is adopted in criticism— it undoubtedly remains so. Artists and connoisseurs are apt to say that good structure cannot be defined but that they can recognize it when they see it. They mean that it cannot be verbally analysed in conceptual language. But if it could not be *ostensively* defined by pointing to examples of its occurrence, it would be valueless as a principle for adjudicating the differences of critical judgement. And if it can be ostensively defined, some property must become apparent which is shared by all those structures which are good and absent from those which are bad. All that can be said is that we have not yet progressed very far towards isolating this common characteristic of structures which are formally beautiful.[2]

The theory involves a second, and less commonly recognized, difficulty. If the difference between a beautiful work and one which is not beautiful is simply a difference in formal structure, why do we *value* a work that is beautiful? We value a realistic work of art (if we are Realists) because it adequately fulfils some utility-function—calls up an exact image of our grandmother or puts us in mind of a pleasant bit of scenery. There is no doubt why we value a work of art if our criterion of excellence is its power to stir up pleasant emotions in us or to translate richer and more complex experiences from the mind of an artist into our mind. But if we judge a work of art to be beautiful merely because it possesses one sort of structure rather than another, why do we *value* the one that is beautiful,

---

[1] *Art* (1914).
[2] The mathematical researches of Matilde Ghyka, Jay Hambridge, J. W. Power and others have necessarily come to nothing.

why are we willing to pay money to possess it rather than some more useful artefact? As M. Paul Souriau saw: 'On me prouvera que toutes les proportions qui me plaisent sont dans tel rapport géometrique. Quoi donc? Est-ce pour cela qu'elles doivent me plaire et que je suis en droit de les admirer? La beauté des proportions, si elle se reduisait à l'application d'une formule arithmétique, ne vaudrait ni dans la nature, ni dans l'art, d'exciter notre enthousiasme.'[1]

Mr. Clive Bell's answer to this latter difficulty was that works of art which possessed 'significant form', a structural property which he could recognize but could not define, were the only artefacts which enabled him to experience a special kind of emotion, and he prized them because he very much liked having this emotion. This is not a solution which has given very general satisfaction. It is, however, pretty generally recognized that certain patterns of shapes and colours, or of musical sounds, or words, do have the power to move men emotionally apart from anything which they symbolize or represent and apart from any associations which they arouse. These 'aesthetic' emotions seem to belong in a class by themselves and are difficult to classify along with emotions aroused in other contexts of life. They may be pleasant or unpleasant in themselves, though most people who make a practice of commerce with the arts enjoy having them. It might be possible to make out a pretty convincing case for the view that human beings have certain ultimate and unexplainable 'tropisms' for particular sorts of visual and aural form-patterns—particularly for those which involve the obscure property of rhythm—and that the appeal of abstract art—the *aesthetic* appeal of all art, if this theory is true—derives from its power to satisfy these alogical and instinctive tropisms. There is no room for doubt that many people do display this sort of emotional sensitivity to the formal qualities of aesthetic objects, and it cannot be plausibly explained away as the result of unconscious associations and the consequent 'transference' of emotions from non-aesthetic objects to works of art. I do not think, however, that this explanation of why men value works of art as they do is ultimately sufficient. First, because neither the artists nor those who appreciate find in general that the emotions aroused in them directly by form account for more than a part of the value they ascribe to works of art, and we cannot legitimately violate the *data* offered by the makers and users of art in order to escape from critical dilemma. Second, because in the actual appreciation of works of art men differ strikingly in emotionality and the more emotional are by no means always the more sensitive; intensity of emotion, moreover, during appreciation

[1] *La beauté rationnelle* (1904).

varies inversely with concentration of awareness. And third, because the most abstract works of visual art—such as those produced by such artists as Malevitch, Mondrian, Nicholson—arouse in most people who are competent to appreciate them less direct emotion than is aroused by the works of Kandinsky, Arp, Lipschitz, which, though non-representational, retain some hint of organic or natural pattern. Direct emotions of visual form are often strongly stimulated by works of the Surrealist artists Miró and Tanguy; yet a large part of the emotional affect from their work is derived from a special mode of incongruity of juxtaposition and space-organization which is reminiscent of the imagery of dreams. It is difficult therefore to know how far the emotions aroused directly by forms may be due to symbolizations in the deep unconscious such as the psycho-pathologists read into the pictorial products of neurotics.

Elsewhere[1] we have attempted to work out a more solid and correct answer to the two difficulties which confront the theory that beauty is a function of configuration and the answer we found may be very baldly summarized as follows:

1. The kind of configuration which constitutes artistic excellence in any mode of art is the configuration which is known as 'organic unity'. An organic unity was defined as 'a configuration such that the configuration itself is prior in awareness to its component parts and their relations according to discursive and additive principles'. The quality of being an organic unity may be possessed by any construct in a greater or less degree and it is this quality which constitutes the beauty or proper excellence of all works of art. Coleridge vaguely anticipated this when he said: 'The Beautiful is that in which the *many*, still seen as many, becomes one.' T. E. Hulme had more than an inkling of it in his concept of an 'intensive manifold'.

2. Any construct which enters into awareness as an organic unity is apprehended 'synoptically' as a single complex whole of multifarious and intricately related parts; it is not apprehended discursively by summation of a series of rapid but discrete particular apprehensions of the parts and their relations. Such synoptic apprehension demands a heightening and tautening of awareness—visual, aural or intellective—far beyond the normal needs of practical life. Only works of art can demand or provide the material for such intense awareness and their apprehension in appreciation causes that heightening of consciousness, that enhancement of mental vitality, which critics have often noticed and attributed to other, inadequate causes. This is why the experience of beauty is valued. It is valued

[1] *Theory of Beauty* (1952).

because it makes us more vividly alive than we otherwise know how to be.

If these contentions are approved, they set the configurational theory of beauty firmly upon its feet and enable it to become a sound basis for criticism.

The historian pinpoints the characteristic style of any epoch or any individual artist, and shows it to reside in a characteristic form-pattern. He traces the evolution of form from one age to another, draws analogies between the form-patterns of epochs widely separated in space and time, and shows that the evolution of form, quite independent of similarities or differences in subject-matter, follows its own laws of development. If he believes, like Élie Faure, that art is an expression or a reflection of social conditions, he draws analogies between the observed changes in artistic form and parallel changes in the field of sociology. And here the job of the historian ends. But within any stylistic period the forms which are characteristic of that style are manifested equally in works of art which are good and in those which are mediocre or bad. As Venturi has recognized: 'Any scheme may be abstracted either from a masterpiece or from a work lacking in art.' It is the critic, not the historian as historian, who intuitively judges which works are good and which are less good within any stylistic scheme. In so far as he judges by form alone he provides pure *data* for the aesthetician who wishes to work out the configurational doctrine of beauty. In practice, however, most critical appreciations combine judgements about formal excellence with moral assessments of subject-matter, the critic's own sentimental responses and associative emotions to the work in its totality and various unformulated assessments of its utility-values, so that it is comparatively rarely that the aesthetician can know just what the judgements of a critic mean or the relative weight which these various factors have been given in reaching them. It is for the aesthetician to generalize from the *data* available to him and to establish those properties of formal configuration in accordance with which the excellence of any work of art is assessed by the intuitive judgement of criticism in any formal style and any epoch. Only after this is done can criticism have a sound basis for explaining and justifying its intuitive assessments. It is with this purpose in view that we shall examine further the conception of artistic beauty as organic wholeness of formal configuration.

1. *On the Nature of a Work of Art*

Unreflective common-sense tends to think of a work of art as some material thing with specific qualities and attributes—a statue as a piece of carved stone or wood with the attribute of beauty, a picture as a piece of pigmented canvas, and so on. But a very little thought even at the common-sense level, and without introducing any philosophic doctrine, serves to show that this naïve view is not tenable.

What material object, for example, corresponds to a work of literary or musical art? A poem is a specific set of words, which need not even become audible for the poem to be appreciated. A musical work is a set of musical sounds, which may be recorded on paper or on a gramophone disc, actualized by performance or merely imagined in memory. Musical and literary works of art are often *recorded* in a physical medium, but the physical recording is never identical with the work of art. There may be many thousands of printed copies of the same poem, but the excellence of the poem is the same whether they are well or badly printed. There may be many printed scores and many gramophone records of the same musical composition, but the musical composition is something different from any one of them. Nor should we try to define a work of art as the class of all recordings which are commonly called recordings of that work of art. For a recording is always a recording *of* something which exists independently of all its recordings and prior to most of them. A work of art may exist without being recorded and a recording may exist although the work of art which it records enters into no man's awareness. A book may never be read and a gramophone record may never be played. In the distant past folk-music was perpetuated solely by memory and even epic poems were handed down by being recited before they were put in writing. Recording is merely a convenient device for perpetuating a work of art and ensuring for it a wider publicity. It overcomes some of the more obvious limitations of human memory and renders unnecessary a personal contact between artist and performers or performers and audience whenever the work of art is to be actualized. Mechanical recordings like the gramophone and broadcasting are extensions of the system of written recordings, rendering unnecessary a direct contact between performers and audience whenever a work of art is to become the object of some person's awareness.

The recording is not the work of art and we do not ascribe beauty to the material recording. If we speak of a 'beautifully' printed book, we are judging it as a separate work of visual art, not as a recording of that which it records. A recording may be more or less accurate or more or less exact, but as a recording it cannot be more or less beautiful. When we speak of a work of art we refer, then, to an enduring possibility of a specific set of perceptions. We say the work of art is *actualized* when somebody reads the poem adequately or when the piece of music is adequately performed to a competent audience. And as we do not ascribe beauty to the recording, so we cannot without doing violence to the language ascribe beauty to any of the immediate physical antecedents of the set of aural impressions which occurs when a piece of music is actualized. We do not ascribe beauty to the bodily movements of the orchestra, to the resultant sound-waves, to the titillation of the aural mechanism or to the consequent cerebral excitation. For the purposes of criticism and aesthetics, at any rate, the work of art must be identified only with a characteristic set of sense-perceptions, and to this only beauty must be ascribed. What there is in common between the recording, the various physical stimuli and the set of perceptions is, presumably, a similarity of structure.

In those art forms where a work of art is not recorded but is *embodied* in a material medium there is usually one material object which is commonly identified with the work of art, and at first sight this identification seems reasonable. A work of architectural art is a physical building, a work of sculptural art is a material piece of shaped stone, a work of pictorial art is a piece of pigmented canvas, and so on. There may, it is true, when sculpture is a metal object cast from a clay model or when a picture is a silver-point or an etching, be a relatively small number of material objects each with equal right to be called the same work of art. And mechanical *copies* of a work of art may be produced in any number, as plaster casts of a sculpture or printed reproductions of a picture; but in such cases there is always a difference between copies and original which enables us to say that the original and not the copy is the work of art. But when a work of art is embodied in a material medium, it can be seen that we regard it as a work of art not in respect of all its properties of a material thing but only in its one function of being a possible means to the actualization of a specific set of sense impressions. A picture is a material thing only incidentally. As a material thing it may be used as a tea-tray or as a screen to cover a blemish in the wall-paper. As a work of art it is the enduring possibility for the actualization of a specific set of visual impression. Picasso's drawings in light may have been works of art but had no permanance except as photographed. A picture may be photographed, but gives permanence to the embodied work of art even without photograph. Thus a little thought serves to show that even when a work of art is not recorded but is embodied in a material medium, the material object is in no case identical with the work of art. It is not the material object of paint and canvas which is beautiful but the set of visual impressions to which it gives rise under suitable conditions. And a work of pictorial art is actualized only when some competent person looks at the material object of paint and canvas and receives the set of visual impressions embodied in it. A picture hanging in an empty gallery is like a gramophone record playing in an empty room or a printed book cast up upon a desert island.

Since the excellent practical work of Mr. I. A. Richards it is a commonplace of literary criticism that any two persons reading 'the same' poem will probably be aware of different poems. The same thing is obviously true of music and painting. This, it should be remarked, is literally true and not simply a manner of speaking. It is only a matter of degree of difference whether a piece of music is performed to a deaf man, a man who is tone deaf, a man who like the mathematician Lagrange uses it to stimulate concentration on something else,[1] or to a man such as Mr. Constant Lambert, who may be presumed to have had a very highly developed capacity for musical perception. It is only a matter of degree whether a picture hangs in an empty room, hangs before a blind or purblind man, or hangs before a man whose capacity for visual perception is little more than what is required for the practical needs of life. In these cases we must, I think, say that the work of art is incompletely actualized if the observer is inadequate and that the full actualization of a work of art requires as one of its conditions an adequate observer. Whether any two ideally competent observers appreciating the same work of art in the sense that they read the same poem, listen to the same performance of a piece of music or look at the same picture would necessarily experience the same work of art in the sense of exactly similar perceptions, is a question of great importance to criticism. So long as we are considering the purely perceptual act involved in becoming aware of complicated constructs of perceptual stimuli to the exclusion of emotional response, imaginal associations and reverie—which is what we intend by the word 'actualization' of a work of art—it is to be assumed that any two ideally competent observers would actualize in awareness exactly the same work of art when looking at the same picture or listening to the same performance of a musical composition. But in literature we are dealing with an art built up from conventional symbols; and words have no fixed and uniform meaning apart from implicit associations which vary from individual to in-

[1] Lagrange said: 'J'aime la musique parce qu'elle m'isole; j'en écoute les trois premières mesures; à la quatrième, je ne distingue plus rien; je me livre à mes réflexions; rien ne m'interrompt; et c'est ainsi que j'ai résolu plus d'un problème difficile.' Those who use music as an inducement to the dance are in no better case.

dividual and which nevertheless form an integral part of the meaning of words and word-groups in writing which is fine art. There can therefore be no assumption that any two ideally competent critics would, by disregarding private associations and affective reactions, become aware of exactly the same poem when reading the same set of printed words, or that either would become aware of the same poem which existed in the mind of the poet when he wrote them. It is, however, reasonably obvious that in practice any two persons looking at the same picture or listening to the same music are almost certain to experience rather different actualized works of art. It is also obvious that these differences are very difficult to communicate. When the difference is great, as between the actualized works of art experienced by a very competent and a very incompetent person when both look at the same picture or listen to the same music, the competent person may indicate verbally certain qualities and certain relations which exist within the total complex of the work of art actualized by him; the less competent person may realize that he is unable to experience these relations or qualities (an extreme instance is the colour-blind person who is unable to experience certain classes of colour relations) or that he has failed to perceive them but with practice and guidance would be able to do so. It is in fact one of the functions of descriptive criticism to induce such realization in readers who are less practised in appreciation than the critic. But when the two observers are both reasonably competent, comparison is apt to become impossible. For words are at present inadequate to describe the less elementary characteristics of works of art, and when critics discuss the relative beauties of works of art, or when they disagree about the degree of beauty possessed by any work of art, it is, as has been said before, proper to remember that there is virtually no possibility for them or anyone else to know whether they have experienced identical actualizations and are talking about the same work of art, or whether they have actualized different perceptive experiences from the same set of complex stimuli. It may be that no two competent critics who had experienced precisely similar actualizations of a work of art would ever disagree about its beauty, and if we exclude the variable idiosyncrasies of personal emotion there are strong *a priori* reasons for thinking that this may be so. But if it is so, we could never know it. Because when two critics seem to disagree about the beauty of any one work of art we can never know whether they have experienced the same or rather different works of art.

We say, then, that for any work of art to be actualized a necessary condition is that it shall be observed by a competent person and that the degree in which it is actualized will correspond with the degree of competence in the observer. Until this happens, and except when it happens, what we are accustomed to call a work of art is, strictly, only the potentiality of a work of art. A work of art is a perduring potentiality for the actualization of a specific set of perceptions.

In the recorded arts, of which music may be taken as typical, actualization requires a stage between the artist who creates and the observer who appreciates. This intermediate stage we call performance. In order for any musical composition to be actualized for a listener the record of the artist's creation must be translated into physical sound-stimuli by the performer. If the composition requires only one performer, the composer himself may fulfil the function of performer or even of performer and listener both. Or the performer may also be the listener though he is not the composer. But if more than one performer is required, this is impossible. And usually composer or artist, performers and listeners who appreciate are different groups of people. Literary art is analogous. The poet creates, the performer recites and the audience appreciates. The poet may recite his own works and act as performer as well as artist. Or, as usually happens when literary art is printed, each man reads the printed recording and recites internally to himself. Musical art consists essentially of the organization of specific structures of aural impressions and is therefore essentially sound, either physical sound heard or physical sound imagined. When a person 'reads a score' he imagines the physical sounds which he would hear if it were performed. As Constant Lambert rightly remarks of Schœnberg's music, 'a contrapuntal device has no more value than an unsuccessful pun if it is not recognizable by the ear alone'. But literary art is concerned primarily with the organization of the meanings of words, and their sounds play a relatively minor though by no means a negligible part. Hence it is possible to read a work of literature without imagining the physical sounds of the words as recited, though in doing so one loses something of the complete work.

Recording systems are of very different degrees of precision. Musical systems are the most precise. In any recording of a musical composition it is possible to indicate with some precision the different timbres of the constituentsounds and their relative pitch. Time relations can be indicated with equal precision, and by means of metronomic markings actual duration may be shown. Though this is not usually done, the degree of loudness may be indicated by 'phon' markings. Theoretically it would be possible to give a metronomic reading for every interval and a 'phon' marking for every note. Yet with the utmost precision of recording some latitude of interpretation is left to the performer, and I think it is true to say that a great executant can produce a finer work of art than that recorded if he is performing an indifferent composition. Probably this is not true when performance is by a number of executants grouped in an orchestra under a conductor. The recording of dramatic art is much less precise, leaving much more latitude to the performer. The record is more or less limited to the set of words which form a constituent element in the drama. In so far as the meaning of the words depends upon intonation, etc., the recording is without precision. And the element of action and mime which is integral to every work of dramatic art is very crudely recorded indeed. In ballet the system of recording is much less precise than in drama, but the latitude left to the performer is less. The inadequacy of recording is supplemented by memory and tradition.

It is characteristic of all art forms which are recorded that they exist in time. By this I do not mean that the recording persists, as a picture also persists, making possible the actualization of the work of art from time to time. I mean that each actualization is itself an extended process lasting through a more or less well-defined period of time. In a musical composition not only is every time-interval defined in relation to all the other time-intervals in the composition, but the total time required to perform the whole composition is more or less definite.[1] Some latitude is allowed to the interpretation of the performer; but if a composition normally requiring half an hour is performed in fifteen minutes, the performance will be bad. The same thing is true of dance, particularly if it is combined with music, and with drama, although rather more latitude of time is allowed to dramatic performance. In literature the words are arranged in a 'before-after' sequence, but the time-interval is quite indefinite; one person may read a book twice or three times as quickly as another. Yet some period of time is always required to read a book. The relation of the plastic arts to time is very different. We may look at a picture a long time or a short time. Usually we look at it for a number of short periods in rapid succession and 'see more in it' on each occasion, as we like to hear a piece of music performed several times in order to know it thoroughly. Yet there is no reason why, if we were good enough, we should not be able to see and appreciate a picture completely in one 'specious present'. The actualization of pictorial art does not require time in the same sense that the performance of music or the reading of literature requires time. Now this characteristic of actualization by performance in time, even if

[1] 'A time-art by its nature demands a period of time within which to be itself.' A. A. Mendilow, *Time and the Novel* (1952).

the period of time required is largely dependent upon the observer as in reading a book, introduces additional complications for appreciation. When you listen to music the attention must be focused and concentrated evenly throughout the period of the performance, as when you read a book your attention must be evenly distributed throughout the period taken to read, even though there may be gaps and resumptions of reading. At each stage of the actualization what has already been heard or read must be present to you in recollection, and at no point in the process can you know or appreciate the work of art as a whole, because the whole work of art is not actualized for you until the performance or the reading has been completed. Your appreciation of the whole must involve the imaginal re-presentation or re-collection of the whole experienced, and although the process of actualization in experience may be extended through a relatively long duration, the act of recollection for appreciation may be psychologically very brief. When you judge a piece of music or think of it as a work of art, you usually combine your recollections of a number of occasions on which you have heard it, each hearing enabling you to know it more fully, to form a more precise and more complete imaginal impression of it; so when you judge a picture, your judgement is usually a result of a composite blending of many occasions on which you have looked at it, each occasion giving you a fuller knowledge of it. But in the case of music, and not in the case of pictorial art, each actualization is extended in time and each particular appreciation is the result of an imaginal recollection in which the time-intervals of the actualized work of art no longer have actual duration. This is a matter which concerns the psychology of appreciation but which arises necessarily from the difference in the nature of various art forms.

I have mentioned two ways in which every work of art is more or less indefinite. The first is due to variations in appreciative capacity. We are all aware that as we come to know a work of art better it changes for us, we see more in it, it becomes richer and more closely and delicately organized. We can never tell just how far this process may go, whether we have achieved the complete actualization of an ideally perfect appreciative capacity or whether we are beginning to get bored because we have reached only the limits of our own appreciative acuity. Nor can any one man know precisely what set of perceptual experiences is actualized by another when both are, as we say, appreciating the same work of art. The second source of indefiniteness is due to the inadequacies of systems of recording and is a liability only of those art forms which are recorded. It is really a limitation of *publicity*. A musical work may be absolutely definite in the mind of the composer and yet each one of innumerable performances will display differences of interpretation. I wish now to refer to a third type of indefiniteness which may be intrinsic to the work of art itself and not dependent either upon differences of appreciative capacity or upon limitations in the system of recording. We have said that a work of art is an enduring possibility for the actualization of a characteristic set of perceptual experiences. It is a specific organization of visual, aural or other experience. Now any set of sense-impressions may be organized with more or less coherence, more or less loosely. If you open your eyes and look out of the window you will obtain a specific set of visual experiences, your visual field, which is very loosely organized. Ordinarily you proceed to organize it unconsciously into the material things of which your percepts are the signs. You see green leaves, trees, a road, houses on the other side of the road, people passing along the road and so on. But the same set of percepts is capable of being organized in innumerable other ways—which is why we can, for example, read strange shapes into clouds and shadows. Nor are the various parts of your visual field closely knit together. If a cart passes along the street obscuring part of the houses opposite, everything else in your visual field seems to go on unaltered. But a work of art is a very highly and tightly organized set of impressions. The organization is not loose but compact, and whenever a change is made, whether by addition or by subtraction, in any part of the set of impressions, the effects of the change involve the whole set. It is this compactness of organization which differentiates a work of art from a mechanical reproduction of a natural scene. The set of impressions which is actualized in a work of art has only one organization, not many possible organizations; and in this statement is involved the statement that if any change is made in the set, the whole organization is upset and not only a part of it.

It is clear that not all works of art achieve the same intrinsic compactness of organization. Sometimes in listening to a piece of music you are aware, like Mr. Clive Bell, of a few scattered melodies, a few pleasant harmonies, an exciting rhythm, and so on, but no superimposed organization and no greater unity. And the limitation of your awareness may be due to the inadequacy of your appreciative powers or it may be due to the inadequacy of the music—there may *be* no greater organizational unity than you have noticed. If that is the case, the piece is a poor work of art. So too a picture, if it is a poor work of art, will lack organizational compactness. Any work of art which is loosely organized is intrinsically indefinite; a number of organizations are equally valid and none is exclusively imposed. Intrinsic indefiniteness is a defect in a work of art and organizational compactness is a large part, if not the whole, of what we mean by beauty. It is that in which a work of art, as a set of perceptual impressions, differs from experience which is not artistically enformed.

Definiteness in this sense must not be confused with sharp differentiations between the parts; a landscape by Turner may be as definite in the sense of organizational unity as a landscape by Canaletto. Nor must it be confused with complexity. An apparently simple drawing by Tiepolo may be more compactly organized than a complicated drawing by Laura Knight. It is manifested in the power of 'coercion', which means that the definite work of art can be actualized in only one way by all competent observers, whereas the indefinite work of art leaves open a variety of possibilities of actualization because in itself it is indefinitely organized and imprecise. We must, therefore, modify our earlier assumption by saying that any two ideally competent observers will actualize the same work of art when looking at the same picture or hearing the same music only provided that the work of art is itself ideally well organized and without any intrinsic indefiniteness or imprecision. If the work of art falls short of this, the experienced actualizations of different observers at the same level of competence are likely to be different.

This definiteness or compactness of organization which allows only one competent actualization is the quality often spoken of as 'organic form' and is the nearest anyone has yet come to a definition of beauty in works of art.

2. Organic Unity as an Aesthetic Principle

In considering the nature of a work of art and how it penetrates to awareness we were led to the view that works of art are essentially *organized* constructs of perceptual impressions and that they are organized at different degrees of compactness. We shall now examine the sort of organization which is characteristic of all aesthetic objects and we shall show that the sort of organization known as 'organic unity' is peculiar to them and constituent of their excellence as works of art.

The conception of an organic unity or an organic whole is not peculiar to aesthetics. It has been rather extensively employed in certain Idealistic schools of philosophy and in certain types of philosophical biology. But it has remained an extremely elusive notion, and precision in its definition has rarely been achieved, so that you can rarely gather what any philosopher intends to mean by it from what he says about it. In aesthetics the idea is as old as Aristotle, who said of plot in drama that 'the fable, being an imitation of action, should be an imitation of an action that is one and entire, the parts of it being so connected that if any one of them be either transposed or taken away, the whole will be destroyed or changed; for whatever may be either retained or omitted, without making any sensible difference, is not properly a part'. In ancient criticism the idea of organic unity became current under the name 'congruity' or 'concinnity' and it has ever remained a subsidiary principle of criticism though never clearly co-ordinated with the other principles by which critics have judged and assessed the excellence of particular works of art.

In embarking upon a new discussion of the place which this idea of organic unity should occupy in aesthetic theory and critical judgement I propose to start from McTaggart's definition of organic unity and Dr. Broad's commentary upon his definition, because those are the only places in philosophic literature where the notion has been expounded with sufficient precision to be serviceable.[1]

McTaggart's account of organic unity is as follows.—Any complex whole is 'manifested' in each of its constituent parts and each of its parts is a 'manifestation' of the whole. He uses 'manifestation' in a special sense, which may roughly be indicated by saying that it belongs to the nature of any whole at all to have just those parts which it does have and as any *part* of the nature of anything is a manifestation of that nature, therefore the characteristic of having any part which it does have is a manifestation of the nature of the whole. It follows that nothing which is a part of any whole could have been a part of it if any other part of it had been different, since *that particular whole* could not have existed if *any* of its parts had been other than in fact it was. McTaggart rightly points out that organic unity in this sense belongs to every composite whole whatever, to a heap of stones equally with a symphony or a living organism. He thinks that people have been apt to notice organic unity more in the case of organisms and works of art than in other things because a relatively slight alteration of the parts of which they are composed may change a healthy organism into one that is diseased or dead and a beautiful work of art into an ugly or inchoate mess. But it is as true, if not so obvious, that the smallest change in the parts which compose a heap of stones will make that particular whole which was that heap of stones into another and different whole which is another and a different heap.

I am in agreement with Dr. Broad when he comments that the notion of organic unity as McTaggart defines it 'is certainly a fact and is perfectly

---

[1] McTaggart, *Nature of Existence* (1921-27), Ch. XX, and C. D. Broad, *Examination of McTaggart's Philosophy* (1933), Vol. I, Ch. XVII.

trivial'. It is certainly not the sort of thing which is meant by those who have used the notion as a guiding idea in aesthetics, for what they have intended—although they have not been able to define their notion very clearly—is a quality which *distinguishes* aesthetic objects from all wholes which are not proper objects of aesthetic contemplation and which is capable of being present in various degrees corresponding to the degree of beauty assigned to any aesthetic object. The notion of organic unity which is—or should be—intended by writers on aesthetics, is, I believe, much nearer to Dr. Broad's definition: 'I believe that other people who have called a whole W an "organic unity" have meant that W is such that no part of it could *have existed* unless all the other parts had *existed* and had stood to each other in the relations in which they in fact did stand.' Whereas McTaggart's notion of organic unity 'is merely that nothing which is part of a whole W *would have been a part of it* if anything else which is a part of W had failed to be a part of it'. I am quite sure, with Dr. Broad, that the latter notion is nugatory and I am sure that the former is important. Dr. Broad agrees that it is important but thinks that it is highly doubtful whether any whole possesses it. I propose to show that aesthetic objects are essentially wholes which possess organic unity in Dr. Broad's sense and that this organic unity is identical with the property which (in this chapter) we are discussing when we speak of beauty. I am inclined to think that human minds or what is commonly referred to as 'personality' may also be organic wholes; but the 'parts' of a human personality are not capable of any sort of separate existence outside the personality of which they are parts—they are analytically separable only —and I do not know whether the notion of organic unity can be defined in such a way as to be applicable to a complex entity such as a human personality which has no concretely separable parts. What is to be discussed here is the application of the notion of organic unity to aesthetic objects and specifically the contention that a beautiful work of art is a configuration such that its constituent parts could not have *existed* except as parts of precisely that whole of which they were in fact parts. Unless exactly this can be demonstrated and is intended, the notion of organic unity is, I believe, not only valueless but conducive to mystification and obscurantism in discussions of beauty.

But first it is necessary to correct the 'facts' about aesthetic objects upon which both McTaggart and Dr. Broad rely. 'The facts about living organisms and beautiful pictures or symphonies', says Dr. Broad, 'are these. A whole which had differed very slightly in the nature of its parts from a healthy living organism, or a beautiful picture, or an harmonious symphony, would have been a monster or a corpse, a mere daub or a mere cacophony, respectively.' McTaggart, in more emotional language, says the same thing. Dr. Broad goes on to point out that in the case of an aesthetic object or a living organism the determination of the qualities of the whole by the qualities and interrelations of its parts is *intrinsic* and not *extrinsic* as in McTaggart's definition of organic unity. 'The qualities of a group might be profoundly changed by a slight *rearrangement* of its members. This would suffice to change a group which was a healthy living organism into one which was a corpse, or to change a group which was a beautiful picture into one which was a hideous daub.' With this we may agree. If you shift about chunks of a picture or a symphony you do as much damage as if you substituted something else in their place. Where we must profoundly and roundly disagree with both philosophers is their assumption that those wholes for which organic unity is apt to be claimed are such that a relatively small alteration in the parts of which they are composed would produce a relatively large alteration in the qualities of the whole. It lies outside our present purpose to discuss the case of living organisms, but in the case of aesthetic objects the facts are precisely the opposite of what is asserted. So far from being particularly susceptible to slight changes, an aesthetic object with any high degree of organic unity acquires a stability which renders it unusually resistant to changes and modifications of its parts. If you have on a sheet of paper a random collection of coloured shapes and lines which has neither representational meaning nor beauty, the change to the properties of the collection will be exactly proportional to the extent of the changes you may make in its parts, by addition, subtraction or rearrangement. If you play a random group of notes on the piano, notes which do not combine into the sort of organic unity which we call a melody, then the change to the group will be exactly equivalent to the amount of changes you may make in the notes of which it is composed. (This language of equivalence is probably not strictly correct, but it is invited by Broad's or McTaggart's use of comparative terms such as 'slight' and 'profoundly'.) A melody on the other hand has a stability and persistence which renders it highly resistant to changes in its parts. Pitch, volume and timbre may be changed and the melody will remain the same, its 'organic' properties unaltered. A melody may be whistled or sung, played on the piano, the violin or the musical saw. Rhythm may be changed without destroying its individuality. The same melody may occur first in duple and then in triple time in the same piece of music and still it remains the same melody. Furthermore, the pitch-intervals, which are the most important constituents of melody, must suffer not slight but pretty considerable changes before the melody as such is destroyed. Any melody can, of course, be played in a major or a minor key and remain the same melody. But more than this, a poor executant may alter many of the intervals by inadvertently striking wrong notes, and still the melody persists. You do not say that a novel group of notes was played but that the player played *that melody* badly. It is impossible to say exactly at what point of badness the melody finally disappears, but in general it seems that the more compact and well organized a melody is, the greater its resistance to badness, the stronger its power to persist through changes to its parts. And the same thing holds true of pictures and sculptures. If a sculptor, lacking bronze for casting, were to purloin a leg from one of the unbeautiful equestrian statues which grace the streets of London, the public would be left simply with a representation of a man on a horse possessing only three legs. But though you remove the head, the arms and the legs of a beautiful statue, its torso will remain a thing of beauty and its beauty will be in a very definite sense the same beauty which once characterized the statue complete. Incomplete statues and fragmentary pictures are preserved in galleries and museums not simply for their historical value but for the beauty that is still seen in them. No more can substitution of parts destroy the beauty of a beautiful statue. If an incompetent restorer were allowed to replace the lost arms of the *Aphrodite of Melos*, the result would be a monstrosity and the aesthetic world would be in uproar. But when you looked at the restored statue the eye would not see a new and monstrous whole; you would still see the organic beauty of the old statue and the restored arm would at most be a distraction. The eye would not combine the old and the added into a new and ugly whole. The sense of incongruity which caused you to speak of it as a monstrosity would result from an *intellectual* judgement of incongruity between two things which, though set in contiguity, it was impossible to *see* as a unity. All works of art have acquired a stoutness of resistance to minor modifications, an individuality which cannot easily be destroyed, and a stability which seems roughly proportional to the degree of their beauty or compactness of organization. It is, I think, possible to draw an analogy, for what it is worth, with the qualities of human personality. A strong and well-organized personality will, as is well known, survive the stress of damage and vicissitudes, retaining those essential characteristics in virtue of which it was distinguished as a personality, where a weaker personality would be disintegrated and driven to lunacy.

All those who have fruitful commerce with works of art are aware of these facts. And what the aestheticians assert about organic unity in works of art is not what the philosophers assume. They assert not that a very small change in a work of art produces a very large change in its beauty, but that *any* change, however small, in its parts causes *some* detraction from its beauty. A typical remark from an aesthetician is the following: 'By this (organic unity) is meant the fact that each element in a work of art is necessary to its value, that it contains no elements that are not thus necessary, and that all that are needful are there.'[1] So put, this is no more than a re-affirmation of the belief which has been an aesthetic common-place since Aristotle, the belief, namely, that a beautiful work of art is such that it is impossible to add or take away anything, or alter any of its parts, without detracting from its beauty. If you substitute 'beauty' for 'value' in Mr. DeWitt Parker's sentence (which is what he intended), and define beauty as organic unity, the statement seems to be a tautology. But I do not think that it necessarily is so. What may be meant is that there exists a quality of compact organization such that, when it is realized, any altera-tion among the parts of the whole would reduce its degree of compact-ness. I think, too, it is fairly obvious that all works of art do not possess this degree of compactness, and if any work of art possessed it, we could not know it. Much as aestheticians and critics are apt to idealize, it remains an undeniable fact that works of art *can* be changed for the better. The great majority of works of art come into being only as a result of many minor and major changes by the artist during the process of creation. Sometimes an artist will make changes in one of his works, and changes for the better, after it has been made and admired for many years. And I do not see how anyone could ever be sure that any work of art was already so perfect that it could not be improved by any conceivable change by the artist. What does seem to be an empirical fact is that a work of art created by one man is rarely improved by changes made by any other man. And this seems to be due not to any intrinsic impossibility but to a peculiarity of the artistic temperament and the fact that no two men are made alike.

The special quality of 'form' which is distinctive not only of any epoch but of an individual artist of merit is known to pervade all the parts of a work of art; it is not only a characteristic of the complete work, and therefore if a work is known only in a very fragmentary state, a com-petent critic or historian can still often attribute it correctly to its author. Literary critics have sometimes asserted that in the case of writers with a highly distinctive style they could recognize any single sentence out of its context and that any sentence written by such a writer could only have

[1] DeWitt Parker, *The Analysis of Art* (1926), p. 34.

been written by him. I think that such assertions are apt to go too far. But there is no reasonable doubt that some single sentences are so distinctive in form that a sensitive critic well versed in the author's writings could tell who had written them. It also seems to be a fact that the formal property of organic unity, in which beauty consists, pervades all the parts of a work of art as well as the work as a whole. This is why sculptures and ceramics which have survived from the past in a very fragmentary state are nevertheless valued for their beauty. And it is why critics are able to estimate the poetic quality of writers like Empedocles and Moschus, although but a few scattered fragments survive from their works.

With these facts in view we may return to the question whether aesthetic objects are configurations of such a kind that the parts of which they are composed *could not have existed* except as parts of precisely the wholes of which they were in fact parts. We shall discuss this first in relation to visual art, because it lacks the added complication of the element of time in its actualization, and in a later chapter we shall apply the theory to literature, which is the most complicated of the arts.

An actualized work of art is, as we have seen, an act of awareness (or more accurately the objective content of an awareness). Except as actualized on successive occasions, a work of art only exists as a perduring potentiality. A work of visual art is actualized in appreciation as the object of an act of visual awareness and its parts are parts of the content of awareness. The quality of organic unity, if it exists, is therefore a quality possessed by a total visual field, as content of an awareness, in virtue of the manner in which the parts of the field, as parts of the content of awareness, are organized into the whole field. There are good and sufficient reasons why organic unity, if it exists, could not by any means be revealed by applying physical measurement, however accurate, to the physical things in which works of art are embodied or recorded.

We will consider then the structure of a visual field in awareness and we will consider first the facts of colour-interaction since these have been the most reliably investigated of the group of phenomena with which we must be concerned. The bare facts are now known to most people. If you look at pieces of uniformly coloured red, orange and yellow paper placed in juxtaposition, the orange paper being between the red and the yellow, your percept of the orange paper will not be uniformly coloured but will show a gradation from redder orange in proximity with the yellow sheet to yellower orange in proximity with the red sheet. The red and the yellow sheets will suffer analogous changes. And this effect occurs only when you distribute your visual attention evenly over the three papers, looking at them together; if you concentrate attention first upon one and then upon another, the effect does not occur. The sensory qualities of your visual field therefore change according to the way in which you fix attention upon it, without any corresponding change in the physical stimulus. Colour interaction works by contrast, each colour-area surrounding itself as it were with an aura of its visual complimentary which modifies in its own sense any other colour which falls within its field; the intensity of the 'aura' diminishes roughly (it has been estimated) in accordance with the cube of the distance from its source. The phenomenon of interaction applies not alone to hue (by which is meant the difference between the colour-quality of red, green and orange) but equally to the three independent variables of all colour sensation—hue, brilliance and saturation. It is therefore the case that what you see in any part of your visual field depends not solely upon the physical stimulus (the thing you are looking at) but partly upon what you are seeing in other parts of the field and upon the way in which your attention is distributed over the field. A similar interaction takes place between shapes in a visual field, although it has been the subject of less extensive investigation than the interaction of colours. But the facts are indubitable and are attested by all who are habituated to inspecting closely their visual experience. Heavy and clumsy shapes seem more clumsy and heavy when they are in the vicinity of shapes that are delicate and trim; square shapes are squarer when in the same field as rounded shapes; sinuous lines are more sinuous against a background of geometric pattern.

The higher, structural properties of those parts of a seen picture which are sufficiently large to have a structure of their own are influenced still more strongly by the structural qualities of all other parts of the picture. Such visual qualities as grace, delicacy, lissomness, obesity, heaviness, clumsiness, sinuosity and its opposite, and the hundreds of perceptible qualities which there exist no words to name, depend to a very large degree indeed upon the qualities of their environment. When you isolate attention upon the part, its structural qualities are very different indeed from when you distribute attention over the whole picture. Finally, every part of a picture has a peculiar quality which is often called 'insistence', which determines its weight or impact in the total system of mutual influences which determines the character of the field as a whole and of its parts as parts of that field. Degree of insistence may depend upon a variety of factors. It may be due to representational significance, it may be due to the fact that this part differs more violently from the parts in its vicinity in respect of some one visual quality (e.g. hue or saturation of colour) than the general scale of variations of difference in that quality through the field as a whole. But insistence is always determined in each part by the field as a whole.

It is therefore a fact that the parts of a visual field are what they are, and have the visual properties which they have, only as parts of the visual field of which they are in fact parts. You do not even need to change the field as a whole (e.g. lop off a chunk of a picture) in order to change the qualities of its parts; you can do this simply by switching attention. The parts are one thing if you attend to them in isolation and something different if you attend to the whole field.

We have spoken of distributing the attention evenly over a whole visual field or concentrating it upon the parts of the field severally. In some cases this can be done; but in most visual fields it cannot be done. In most visual fields the relation of interaction between the parts is such that the influences bearing upon any one part of the field are mutually conflicting, determining it to have different and incompatible qualities. If you *were* able to concentrate your attention evenly over such a field, to see it as a whole, no part which you saw would have any specific character at all because it would be determined to having mutually exclusive qualities by the various other parts of the field—which is clearly an impossible state of affairs. The result is that in looking at such fields (and almost all visual fields are of this type except works of art), you do not, although you may think you do, in fact see them as a whole; what you in fact do is to switch your attention rapidly from one section of the field to another section, never holding it still, and *apprehend* the field as a whole by a series of rapid intellectual comparisons and analogies between the parts you have attended to in segregation. But *apprehending* a field in this way is a very different thing from *seeing* it as a whole. We call the former process seeing it 'discursively' and the latter seeing it 'synoptically'. You can only look at a field synoptically if it is such that the mutual interaction between all its parts determines each part, large or small, structurally simple or complex, to have definite and specific qualities. It is this sort of structuring of a visual field which ought to be meant when it is called an organic unity. It is not merely that each part is influenced as to its seen quality by the parts of the field in its vicinity, or that the properties of the field as a whole are determined by the properties of its parts and their relations. This is true of every visual field. In a visual field which is an organic unity the field as a whole can enter into awareness in a single act of evenly distributed attention and the relations of the parts to each other and to the whole are such as to make this synoptic seeing possible by determining the qualities of each part (and of the whole) unequivocally and coherently.

I think it is as certain as any proposition in philosophy can well be that the parts of any such whole could not have *existed* except as parts of just that whole of which they were parts. In any other whole, in any other context, they would inevitably have been in some respects different from what they were. (This is of course not asserted of pieces snipped out of a pigmented canvas but of the visual impressions usually held to be determined wholly by the corresponding parts of the canvas when attention is concentrated upon the whole picture.) This configuration which we have tried to indicate by the term 'organic unity' is another aspect of the quality we have already referred to as *compactness*. It is, I think, the most important element in (possibility the whole of) what we mean by beauty as configuration. It is the common aspect of those things which are rightly classed by the critics as beautiful or excellent works of art within the many and various formal styles of artistic production which the historians of art have traced down the ages. It is a quality which is capable of existing in various degrees, as any quality proposed for clarification of what the critics mean by beauty quite obviously must be. There are pictures which you can look at synoptically and see as a whole only at the expense of some fading of definition in the parts, or if you concentrate attention to render the parts specific it is at the expense of some recession in your awareness of the whole. This is because they are not organized into perfect organic unity. Perhaps no picture has yet been made which is perfectly organized in this way; if there is, it will be a perfectly beautiful picture. On the other hand I believe that only works of art are capable of being seen in this way at all; the degree in which any work of art can be seen in this way is the degree of its beauty. The extent of the 'interference' between simultaneous synoptic awareness of the whole and attention to the parts is the extent of its failure to achieve beauty.

There are those assuredly who will complain that this account of an organic whole is too abstract, will ask that we display an example of an organic whole concretely, take it to pieces, hold up the parts to inspection, show how they are fitted together, then assemble them again, so that everyone may see and understand 'the works'. Unfortunately this cannot be done, and if it could be done, the whole would not be an organic whole. T. E. Hulme once said that 'if the intellect came across an intensive manifold'—which he defined somewhat as we have defined an organic whole, though less exactly, as 'a finite thing of such a nature that its parts interpenetrate and cannot be separated out'—then it would 'endeavour in roundabout ways to replace them by complicated extensives, and so would distort reality'. An organic whole cannot be broken down, because in the breaking down the parts of which it is composed change their nature and become something else. The relations in which they now stand, each set of relations being displayed in isolation from the whole, have become other than the relations in which they stood within the whole. And when you put them together again, these new parts and relations, you obtain another and a different whole, similar to the original whole in many superficial characteristics but lacking precisely the coherence and unified compactness which made it an organic unity. Hulme therefore concluded that: 'Obviously you can't understand, or be said to know in any way, an intensive manifold by means of logical intellect because by the very nature of the thing you can't analyse it, and so it is indescribable.' I think that this is true. You can know and describe logically in the abstract what an organic whole *is*, and this I have tried to do. But you cannot know by logical reason any specific concrete organic whole, and you cannot describe it analytically. You can know it only by intuitive apprehension of it as a whole in direct acquaintance. And the manner of this apprehension—which is what we call aesthetic appreciation—will now be described.

3. *Appreciation*

Appreciation of the beautiful is a skilled capacity which can be trained to greater sensitiveness and acuity by appropriate exercise or, as is more usual, thwarted and starved. Training is the acquisition of skill, and skill is acquired not by the learning of theoretical rules or emotional habits but by the proper conditioning of attention.

In ordinary life we waste no more attention upon what is presented to our perception than is necessary to becoming aware of its practical significance. We use our sensations as signs or 'clues' to that world of external causality by which our lives are adjusted, and it is a psychological law that as we are conscious of the meaning of a sign we are no longer conscious of what the sign is in itself. If you ask anyone what he hears at a given moment, he does not mention characteristics of sound—qualities of pitch or timbre—but he tells you, 'I hear a bell ringing' or 'I hear a cow low-ing'. It is almost impossible for a normal man without previous training to see the picture presented to him by his eyes. What we see is a field of external objects standing in certain spatial relations to each other and to the observer; we do not even see them in the shapes and sizes in which they are presented to our eyes but in the shapes and sizes we know them to be. We are aware of objective situations and not of sensory presentations.

In aesthetic appreciation awareness is concentrated upon the perceptual situation as it is presented, as the connoisseur savours the bouquet of a wine or the Chinese savour the qualities of jade. When you begin to attend to the sensations themselves, to see the picture which is before your eyes and to hear the sounds which your ear presents, you are making the first step in appreciation. If someone asks you what a picture by Kandinsky means, he is not looking at it in order to see it and probably lacks the capacity to see the familiar pictures of the National Gallery which he thinks he can interpret. Nor is it any otherwise with literature, which is apprehended by intellective and imaginal awareness. In ordinary life we habitually attend only to the fragmentary meanings of spoken or written sentences which have practical implications for the situations in which we find ourselves. But when language is literature and we attend to it as literature, our minds must be opened to uninhibited awareness of the full meanings of words and sentences. The man who asks what a poem means is asking a ridiculous question; for unless the poem is a bad one, the poet himself cannot say what he meant except in precisely the words of the poem.

In practical life we 'get to know' a presentational field by rapidly switching attention from one small segment of the field to another, picking out prominent objects in the field, noticing the relations which maintain between them, and thus by a series of discrete acts of awareness we attain a summative understanding of those aspects of the field which have practical significance for us. The older facultative psychology was apt to explain all perceptual awareness in this way as a summative process from discrete atomic perceptions. But the more recent 'configurational' psychology has drawn men's attention to the fact that in all awareness certain patterns or configurations immediately and directly leap to awareness without this summative process. When you become aware of the five-pattern on a die you do not first notice five individual spots, count them, and notice the relations of distance and direction in which each of the five stands to the remaining four, thus building up the five-pattern from a large number of separate and discrete awarenesses. Your perception of the five-pattern is immediate and primary. This is the mode of aesthetic awareness.

It is the essence of aesthetic contemplation that the whole field of presentation is seen as a single unified pattern-configuration with the same immediacy and directness (though not, of course, with the same ease and speed) as you see the five-pattern of a die. Such an over-all configuration cannot enter into awareness by means of the discursive summation of a number of discrete awarenesses of the parts of the field and the part-relations which unite them, because the parts are something different when perceived as parts in isolation from what they are perceived to be when they are seen in a synoptic act of awareness directed to the whole field. And this statement that they are different things when attended to as parts of the whole and when attended to in isolation is not a metaphor but plain and literal truth.

But only a field of presentation which is an organic unity can become the object of synoptic awareness as a single pattern-configuration; for the field must *be* a configuration in order to be seen as one. The essence of an organic whole, as has been said, is that it is a configuration such that the whole is logically prior to the parts and the relations between the parts; the parts are what they are in virtue of the over-all properties of the whole of which they are parts. So far as is known for certain, the only organic wholes that exist are presentational fields. And works of art are, by definition, presentational fields which are organic wholes. A work of art is a very complex and subtle organization of configurational patterns into a single organic whole and its apprehension with immediacy as an individual, not analytically by the classification and summative comparison of its parts, is what we have called 'surview'. This is what is intimated in the old definition of beauty as 'unity in diversity'. The excellence of aesthetic contemplation lies in attaining maximal awareness of the complexity and richness of the parts and the contained relations without losing grip of the essential prior unity of the configurational whole. Any relaxation in awareness of the whole distorts awareness of the parts on which attention is deflected; any inadequacy in awareness of the parts leads inevitably to imperfect, and not only imperfect but false, awareness of the whole. This is why a fine work of art is not easily exhausted, why you continue to see more in it the more often and the more intensively you contemplate it.

In the practical conduct of life but a small part of the mind is devoted to awareness of perceptual situations. We are also conscious of much else as well—of memories and prognostications, of emotions and impulses, of a whole range of practical interests and implications. Mental energy is divided. And in general the smaller the field upon which awareness is directed, the more vivacity our awareness displays; the more extended the field the more hebetant our awareness of it. In aesthetic awareness the whole energy of consciousness is focused into the act of awareness by the exclusion of all other interests and we endeavour at the same time to render awareness as vivacious as possible and to extend its scope to an object which taxes its powers to the uttermost and beyond. It is only in the contemplation of aesthetic objects that the full exercise of a trained perceptive faculty is called forth and stimulated to ever greater keenness. And herein lies the source of that high value which is universally ascribed to aesthetic commerce with the arts. For supreme human value is attached to the most complete and successful activation of the higher human faculties; and the intensification of consciousness focused wholly into the narrow channel of a trained faculty of apprehension has a value for us far beyond the ordinary practical values of daily life in which we are but half or three-quarters conscious and never fully ourselves. Only works of art can stimulate and offer scope for this heightening of consciousness in awareness. It is this effect, though not the true reason for it, that has been frequently noticed by critics who have recorded that they are never so 'fully alive' as when they are occupied in the appreciation of works of art.

Appreciation brings, in Pater's words, 'a quickened, multiplied consciousness'.

4. *Configurational Criticism*

From what has been said it will be apparent that the actualization of a work of art in awareness, which is its appreciation, is not to be achieved with fullness and integrity apart from great natural aptitude, concentration and cultivated ability. We do not, for example, regard the mild delight which people derive from seeing a rainbow or a pleasantly rounded pebble as exercises of aesthetic contemplation. Facile emotional reactions to hymn tunes or jazz rhythms have little or nothing to do with aesthetic appreciation. The act of entering into awareness of a complex aesthetic whole often indeed appears to introspection as an emotion. But it is an emotion different in character from the fickle and fleeting disturbances enjoyed by many people in passive response to the changing moods of a musical composition during the time of its performance and different too from the sympathetic reactions of an audience to the varied fluctuations of emotion symbolized by the actors on a stage. It is an act of unverbalized awareness so intense and so overcharged that it merges into emotion. The object of such an awareness can only be a complex organic whole re-created imaginally after a process of actualization which continues, in the case of the recorded arts such as literature, ballet and music, through a period of time or, in the case of architecture and sculpture, as the result of a number of partial observations which are imaginally combined into a single synoptic awareness. The organic construct which is the object of aesthetic awareness is always contemplated not as a collection of discrete parts but as a unity and a whole.

In a previous book I quoted a passage from Professor Santayana in which he speaks so pertinently about the nature of musical appreciation that I cannot forbear to reproduce it here. 'Both in scope and in articulation', he says, 'musical faculty varies prodigiously. There is no fixed limit to the power of sustaining a given conscious process while new features appear in the same field; nor is there any fixed limit to the power of recovering, under changed circumstances, a process that was formerly suspended. A whole symphony might be felt at once, if the musician's power of sustained or cumulative hearing could stretch so far. As we all survey two notes and their interval in one sensation . . . so a trained mind might survey a whole composition. This is not to say that time would be transcended in such an experience; the apperception would still have duration and the object would still have successive features, for evidently music not arranged in time would not be music, while all sensations with a recognizable character occupy more than an instant in passing. But the passing sensation, throughout its lapse, presents some experience; and this experience, taken at any point, may present a temporal sequence with any number of members, according to the synthetic and analytic power exerted by the given mind. What is tedious and formless to the inattentive may seem a perfect whole to one who, as they say, takes it all in; and similarly what is a frightful deafening discord to a sense incapable of discrimination, for one who can hear the parts, may break into a celestial chorus. A musical education is necessary for musical judgement. What most people relish is hardly music; it is rather a drowsy revery relieved by nervous thrills.'[1] The sort of appreciative experience which Professor Santayana describes is what Mozart was describing when he said—if he did say—that he used to hear one of his symphonies complete in the imagination and survey it at a glance. It is an ideal of concentrated awareness which few men, if any, are capable of achieving. But it is an ideal to which the critic must constantly aspire if he would progress to fuller awareness of the works of art which he alleges to interpret to others.

On the difficulty of grasping a literary work in synoptic awareness Professor Tillotson has recorded with engaging candour: 'When I think of this read book or that my memory throws up what I can only call a cloud, a cloud not very luminous, sometimes a darkness more or less "visible". If I think, say, of *Hamlet*, which like most students of English literature I know almost by heart, the nearest I can come at any one

[1] *Reason in Art* (1905), pp. 50-1. Quoted in *Theory of Beauty* (1952), p. 110.

moment to seeing it as a whole is to see a cloud, rich like shadows painted by Matthew Smith, a cloud that strikes awe as if it were of incense, but vague and ungraspable, a thing possessed clearly only in so far as I recall details of the play during the time I devote to musing on the cloud.'[1] It is certain that Professor Tillotson is not alone in experiencing this difficulty. And to know a work by heart, whether it is a work of literature or a musical composition, is not enough in itself to ensure synoptic vision of it as a whole. Nor is the difficulty of apprehending an aesthetic whole due entirely or mainly to the length of time occupied in the performance of the recorded arts or to the difficulty of carrying in the mind and recalling simultaneously to memory the successive features which went to make up the performance. A short work may contain a concentrated abundance of material implicit in its every part which may demand more effort in the unified apprehension than is needed for a work which displays a more leisurely development. Nor does the fact that a painting can be seen in the *coup d'œil* make it easier to apprehend as an organic unity of structure than a cathedral or a sculpture, in whose apprehension many successive glances must be combined, or than a poem or a symphony in whose actualization attention must be held taut over a greater or less duration of time. It is not.

The method which we have advocated of entering into complete awareness of a work of art as an organic unity is patently a counsel of perfection. Such synoptic vision can be fully achieved very rarely and by exceptional persons, if at all. And it must be remembered that the critic who would assess the value of individual works of art by setting them in comparison with others must hold side by side and simultaneously in his mind two or more works of art imaginally re-created. Then if this were not difficult enough, those critics who, as many critics do, would compare the whole output of one artist with the whole output of another must be prepared to grasp and hold a very large number of imaginally re-created aesthetic wholes for simultaneous assessment. But if it is an ideal which is beyond frequent realization, appreciation as we have depicted it must still remain an ideal towards which the critic must strive in his own contacts with works of art and to which he must endeavour to guide those who read his criticism. Appreciation is a constant struggle towards a perfection that is never achieved, and no man's critical work is successful beyond the measure of his own progress in appreciation.

It is a function of criticism to record and compare the results of complete synoptic awareness of aesthetic wholes and to describe those wholes in such a way as may aid others in their turn to enter into awareness of

[1] *Criticism and the Nineteenth Century* (1951), p. 25.

them more fully. Within the limits of each critic's appreciative powers it seems that configurational criticism may fulfil this function in three ways.

1. Although the literary critic's awareness of a composition may be as vague as a cloud, Professor Tillotson thinks that he 'must be aware of how the vagueness of one book differs from the vagueness of another'. And, he goes on, 'it is partly because he feels an inexplicable but reliable confidence in his capacity to keep these vague and subtle things apart that he is a good critic'. As an instance of successful and profitable description of a literary whole he adduces the phrase 'happy valiancy of style', used by Coleridge in criticising *Antony and Cleopatra*. This method of trying to crystallize the essential observed character of an aesthetic whole in a descriptive phrase is common to criticism of all the arts and is often referred to as 'impressionistic' criticism. It would be better to use the word 'suggestive' of it, reserving the word 'impressionistic' for that sort of criticism which purports to convey by verbal artistry the critic's individual and subjective responses to a work of art. For the descriptive characterization of aesthetic wholes is *objective*. It purports to name qualities perceived in the aesthetic wholes which from time to time enter into the critic's awareness. If it may sometimes be illuminating, it may also be crude, muddled, imperceptive or positively misleading. But epistemologically the statements which it makes are on a par with such statements as 'this apple is red' or—in bad cases—'this penny is virtuous'. Such statements are sensible or nonsensical, and if they are sensible, they are right or wrong, veridical or mistaken. As descriptions they are more or less complete, more or less apposite.

Apart from the usual vagueness of the critic's awareness, descriptive criticism of the sort which describes the characteristics of aesthetic wholes as wholes has two other inherent sources of vagueness. In the first place, by the very nature of the case all descriptive language necessarily names properties which, in order to be named, must be common to a large number of objects. But aesthetic wholes are in a high degree individual, no two are exactly alike and although they have properties in common, the unique quality of any aesthetic whole—which is what the critic would like to describe in words—does not consist in a unique selection among aesthetic qualities which many such wholes possess in common, but is itself a new 'emergent' property arising from a unique organization of such common properties. For this reason the 'essence' of any aesthetic whole—which is what the critic strives to define or to display—cannot be put into words, and the verbal descriptions of the critic are never more than approximations to an ideal limit. In the second place, the languages which men use have no vocabularies which cover even the moderately complex contained aesthetic qualities, much less the total or over-all qualities of complete aesthetic wholes, and for this reason all descriptions of such wholes must make use of metaphorical language. Linguistic characterizations of aesthetic wholes are therefore necessarily suggestive and lacking in exactness. But they are not for this reason subjective. They do not refer to individual reactions, which must always and inevitably differ from man to man. They suggest and endeavour to communicate qualities of which every man who is fully and correctly aware of the same aesthetic whole must be aware. They are right or wrong, not subjective 'impressions' which have neither rightness nor wrongness. They are vague and imprecise not only because the object which they characterize is vaguely before the consciousness but also and much more because the linguistic instrument is inadequate to precision in such matters. But it implies no condemnation to say that they are suggestive: indeed it is because they are suggestive that they may be profitable.

A critic who is able to crystallize his appreciations of aesthetic wholes in such phrases as Coleridge's 'happy valiancy of style' is commonly admired. The admiration is accorded, I think, to the linguistic artistry which enables him to express in words an appreciation which the reader, having experienced it, has been unable to verbalize to himself. And such partial verbalizations of shared appreciative experiences which the ordinary man, ungifted with linguistic deftness, is unable to put into words for himself no doubt have a real value. But I am inclined to doubt—though I am not sure of this—whether such linguistic characterizations of aesthetic wholes can ever lead another person to a correct appreciation which he has not already achieved.

2. The second mode of configurational criticism consists in the analysis of artistic form in the specialized sense of that word, and in this mode criticism overlaps the province of technique.[1]

---

[1] It is to be observed that the word 'technique' is apt to carry different implications in the recorded and the embodied arts. In the latter arts it is customarily used with reference to methods of manipulating the material—in painting with reference to the composition of the artist's palette, the manner of spreading pigment on canvas, etc. The analogy in music would be ways of lipping a flute or of bowing a violin. But in music 'technique' is used by the critics primarily to refer to the manner in which certain arbitrary rules and conventions in the combination of sounds are used in particular cases for the construction of aesthetic wholes of sound. In literature 'technique' commonly refers to the ways in which in individual cases the universal rules of grammar are adapted for the expression and combination of units of group-meaning or evocation.

The school of criticism which occupies itself with studying the technique of form—musical form or poetic form—easily degenerates into a barren and purblind academicism. External perfection of form is never enough to constitute aesthetic excellence, and nobody has ever brought to being a work of art by successfully adhering to correct rules of composition. The most technically perfect *seguidilla* is not necessarily a good poem. A figured chorale which achieves faultless quasi-mathematical perfection in inversions and fugal counterpoint may be no more than an academic exercise, although the same type of formal perfection undoubtedly contributes to the beauty of Bach's chorales. The form which can be analysed and submitted to rules is a mechanical thing which in itself is devoid of organic configuration. But perception of formal structure is an essential element in the awareness of any aesthetic whole, and the study of form, if it is pursued not for its own sake but as a propaedeutic to the appreciation of each highly individual aesthetic whole which an artist had created, may contribute much to the apperception of beauty while its neglect may stultify and enfeeble appreciation. It is significant that poets who write about poetry and musicians who write about music tend more often than lay critics to concern themselves with the technical aspects of the works before them. And in this sense technique, or formal construction, comes very close to organic configuration although it is not organic configuration. I have seen the truth of this matter nowhere better expressed than in the following words of Professor D. F. Tovey, musician and critic: 'The line between the technical and the aesthetic is by no means easy to draw, and is often, even by musicians themselves, drawn far too high, so as to exclude as mere technicalities many things which are of purely aesthetic importance. The greatest musicians, whether composers or performers, have often not cared to draw the line at all. They prefer modestly to regard everything as technique.'[1]

After giving a structural analysis of the first movement of Berlioz's *Symphonie Fantastique*, a piece which in 1835 seemed new and incomprehensible to many, Robert Schumann wrote: 'I believe that Berlioz, when a young student of medicine, could never have dissected the head of a handsome murderer with greater distaste than that which I feel in analysing his first movement. And has my dissection in any way been useful to my readers? My intention was threefold: first, to demonstrate to those to whom the symphony is wholly unknown how little in music can be clarified with a piece of analytic criticism; second, to point out a few high

[1] 'Musical Form and Matter', Philip Maurice Denecke Lecture (1934), published in *Essays and Lectures on Music* (1949).

spots to those who had superficially looked the score over, and then possibly laid it aside because they did not quite see their way about in it; and last, to prove to those who know the work, yet do not recognize its merit, that, in spite of an apparent formlessness, there is an inherent correct symmetrical order corresponding to the great dimensions of the work—and this besides the inner connection of thought.' Beyond this there is perhaps little to be said. The study of form is one aspect of the wider study of the use of conventions, traditional or personal, in the creation of works of art. If you do not perceive the form you can in no way enter into awareness of a work of art as an aesthetic whole. You cannot appreciate it. But if you direct attention to the form in isolation, as a mechanical and external thing imposed upon the material, you are again impeded from entering into awareness of the unity which is a beautiful work of art.

There is no doubt that configurational criticism can, by guiding attention appropriately to the formal aspects of works of art, facilitate and enhance the appreciation of them as aesthetic unities and objects of beauty. There is equally no doubt that the study of form in isolation (except as a preparatory exercise), attention to verse form apart from attention to the way in which the poet has in each poem individually utilized his form to heighten the compactness of organized meanings or attention to the quasi-mathematical aspects of pictorial form apart from attention to the way in which that form is made to contribute in each picture individually to the organic unity of presentation which is the picture's beauty—there is no doubt that such academic preoccupation with form frustrates appreciation no less than a correct apprehension of the functions of form enhances it. The critic must always endeavour to draw attention to form as an essential element in compactness of total organization.

3. The third way in which configurational criticism may function to facilitate appreciation is by the discussion and illumination of details. And for obvious reasons the bulk of all critical writing will be about details, about the contained isolable parts of any work of art large or small and the subsidiary relations in which one part stands to the other parts. For the analysis of abstract form is a specialized study which, while necessary to appreciation, cannot be fruitful if it stands alone; but the amount which can be said descriptively about any aesthetic whole, as a whole and undivided, is very restricted. Therefore the greater volume of critical work will certainly consist of detailed discussion of prominent contained parts and the means by which they are set and moulded together.

But here criticism is faced with a seemingly intractable difficulty. For according to the configurational conception of artistic beauty the contained parts of a work of art are what they are only in virtue of the place they occupy in the organic whole which is that work of art. The parts are what they are only as parts of the whole of which they are parts. When attention is directed upon them in isolation and they are looked at for themselves, they become something else from what they are as parts of the organic whole in which they occur. It is for this reason that common quotations often repeated from memory while their context is forgotten change violently in character, and melodies which are frequently whistled or sung out of their context may become banal and jejune. No isolable part of any compact work of art can be perceived as it is except within a total apperception of the aesthetic whole of which it is a part; specialized attention to detail not only deflects attention from the whole but distorts the detail which is being observed. And yet it is not possible to enter into full and complete awareness of a whole as a whole except as each detail is fully and clearly present to awareness, and a vague and indeterminate impression of an aesthetic whole can be articulated to greater precision and opulence only by achieving clearer and more vivid perception of all its parts and of the relations in which part stands to part.

The antinomy is mitigated by the fact that the quality of organization which pervades the whole and makes it what it is is to some extent reflected in each of its parts. There is a beauty in the torso of a fine piece of sculpture even though the head and limbs have suffered annihilation; and the beauty of the torso is in some sense the same as the beauty which belonged to the statue. In some sense and to some extent the characteristic quality of any highly organized, compact literary whole is recognizably reflected in each and every paragraph. When a musical composition is compactly integrated the quality of the composition is present in every section and you cannot without ruining it take out any phrase or segment and substitute some corresponding phrase from another composition—and this is as true of the superficially 'formless' tone-poem as of a Mozart concerto. It is owing to this universal pervasiveness of structure that attention can be allowed to oscillate between the whole as a whole and the various contained parts which compose the whole. And it is by this process of oscillation that aesthetic objects are studied and appreciation matures, as the whole in awareness becomes an increasingly vivid integration of articulated parts. It must be a process of oscillation. Exclusive and continual attention to the whole can hardly result in a more vivid and opulent awareness of the whole; the normal mind is limited in its grasp and capacity. But attention to details out of relation to the whole distorts the details themselves and their subsequent mechanical assembly results in the recreation of a bastard product lacking in unity and compactness.

The object of the critic must be therefore to direct attention upon the parts in their functional capacity with a view to clarifying perception of each part, and each grouping of parts, as parts of just that whole of which they are parts, inviting more vivid and alert apprehension of each part but at the same time displaying the nature of each part as moulded by its position within the whole. In literary criticism this method has been applied with considerable success to the study of relatively short poems by Mr. Cleanth Brooks. The critic who attempts it is attempting something which cannot be set forth in words. The words he uses must be suggestive. They must enable and induce the reader to see for himself more vividly, more correctly and more completely something—the work of art—which is not contained within the words of the criticism. If they do not have this effect upon a competent reader, the critic has strayed from true aesthetic criticism into the morass of academicism. But the critic cannot succeed unless he also has both seen the parts vividly and seen the whole with clear and undivided vision. Professor Tillotson has said: 'After all, the main reason why we read a book is to meet the moments in their vividness. We do not read it to have a memory of it, but to accompany its sentences from cover to cover.' This is as though we were to say that we do not look at a picture in order to see a picture but in order to discover how many delightfully drawn or interestingly reminiscent incidents we can find in it. Undoubtedly many people read books and look at pictures in this frame of mind. But we regard it as an attitude of approach which is antithetical to appreciation. While we admit that some critical writing which concerns itself with displaying and illuminating the details of a work of art may contribute much profit, we believe that the critic who sees the value of a work of art primarily in the details is impeded from achieving appreciation himself and is likely to obstruct others in the attempt to achieve it.

Chapter X

ANATOMY OF LITERATURE

In all speech, words and sense are as the body and the soul. The sense is as the life and soul of language, without which all words are dead.

BEN JONSON

But the aim of technique is that it establish the totality of the whole.

EZRA POUND

LITERATURE is the most complex of the arts because the material out of which it is constructed—the instrument of intercommunication which we call language—is not a purely sensory material of colour, shape or sound, but a compound of sensory and ideational material. The principles of structure which make any linguistic artefact a work of art are therefore inherent on various levels. In this chapter we propose to analyse those principles, which are the basic aesthetic principles of literary excellence with which the criticism of literature is concerned.[1]

1. Literature we call any structure in language which is fine art. Its characteristic excellence is literary beauty.

Language is composed from words, which are its material elements, as a house is built from bricks and an organism from living cells.

Words are vocal noises which have been adopted as symbols in the conventions of a group of human beings. A symbol is a thing which, becoming the object of attention, 'stands for' and therefore evokes in the mind an image or a thought of something not itself. There are, therefore, two things and not one thing. There is the thing which is the symbol and the thing which, by being evoked in thought or imagination, is the referent of the symbol. Words as things are modifications of vocal noise. The referents of words may be anything which can be thought or imagined for thought. We shall call the referents of vocal symbols their 'meanings', not intending this word in an exclusively logical or conceptual sense. The meaning of a word may be simple or complex, circumscribed or imprecise, primarily conceptual or primarily imaginal. The relation of verbal symbols to their referents is conventional, i.e. the

[1] This chapter is written from the point of view of configurational criticism.

referent of any verbal symbol is determined by the linguistic habits of the person for whom it is a symbol. If you hear a person speaking a language you do not understand, the words are *merely* vocal noise; they are not symbols for you and they have no referents in your mind.

The raw material of literature is therefore dual, the word-things which are the symbols and the meanings which they symbolize. Its beauty is also necessarily dual. There is a beauty of the words and a beauty of the meanings, and each of these beauties resides in the enforming of the material into configurations which have organic unity. In the most highly organized examples of literary art the beauty of the words and the beauty of the meanings are, it is claimed, organically co-ordinated and enformed into a higher, second-degree unity.

2. Of the two beauties the beauty of meanings is more important and contributes more to literary excellence than the beauty of words. Words as things are very trivial modifications of uninteresting noise and their efficacy as symbols depends largely upon their intrinsic insignificance as things. They do not ordinarily attract attention upon themselves. They can become the material of art only in so far as they overcome this habitual neglect and hold awareness to themselves as aural phenomena; but to the extent to which they do this their efficiency as symbols wanes. They become dense and lose transparency. Some attention to the sensuous quality of word-sounds seems nevertheless to be a *sine qua non* of most literary art, and some poets have concerned themselves with the endeavour to heighten awareness of the sensory qualities of words without detracting from their symbolic efficacy.

Physical language provides little scope for organization into constructs of beauty because as sound it is jejune, because it has no standard of uniformity and because its recording is extremely crude. Word-sounds are varieties of noise without the definition of outline that characterizes the specially produced sounds which are the raw material of musical art. They lack precision of timbre, pitch and volume. The 'same' word-sound may be sensually attractive when vocalized by one person, harsh and grating when pronounced by another. There is no ideal of excellence to which individually different pronunciations may be asymptotically related, as the production of good tone on a flute or even good singing tone. And finally, the recording of word-sounds in writing is immeasurably less precise than recordings of musical sounds. Writing has no means of indicating time-interval or speed, makes no provision for specifying pitch, timbre or volume. Therefore a literary artist who publishes his compositions must expect immeasurably less uniformity among their performances—their internal or audible pronunciation on various occasions—than is justifiably expected by a musician, and one who sets high value upon the beauty of his compositions as constructions of vocal sound should logically refrain from publication and have them recited to a gramophone. The reason for the inadequacy of the recording system in use is not far to seek. Writing was invented and perfected by men who were interested in perpetuating and communicating the meanings symbolized by words and interested not at all in the sensuous qualities of words as such; therefore they omitted from their recording systems anything which was irrelevant to the symbolic function of words. But whatever its explanation, the inadequacy is there and there to stay. And from elements lacking in intrinsic precision no very highly configured structure can be built.

Nevertheless and despite these initial drawbacks, some poets have set a very high value on the sensuous beauty of their words, a few going so far as to ascribe greater importance to it than to the beauty of meanings. And some critics have followed their lead, while all critics and all poets insist upon assigning some importance to aural beauty in the total excellence ascribed to any work of poetic art. We are therefore bound to examine what potentialities for the sensuous organization of word-sounds survive the imprecision of literary recording.

The aural qualities of words consist of some dozen different vowel sounds in any language, interspersed with guttural, labial and sibilant consonantal sounds. Verbal beauty is derived from the permutations of these elements, which have no very precise fixation but vary within pretty broad limits according to individual habits of pronunciation. The most important principle of their organization into configurations of beauty is *rhythm*. Rhythm is a characteristic of all modes of art which are recorded and where time-duration enters into the sensory material which is structured for appreciation. An analogous quality occurs in the visual arts and we speak metaphorically of 'rhythm' in architecture, painting and sculpture, but in its primary sense rhythm involves essentially the patterning of time-intervals throughout some continuous movement. It is a quality by no means easy to describe, and although it involves time-patterning, it is not identical with symmetrical regularity of patterning. With regard to the configuration of words in their sensuous aspect and in abstraction from the meanings they symbolize, I think that what is meant by rhythm can most usefully be indicated ostensively as follows. If you are in a foreign country and listen to the people speaking without understanding what they are saying, your attention fixes itself upon the *sound* of the words in a way in which it never does when the sounds of language function for you as symbols of meanings. And almost always, when this happens, the language—any language—seems rhythmical, more like music than a language which you know. The quality of which you become aware on such occasions is a quality that is present in all spoken language; but once a language has become symbolic for you, once the word-sounds have acquired meanings, your awareness of its rhythm lapses. Poetry which is dependent upon word-beauty requires the reader to image the word-sounds in his mind and to attend to their quality of sensuous rhythm more earnestly than he usually does in the day-to-day commerce of linguistic intercourse. Many poets and critics believe that the poet intensifies the rhythmic quality which is present in all or most spoken language and fashions configurations of word-sounds which are more rhythmical than the spontaneous utterances of discourse. It may be so. But so long as the present methods of recording are used it is obvious that poetry will have incalculably smaller potentialities of rhythmic structuring than music, simply because writing allows no precision in the indication of the time-intervals which are the essential constituent of rhythm in all aesthetic objects which are appreciated through time. When literary critics discuss word-rhythm they are always in fact talking about a quality possessed by sequences of words as bearers of meanings and this quality we shall discuss separately.

In spite of the poverty of the sensory material, some poets and many readers of poetry have professed themselves to be intensely aware of the configurational beauties of word-sounds and to have been moved by them to the point of ecstasy as pure structures of sound and apart from any consideration of meaning. In the Preface to *Fleurs de Mal*, Théophile Gautier wrote: 'Pour le poète les mots ont en eux-mêmes, et en dehors du sens qu'ils expriment, une beauté et une valeur propres, comme des pierres précieuses.' Some poets have gone so far as to claim that poetry should exclude meaning as antithetical to verbal beauty and have made obscurity their ideal.

'La clarté confine à la sottise; la vie des chiens,' cried André Breton in the *Manifeste du Surréalisme*. The cult of the obscure, the repudiation of meaning, goes back to the Symbolists, who were, however, never able to make up their minds whether they wished to exclude all meaning, only logical and conceptual meaning, or only meanings which had become trite and hackneyed. Their rather ambiguous attitude is reflected in the declaration of the Abbé Brémond that in order to appreciate poetry 'il ne suffit pas et d'ailleurs il n'est pas toujours nécessaire d'en saisir le sens'.[1]

[1] *La Poésie Pure.*

263

The more extreme 'purists' about poetry have claimed that a poem should, or may, evoke in the reader certain affective states intended to be evoked by the author yet unattached to any conceptual or imaginal content other than the (actual or imaged) sounds of the words themselves, as music (it is sometimes thought) evokes affective states by means of sound alone without the aid of any associative stimulus of ideas or images. The claim seems to be false and the ideal impossible of fulfilment. It is impossible first because vocal noises are too vapid, too void of malleable sensory quality, and their recording is too imprecise, for them to be made suitable material for configuration into artistic structures; and secondly because, even if the sequences of words used by the poet are innocent of conceptual or ideational meaning, yet the individual word-elements inevitably retain meaning and associations.[1] The only way to eliminate meaning entirely from poetry is to construct a poem of nonsense-syllables—of vocal noises which are not words—as was attempted by the Russian Futurists and a very few others. The fact that no 'Jaberwocky' poetry has ever been judged by criticism to have literary importance, and that all poets who have experimented with this kind of writing have abandoned it, sufficiently attests that there can be no significant possibility of beauty in word-sound

[1] Julien Benda has said very sensibly: 'Il existe des états sentimentaux exempts de représentation, des états d'"affectif pur"; des états d'angoisse sans objet, de joie sans objet, d'enthousiasme sans objet, de tristesse sans objet; outre qu'on peut les observer dans certaines maladies ou sous l'action de certain stupéfiants, on le peut, pour nous tenir au domaine de l'art, sous l'action de la musique. *Or un art qui procède par des mots est incapable de nous procurer de tels états*; d'abord parce que, si nous comprenons ces mots, ils nous imposent une signification; puis parce que, si nous ne les comprenons pas, la nature musicale du mot—profondément distincte de celle du son—est beaucoup trop pauvre, beaucoup trop plate, pour nous faire à elle seule connaître un sentiment.' *Du Poétique* (1946), p. 21. Benda's grasp of this whole matter is exceptionally acute. He sees, for example, that though it may enhance the beauty of language used symbolically, musicality of word-sound is in itself neither a necessary nor a sufficient condition for poetic quality. It is not a *necessary* condition because we often judge works to have poetic excellence without apprehending musicality of word-sound—as in Latin and Greek poetry, although we no longer know how the words were pronounced or how the metres were vocalized. It is not a *sufficient* condition because there are works which we judge to be musical but not highly poetic. 'Cette musicalité peut même exister sans ce sentiment (poétique) et nous causer un affet agréable, en accompagnant des écrits dont le contenu est le plus dépourvue de teneur poétique; par exemple, eux de Boileau ou ces dissertations versifiées du xviiie siècle qu'on a appelées de *l'éloquence harmonieuse*. Réciproquement, la chose écrite peut nous donner le sentiment du poétique alors que cette musicalité lui manque, comme on le voit par ces œuvres qui demeurent poétiques dans une langue étrangère, où leur musicalité originelle, et peut-être toute musicalité, disparaît.'

alone, analogous to the beauty of music and entirely divorced from sense.[1]

The once exasperated controversies about the critical assessment of obscurity and lucidity led on to somewhat wider terrain. In an essay on 'Obscurity in Poetry',[2] Sir Herbert Read argued in support of the belief that obscurity cannot be simply deplored as a purely negative quality and a blemish, as mere failure to achieve that clarity of communication which is the primary virtue of language. In poetry, on the contrary, some measure of the right kind of obscurity may have a positive value by occasioning the 'direct impact of a sudden glory', may convey 'vision without meaning, concrete, synthetic, but held in suspense, contemplated without question'. He quotes Rainer Maria Rilke, who described the sensation as 'the vision of an unknown garden, embedded in glass, clear but unattainable'.[3] But the obscurity of which Sir Herbert Read speaks is a lack of logical coherence in conceptualisable content; it is not an absolute incoherence of content and still less the absence of any content whatsoever. Logical coherence is certainly not essential to poetic content; but content is essential to poetry. And *some* kind of coherence is involved in the organization of content which is the excellence of poetic art. The difference between non-logical cohesion and the absence of cohesion may be illustrated by the two following passages quoted by Julien Benda from the Surrealist poet Tristan Tzara:

> *l'année sera parmi les palmiers et bananiers jaillis du halo en cubes d'eau*
> *simple productive vaste musique surgissant à bon port*

and

> *la terrasse est pleine*
> *de rumeurs salines*
> *la robe et même*
> *les plis du soleil.*

In the second passage there is no logical but some ideational coherence and the lines may be thought to have some poetic quality. In the former

---

[1] Mr. C. M. Bowra summed this up fairly when, writing of the nonsense-poetry of Alexander Kruchenykh, in his *The Creative Experiment* (1951), he says: 'The trouble with "trans-sense" is that, although it is often amusing and sometimes effective, its range is extremely limited. It succeeds only when it deals with irrational, unintelligible sensations, and these form so small a part of poetry that they can almost be discounted.'

[2] Published in *Collected Essays in Literary Criticism* (1951).

[3]   *Singe die Gärten, mein Herz, die du nicht kennst;*
        wie in Glas eingegossene Gärten, klar, unerreichbar.

passage, although the words still retain sense and associations individually, there seems to be no coherence of any sort and it is probably devoid of literary value.

In the same essay Sir Herbert Read speaks of the incantatory use of language, quoting Paul Valéry as follows: 'What is sung or articulated in the most solemn and the most critical moments of life; what we hear in a Liturgy; what is murmured or groaned in the extremity of passion; what calms a child or the afflicted; what attests the truth of an oath—these are words of a particular tone and expression which cannot be resolved into clear ideas, nor separated out, without making them absurd or silly. In all these cases, the accent and inflexion of the voice outweigh anything intelligible conveyed to us; it is our life rather than our mind which is addressed—I would say that such words incite us to *become* rather than incite us to *understand*.' The facts are incontestable, as witness the mother's lullaby to her child or the Latin liturgies of the Roman Church. Not only Valéry and Brémond, but many poets and critics besides, have believed that poetry should have this incantatory quality, affecting the reader as a liturgy or the recitation of a magical formula affects him. But the incantatory effect belongs to *spoken* language, and usually depends to a greater or less extent upon the circumstances of its use, an accepted system of beliefs, and so on. Meaning may indeed be quite irrelevant to it and any sequence of meaningless words *may* serve equally well for incantation. Some poetry does rely in part upon incantatory effects, requiring to be spoken either audibly or internally. When it does so, it is limited by the imprecision of written recording and the unreliability of performance. There exists no one capable of saying that one sequence of words which he does not understand is more or less incantatory than another, since *any* sequence may become incantatory if spoken in the right way and in suitable circumstances to a person who does not attend to the meaning.

'Words', as Mr. Bowra has admirably said, 'are limited by their meanings. The most melodious and associative poetry cannot hope to snatch his honours from the musician. Attempts have been made to justify Mallarmé's belief, but the facts are against him. His own confession "Mon art est une impasse", his failure to write his great poem, the failure of his apologists to show that poetry can achieve effects comparable to those of music, the unalterable truth that words cannot be divorced from their meanings, all these show that his doctrine was faulty.'[1] If there *could* be a melodious beauty of words as pure aural sensation divorced from symbolic function, it would be most effectively manifested in configurations of

[1] *The Heritage of Symbolism* (1943).

vocal sounds made up from elements which were not known words, that had no sense. But there seems not the least likelihood that nonsense poetry has any future.

3. Apart from their sensuous qualities, words are instruments for the symbolic communication of meanings. And as instruments their use may be efficient or slovenly, artistic or inartistic. There is therefore a second principle in the organization of words into linguistic structures which is identical neither with their aesthetic structuring as independent aural things nor with the structuring of symbolized meanings into organically unified aesthetic wholes. We are to speak now of the arrangement of words into sequences such that the atomic referents of individual words combine into units of coherent meaning. And the meanings into which they combine may be units of conceptual thought or units of imaged thought (sometimes called 'mental pictures') or awarenesses of emotion or mood, which are also imaged though not pictured. (I do not include the evocation of emotion and mood, because I do not believe that poetry evokes other than 'aesthetic' emotions directly but invokes them through sympathetic reaction by presenting an awareness of a certain emotion in relation to a presented situation.) I am inclined to regard the principle of configuration with which we are now concerned as belonging to the province of craftsmanship rather than to that of artistic beauty, but with the proviso that I do not know how to draw a hard and fast line of demarcation between craftsmanship and artistry. There are in all the arts some constructs judged to be beautiful though they reach no high level of craftsmanship, there are masterpieces of craftsmanship which are antithetical to beauty and there is fine craftsmanship which is contributory to beauty. In making this necessary distinction between beauty and craftsmanship I do not wish to decry the admiration for good craftsmanship as such. I believe that delight in workmanship for its own sake has an important social value, and that our own society suffers from its deprivation. I believe that satisfaction with slovenly workmanship can rarely be excused even on the score of great beauty. Attention to craftsmanship is misplaced only when it ceases to be ancillary to beauty—or to some extrinsic utility-function—and is confused with aesthetic appreciation. A great deal of that part of criticism which is devoted to the analysis and appreciation of literary style, prosody, technique, is in fact an assessment of the qualities of craftsmanship. It is a necessary and important part of criticism. But it becomes aesthetic criticism only when, in each work of art under consideration, it displays the bearing of workmanship good or bad upon organic configuration into a structure fraught with beauty.

Libraries have been written about the principles of good writing, many contradictory opinions have been expressed and there is probably nobody who would dare to assert that he knows exactly what it is that makes some writing good and some bad. I have myself read a good deal of critical exposition of good and bad literary style, I have read a more than average amount of literature good and bad, and I believe that up to a point and in different degrees I can discriminate good and bad workmanship in six languages. But I do not know what it is that makes some writing very good, although it is more often apparent why other writing is very bad. I believe, however, that in the sphere of craftsmanship with which we are at this moment concerned there are objective principles of good and bad and that assessment is not a matter purely of individual taste.

In enunciating the following three basic principles of craftsmanship I am prepared, therefore, to be accused of niggling dogmatism although I am myself convinced that they cover, not certainly the whole but the greater part at any rate of what is meant by good writing—the more so because they are integrated with the aesthetic principles by which the literary excellence of a composition is assessed. And in basing myself upon these principles I have, I believe, the support of the practical judgements of criticism to a far greater extent than the theoretical lucubrations of many critics.

3.1. First *precision*. Precision or exactness is often claimed to be the supreme excellence of poetic writing and has become a fetish with certain critics. Yet the exactness of poetry is not identical with the exactness to which philosophical or scientific writing aspires and just what it is has never, so far as I know, been satisfactorily defined.

To clear the ground we may say at the outset that it is *not* what was in the mind of Mr. Stauffer when he wrote: 'To say that the language of poetry must be exact is to say no more than that it must truthfully reflect the mind of the poet.' As we have seen in discussion of the Expressionist theory of beauty, only the poet can tell whether or no his poem truthfully reflects his mind and he can only tell whether it truthfully reflects his mind to himself. When Mr. Stauffer goes on to claim that a poet's readers are to be the judges of his exactness, he is, therefore, imposing on them a task which is in the nature of things impossible to fulfil. He does indeed admit that the reader's 'pleased conviction that he has caught the unique personal thought of the poet in all its precision and completeness may be an illusion', yet he believes that this does not make the standard 'purely relative'. But when two critics disagree, each with pleased conviction, who is to judge, and by what standard is he to judge, between them?

The precision of language which is contributory to poetic excellence, the precision which is consciously sought by those modern poets who profess it as their aim, is, I believe, a combination of two qualities, which I shall call *conciseness* and *univocacy*.

3.11. Conciseness as we shall use the term does not mean aphoristic brevity. We do not refer to the quality of language exemplified by the famous message of the Spartans, 'Dionysius in Corinth' which, as Demetrius said, was more forceful than if they had spelled the meaning out in full: 'Dionysius, who was once a famous tyrant like yourself, is now living as a private citizen in Corinth.'[1] Sir Thomas Browne is in our sense of the word one of the more concise writers in the language. The meaning which we shall attach to the word is perhaps best indicated saying that it involves the absence of redundancy. In concise writing there is nothing which does not function, everything pulls its weight and contributes to the purpose of communication, there is no upholstery, nothing whose removal would not diminish the clarity and coherence which it is the object of good writing to achieve. Conciseness is of course a wider concept than verbal exactness, since it may also cover the absence of redundancy in the conceptual or ideational content which is structured into aesthetic unity. There is a conciseness of referents as well as the conciseness in the use of symbols which we are now discussing. Without confusing the two sorts of conciseness, the *Wen Fu* recommends both sorts as essential to good writing.[2] Mr. Ezra Pound was thinking of conciseness in the narrower sense when he said: 'Great literature is simply language charged with meaning to the utmost possible degree.' And he draws the perfectly valid conclusion that: 'Good writers are those who keep the language efficient. That is to say, keep it accurate, keep it clear. It doesn't matter whether the good writer wants to be useful, or whether the bad writer wants to do harm.' And, further: 'Incompetence will show in the use of too many words. The reader's first and simplest test of an author will be to look for words which do not function; that contribute nothing to the meaning *or* that distract from the *most* important factor of the meaning to factors of minor importance.'[3] When this has been said, the most of what needs to be said about efficient writing has been said. There-

[1] Demetrius, *On Style*, 8.

[2] 'Also, in both parts of the poem, the author again and again emphasized that good writing, poetry included, is always both cogent and concise.' Professor E. R. Hughes in his excellent commentary *The Art of Letters, Lu Chi's 'Wen Fu'*, A.D. 302 (1951). There is an almost verbal parallel to Professor Hughes in Quintilian: Ornatum est quod perspicuo ac probabili plus est.

[3] The quotations are from *A B C of Reading* (1934).

fore instead of breaking the canons of good writing by attempting to amplify what is already as explicit as it can well become, we shall be content to illustrate with a couple of concrete examples.

But first a word is called for on 'clarity'. Clarity does not mean easiness to be understood. The content of good writing may be difficult to understand because the meanings which it communicates are intrinsically difficult to apprehend, because they are new and strange or because they demand the jettisoning of ingrained and unconscious mental habits. In such cases good writing is difficult writing, writing that demands concentration and effort. Clear writing is writing which to a competent reader expresses fine shades of meaning with greater precision and univalence than ordinary people are able to achieve or writing which communicates complicated and abstruse meanings unambiguously. This is the skill which is claimed, not uniquely, for the poets. There may be a false clarity, as occurs perhaps in much of Mr. George Bernard Shaw's *The Intelligent Woman's Guide to Socialism and Capitalism*, where the style creates the illusion that the reader apprehends with precision meanings which are not in fact coherent. 'Meaning', again, as we have previously said, does not refer to logical or conceptual content only. There may be clearness or incoherence of imaginal presentation. Mr. Ezra Pound has made this point too: 'The term "meaning" cannot be restricted to strictly intellectual or "coldly intellectual" significance. The how much you mean it, the how you feel about meaning it, can all be "put into language".'

To illustrate the effect of blatant offence against the principles of conciseness we will choose—out of an abundance of material—a criticism made by Joseph Conrad not by applying text-book rules but from his instinctive feeling for good writing. The criticism occurs in a letter to Sir Hugh Clifford, who had sent Conrad a copy of his book of stories *In a Corner of Asia*.[1] Conrad praises the matter of the book but is severe upon the style: 'Words', he writes, 'should be handled with care lest the picture, the image of truth abiding in facts, should become distorted—or blurred.' He illustrates his censures by analysing two or three sentences from the story *The Vigil of Pa' Tua, the Thief*.

'. . . "When the whole horror of his position forced itself with an agony of realization upon his frightened mind, Pa' Tua for a space lost his reason." . . . In this sentence the reader is borne down by the full expression. The words: *with an agony of realization* completely destroy

[1] The letter is dated the 9th October 1899 and is printed in *Joseph Conrad, Life and Letters* (1927), by G. Jean-Aubry.

the effect—therefore interfere with the truth of the statement. The word *frightened* is fatal. It seems as if it had been written without any thought at all. It takes away all sense of reality—for if you read the sentence *in its place on the page* you will see that the word "*frightened*" (or indeed any word of the sort) is inadequate to express the true state of the man's mind. No word is adequate. The imagination of the reader should be left free to arouse his feeling.

'... "When the whole horror of his position forced itself upon his mind, Pa' Tua for a space lost his reason. ..." This is truth; this it is which, thus stated, carries conviction because it is a *picture* of a mental state. And look how finely it goes on with a perfectly legitimate effect. ... "He screamed aloud, and the hollow of the rocks took up his cries. ..." It is magnificent! It is suggestive. It is truth effectively stated. But "*and hurled them back at him mockingly*" is nothing at all. It is a phrase anybody can write to fit any sort of situation; it is the sort of thing that writes itself. ...'

Those who would see an example of true conciseness, as we intend the word, may read the opening paragraph of the *Religio Medici* or—in poetry —such poems as Vaughan's *The Night* or Herrick's *Corinna's Going a Maying*.

3.12. The second quality which goes to make up preciseness of writing is that which we have called *univocacy*. We are discussing now the fashioning of relatively short sequences of words in which the atomic meanings of individual words shall be combined according to the rules of grammatical structure into coherent units of apprehensible meaning. Univocacy is, in its primary application, a property of these *units of meaning* and is the property of having one and only one meaning, of being sharply defined and unambiguous of meaning. The meaning of a sequence need not, it goes without saying, be simple in order to be univocal. Some units of meaning are highly complex in their ramifications, many units of poetic meaning are so profound, reaching to the deepest levels of subconscious thought, that it has taken generations fully to plumb them. But, simple or complex, the meaning must be unequivocal. If a sequence bears three or four different and equally likely meanings, it is ambiguous and not univocal; if it bears three or four part-meanings, each contained in and contributing to its one full meaning, each part-meaning necessary to its full apprehension, it is univocal.

Words are not rigid and univocal symbols in isolation. They have not pre-formed shapes like the bricks of a house, but are rather like lumps of clay which are moulded into shape by the weight and tension of their neighbours. Some words have several primary meanings, but all words have a wealth of associated meaning, logical and emotional, an umbra of subsidiary implication which gives them as it were a distinctive character and a flavour but reduces the definition of their symbolic reference. When they are concatenated with other words into univocal sequences the effect of the organization into which they fall is to select and order the vague conglomerate of meaning which belongs to each word individually, emphasizing some meanings which it bears, rejecting others and instituting an order of importance among the survivors. It is usually obvious 'from the context' whether the word 'bow' has as its referent an instrument for shooting arrows, a part of a ship or an act of obeisance. What good writing does is to institute a similar order of selective preference among the multifarious and intangible secondary meanings which have become attached to individual word-symbols.

One of the aims of 'modern' poetry is to communicate with realism or 'truth' certain very subtle and unusual states of mind which existing language is incompetent to symbolize directly and which must consequently be indicated or suggested by imagery and allusion. The 'truth' to which writers of this school aspire demands extreme precision of language, for the slightest equivocality in the unitary meanings would make it impossible for them to get across to the reader the delicate and subtle referent they intend. For they wish to convey in language rare moments of experience in which sensation, thought and emotion so interpenetrate as to be fused into one, mental events which have not been communicated in language before. And for this reason contemporary writers are, on the whole, more self-conscious about precision than writers have been in the past. They seek

> The common word exact without vulgarity,
> The formal word precise but not pedantic,
> The complete consort dancing together.

It is the desire for univocacy which induced Pound and Eliot to harness together in seemingly incongruous pairing homespun phrases from common speech and extremely recondite literary allusions. They do this because the complex of meanings symbolized by a literary word—or by the literary words they choose—is usually more definite, more to be relied upon for precise communication to those who are familiar with the literary tradition in question and also because phrases of common speech and dialect, though often vague of logical content, are frequently very precise in their emotional implications. Thus precision is achieved. But it is precision at the expense of general communicability. For the literary element in this poetry speaks only to the learned and those who are well read, while the phraseology of common speech changes rapidly from year to year and what is completely precise when it is written may within a generation become strange and antiquated, demanding the merciless interpretation of a commentator. The only poet I have read who has succeeded in writing in this modern style poetry with a wide and spontaneous appeal to the unlearned is the Spaniard Federico García Lorca. His poems, though unpolitical, were spoken and loved during the Spanish Civil War by those who read no books. Señor Arturo Barea relates that a member of the Republican militia, forty-six years old and illiterate, would visit him with a tattered copy of Lorca's *Romancero Gitano*, asking: 'Explain this to me. I can feel what it means and I know it by heart, but I can't explain it.'[1]

> *Los caballos negros son.*
> *Las herraduras son negras.*
> *Sobre las capas relucen*
> *manchas de tinta y de cera.*
> *Tienen, por eso no lloran,*
> *de plomo las calaveras.*
> *Con el alma de charol*
> *vienen por la carretera.*
> *Jorobados y nocturnos*
> *por donde arriman ordenan*
> *silencios de goma obscura*
> *y miedos de fina arena.*[2]

[1] *Lorca, The Poet and his People* (Eng. Trans. 1944).

[2]
> *The horses are black,*
> *Black are the horse-shoes.*
> *On the police-capes glitter*
> *Stains of ink and wax.*
> *Their skulls are of lead,*
> *Therefore they do not weep.*
> *With souls of patent leather*
> *They come on the highway.*
> *Hunch-backed and nocturnal,*
> *Where they stir they command*
> *Silences of dark rubber*
> *And fears of fine sand.*

(The opening lines of the *Romance de la Guardia Civil Espanola*.)

Another method by which the modern poet strives to achieve uni-vocacy is by a special use of poetic imagery, and it is important to realize that imagery may be univocal or ambivalent. The good writer strives to make it univocal, however complex or profound be the meanings which it univocally bears. To illustrate, let us compare Shakespeare's familiar image 'Morn in russet mantle clad' with Eliot's

> When the evening is spread out against the sky
> Like a patient etherised upon a table:

Dawn has been personified in poetry since Homer's *Rhododactylos Eos*, and Shakespeare's image incites (without compelling) a mental picture of a healthy young woman in a brown robe walking amid the early morning dew, the word 'russet' arousing associations of autumn fruitfulness. But there is no great precision in the image evoked or in the emotional attitude to be taken up towards it; nor was greater precision necessary to the poet's purpose. In Eliot's image, however, the pictorial analogue of the first line is far less readily available, but the state of mind presented by the simile in the second line is much less equivocally defined. In the past poets were often able to rely upon familiarity in their readers with a traditional imagery in order to achieve symbolic univocacy. This was the case, for example, in George Herbert's

> O all ye who passe by, behold and see;
> Man stole the fruit, but I must climbe the tree;
> The tree of life to all, but onely me:
> Was ever grief like mine?[1]

As Professor Rosemond Tuve[2] has ably shewn, Herbert could presume that any reasonably competent reader of his day would apprehend the rich layers of contrasted allegorical meaning, with the combination of irony and pity, in these lines, because readers in his day were familiar with the allegorical imagery of Christian iconography, of medieval Complaint of Christ poems and of the Church liturgies for Holy Week. But there is now no traditional imagery, literary, religious or secular, with which the modern poet can presume the generality of his readers to be familiar. And the modern poet often, too, wishes to present with realism and truth states of mind which have not before been made explicitly the subject-matter of poetry; therefore no traditional imagery could exactly serve his purpose. But whatever the method, whether by imagery of by the careful

---

[1] From *The Sacrifice*.   [2] *A Reading of George Herbert* (1952).

selection of words, whether self-consciously or by an instinctive apprehension of the nature of good writing, univalence in the unit of meaning has been and is a main principle of stylistic craftsmanship.

The converse of univocacy may be illustrated by Mr. Ezra Pound's remark that: 'There are scores of lines in Pope that hundreds of people can quote, each person meaning thereby something different, or something so vague and general that it has almost no meaning whatever.'

3.2. We have now endeavoured to illustrate what is meant by *precision*, a conjunction of verbal *conciseness* and *univocacy* of unit meaning, as a principle of good literary craftsmanship. For the second principle to which we shall direct attention I know no name, but it may be indicated by the Horatian tag *ars est celare artem*: the art consists in concealing the art.[1]

It is a principle which is valid in all the arts and says, briefly, that that craftsmanship is good which is not noticed in appreciation; craftsmanship which is so good as craftsmanship that it is obtrusive and draws attention to itself is aesthetically bad. The reason for this is that in the appreciation of an aesthetic object the whole attention is needed for awareness of the organized configuration presented to awareness, and when you notice or admire the skill and the means by which the material is structured into an organic configuration, your awareness of the configuration itself to that extent lapses. You cease to be fully aware of the object in attending to the workmanship. There is, I suppose, a certain relation of balance which might be established between interest of matter or complexity and tightness of organization and sheer brilliance of workmanship; if the workmanship is too intricate, too finished and fine, for the particular configuration in which it is displayed, it becomes obtrusive and a person sensitive to literary style can hardly help being distracted by it.

Anyone who would observe for himself the quality of which we speak should read one of the *Shorter Poems* of Robert Bridges—or better still, if he is a classicist, one of the *Poems in Classical Prosody*—and then read alongside it a poem by Thomas Hardy. We will illustrate the quality in prose by three short selections, neither very good nor very bad, from the literature of charactery. In the seventeenth century it became the mode to write short character sketches in the manner of Theophrastus and a special style was developed for them, combining on the one hand acute observation set forth in pithy and pungent sentences and on the other all manner of literary artifice of wit, satire, humour, punning and so forth.

[1] In reference to the art of music D. F. Tovey has very finely said: 'The process miscalled by Horace the concealment of art is the sublimation of technique into aesthetic results.'

It was rarely that the artifice and the substance, the matter and the manner, were nicely balanced.

(i) A GOOD OLD MAN is the best antiquity, and which we may with least vanity admire. One whom time hath been thus long a-working, and like winter fruit ripened when others are shaken down. He hath taken out as many lessons of the world as days, and learnt the best thing in it, the vanity of it. He looks over his former life as a danger well past, and would not hazard himself to begin again. His lust was long broken before his body, yet he is glad this temptation is broke too, and that he is fortified from it by this weakness. The next door of death sads him not, but he expects it calmly as his turn in nature; and fears more his recoiling back to childishness than dust. All men look on him as a common father, and on old age for his sake as a reverend thing. . . .

(ii) AN OLD MAN is loath to bid the world goodnight; he knows the grave is a long sleep and therefore would sit up as long as he could. His soul has dwelt in a ruinous tenement, and yet is so unwilling to leave it that it could be content to sue the body for reparations. He lives now but to be a burthen to his friends, as age is to him, and yet his thoughts are as far from death as he is nigh it. Howsoever time be a continued motion, yet the dial of his age stands still at 50. That's his age for ten years afterward, and he loves such a friend that like a flattering glass tells him he seems far younger. His memory is full of the actions of his youth, which he often histories to others in tedious tales, and thinks they should please others because himself. His discourses are full of parenthesis, and his words fall from him as slowly as water from an alembic; drop by drop. He loves the chimney corner and his chair, which he brags was his grandfather's, from whence he secures the cupboard from the cats and dogs, or the milk from running over, and is only good to build up the architecture of a seacoal fire by applying each circumstant cinder. . . .

(iii) AN ANTIQUARY is one that has his being in this age, but his life and conversation is in the days of old. He despises the present age as an innovation and slights the future, but has a great value for that which is past and gone, like the madman that fell in love with Cleopatra. He is an old frippery-philosopher, that has so strange a natural affection to worm-eaten speculation that it is apparent he has a worm in his skull. He honours his forefathers and foremothers, but condemns his parents as too modern and no better than upstarts. He neglects himself because he was born in his own time and so far off antiquity which he so much admires, and repines, like a younger brother, because he came so late into the world. . . .

The first of these passages is from John Earle's *Microcosmographie; Or A Peece of the World discovered in Essays and Characters*, published in 1628. It ran to eight editions in the author's lifetime and has maintained a position in English literature. The second is from Wye Saltonstall's *Picturae loquentes: or Pictures drawne forth in Characters*, published in 1631, with a second edition in 1635. It is now forgotten, not altogether justly. The third was written by Samuel Butler and survives only because Butler also wrote *Hudibras*.[1]

3.3. We have discussed precision and the unobtrusiveness of craftsmanship as principles of good writing. The third principle is the control of word-sound for the enhancement of meaning. There is no doubt that the aural qualities of word-groups may add to or detract from the beauty of literature. When correctly used, the function of word-sound is to make the pattern of configuration sharper, tighter. But they do not effect this by adding a separate beauty of sound, which exists in the sound independently of the meaning, to another beauty of meaning which exists independently of the sound. The beauty of sound to which we now refer exists only in relation to meaning and emerges as an intensification of meanings or of the relations among fused meanings. While it is not limited to poetry, this element in literary craftsmanship is far more prominent in poetry or in poetical prose. Vernon Lee has rightly said: 'it is only in verse that any large and active effects can be obtained by the arrangement of words with reference to their sound'.[2] It is an aspect of poetical craftsmanship about which so much has been written, and on the whole so justly, by literary critics, that we do not propose to discuss it further than to say—what is evident—that it may be used to good or bad purpose. The manipulation of word-sounds may blur and confuse meanings as well as intensifying them; it may tend to disjoin or set in contrast meanings which should be fused; or it may tend to weld together meanings which should be sharply distinct. It is an element of good writing only when it functions to render the compact configuration of meanings which is the work of art more and not less compact.

The most important aspect of the adaptation of sound to meaning (we do not speak of onomatopoeia but of the enhancement of structured mean-

---

[1] All three extracts are taken from my little anthology *A Mirror of Charactery* (1935).

[2] *The Handling of Words* (1923).

ings by the configuration of sound) is that element of literary craftsmanship known as rhythm. In the sense in which we are now using it, the
word rhythm refers to a quality of word-groups as conveyors of meanings
and not a quality of word-sounds in isolation from meaning. It is very
difficult to define this rhythm even ostensively and its discussion is best
approached by examining the traditional distinction between poetry and
prose.

It is important to understand that the word 'poetry' commonly bears
a double meaning in the vocabulary of literary criticism. Almost all
literary critics sometimes use the word 'poetry' as a synonym of 'literature'
in the sense in which we have used that word, implying that the critic
judges any work called 'poetical' to have a relatively high coefficient of
literary excellence, to be a work of literary art. But as the antithesis of
'prose' it is often used to mark a technical distinction between two modes
of literary composition, each of which has its own excellence or badness
as art. From the technical point of view there is no clear line of demarcation between poetry and prose but a wide debateable borderland, and we
often hear such phrases as 'poetic prose' and 'prosaic poetry'. Poetry is also
sometimes discriminated from prose on the score of content or subject-
matter[1] and confusion is prevalent when these several methods of classification are combined together. On the *technical* side, which here concerns
us, according to the linguistic habits most general among critics, poetry is
language which is metrical and prose language which is not metrical.[2] Dr.
Johnson defined poetry as 'metrical composition'; this was accepted by
Wordsworth as the broad antithesis between poetry and prose and it is
accepted, with qualifications, by most critics still. Metre is not, however,
sufficient to make a verbal construct technically poetry, and there is a
rather surprising unanimity among critics in judging that any writing
which is metrical but which has not the other technical requirements of
poetry is necessarily bad literature. The word 'verse' is often nowadays
applied in a pejorative sense to metrical language which is judged to be
not technically poetry, and when such a judgement is made it is always, I
think, implied that verse which is not poetry is devoid of literary excellence. It seems to be a universal assumption of contemporary criticism that,
while non-metrical language may have literary excellence, no metrical
language is good literature unless it has the full technical apparatus of
poetry.

[1] See, for instance, Julien Benda's *Du Poétique* (1946).
[2] Mr. Edmund Wilson has a penetrating discussion of poetry, prose and verse
in his essay 'Is Verse a Dying Technique?' (In *The Triple Thinkers*, 1952.)

The quality which is necessary to poetry in addition to metre is rhythm. Yet rhythm is not confined to poetry but may characterize prose composition also: in fact, all elevated and impassioned prose tends to be rhythmical. It is the combination of metre and rhythm which makes a composition technically poetry. There is, I think, little to be added to the clear-sighted discussion of this topic by Professor J. W. Mackail in his essay on *The Definition of Poetry*.[1] 'The essence of poetry technically', he says, 'is that it is patterned language. This is its specific, central, and indispensable quality as a fine art. Pattern, in its technical use as applied to the arts, is distinct from composition generally. It is composition which has in it what is technically called a "repeat". The artistic power of the pattern-designer is shown in the way he deals with the problem of his repeat: the problem being, stated baldly, to make the rhythm of his repeat felt in such a way that the pattern which is based on and consists of a repeated unit may at the same time not fall asunder in separate units, but move and spread in a continuous and longer composition over the whole surface which is covered by the pattern.' He therefore defines poetry as language which combines both rhythm and metre: 'In verses that are merely mechanical there is not the rhythm; in rhythm which is not in verses there is not the quality which constitutes pattern. Neither apart from the other is technical poetry.' As Professor Mackail himself recognizes, this definition does not strictly accord with the linguistic habits of critics. There are literary constructs which are not metrical but which are commonly classified as poetry rather than prose. Compositions in 'free verse' are called poetry if they are judged to have literary excellence, and many writings which are technically prose—passages from the Authorised Version of the Bible, for example—are habitually referred to as poetry. Usage in these matters is not logical, and strictly logical definitions cannot be constructed so as to be conformable with illogical linguistic habits. What is meant, I think, when a passage from Isaiah or a composition by Walt Whitman is called poetry is that it conforms to the critic's idea of poetical *content*, that it has a relatively highly literary value and that it is highly rhythmical.

Rhyme is a subsidiary device of patterning, making the pattern more rigorous when it occurs. As Mr. Ezra Pound has said: 'Rhyming can be used to zone sounds, as stones are heaped into walls in mountain plough-land.' Like pattern itself it may either enhance and intensify rhythm or it may be devoid of rhythm. In general, the more complex and rigid the pattern, the harder the poet's task to infuse it with rhythm.

As to what rhythm is, everyone who has enjoyed successful commerce

[1] *Lectures on Poetry* (1911).

with the arts knows what it is in the sense of having experienced it. Nobody has succeeded in defining it. It is closely allied with pattern but is not identical with pattern. There are non-rhythmical patterns, such as the patterns of crystallography, organic chemistry and non-poetical verse. There may be rhythm without formal pattern, although rhythm seems always to produce a tendency towards pattern. In the recorded arts rhythm is primarily an ordering of time-intervals within a total duration occupied by a complex movement. More than this I do not think can be usefully said about the nature of rhythm. But about the *effects* of rhythm in literature, the way in which it works, two things may be noticed. (We do not here speak of the effects of rhythm in *spoken* language in so far as these transcend what is capable of being recorded.)

(1) Rhythm seems to be the most potent isolable factor in inducing the semi-hypnotic state of suggestibility which is characteristic of aesthetic appreciation and which predisposes the reader to the influences which poetry exerts upon him.[1] It is in virtue of this attitude, which we have earlier called 'make-believe', that the poet can incite in the reader, not emotional states directly but mental attitudes—acceptance or repudiation, indignation, respect, contempt, and the rest—with far more delicately modelled precision than any language can forthrightly describe, towards the logical, perceptual or emotional situations which his words present to the reader's awareness. It is because of the potency of rhythm in this respect that poetry is so much more effective than prose in controlling mental attitudes, but has so very small an influence upon the man of unpoetic temperament.

(2) Rhythm is also more potent than any other element of word-sound in aiding (or obstructing) the configuration of meanings into aesthetic constructs. It can give emphasis and 'position' to individual words and word-groups, relate them or disjoin them, oppose them or weld them, far more effectively than grammatical structure alone. The 'repeats' of rhythm recall not merely words and phrases but the contexts of meanings in which the words and phrases were previously used, welding and fusing

---

[1] The word 'hypnotic' is frequently used in this connection, being sometimes replaced by the word 'reverie'. It is a valid metaphor so long as it is intended to convey a heightening of suggestibility. It is invalid if it is understood to imply a relaxation in the tension of awareness. In appreciation of an aesthetic object awareness is tautened and fulfilled, not slackened. Poetry whose rhythm induces a sort of mental drowsiness and as it were a numbing of perceptive keenness is bad or indifferent art. It goes against the primary function of all art, which is to stimulate perceptive awareness to more than usual alertness while affording to it an adequate object of awareness.

meanings into a structural whole. Prosody and rhyme may work to the same effect. If used effectively as an ancillary to the structuring of meanings which is the poem, the importance of prosody is unbounded. But a poet's rhythms may go astray, jarring with the sense-configuration, or his verse-form may be unrelated to the structuring of meanings, and this is one of the cardinal points to which the critic should direct the inexpert reader's attention, but rarely does.

4. We have now said all that can usefully be said in a work of this compass about the technical aspects of good composition. Some may think that disproportionate attention has been given to this. The importance of its contribution to literary excellence may, however, be gauged by considering what remains when a poem is translated from one language to another, from Chinese, say, or ancient Egyptian into English. That something remains is certain. That what remains is not literature is equally certain. There are, of course, translations which have high literary excellence. But when a translation has literary excellence it is always *another* excellence than that of the original; the subject-matter has been made into a different work of art, which, though it be better than that from which it was derived, cannot be the same. How far it can be away may be seen from Professor Gilbert Murray's romantic renderings of the Greek tragedians in verse or George Rapall Noyes's prose version of *Pan Tadeusz*. What cannot be given in translations is the contribution of craftsmanship, for that is peculiar to the language in which it operates.

It remains now to discuss the most important aspect of literary art: the enforming of meanings into aesthetic wholes. This is far too large a subject to cover at all fully here and the most that can be done is to indicate suggestively what it is all about by touching briefly upon two points—the types of poetic presentation and the alogical fusion of poetic meanings.

4.1. Mr. Ezra Pound mentions three modes of poetic presentation and names them melopoeia, phanopoeia and logopoeia. I propose to adopt these terms but to use them in a slightly different sense from his.

Melopoeia roughly corresponds to what we have described as the beauty of sound, including rhythmic sound, in the expression of meanings and no more will now be said about it.

Phanopoeia is described by Mr. Pound as 'throwing a visual image on the mind'. We shall use it in a rather extended sense as the presentation to awareness of a perceptual or an emotional situation, but with two provisos. Visualization (or the 'imaging' of any mode of sensation) varies from person to person; some people are visualizers and some not, and the extent to which a situation is visualized does not greatly affect appreciation. Even with a confirmed visualizer past experience will have a profound effect upon visualization; for instance, a person who has visited a French *bistro* would inevitably visualize the situation presented in the poem by Rimbaud quoted below differently from a person who had not. In general, moreover, the formation of mental images is inversely proportional to the intensity with which awareness is concentrated upon the literary object. So far as I can tell, from personal experience and from enquiry, it has little bearing upon appreciation. It must also be remarked that the primacy of the visual sense, which is a heritage of Western culture from the Greeks, must not be presumed in poetry. A poet may mould his experience with preponderance for the visual or, as J. M. Valverde justly remarks of Spanish-American poetry in general, optical perception may have no primacy over other modes of perception. The reader must be prepared to 'image' in every mode of sensation. Valverde points out, for example, that the poetry of Neruda is tactile rather than visual, quoting his 'y en tu catedral ciega me arrodillo—golpeandome los labios con un ángel'.

It must also be repeated that when an emotional situation is presented the reader does *not*, as is too often assumed, become aware of the emotion by experiencing it. To do so would disrupt awareness, obliterate the object and annul appreciation. He is aware of the emotion imaginally, as he is aware of a presented perceptual situation imaginally. An emotional situation is presented in the sentence quoted earlier from Joseph Conrad's letter to Sir Hugh Clifford. The reader does *not* experience Pa Tua's intensity of fear, although he is aware of the fear-situation and *may* image the fear.

In all literary *phanopoeia* an attitude of mind, often called a mood, is induced in the reader in relation to the presented situation. The mood is not apart from the situation as a thing external to it, but is as it were fused with it and presented as part of it. But while the mood is experienced directly by the reader, the presented situation is not. Thus we may experience pity, contempt, indignation, towards a fear-situation, but we do not experience the fear although we are aware of it as fear in somebody else and may 'image' it.

I will now give two illustrations of *phanopoeia*, one from a French and one from an English poet.[1]

---

[1] In both these examples a (relatively) static situation is presented. When language presents a situation of movement, it becomes narrative. An example has been quoted on p. 185 n.1.

(i) *Au Cabaret Vert*

Depuis huit jours, j'avais déchiré mes bottines
Aux cailloux des chemins. J'entrais à Charleroi,
—Au Cabaret Vert: je demandai des tartines
De beurre et de jambon qui fût à moitié froid.

Bienheureux, j'allongeai les jambes sous la table
Verte: je contemplai les sujets très naïfs
De la tapisserie.—Et ce fut adorable,
Quand la fille aux tétons énormes, aux yeux vifs,

—Celle-là, ce n'est pas un baiser qui l'épeure!—
Rieuse, m'apporta des tartines de beurre,
Du jambon tiède, dans un plat colorié,

Du jambon rose et blanc parfumé d'une gousse
D'ail,—et m'emplit la chope immense, avec sa mousse
Que dorait un rayon de soleil arriéré.

RIMBAUD.

My second example is a poem by Sir Herbert Read:

(ii) *The Pond*

Shrill green weeds
float on the black pond.

A rising fish
ripples the still water
And disturbs my soul.

In both these poems the mood is definite and precise; in both it is completely fused with the presented situation, so that it cannot be separated from it and cannot be described in any words other than the words of the poems. I know no other mark than this to distinguish literary and non-literary *phanopoeia*, *phanopoeia* which is art and *phanopoeia* which is not art.

A special case occurs when the poet desires to communicate a very intense or unusual emotion of his own which is not directly linked with external things and does this by means of metaphor or imagery. In this case the presented situation is not only the bearer of the emotion but becomes in a certain sense a symbol of it. We have seen that this is one of the preoccupations of modern poets and have given an example from Eliot. In his study of modern poetry *The Creative Experiment* Mr. C. M. Bowra quotes an outstanding example from the Spanish poet Rafael

Alberti, who thus portrays the crisis of desolation which inspired his book of poetry *Sobre los Ángeles*:

> *Cuando para mí eran los trigos viviendas de astros y de dioses*
> *y la escarcha los lloros helados de una gacela,*
> *alguien me enyesó el pecho y la sombra,*
> *traicionándome.*
>
> *Ese minuto fué el de las balas perdidas,*
> *el del secuestro, por el mar, de los hombres que quisieron ser pájaros,*
> *el del telegrama a deshora y el hallazgo de sangre,*
> *el de la muerte del agua que siempre miró al cielo.*[1]

By *logopoeia* we shall mean the presentation of a conceptual situation or the presentation of an emotional situation in conceptual terms, i.e. an emotional situation which has been conceptualized. In this mode also the artistic use of linguistic communication is distinguished from the non-artistic use only by the fusion of an attitude of mind with the presentation so that the two are inseparably presented as one. The mood may be intense, like horror or exaltation; or it may be no more than an attitude of unusual *interest*. But unless it is there and unless it is fused, I know no way of distinguishing artistic from non-artistic *logopoeia*. The philosopher who presents sequences of ratiocinative thought with the *external* implication 'this is true, and you should adopt towards it the attitude of accepting belief', is not writing artistically. A logopoeic sequence which, taken in isolation, is not artistic, may nevertheless be a part of a larger artistic whole. When this happens a mood is reflected upon it from the whole and infuses it. It is not the same thing outside the whole of which it forms a part as it is within it.

I give now two examples of artistic *logopoeia*.

(i)   *Je suis l'esclave heureux des hommes dont l'haleine*
      Flotte ici. Leur vouloir s'écoule dans mes nerfs;
      Ce qui est moi commence à fondre.

[1]   *When for me the wheat was the home of stars and gods*
      and the rime the frozen sobs of a gazelle,
      someone smeared my chest and shadow,
      betraying me.

      That was the minute of the shots that went astray,
      the minute when the sea kidnapped the men who sought to be birds,
      of the untimely telegram and the discovery of blood,
      and of the death of the water which always looked on the sky.

These lines were written by M. Jules Romains, and Mr. Ezra Pound has said of them: 'This statement has the perfectly simple order of words. It is the simple statement of a man saying things for the first time, whose chief concern is that he shall speak clearly.'

The second is from the *Scopas* of Franz Tamayo and is a conceptualized description of the emotional effort involved in artistic creation.

(ii)   *Conoces la agonía del artista*
Al instante fatal que inspira y crea?
Fluye su genio como sangre vívida
De vientre maternal que alumbre a gritos.
No hay dolor igual. De las tinieblas
Se arrancan formas cual jirones mútilos
De alma. Y esas tinieblas desgarradas
Son el artista mismo. A sus criaturas
Si da un contorno, de su carne talla,
Y si un gesto, es la mueca de su pena
Transfigurada en luz. Cada sonrisa
Que en barro admira el vulgo cuesta lágrimas
Ocultas, y si es Niobe estupefacta
La desesperación en Paros fúlgido,
El creador desesperó al crearla![1]

4.2. It has been often and truly remarked that the concatenation of meanings in poetry is not in accordance with logical coherence. Yet poetry has meaning. Not only are the unit-meanings apprehensible, but the larger constructs into which they are built are cemented together wholly or in part by other principles of cohesion than those of logical reason. And yet these larger constructs are themselves apprehensible to awareness and have meaning and import. All this is true. But when it is added that the unit-meanings are organized into larger wholes in accordance with the laws of affectivity, this leaves the matter where it was and is, moreover, false. It is true of the language of propaganda, advertising, politics; of all language

---

[1] Franz Tamayo, *Scopas: tragedia lírica* (La Paz, 1939).

'Do you know the agony of the artist at the fatal moment of inspiration and creation? His genius flows out like the vivid blood from the mother's belly which gives birth with cries of anguish. There is no pain to equal it. From darkness the forms are snatched like mutilated shreds of the soul. And that lacerated darkness is the artist himself. If he gives a contour to the children of his creation he carves it from his flesh; if a gesture, it is the grimace of his pain transfigured into light. Every smile which the public admire in the clay costs hidden tears, and if Niobe bemazed is desperation in luminous Paros, the creator despaired at its creation.'

which convinces against logic. It is not true of good poetry. Poetic meanings are organized in accordance with principles of the human reason which are not less fundamental, and more universal, than the principles of logic; which do not conflict with the principles of logic, although when illegitimately conceptualized they may seem to do so; and which are independent of logical thought. They are principles which, although neither 'primitive' or 'abnormal' in the sense of being peculiar to primitives and psychotics, have recently come to light particularly in the spheres of abnormal psychology and anthropological investigations of primitive mentality.

Men who are living in that condition of culture known to the anthropologists as 'primitive' do not think with our categories. They do not reason in terms of subject and object, property and substance, regular sequence of cause and effect. They know nothing of the strange idea of immaterial substance which we have inherited from the Greeks. The primitive makes no ineluctible separation between matter and spirit, body and soul, animate and inanimate, the reality of sense and the reality of dream. Even the gap between human and animal is flickering and evanescent, as is apparent from the religion of totemism, folk-stories and the animal gods of maturer civilizations. His one important distinction, his dichotomy of being, is into the sacred and the profane. The sacred is the realm of power that is mysterious, incalculable; the profane is the customary, the ordinary, the familiar. Man has had little interest ever to spare for all that happens according to his unconscious expectations and without frustrating his desires. But whatever happens out of the ordinary, the unexpected, the disastrous, arrests his attention and tends to be regarded—not only by the primitive mind—as miraculous. The power to concentrate interest upon the usual and ordinary and to observe the 'laws of nature' in the customary course of events comes only with great maturity and in the mature man is never more than a superficial veneer covering a small part of his mind. For the primitive the world is a battleground of warring wills. There is a great barrier fixed between the conceptual world which we call logical and that of the primitive man. The questions we instinctively ask he does not ask. The concepts which are the tools of our thought are not his tools and our very language has no words with which to express the mental categories he uses. Anthropologists in the last thirty years have become more and more conscious of this chasm —and at the same time more convinced about the essential rationality and practicality of the primitive mental world. In the Preface to his illuminating *Kingship and the Gods*, Henri Frankfort writes: 'The creations of the primitive mind are elusive. Its concepts seem ill defined, or, rather, they defy limitations. Every relationship becomes a sharing of essentials. The part partakes of the whole, the name of the person, the shadow and effigy of the original. This "mystic participation" reduces the significance of distinctions while increasing that of every resemblance. It offends all our habits of thought. Consequently the instrument of our thought, our language, is not well suited to described primitive conceptions.' In the primitive thought-world the part is, and is not, the whole; the symbol is, and is not, that which it symbolizes; the manifestation is, and is not, what it manifests. An embodiment may be identical with what is embodied and yet remain distinct; an expression becomes one with what is expressed, but without losing its distinctness. Yet these 'illogicalities' are not just failures of the untutored and undisciplined mind to achieve coherence. That they do not impede man's efficiency to cope practically with his environment is apparent, since by them he has come where he has. They persist with unabated strength in the religious, magical, mythological and mystical traditions of all races and in the deepest and most powerful psychological habits of modern man, beneath the superficial levels of conscious rationality. It is to these modes of mentation that the language of poetry speaks and in their light the seeming incoherences and absurdities of poetic meanings evanesce.[1]

What has so far been said is mainly negative. It is not, I think, yet possible to set forth, in the manner of the primers of logic, the positive principles of alogical coherence. There exists here a wide field of human mentality which cries out for investigation. And until it has been investi-

---

[1] With what is said here may be compared two passages, which I set side by side, from Professor Rosemond Tuve's critical commentary on the poetry of George Herbert. The first is from page 202 and the second from page 105. 'This kind of organic unity will always characterize the work of a man who interprets life by the aid of metaphor, because metaphor does not "compare" one thing with another, it states that one thing is another. Metaphor (and allegory, which is metaphor) deals not with likenesses but with essences. So, of course, do symbols, the extreme of metaphors. They can reconcile seeming contradictions because their terms can be "different from" and "the same as" simultaneously; nor is this in defiance of logic, for metaphors deal with reality at the level of universals.' And: 'The insight into truth by means of metaphor marks the "aesthetic" province and method *par excellence*, is poetry's *modus vivendi*, but all the great religions have used it, and in that connection we meet it when we study "myth"—in the re-habilitated modern sense of that word. The history of all modern poetry with any claim to be called great is the history of our attempt to recapture this way of viewing the world; and it has been the extreme of the method, the symbolical rather than simply the figurative mode, which our poets have embraced.'

gated that branch of literary criticism which concerns poetic coherence in the concatenation of unit meanings must remain intuitive rather than the application of known laws.

5. The unity of a work of literary art originates in the unity of the experience which the work of art presents. The components of the total experience are not externally linked but interact organically, react and respond by mutual influence, are each determined for what they are by the interplay of all the other parts and by the whole of which they are parts and which they together compose, as the parts of an organic whole which is a picture or a piece of music. An idea, a presented emotion or a presented perception taken out of its context in a literary work is something different from what it was in that work; if it is not different, the work from which it was taken was not a work of art. Quotations and excerpts cannot ever say the same thing when used as quotations in isolation from the context of the whole from which they were abstracted. It has been frequently observed that the poet fuses his sensory experience, his intellectual experience and his emotional experience, so that the one may stand for the other and they cannot be disjoined. This is particularly true of the short poem whose ostensible subject is a direct experience in the mind of the writer—the type of poetry upon which modern poetic theory is chiefly based. This is one method among others of fusion, but there is, ultimately, no sharp demarcation between the short personal poem and the long narrative or philosophical poem, no line between the art of the poem and the art of prose. Coleridge said that the distinguishing feature of poetry is 'the property of exciting a more continuous and equal attention than the language of prose aims at, whether colloquial or written'. If 'poetry' is understood in the sense of 'artistic writing' to include prose art as well as writing in verse, this statement is as near to the truth as it is possible to come. A work of literary art cannot be appreciated as a conglomeration of externally conjoined parts any more than a musical composition can be appreciated as a conjunction of melodies. It must be seen as a single unified whole and each separable part can only be seen as it is when it is seen within the whole as a part of the whole. As the work of art enters into awareness through a period of time, attention must be evenly distributed throughout the time of reading if the balance of parts is not to be disturbed. Appreciation of the whole and of the parts—and appreciation is nothing more nor less than perception—can only be achieved when the whole is before the mind as a whole composed of parts each with its proper place and prominence, each what it is within the whole and not what it might be if taken outside the whole.

No criticism can *describe* such a whole as is a work of literary art and no other form of words can be substituted for it. The most criticism can do is to provide pointers and guidance to lead the reader to see further into it, to see particular reflections and interactions which would otherwise have escaped him and to encourage him to look at it as a whole and not as a collection of quotations. Criticism of this type is exemplified in Mr. Cleanth Brooks's *The Well Wrought Urn*, and I know no better description of practical and effective literary criticism than the description he there gives: 'To sum up: our examination of the poem has not resulted in our locating an idea or a set of ideas which the poet has communicated with certain appropriate decorations. Rather, our examination has carried us further and further into the poem itself in a process of exploration. As we have made this exploration, it has become more and more clear that the poem is not only the linguistic vehicle which conveys the thing communicated most 'poetically', but that it is also the sole linguistic vehicle which conveys the things communicated accurately. In fact, if we are to speak exactly, the poem itself is the *only* medium that communicates the particular "what" that is communicated.'

From the point of view of configurational criticism the old conflict between 'form' and 'content' is unreal. The form of a poem, the prosodic structure, the rhythmic interplay, the characteristic idiom, are nothing any more when abstracted from the content of meaning; for language is not language but noise except in so far as it expresses meaning. So, too, the content without the form is an unreal abstraction without concrete existence, for when it is expressed in different language it is something different that is being expressed. The poem must be perceived as a whole to be perceived at all. There can be no conflict between form and content in configurational criticism, for neither has existence without the other and abstraction is murder to both.

Chapter XI

ANATOMY OF CRITICISM

The content and the 'importance' of a work of art are in fine wholly dependent on its being one: outside of which all prate of its representative character, its meaning and its bearing, its morality and humanity, are an impudent thing.

HENRY JAMES

The function of a genuine critic of the arts is to provoke the reaction between the work of art and the spectator. The spectator, untutored, stands unmoved; he sees the work of art, but it fails to make any intelligible impression on him; if he were spontaneously sensitive to it, there would be no need for criticism.

H. L. MENCKEN

... considerar el menester crítico, no como una explicación aparte, como otra obra, o la traslación a otros paralelos y meridianos, sino como una simple ayuda al lector, como un ahondamiento y enriquecimiento en la lectura—lo único que interesa—, pero dentro del mismo camino de la palabra poética.

JOSÉ M. VALVERDE

Excernment. The general ordering and weeding out of what has actually been performed. The elimination of repetitions. The work analogous to that which a good hanging committee or curator would perform in a National Gallery or in a biological museum; the ordering of knowledge so that the next man (or generation) can most readily find the live part of it, and waste the least possible time among obsolete issues.   EZRA POUND

The 'greatness' of literature cannot be determined solely by literary standards; though we must remember that whether it is literature or not can be determined only by literary standards.   T. S. ELIOT

A FTER surveying the general practice and profession of critics we argued that the criticism of literature and the arts has two principal functions and we have continually assumed that the excellence of any piece of critical writing is to be judged by the extent to which it contributes to the fulfilment of either or both these functions. Before enquiring into the various modalities of criticism it will be well to re-state the two functions of criticism as such. If anyone does not accept that these are the functions which criticism exists to fulfil, he will be out of sympathy with the greater part of this book and will not be found to assent to what follows.

In the first place, after having discriminated genuine works of art within the class of all putatively artistic artefacts, criticism is to exhibit a true order of merit among them in respect of those qualities of excellence which they possess specifically as works of art. This is the juridical or axiological function of criticism. Secondly, criticism *describes* works of art, but describes them in a special way, calling attention in its descriptions not to any and every characteristic which they possess but signalizing those characteristics in virtue of which they are judged to be excellent or indifferent works of art. A person who describes the physical dimensions of a picture and the chemical composition of the pigments is not, for example, writing as a critic of painting; and one who comments on the binding and layout of a book is not indulging in literary criticism. In addition to but largely through the exercise of these two functions criticism also serves the practical purpose of interesting and aiding its readers to achieve a more complete and correct appreciation of the works of art which it evaluates or describes.

In practice there is a rather low measure of agreement among critics about the relative merits of individual artists or works of art. If you take a cross-section of critical writing at intervals of fifty years or so, you will indeed find a larger measure of broad general agreement among critics who are contemporary with each other than among those who belong to different periods; but this agreement seldom goes very deep and the history of criticism reveals no steady progress of accumulated knowledge but continual swings of fashion or alterations in sensibility from one generation or another. Among critics writing to-day, except for the few very good and the many very bad, there is less general agreement than at any time in the past about the axiological placing of individual artists and works of art and there is less agreement still about the reasons for which individual works of art are judged to be good or less good. We have seen that critics work with a number of different assumptions about the nature of beauty or artistic excellence and that their critical judgements and descriptions vary in accordance with the assumptions which they adopt. Some of these assumptions are more convenient and workable than others, but none of them is right or wrong in itself; for they are in the last resort merely definitions of linguistic usage. But until you know what assumptions about the nature of artistic excellence any critic is making, it is not possible to know what he means when he says that any work of art is good or not good. Nor is it possible to know whether disagreements among critics are real or apparent until you know what they mean when they advance judgements of good and bad about works of art.

We will recapitulate the main aesthetic assumptions which are embodied in modern criticism.

1. The *Realist* assumption makes the excellence of any work of art dependent upon the veracity with which it copies or symbolizes something not itself. It affords a coherent basis for criticism, but if it were consistently applied it would lead to critical assessments widely at variance with those which are currently accepted by critics. For it would exclude music, architecture and all purely decorative plastic art from the category of aesthetic objects and would demand that photographs, waxwork figures, white papers and scientific treatises should be ranked high in the scale of art. No critics apply the Realist assumption consistently. But many critics, having classified certain artefacts on other grounds as works of art, illogically judge them to be excellent because they veraciously copy something not themselves or alternatively stigmatize symbolic inveracity as an artistic defect.

2. The *Emotional* assumption makes the excellence of any work of art depend upon the intensity or the pleasantness of the emotion which it arouses in an observer. In its naïve form this assumption would lead to a very strange classification of works of art; dentist's chairs, mink coats and very many other objects not commonly classified as aesthetic objects arouse strong emotions in many people. But it is not consistently applied in practice. Like the Realist assumption, this criterion of excellence is usually applied illogically by critics who have already discriminated the works of art to which they apply it on other and less apparent grounds.

A more recondite form of the Emotional assumption maintains that there exists a special type of emotion which is experienced only in contact with aesthetic objects and which therefore serves to discriminate works of art from non-artistic artefacts, while the intensity with which it is experienced serves as an indication of their excellence as works of art. Mr. Clive Bell was content merely to affirm the existence of such a special emotion while professing to be unable to define it. Mr. A. E. Housman, in his lecture on *The Name and Nature of Poetry*, claimed to be able to define this special emotion by reference to a combination of physical symptoms such as bristling of the skin, a shiver down the spine, a constriction of the throat, a precipitation of water to the eyes and a peculiar sensation in the pit of the stomach.

The Realist assumption provides an objective basis for criticism and critical judgements based upon it are as little subject to the vagaries of personal opinion or predilection as the verdicts of any other science. Emotional theories of beauty are on the other hand ultimately and inescapably subjective. They lead to the discrimination of a different class of aesthetic objects for every observer and different gradings of merit within the classes. Professor Frederick A. Pottle has, for example, shown that there is every reason to suppose that eighteenth-century critics experienced emotions when reading Pope or Dryden very similar to those which Mr. Housman says that he experiences when reading Wordsworth or Shelley. For this brand of criticism individual differences in emotional sensibility are ultimate and decisive. Critical judgments become concealed autobiography and have no normative validity from person to person.

3. The *Expressionist* assumption makes the excellence of a work of art dependent upon the exactness with which it causes to be reproduced in the observer an experience which previously occurred in the mind of the artist. It professes to escape the subjectivity of Emotional criticism by providing an objective criterion in the degree of similarity between two concrete experiences. Such a criterion is indeed objective. But since the artist's experience cannot be communicated otherwise than through the work of art or known by any other means except by responding to the work of art, no objective comparison of the two experiences is ever possible. In practice, therefore, Expressionist criticism is on all fours with Emotional subjectivism.

4. *Transcendentalism* is a special type of Emotional assumption, which makes the excellence of any work of art dependent on the intensity with which it evokes the special type of mystical emotion which we have called Revelatory. Since different people experience such emotions in contact with different objects, and at different intensities, this assumption also leads to a subjective standard of criticism.

5. The *Configurational* assumption makes the excellence of any work of art dependent upon the compactness with which it is organized into an organic unity. It affords an objective standard of criticism, since organic configuration is not constitutively dependent upon emotional response, and it seems to lead to critical assessments less violently at variance with the usual judgements of critics than those which would result from a consistent and logical application of most other assumptions about the nature of artistic excellence. The qualities of organic configuration are, however, necessarily extremely difficult to describe or demonstrate in particular works of art.

Anyone who describes or arranges works of art in accordance with any one of these five criteria, or any combination of them, is writing what may properly be described as criticism. But unless he makes it clear which criterion he is adopting on each occasion, his writing will be meaningless and his judgements will assert nothing. If, again, he combines a criterion which yields an objective classification with a criterion which yields a subjective classification, he is likely to fall into the insidious error of erecting his personal propensities into normative principles and confusing autobiography with judgement.

There are, however, other modes of writing about works of art which are popularly confused with criticism but which do not belong to criticism as we have defined it. For they profess to classify and assess works of art in accordance with criteria which cannot by any stretch of the imagination be thought to be specific to works of art and whose acceptance is logically incompatible with any classification of artefacts into art and not-art.

We have mentioned from time to time that many works of art serve utility-functions, defining a utility-function as any purpose served by a work of art other than that of existing as an aesthetic object for appreciation. All such utility-functions are served also by things which are not classified as works of art; none of them is served by all works of art and only by works of art. The proper excellence of works of art must therefore be something other than any or all the utility-functions which some works of art in fact serve; for if it were not so, there would be no sense or reason in classifying as works of art all and only those things which we do classify as works of art. The term 'work of art' would, in fact, hold no coherent meaning. If, on the other hand, the class of all works of art is a real class, composed of things which have some common property not possessed by things which are not works of art, criticism is clearly concerned—as we have said—with that common property which is their specific excellence as works of art. And from this it follows that the critic who writes about the utility-purposes served by individual works of art is not, in the strictest sense, writing criticism.

In many cases the irrelevance of utility-functions to artistic excellence is pretty generally recognized in spontaneous judgement. A piece of architecture may be a house built to live in; and it can be a very good house to live in without being a thing of beauty. It may be comfortable and ugly, convenient for habitation though in the most execrable taste. A lecythos is not judged to be more beautiful because once it was a useful container for perfume, and the music of saxophones is not always judged to be good music if it provokes many people to the dance. A poem does not acquire literary merit because it is printed on fine paper; nor is any piece of writing commonly judged to be literature because it serves to call public attention to an abuse or to inflame political passions. Yet there are many other cases where works of art are frequently commended for the utility-functions which they serve, as though these functions were integral to artistic excellence. Pictures have been praised by competent critics because they were effective substitutes for the contemplation of pleasant landscapes or because they were admirable aids to the imaginative reconstruction of some historical or religious scene. Music is often esteemed as a source of pleasant relaxation or because it serves as an antidote to mental depression by setting up a chain of pleasant recollections. But the most tenacious and widespread confusion in this field is that which is connected with the didactic and heuristic functions of literature. There is probably not a single critic who does not from time to time commend works of literature because he approves of the moral views they express or because their contained philosophy seems to him to be true and good; and many literary critics have argued expressly that moral profundity and philosophic insight are qualities integral to the correct assessment of literary excellence.

The didactic function of literature has long been recognized. 'Poets', said Horace, 'desire either to improve or to please, or to unite the agreeable and the profitable. . . . You will win every vote if you blend what is improving with what pleases, and at once delight and instruct the reader.' Sir Philip Sidney assumed that the historian, the philosopher and the poet 'al endeavour to take naughtiness away, and plant goodnesse even in the cabinet of our soules'. But the poet, he thought, is the most efficient of the three because whereas the historian works by example and the philosopher by precept, the poet is more concrete and 'gives a perfect picture of it by some one, by whom he presupposeth it was done, so he coupleth the generall notion with the particular example. A perfect picture I say, for hee yeeldeth to the powers of the minde an image of that whereof the Philosopher bestoweth but a wordish description, which doth neither strike, pearce, nor possesse the sight of the soule so much as the other doth.'[1] The 'new' criticism of to-day is vigorously opposed to the view that a work of literature expresses vividly and concretely something which could also be expressed by a philosopher in abstract and general terms. In direct contradiction to Pope's phrase 'what oft was thought but ne'er so well expressed', it holds that what is expressed by any genuine poem is something unique to that poem, something which could not be expressed in any other way or couched in any other words. 'Poetry', said Mr. Richard P. Blackmur, 'is idiom, a special and fresh saying, and cannot for its life be said otherwise; and there is, finally, as much difference

[1] *Apologie for Poetrie* (1595).

between words used about a poem and the poem as there is between words used about a painting and the painting.' Yet critics to-day continue to believe that the moral profundity of any writing or the quality of wisdom contained in it is relevant to a just estimate of its literary value. Mr. Edmund Wilson records the response of Mr. Paul Elmer More when asked why he could not admire Baudelaire. 'Why,' he replied—he had an abrupt hesitation, as over the difficulty of dealing urbanely with a subject about which he felt so strongly, with an author of whom he so greatly disapproved, and upon whom, if he had been writing an essay, he would certainly have visited his stinging indignation—'I'm old-fashioned about Baudelaire. I recognize his power—and his significance in his time —but as a guide to life—!'[1] This is extreme, but it is typical of a mode of judgement which still exerts an important influence on the main body of critical writing.

A similar confusion of opinion exists about the intellectual content of literature. Mr. Lionel Trilling thinks that Mr. T. S. Eliot was exaggerating for effect when he wrote: 'I can see no reason for believing that either Dante or Shakespeare did any thinking on his own. The people who think that Shakespeare thought are always people who are not engaged in writing poetry, but who are engaged in thinking, and we all like to think that great men were like ourselves.' He himself is more inclined to the view expressed in a sentence of Carlyle's: 'If called to define Shakespeare's faculty, I should say superiority of Intellect, and think I had included all in that.' And he enters upon a painstaking argument to show that 'ideas' are proper and germane to literature. 'The most elementary thing to observe is that literature is of its nature involved with ideas because it deals with man in society, which is to say that it deals with formulations, valuations, and decisions, some of them implicit, others explicit".[2] That a critic of repute should find it necessary to argue and debate a question of this sort is symptomatic of the state of muddle into which criticism in general has fallen. Literature, as Henry James would say, is 'all of life'. In the words of Mr. John Crowe Ransom: 'The ostensible substance of the poem may be anything at all which words may signify.' Man is a thinking being and a being who forms ideas about metaphysical problems, problems of conduct and practical problems. Ideas of all these kinds are, therefore, obviously proper subject-matter of any literature written about human beings and for human beings. And empirically one may see that a great deal, though not all, of the literature which has been judged to be of high

[1] 'Mr. More and the Mithraic Bull' in *The Triple Thinkers* (London, 1952).
[2] *The Liberal Imagination* (1948).

excellence by the critics contains ideas of all these kinds explicit or implicit in its subject-matter. The only question which is at all open to discussion is the question whether any piece of literature is better as literature because it has more ideas rather than less, because its ideas are profound rather than banal, because they are original and new rather than trite, or because they are true rather than false.

Yet the answer even to these questions is not really obscure and the perplexities they have engendered need not really perplex. No poem, we will agree, can be paraphrased without destroying it as a poem. An idea, on the contrary, can always be paraphrased. Whether it is a metaphysical idea, a moral generalization or a proposition about matters of empirical fact, an idea can always be expressed in a variety of ways, some more exact and lucid than others but all expressions of the same idea. The intellectual content of a poem can, therefore, be re-stated without loss or distortion in a prose paraphrase and the paraphrase is not itself literature, however novel, profound or true be the ideas. Ideas which occur in the context of a poem are always modified to an appreciable extent by the alogical influences reflecting upon them from other ideas in the same poem, just as patches of colour in a picture are modified by all the other colour patches in the same picture, and are fused with attitudes of mind which pervade and give its character to the whole. If you isolate them from their context—and the actual words of a genuine poem are an essential part of the context—you cause them to be something other than they are in the context. When you separate the intellectual content of a poem from its other content and isolate the logical concatenations of concepts from the interplay of alogically controlled influences among them, you may achieve a true paraphrase of the intellectual content but you destroy the organic conformation which is the poem. For the excellence of the poem consists in the compactness with which its word-meanings are moulded into an organic unity and not in any quality which belongs to the individual constituents of its material when they are taken in isolation after the organization has been disrupted. Truth, originality and profundity of ideas are not, and cannot be, in any way integral to poetic excellence. We need not ask, with Mr. T. S. Eliot, whether Shakespeare or Dante thought.[1] But we must affirm—which may be what he meant—that whether their ideas were true or false, original or plagiarized, trite or

[1] 'As statement of historical fact José M. Valverde comes closer to the mark than most: 'La realidad histórica es que la mayoría de los poetas verdaderamente respetables tuvieron una cabeza muy clara, aunque no pensaran que la poesía fuera un resultado de la inteligencia.' *Estudios sobre la Palabra Poética* (1952).

profound, makes no difference to the artistic excellence of their poems. We need not believe that a poet's philosophy is true in order to appreciate the excellence of his poetry. We need not be prepared to take a poem as a guide to life before we can accept that it is a good poem. Nor, if we think Baudelaire's poems are good poems, must we—as Mr. I. A. Richards would have us—study M. Jean-Paul Sartre's examination of his psychology in order that we may make ourselves as like him as possible.

And as a corollary of this it follows that any critic who writes about the excellence or defects of a poet's ideas, about his contained morality or his wisdom, is not writing literary criticism but something else. He is discussing something which may be of genuine interest and importance but which is irrelevant to an estimate of literary excellence. One of the few critics who have seen this clearly is Mr. Cleanth Brooks, who, in an Appendix to *The Well Wrought Urn*, wrote: 'Why may we not, then, generalize on the basis of the attitudes adopted in the great and more important poems and thus get a world view which will provide a set of basic values? Cannot we catalogue and categorize the wisdom included in the great poetry in this fashion, and thus make poetry yield a directive wisdom, after all? We may, of course, if we like. But it needs to be pointed out that we are moving out of the realm of literary criticism if we do this. The real point is that, though any wise philosophy will probably take the greatest poetry into account, still this is a problem for philosophy or religion, and not for art.' In assessing literary excellence, criticism is not assessing the truth, the originality or the profundity of ethical or philosophical propositions. Original and profound concatenations of intellectual propositions occur in much writing which makes no claim to literary excellence and is not judged to be literature. Hence to say that any piece of writing sets forth true and original philosophy or displays deep moral insight is not to say that it is good literature; and to say that its ideas are unoriginal, untrue or banal is not to say that it is not good literature.

On the other hand it is certain that much writing accepted as good literature has in fact been composed with the main or the subsidiary purpose of causing people who read it to become convinced of the truth of certain philosophical ideas or to mould their lives in accordance with certain ethical principles. Sometimes the ideas are directly formulated in abstract propositions and the ethical principles are stated as moral precepts. Sometimes they are inculcated indirectly by illustrations, examples or analogies. But in one form or another the didactic and the heuristic functions of literature have been one of the main inspirations of the more successful producers of literature. This is an empirical fact which cannot be controverted. To-day, it is true, any person whose main purpose was to advocate philosophical beliefs or an ethical code would be rather stupid to try to do so through the medium of poetry, because nowadays entertainment fiction and books of popular science or philosophy are much more widely read than poetry, are read with greater care and understanding and have a wider influence upon a wider public. But even to-day a person whose main purpose was to write poetry might still endeavour as a subsidiary aim to recommend a philosophy he believed to be true or to promulgate moral principles which he believed to be right.

It is also certain that much writing which has passed as literary criticism has been primarily concerned with the asserted ideas and the logically formulable thought which are the paraphrasable content of literature. It is a propensity which has been particularly blatant in indigenous American criticism. At the end of the last century William Dean Howell was preaching the aesthetics of Realism and maintaining that for the American the best, because the truest, Realism was that which displayed the 'large cheerful average of health and success and happy life', since the more smiling aspects of life were the more typically American. Following William Cary Brownell, the generation of critics who wrote during and in the decade which followed the First World War were more lively to the deficiencies of the American character. Men like Van Wyck Brooks, Randolph Bourne, H. L. Mencken, Lewis Mumford, set themselves up as castigators of the national obtuseness to cultural values, attacking the puritanism, the commercialism, the social snobbery, the philistinism, the vulgarity and the smugness and complacence of the American people. What they spoke of as the 'discovery of the American spirit' was, quite patently and openly, an attempt to modify and civilize the then spirit of the average American. It was an active propaganda for culture as they understood it. The literary critic was first and foremost a critic of ideas and valuations, a social reformer, a lay preacher. 'But, then, isn't every critic a lay preacher?' asked James Gibbons Hunecker. Morton Danwen Zabel appropriately describes Mencken's output as the 'hilarious *Dunciad* of an age' and Lewis Mumford as one who has 'fallen glibly into the prophet's rôle'. Critics of this sort assess literature in accordance with their estimation of the ideas which literature contains, and Paul Elmer More was not giving utterance to a hysteron-proteron when he said: 'Before we can have an American literature, we must have an American criticism.'[1] For, by the criteria and standards which this sort of criticism employed, American literature must mirror forth the spirit of America, and it could

[1] *Shelburne Essays* (1904).

only be good literature if that spirit was a good spirit, and it could only become a good spirit when the reforming zeal of the critics had made it so.

Of course literature does incorporate and embody intellectual beliefs, moral attitudes, valuations of all kinds, sociological, religious and even scientific doctrines, and tends to induce in its readers specific attitudes of mind towards this intellectual content. It has the value of propaganda. It is a social force, though now but a feeble force compared with the influence of the various sorts of pseudo-literature. This is a fact which it would be idle to deny. And the criticism and discussion of ideas and valuations, whether embodied in literature or otherwise disseminated, is a necessary and healthy operation in human society. Far be it from us to exclude literature from such criticism. So long as literature works for the propagation of ideas and beliefs, influences human conduct and the motives of conduct, whether intentionally or unintentionally, whether as a main purpose or as a subsidiary purpose, it must and should be assessed as a social instrument. But this type of criticism is sociological criticism and has nothing to do with the aesthetic criticism which judges literary excellence. It is an accident that a large and vociferous group of sociological critics have been primarily interested in assessing the ideas they found expressed in books which they regarded as literature rather than similar ideas spoken in pulpits and law-courts or written in popular fiction or philosophical and moral treatises. The sociological assessment of literary content, the estimation of the truth or the validity of what literature 'says' has no part or parcel in the aesthetic criticism of literature as a mode of fine art. To say that one poem is a better poem than another because its contained fact or philosophy is truer is as silly as to say that a picture of a cathedral is a better picture than a picture of a cottage. When we read Darwin's *The Origin of Species* we are concerned to decide whether his theories and the facts upon which he bases them are correct; we are not concerned with the language except in so far as it sets forth his theories unambiguously. When we read *The Ancient Mariner* we are not interested to know whether the contained statements about the habits of the albatross could be scientifically verified. In so far as we regard Defoe's *A Journal of the Plague Year* as a work of literature we do not seek to verify whether the events he describes occurred as he describes them. If we read *The Decline and Fall of the Roman Empire* as a book of history, we are interested to know whether the facts occurred as they are there stated to have occurred, whether the analyses of their causes and their effects are correct. If we read it as literature, this is irrelevant: we judge it as a unified and imaginatively integrated presentation of the pomp of events and judge it for what it is without any justification from events which occurred or did not occur more than a thousand years before it was composed.

Literary critics have for obvious reasons been most prone to be deflected from the criticism of literary excellence to the criticism of ideas. But there is a certain school of historical criticism applied to all the arts which holds that, as in the artistic achievements of the race man's loftiest intimations of value are concreted and preserved like ants in amber for our inspection, so the artistic products of any epoch body forth most surely the finest flowering of sensibility and intellect in that epoch. Man's attitude to the word and to man, his most cherished ethical convictions, the pattern of his philosophy, his most secret aspirations and his dreams, are inexplicably carried over into the shape and structure of things appreciated through the senses. And those who know how to read the language of form can, it is claimed, derive from the artistic style of a period the pattern of its thought, its economics and its social structure, tracing from its art as from a map the main lineaments of that clumsy invention of Teutonic vapidity, the *Zeitgeist*. This cheiromantic mode of criticism is beset by many dangers, not the least of which is its tendency to *petitio principii*: you first deduce your spirit of the age from the art of the age and then you rediscover and verify that spirit in the art from which you have derived it.[1] But if all dangers are avoided, if the method is as successful as its most enthusiastic advocates have hoped it would be, it is still a method of determining the history of ideas, the sociology of culture or the phenomenology of thought and belief from the consideration of a rather special type of *data*. It has nothing to do with aesthetic criticism and it can never allege that the mysterious 'spirit of the age' is more fully or more genuinely manifested in the good than in the bad art of the age, since it has no criterion for distinguishing good art from bad. For that it must go to the true critics of art.

We see therefore that wisdom and moral elevation are neither a necessary nor a sufficient condition for literary excellence. There is much writing which contains wisdom, insight and moral profundity but is not regarded as literature; and there are works of recognized literary excellence which make no claim to wisdom or moral rectitude. Yet almost all critics discussing literature do desire to appraise it for the excellence of its wisdom or for the integrity of its moral insight when these qualities are present. There need be no conflict here. On the one hand a work of literature is

[1] A salutary antidote to the wilder flights of cheiromantic criticism will be found in Levin L. Schücking, *The Sociology of Literary Taste* (Eng. Trans. 1944).

assessed for its excellence as literature, its aesthetic value. On the other hand it is assessed for certain utility-values, the values of wisdom and moral illumination. The former mode of assessment, and the former mode only, is literary criticism proper; the latter mode differs in no respect from similar assessments of a human being or a non-literary treatise; it is the function of the philosopher, the moralist or the preacher. There is no reason why one man should not combine the two functions, unite the two types of assessment in one piece of writing; but unless he keeps the two types of judgement reasonably distinct, what he means to say will not be apparent in his words. One might reasonably claim that a piece of literature which has utility-values in addition to its literary excellence possesses an increment of total value over another piece of literature which has equal literary excellence but no other values, and the assessment of these adscititious values is no doubt a useful procedure. It is usual to find the word 'greatness' applied to writing which is judged to have deep wisdom or moral profundity in addition to high literary value. Nor is there any reason to object to this linguistic practice. It is necessary only that the critic who predicates greatness should bestir himself to analyse the values in which that greatness consists on each and every occasion when it is predicated. For this is the analytical task of criticism, and unless this is done, the critic's own impression will remain vague and obscure, while his predication will carry no meaning for others.

What we have, therefore, is two disciplines and not one discipline. On the one hand is literary or aesthetic criticism which assesses or describes works of art in respect of the qualities in virtue of which they are good or bad as works of art. On the other side is the criticism of ideas and attitudes. Ideas and attitudes may be embodied in literature and may be embodied in writing which is not literature. An idea, a belief, a moral attitude, a sociological, religious, philosophical, scientific or human doctrine, an aspiration or an ideal may be formulated in a hundred or a hundred hundred different ways, some more cogent and persuasive than others, some appealing to one group of men and others to another group; but the idea, attitude, belief is the same in all its formulations. If you describe or assess the extractable, paraphrasable 'content' of a work of literature, you are dealing with something which is not peculiar to it. If you assess or describe its quality of organic unity, the compactness of its organization, you are dealing with that which is unique to it; you are dealing with it as an aesthetic object and not with an abstraction taken from it. There need be no confusion between these two disciplines, both of which are commendable. But if you write about ideas purporting to write literary criticism, there must be confusion. And if, when you say any piece of writing is good or bad, you do not specify whether you mean that you think that the statements it makes are true or false, whether you think that the moral precepts deducible from it are right or wrong, whether you think that its general effect on society is desirable or deplorable, or whether you think it has a high or low degree of literary excellence, then what you write has no meaning and misunderstanding and confusion must result.

Against this background we will conclude with a brief examination of the competence and the contributions which can in principle be made by the various modes and techniques of criticism at present in vogue to the main task of criticism as such, which is—if our contention is right—assessment or description of the characteristic excellence of works of art as works of art rather than the general assessment of their 'greatness' in terms of non-aesthetic values.

Psychological Criticism

'Concern with his own mind is an occupation characteristic of modern man. Only recently, interest in the psychological motives and rules of artistic activity has begun to complement and even to overshadow the tradition and search for norms of apt and beautiful representation.' These words are quoted from a book published from the University of Buffalo, where a library of poets' worksheets and other biographical material has been formed which is intended to be a 'kind of laboratory' for the study of the 'intellectual activity which gives birth to the works themselves'. It is symptomatic of the growing interest in the psychological processes of artistic creation which, arising partly from the popularization of psycho-analytic theories and partly from a general increase in psychological interest through all walks of life, has done more than anything else to lend its distinctive tone and colour to modern criticism. Some critics indeed set up to be as it were obstetricians of artistic production. And even those who do not wholly ascribe to the psychological method of criticism are seldom entirely uninfluenced by the new interest in psychology and the new psychological theories. It cannot therefore be otiose to examine what psychology has to contribute to criticism and in what ways it can legitimately contribute.

The psychological study of artistic production may be undertaken from either of two opposed motives. On the one hand works of art and the known processes of their manufacture may be studied for the indications they afford about the mental dispositions of the men who made them. On the other hand known psychological facts about the artist other than the fact that he made certain works of art may be used as *data* from which to draw inferences about the works of art which he made. In the one case the purpose of the investigation is to know more about the mentality of the artist as a man and in the other it is to know more about the work of art as a work of art. Works of art, and particularly works of literary art, are without any doubt important *data* for the understanding of the psychological processes of the men who made them and for a fuller understanding of human psychology in general. Only it is to be remembered that the study of human psychology is something else from the assessment of artistic excellence and it is still to be proved that a fuller knowledge of psychological processes can facilitate the assessment of artistic excellence which is the function of criticism.

The discipline which has come to be known as 'ontogenetic criticism', that is the study of what takes place in an artist's mind during the processes of gestation and production of a work of art, is certainly an interesting branch of psychology. It can only become relevant or helpful to criticism if it can facilitate the discrimination of good from indifferent works of art, if for example it were possible to establish generalizations of the form 'all artefacts created as a result of such and such mental processes are good works of art' or 'all artefacts created as a result of such other mental processes are artistically defective'. No such generalizations have yet been established. Genius and inspiration are not the prerogatives of men who produce artistic works of high excellence. All the many studies of artistic creation detect precisely similar mental processes attendant on the creation of good art, indifferent art and bad art. The bad artist describes his mental processes, his inspiration, in no different terms from the good artist, and no psychologist has yet detected any significant difference between them. The same thing is true of general psychological theories about the source of creative power such as Freud's theory that the artistic gift is a compensatory function of neurosis—a theory which has been formalized by Mr. Edmund Wilson in terms of the Philoctetes legend. It has been sufficiently substantiated that many of the artists who enjoy the highest estimation of the critics have displayed characteristic symptoms of neurosis and it is not difficult to trace some sort of plausible connection between their artistic activities and their neurotic tendencies. It would be remarkably difficult to prove that all men who have been recognized to be great artists or poets were neurotic in any sense other than the senses in which all men can be accused of neurosis. But even if it were conceded that there existed a concealed neurosis wherever there has existed a capacity to create works of high artistic excellence, it is still certain beyond any shadow of doubt that precisely the same symptoms of neurosis are displayed by very many people who either have no impulses at all to create artistically or who having impulses produce very bad works of art. This being so, and it is a fact which I have never seen disputed, it is merely silly to refuse the logical implication that the neurosis which is common to artists and men who are not artists, to good artists and to poor poetasters and indifferent daubers, cannot be the source of the difference between the man who has and the man who has not the artistic gift. Most of the more competent psychologists who have given their attention to this matter have recognized that there is as yet no discernible psychological difference between the mental processes attendant on the birth of a work of art which the critics judge to be of high excellence and those which accompany unsuccessful attempts to produce works of art. Freud has said that psychoanalysis 'can do nothing towards elucidating the nature of the artistic gift, nor can it explain the means by which the artist works—artistic technique'. And Jung asserts: 'Any reaction to stimulus may be causally explained; but the creative act, which is the absolute antithesis of mere reaction, will for ever elude the human understanding.' I would not go so far as to claim that no psychological differentia will ever be discovered. But none are as yet known, and until they are discovered psychogenetic research into the origins of aesthetic objects can hold nothing of use for criticism which is concerned to differentiate good works of art from bad and to describe those qualities in which the artistic excellence of individual works of art resides.

The prevalence of the psychological biography is one of the signs of the popular interest in practical applications of psychology. And there is every reason to welcome the tendency to make artists and writers the subjects of such biographies, for this is one of the most effective means of stimulating interest in their production. Nor is there any reason why both psychological biography and criticism should not be written by the same man or even combined in the same book, provided that the two are kept distinct. The critical essays of Mr. T. S. Eliot are striking examples of a form of writing where psychological biography and criticism are set side by side as it were in distinct wedges. Mr. Eliot holds the somewhat dubious belief that if a writer's mental reactions are specially typical of his age, and if he has succeeded in embodying those typical reactions in his writing, then his works are particularly 'significant' and that writing which is in this way significant has always a high level of literary excellence or at any rate greatness. In general he is meticulous to keep

U

psychology and criticism distinct, although even he is liable to occasional lapses. Thus he tells us that Jonson's *Catiline* fails 'not because it is too laboured and conscious, but because it is not conscious enough; because Jonson in this play was not alert to his own idiom, not clear in his mind as to what his temperament wanted him to do'. Now these statements are inferences from the play as we know it to certain mental processes presumed to have happened in Jonson's mind when he composed it. They may or may not be correct inferences. If they are correct, they may or may not be the cause of certain features in the play which Mr. Eliot judges to be artistic faults. But the psychological causes which he infers are not themselves qualities of the play, and the attribution of causes for deficiencies cannot take the place of descriptive criticism which could point to the alleged defects in the work. Again he says of Blake: 'It is only when the ideas become more automatic, come more freely and are less manipulated, that we begin to suspect their origin, to suspect that they spring from a shallower source.' Now if your purpose is to understand the workings of Blake's unconscious mind, ideas which are thought to spring from a shallower source will be less significant *data* than ideas which are thought to spring from a deeper source in the unconscious. It may also be true that in general the ideas of Blake which spring from a source deeper in the unconscious are those which are more highly manipulated. But no inferences about the level of consciousness at which ideas originated can take the place of judgement about the artistic excellence or defects of the poetry or supply the place of a descriptive indication of what those defects are. Inferences about psychological causation are not germane to criticism. Yet few writers of criticism have maintained the distinction as meticulously as Eliot. Whenever one reads that 'inspiration has failed' or that 'the artist was insincere', one should suspect that the critic has failed in his task: he has judged that a work of art is defective, has failed to find words in which to indicate the deficiency descriptively and has offered instead an inferred psychological cause of the undescribed defect. 'You can spot the bad critic', says Ezra Pound, 'when he starts discussing the poet and not the poem.'

Anyone who claimed that knowledge of the artist's psychology is essential to criticism would have to admit that there can be no criticism of works of art whose author is unknown. Anyone who claimed that knowledge of the artist's psychology is useful to criticism would have to admit that critical assessment of the excellence of anonymous works is less effective, more tentative, than critical assessment of works whose author is known and that when a great deal is known independently about the artist's psychology assessment of his works is more effective than when little is known. In practice, of course, criticism assumes itself able to assess works of art even although nothing at all is known about their authors. In the case of all anonymous literature, the poetry of Homer, the poetry of Shakespeare for those who are uncertain whether or not William Shakespeare composed the writings which are commonly published under his name, in the case of all folk-music, all works of plastic art which have survived anonymously from the past—in all these cases it may be possible to make unverifiable inferences from the works of art to the psychology of the artist, but it cannot be possible to make inferences from the unknown psychology of the artist to his work of art. Nor in general do critics feel themselves less capable of estimating the artistic merits of works when very little is known about the artist than when they are in possession of much independent information about his life and his psychology. Confusion about the contribution of psychology to criticism prevails because critics intermingle inferences from the work of art to the artist with inferences from the artist's psychology to the work of art and when they are writing biography do not realize that they are not writing criticism. It is often stated, for example, that one of the tasks of the critic is to determine the artist's purpose and then to decide how far he succeeded in realizing that purpose. Yet it must now be obvious both that the critic can never determine the artist's purpose in creating any work of art and that what his purpose was is irrelevant to the artistic excellence of what he produced. The ulterior purposes of an artist may be recorded by him and the critic may decide how far he has fulfilled them. But these are the adscititious, utility-values of the work of art, which are not integral to its excellence. The artistic purpose of an artist cannot be stated by him except by pointing to his work of art, and no critic can know it except in so far as it was in fact realized in the work of art.

Psychology has, however, very much more to say in the clarification of those assessments of the 'total value' of works of art which include their adscititious uses in providing various gratifications and in satisfying various deep-seated needs. The needs which they satisfy vary from person to person. M. Charles Lalo has distinguished a number of aesthetic types among both producers and critics of art, each type requiring its art to serve different ulterior purposes. To put it baldly, different people want (or make) their art for different reasons and want it to do different things to them. And according to the kind of thing you want your art to do, you will prize one sort of art and find no use for another. Your wants are likely to be largely subconscious, in the sense that you have not thought very much about them and take them mainly for granted. You go to your art with subconscious expectations and value it as it manages to fulfil what you subconsciously require of it. The critics no less than the artists and amateurs belong to different aesthetic types; and those critics who purport to give you an assessment of the total value of a work of art will inevitably judge according to the type to which they belong. There will be no common standard among them and it will be very difficult to understand the meaning of their judgements until you know their aesthetic type. There is no final and complete classification of personality-types, and the following summary division is offered as an illustration only.

1. *Art as substitute-gratification.* The literature of psychoanalysis has given special prominence to the function of art which is analogous to that of the day-dream—the creation of an artificial pseudo-reality which when life fails to come up to the mark can be substituted imaginatively for it and can afford temporarily the adventitious satisfactions which life denies. This attitude to art, which is popularly known as escapism, may take any of several forms. There is a type of person who is reasonably at home with life but, as the most seductive environment becomes tedious in time, likes from time to time to make an excursion into the imaginative world of art in order to return refreshed and invigorated to the world of reality. For people of this type art serves as a relaxation, a diversion, a mental holiday. Such people have little use for a strictly realistic art and set a high value on novelty and strangeness. They desire contrast between the world of reality and the world of art, as men desire a change of scene when on holiday. There are others whose discontent is more settled and permanent, who find life if not a prison and a torment, at any rate insipid and little to their taste. For them the world of artistic imagination is not a frolic recreation from a genuine life they love, but the more serious and satisfactory of the two. They seek to find in art a separate and superior life to the life of reality and worship art for its own sake because it frees them from the fetters of the real. Mr. T. S. Eliot has rightly said: 'If you read carefully the famous epilogue to Pater's *Studies in the Renaissance*, you will see that "art for art's sake" means nothing less than art as a substitute for everything else, and as a purveyor of emotions and sensations which belong to life rather than to art.' And M. Henri Delacroix has mentioned the religious attitude which such people are apt to adopt towards art. 'Nombreux sont ceux qui se sont organisé dans les émotions esthétiques une sorte de monde supérieur où se réfugier, où trouver consolation et expression adéquate de soi-même; ils n'y pénètrent qu'avec cette exalta-

tion solennelle qui marque le passage du profane au sacré.'[1] The extremes of this type are those who suffer from pathological ennui, acedia or melancholia. Ennui is a mental illness and may be a very serious illness. It manifests itself in loss of mental appetitite, in an uneasiness devoid of definite desires whose satisfaction might bring relief. The sufferer seeks to stimulate his flagging interests by ever more artificial, more novel and more recondite enjoyments. As with the drug addict, the more he gives way to his passion for the recherché the less can his craving be satisfied until, in the words of Baudelaire, the world of reality seems

Une oasis d'horreur dans un désert d'ennui!

Then escape, any escape, escape at all costs, is a necessity:

Plonger au fond du gouffre, Enfer ou Ciel, qu'importe?
Au fond de l'inconnu pour trouver du nouveau!

It should not be thought that all creative artists who have been the victims of pathological boredom or melancholia have been makers of escapist art. Such men as Leopardi, Novalis, James Thomson, have tried to express realistically the mental distress which afflicted them. Their works may have escapist value for others but were not written by them as a reality-substitute. Contrariwise, works of art which were created from escapist motives may have other values for those by whom they are appreciated. Many men of creative ability have been inept in coping with the exigencies of practical life and have sought in artistic creation a means of escape from their practical deficiencies; yet the imaginative works which they have created have served as an inspiration to others in coping with the life of reality. To escapism in the artist we owe much of the extensive literature of Utopias, the idealistic literature of love, the imaginative transformation by which the strenuous and drab world we know

doth suffer a sea-change
Into something rich and strange.

Yet such art may provide others with ideals and inspiration to labour realistically to make the drab world less drab.

From the point of view of the psychoanalyst, escapism is retrograde

[1] Certain Revelationist or Transcendental art arises from this need. Lalo instances as typical of the religious or mystical attitude the painting of Puvis de Chavannes and of Maurice Denis and the music of Vincent d'Indy. One might add Odilon Redon and Paul Klee in painting, Scriabin and Delius in music.

and anti-social in principle. It absolves a man from the urge to cope with reality and the need to come to terms with the world as it is and enables him to live a factitious life in a world of illusion. It is the enthroning of phantasy in the seat of the real. This over-all judgement is outside the purview of an examination into the meaning of those comprehensive assessments of particular works of art which include an estimation of the psychological purpose which they serve. What is important to observe is that a work of art may fulfil different functions for different observers and the unconscious motives of the critic's appraisal may not be the same motives as moved the artist in its creation.

It is clear, therefore, that the values which works of art may possess as 'reality-substitutes' vary from person to person. It is clear, too, that they do not possess these values as works of art. There are many other ways of escaping reality besides immersion in art. Men have made a religion of art, but they have made a religion of gold, of science, of the theories of psychoanalysis. Bad art and pseudo-art can be no less valuable as a reality-substitute than good art. Hollywood films and romantic novelettes offer a more effective escape to many than fine works of creative art. The utility-function of escapism is not in any sense integral to artistic excellence. A work of art is neither a better nor a worse work of art because some people use it as a reality-substitute.

2. *Art as Compensation.* Different from the foregoing, though closely allied to it, is the compensatory function of art. We know that men habitually seek in their reading matter and their films vicarious experience of those things which life denies them. The criterion is contrast. Thus at the height of a campaign Napoleon wrote a congratulatory letter to the author of *Paul et Virginie.* Your stay-at-home reads tales of adventure for preference; the law-abiding citizen plumps for the hard-boiled novel of American gangsterism; the tweenie thrills at films of high romance. Society could not without disruption provide an outlet in the sober world of reality for all the unsatisfied and half-realized cravings of the little man, and art—or pseudo-art—serves the ulterior purpose of a safety-valve.

It is known, too, that a great part of the art which is produced is not an expression of the artist's ostensible personality but an outlet for the hidden and contrasting personality which modern psychology has taught us lurks in the deep subconscious beneath the superficial dispositions and impulses which erect a façade before the eyes of the world. Every man, it is said, has a 'shadow' personality, which is often the obverse of his ostensible character. And the study of the biographical material available in the case of artists shows that their artistic production more often than not springs from this compensatory self. Schiller wrote his *Ode to Joy* at a time when he was in the throes of despair and contemplating suicide. Beethoven's seventh and eighth symphonies were composed during years when his projects of marriage were frustrated, when he was in financial difficulties and had thoughts of suicide. Schubert, whose music speaks to everyone of a romantic sadness, was a gay and lively tavern-companion. John Field is described as the type of a modern Falstaff. Watteau was of a lugubrious and puritanical temperament. Emily Brontë was a repressed spinster. It is never possible to make deductions from artistic output to the mentality of the artist unless you already know a great deal about his ostensible personality from independent sources.

Nor is there any possible reason to believe that good art provides compensatory satisfaction either to the artist or to his public any more effectively than poor art. Products which spring from or appeal to the hidden unsatisfied cravings of a man's psyche are not better or worse in themselves than the uncomplicated expressions of his conscious thoughts and emotions.

3. *Art as Cathartic.* Contrasting with the compensatory function of art is its *homoeopathic* or *prophylactic* function. The normal social man has always a fairly extensive reservoir of untapped impulses and emotions, of which he may be fully conscious but to which he feels that it is not safe to allow an outlet in real life. The altruistic emotions are an important case in point. You cannot after all allow yourself to feel profound and genuine pity for those who have suffered catastrophe without at any rate trying to do something to remedy their case or else feeling distressed and guilty at your apathy. To offer practical help in all such cases would involve the individual in economically undesirable sacrifices, and if he allowed free play to pity whenever pity was called for, his economic resources would soon be exhausted. But to feel unhappy is unpleasant, and unhappiness at one's unwillingness to help effectively those whom one pities lowers the vitality and leads to depression. Therefore most men in practice keep a tight rein on their altruistic emotions, allowing themselves to feel just enough for indulgence but not enough to lead to remorse. So it is that in many people there are large reserves of altruistic emotion battened down and suppressed. And these unsatisfied emotions are served by the imaginary creations of art, where indulgence can be unleashed upon the illusory and fictitious situations which are presented. This is, baldly and unsympathetically but correctly stated, the interpretation which most critics have put upon Aristotle's doctrine of *catharsis*. Tragedy, said Aristotle, works for

the purgation of pity and terror. The impulses to pity and terror are bottled up by the conditions of practical life, say the critics, and fester like pus in the subconscious; tragedy pricks the boil and we return from it liberated of the dangerous infection.

It has often been claimed too that those artistic productions which display diabolism, sadism, erotic abnormalities and anti-social impulses may also provide an artificial and innocuous outlet to suppressed tendencies which else would prove damaging. If the one is true, the other may well be true. What is certain is that the cathartic value of any work of art must necessarily vary from individual to individual and will depend upon the nature and quality of the impulses which each man is required to suppress by the conditions of his life.

4. *Art as Reality.* A man may, finally, approach a work of art in the same attitude he takes up towards the realities of existence, treating it as a chunk of life like any other. The attitudes which the realists of art take up are as various as the attitudes they take up to life. There are those who, reading an artistic presentation of social abuses, oppression and misery, are influenced by it to do something to set matters right—as men were influenced by *Uncle Tom's Cabin* to condemn the iniquities of the slave trade. And there are schools of criticism which evaluate works of art in accordance with the direct results they are thought to have had for the betterment of man's condition. This is to treat art as one would treat a newspaper report or a conducted tour of inspection. There are others who, reading the story of the drabness and joylessness of the lives of others, or seeing it reproduced in pictures, are soothed to greater contentment with the monotony of their own lives by the thought that at least there are some whose case is worse than theirs. There are those again who in their reading and their pictures wish nothing better than to see mirrored there the personality they believe to be their own and the environment they regard as theirs, in order that so mirrored it may multiply in importance before the eyes of men. Others would satisfy their curiosity and learn of new scenes, new manners, new facts, extending their knowledge and their experience through the medium of artistic representation in order to save themselves the labour and effort required for first-hand observation. All these are ulterior uses which can be served by bad art as well as by good art and which are merely substitutes for other more complicated methods of achieving the same end.

We claim neither completeness nor originality for this analysis of some of the ulterior functions of works of art, but there can be no question that men do derive satisfactions such as these from works of art.

It is obvious too beyond question that none of these satisfactions is peculiar to works of art. There are other ways of dealing with starved altruistic impulses than attending a performance of Mr. Eugene O'Neill's plays, other ways of relieving suppressed sadistic impulses than reading the works of the Marquis de Sade or writing the *Cenci*. There are other ways of learning about the atrocities committed by the Nazis than by reading *The Wall*, other ways of enjoying relief from the horrors of Hounslow than by contemplating the pictures of Gainsborough in the National Gallery. All these ulterior functions are shared by works of art with things which are not works of art; all can be performed as well by bad art as by good art, as well by pseudo-art as by masterpieces. Indeed, the majority of people to-day, who have not what is considered good taste in art, find that those works of art which the critics judge to be best often make too great demands upon them, require too much concentration and attention. Their needs are satisfied equally well and with far less effort by ephemeral best-sellers, jazz tunes, sentimental or gangster films, magazine pictures. That these needs could also be satisfied by a selection among the works of genuine art if they would undergo the necessary discipline of training themselves in appreciation is a matter of just indifference to the majority. They do not want, or do not know that they want, that which true art alone can give; and that which they do want is purveyed more easily by the masquerading substitutes for art. Nor can criticism be held wholly guiltless for directing attention too lavishly upon these subsidiary functions of art and encouraging the neglect of those satisfactions which art alone can offer.

It is for these reasons we insist that consideration of the ulterior functions which a work of art may be induced to fulfil must be held separate from the assessment of its excellence as a work of art. Any work of art may give various and different satisfactions to various people and these may be different from the satisfaction which its creation gave to the artist. None of these satisfactions is illegitimate and none is integral to its excellence. The only satisfaction which is common to all in appreciation is the heightening of awareness which derives from intense 'synoptic' perception of it as an organic unity. We do not, of course, maintain that a critic may not estimate the social or human usefulness of works of art in accordance with his own standards of usefulness. He has as much right as another to do this and more right than most. But in doing this he is not writing as a critic but in some other rôle. And the reader is entitled to know what rôle he is assuming on every occasion and what are the standards of judgement he is applying.

Historical Criticism

Under the heading of historical criticism we shall include all attempts to 'explain' works of art in terms of their antecedent causes from purely artistic or literary influences to general sociological conditions.

Sociological criticism is generally thought to have originated with Vico, whose *La Scienza Nuova* was published in 1725. It was developed in Germany by Herder and was formalized by Taine, who claimed that all art can be fully explained as the resultant of three interacting conditions: the moment, the race and the milieu. To this Marx and Engels added a preponderant interest in economic conditions regarded as the basis of class distinctions. What in principle this type of criticism proposes to do is to explain why any work of art was made as it was made by showing all the various factors which influenced the mind of the artist and made him the sort of man he was. Now it is entirely certain that if knowledge of the psychology of the artist is not able to offer guidance to the critic in assessing the artistic merits of what he has produced, knowledge of the more remote causes which supposedly made the artist what he was will be unable to offer guidance to criticism either. And in fact no such guidance has ever resulted from historical or sociological criticism. The same general causes determine the good and the bad art of any age and no difference of historical or sociological causation has ever been adduced between works of art which are good and works of art which are bad. Not only does historical criticism afford no principle of assessment, but it is itself bound to assume assessments made by the critics on some other basis. The very selection of significant material by the historian implies a critical assessment of excellence. 'There are simply no data in literary history which are completely neutral "facts". Value judgements are implied in the very choice of materials: in the simple rudimentary distinction between books and literature, in the mere allocation of space to this or that author.'[1]

There is a kind of sociological criticism which assesses works of art not in terms of antecedent causes but in terms of the effects which they themselves have exercised upon men and society. In our own day this type of criticism is applied in practice by the régimes of totalitarian states for the suppression of art and artists whose probable effects upon society are judged to be contrary to the political ideology favoured by the régime. Such criticism, whether theoretical or applied, is an assessment of a particular group of ulterior functions which some works of art may serve; it

[1] René Wellek and Austin Warren, *Theory of Literature* (1949).

has no relevance to their excellence as works of art. A very bad work of art may exercise an influence which the adherents of a particular sociological or political theory hold to be desirable, while a very good work of art may appeal to few people and so have very little influence or its social influence may not be in keeping with a prevailing conception of social good. There are, too, very many works of art which have little discernible influence on society at all, which have neither a social nor a political implication, and yet they are judged by the critics to be good—or bad—works of art.

There is another conception of historical criticism which holds that the critic's task is not to assign causes, not to 'explain' works of art in terms of their antecedent conditions nor to assess them in terms of their social effects, but to collect and record the judgements made in each age about the art produced in that age and in preceding ages. He is, in effect, to produce a history of taste. The works of any age are not to be assessed according to the way in which men respond to them to-day but in terms of the response of critics who were contemporary with them. This mode of writing criticism was popular during the nineteenth century in Germany, where it was criticized by Ernst Troeltsch, and has proved to have considerable vitality. Now it may well be that if a critic is wedded to a subjective aesthetic of beauty, this is the most sensible and interesting mode of criticism open to him. For if he sets himself to arrange works of art in an order of merit on the basis of his own emotional response to them, what he says will be of interest primarily to himself and to other men only in so far as they happen to respond in the same way as he does. If, however, he investigates and records how in the past men have responded to the art of their day, he will be writing something which has general historic interest. It is as the difference between writing autobiography and writing specialized history. Yet writing of this sort cannot justly be called criticism. For a man who takes this path has decided to refrain from criticism and in its place to write a history of criticism in the past.

Exegetical Criticism

Under the heading of exegetical criticism we shall include textual emendation, the application of scholarship for the elucidation of symbolic significance and the investigation of artistic technique. Exegetical criticism has latterly tended to be held suspect owing to a recurrent tendency in universities and places of learning for scholarship to usurp the place of appreciation. The suspicion is not entirely ill-founded, but is exaggerated beyond measure by a tacit and false assumption that it is the function of the critic to communicate to others the results of appreciation. Appreciation cannot be communicated. It is the exercise of a skill which can be guided and trained by the critic where the capacity and the desire and will to develop it exist; but the exercise of this trained skill by the critic cannot take the place of a similar exercise of skill on the part of his readers. The scholar may be without the power to appreciate—by no means all scholars are without this power—and may yet contribute much that is essential to the critic. Scholarship is, indeed, an indispensable ancillary to criticism and can in no way be evicted. As Mr. R. P. Blackmur has rightly said: 'Upon scholarship all other forms of criticism depend, so long as they are criticism, in much the same way that architecture depends upon engineering.'[1]

Textual emendation is responsible for clearing the recordings of literary works of art from casual inaccuracies and restoring them to their original state. A literary recording, a printed poem or play, is not a work of art but is a perduring potentiality for the actualization of a work of art. An imperfect text is like a picture that is browned with varnish or grimed with filth: the work of art which it records cannot be perceived until the record has been purified. An appreciator, whether he be a critic or a member of the reading public, will necessarily actualize something other than the work of art which the artist invented if he reads an erroneous text. Textual emendation of music and literature, restoration of pictures, are therefore simply the removal of haphazard blemishes in the physical media by means of which the possibility for actualizing works of art is perpetuated.

The elucidation of symbolism becomes necessary because the referents of all conventional symbols such as words and of all semi-conventional symbols, being to some extent arbitrary, tend to change with time. Some words which were once common counters drop out of use and are no longer understood; others continue in use but with changed meanings. And to read a word with meanings other than those which it bore in the recording made by the artist is as deleterious to the actualization for the artist's work of art as reading a text in which words have been changed. Therefore the services of scholarship are needed to recover the meanings which words bore at the time when they were written just as the services of a dictionary are needed in order to read a language imperfectly understood. This work of elucidation goes much further, however, than the mere construction of a dictionary of past meanings of words, for words

[1] *The Double Agent* (1935).

and phrases have secondary and recondite meanings in addition to their primary meanings, meanings deriving from associations, from habits of thought and modes of feeling, from social customs and ways of behaviour which also change with the changing times. In all these cases the help of scholarship is needed in order to reconstruct the full symbolic implications of the language and to actualize the written record. As an example of this type of criticism one might compare the critical interpretations of George Herbert's words 'Man stole the fruit, but I must climbe the tree' proposed by Rosemond Tuve with that earlier proposed by William Empson. Professor Tuve[1] uses her wide learning in Christian iconography and symbolism to elucidate the probable implications which this verse bore for Herbert and for his readers—implications which the modern reader could not recover without such learning. Mr. Empson[2] uses his knowledge of the theories of psychoanalysis to draw inferences from the verse to the hidden psychology of Herbert. Professor Tuve directs attention upon the work of art and helps the modern reader to actualize the work which Herbert invented. Mr. Empson directs attention away from the work of art and endeavours to elucidate the psychology of the artist on the basis of an actualization of his written words which is very unlikely to have been that given to them either by Herbert or by the people for whom he wrote.

All poets tend to use language in a personal way and to create their own idiom, but in many the implications of their words can be recovered fairly easily from a full knowledge of the implications and associations which those words generally carried in their day. There are other writers, however, who use a private or esoteric symbolism which is much more difficult to recover, and in such cases an intimate knowledge of the writer's personal linguistic habits may be necessary in order to actualize his works of art. Blake is an outstanding example of a writer with a private mode of symbolism and the sort of exegesis which is necessary to facilitate the actualization of his works from his written records is that of S. Foster Damon in his *William Blake: His Philosophy and Symbols* (1924).

Much literature, particularly works of fiction whether written in prose or in verse, requires for its actualization a thorough knowledge of the manners and customs of the age in which it was written, without which the implications of the language are lost to a reader in a later age. Hence the contributions of the social historian are required to give 'background' for the interpretation of the literature of the past. But this use of history differs from the forms of historical criticism previously discussed; in this

[1] *A Reading of George Herbert* (1952).
[2] *Seven Types of Ambiguity* (1930).

case history is found necessary for the effective and accurate actualization of the work of art from the written record in which it is perpetuated. It is necessary—as scholarship in general is necessary—because recordings are by their nature partial and imperfect. For any written recording of a work of literary art embodies only a small nucleus of the symbolized meanings; the rest must be supplied by mutual consent between writer and reader, and as language and customs change the ordinary reader becomes less and less able to supply what was left for him to supply without the aid of the scholar.

Such elucidation is less necessary in the case of painting and still less necessary in the case of music, because the natural symbolization of painting is less liable to distortion through the influences of time while the semi-conventional symbols of painting and music play a much less important part.

An artist's technique is the manner in which he utilizes his medium in order to mould his material into an organic whole. It is the essence of his individuality and personality as an artist and is closely allied to what is known as style. Study of technique tends to focus attention upon the heart of the aesthetic object. It cannot take the place of appreciation—no criticism can do that. But more than any other mode of talking about an aesthetic object it encourages the reader to observe it as a single entity of inter-related and inter-acting parts, to see it synoptically and not discursively. And a small body of contemporary criticism is becoming more and more concerned with technique. It is the critics who are also poets who stand as the chief advocates of the view that 'poetry is idiom'[1] and encourage the detailed study of poetic language—and although poetry is more than idiom, this view and this mode of study are more likely than any other to deflect attention from the accidentals to what poetry is. It is the musicians who most vigorously encourage that form of musical criticism which concerns itself with technique rather than with emotions and literary associations. And although in painting and sculpture little attention has been given to technique apart from mechanical techniques of manipulating materials, there are signs that with the growing interest in form a serious study of artistic techniques may be on the way.

Impressionist Criticism

The Impressionist critic is one who, having contacted a work of art in appreciation, regards it as his function to communicate his experience to

[1] R. P. Blackmur. As Mallarmé warned Degas, who had ideas for poetry: 'Poetry is not made with ideas but with words.'

other men in written words.[1] In this country the Impressionist critic is apt to be regarded as the type of the 'exquisite' represented in the last generation by Arthur Symons, of whom Robert Hichens wrote in his Autobiography: 'He always seemed to me to be moving softly along the fringes of life, and mentally dwelling in days that were dead.' He is not always such. James Gibbons Hunecker in the United States was very much a man of his own age.

Impressionist criticism is impossible unless the critic is an artist, and if he is an artist it is doubtful whether this form of criticism is properly classed as criticism at all. However you think of a work of art, there is presumably only one correct way of actualizing it, of seeing it as it is and making it your own. And the work of art is identical with the set of impressions embodied or recorded in the physical medium which perpetuates it. The poem *is* the specific arrangement of words which we call the poem, and the picture *is* the specific arrangement of coloured surfaces which we call the picture. Appreciation is the process of becoming fully and completely aware of them as they are, as unified wholes. No other set of words can be substituted for the poem and no set of words can be substituted for a picture or a musical composition. All that the critic could do, therefore, if he wished to communicate to others his 'experience' in making appreciative contact with a work of art, would be to point in silence to the work of art he is criticizing. In fact, however, most Impressionist critics have set themselves to convey to others certain *indirect* effects exerted by works of art upon themselves. In the words of James Gibbons Hunecker, the critic must 'spill his soul' upon paper and 'humbly follow and register his own emotions aroused by a masterpiece'. The critic presumably regards his own emotions experienced in contact with works of art as being of interest and value to others, or he would not trouble to communicate them; and because he does so, he often becomes a very effective aesthetic propagandist. Since that which he wishes to communicate is too subtle to be communicated in scientific language without destroying its value, he is apt to become a belletrist and his critical writing if itself a minor form of literary art. But it is written about the critic and his emotions, not about the work of art. It is the material of autobiography

[1] See Alfonso Reyes: 'Impresión es el impacto que la obra causa en quien la recibe. . . . Es el efecto que nos causa la obra, efecto anterior a toda específica formulación literaria, y que puede o no alcanzarla o pretender a ella. Cuando la impresión se expresa fuera del arte, se confunde con las manifestaciones sociales de la opinión. Cuando adquiere una formulación literaria, es la crítica impresionista o, más brevemente, el impresionismo.' *El Deslinde* (1944).

rather than criticism. Yet although Impressionist criticism does little to direct the ignorant *how* to appreciate works of art, it does often succeed more than most in stimulating the interest to appreciate, and the importance of this is too often under-estimated by those critics who write primarily for scholars and students. For until a man is interested in the arts and their appreciation, he is unlikely to devote much precious time and energy to developing the necessary skills and aptitudes.

When Socrates was on trial for his life he described before his judges how he used to go to the poets and ask them to explain what their poems meant in order to prove to himself that they were wiser than he. But to his surprise he found that poets were unable to explain what their poems meant and that indeed 'almost all the bystanders could have spoken better about the poems than the men who made them'. From this discovery Socrates wrongly assumed that, although poetry contains much wisdom, poets do not compose their poems through wisdom but like seers and prophets speak truth by inspiration of the gods and utter glorious sayings without understanding what they mean. What we now understand and Socrates did not understand is that any work of literary art says something which cannot be said so exactly or so clearly in any other words, and it is for this reason that the poet can no more tell you what his poems mean by verbal paraphrase than the painter or the musician or the choreographer can tell you what his artistic creations mean. The poet, if not always the bystander and the critic, is inclined to realize this and refuses to substitute another set of words for the words of his poem in explanation of what it means. For if there had been any other set of words capable of expressing more clearly or more adequately the meaning he intended in his poem, he would have used that set of words instead of the words he did use. A poet who says something differently is saying something different just as a painter who paints something differently is painting a different thing. Nor can any set of words explain what a picture means, what a statue means or a dance or a song or a musical composition. Works of art cannot be described or explained. They must be perceived. And the most the critic can do is to offer hints and directions for focusing the attention in the very difficult art of exercising and cultivating the skill to perceive.

APPENDIX

A FURTHER word may be said about the dual aspect of literary art. There is a sense in which it is certainly true that all literature is a record of recollected or imagined experience, the word 'experience' being understood in its widest sense. And to be good literature the experience recorded must be selected and unified into an organic whole.

Now the musician composes organic wholes of musical sounds and thinks directly in elements of musical sound. He does not first recollect or notice certain natural sounds and then try to translate them so far as he can into musical sounds. His music is not both an organic whole of musical sounds and a natural symbol of an organic whole of natural sound. It is an organic whole of musical sound only. The case of the painter is somewhat different. Some painters by selective vision see natural colours and shapes as organic wholes, see landscapes, still-life groups or the bodies of human beings as 'pictures'. They then have to translate the pictures they see into pigments laid upon canvas. The translation can never be exact because pigment colours have a narrower range of luminosity and saturation than natural colours, because painted pictures have only two dimensions while nature has three dimensions, and so on. The problem of the artist who works in this way is to create an organic whole of pigmented surfaces which, although more limited in various dimensions, will in some way suggest the natural organic whole which his selective vision of natural objects has shown him. Other artists think directly in pigment colours and their problem is simply to create an organic whole of pigmented surfaces which may or may not symbolize certain natural objects. In both cases the picture which the artist creates must be an organic whole, and necessarily an organic whole of two-dimensional pigmented surfaces; whether or not it partially translates a natural organic whole seen by the artist prior to his invention of the picture is irrelevant to its excellence as pictorial art.

With the literary artist the case is still different. Since words, which are the material in which he works, are mere vocal noises and devoid of aesthetic significance when taken apart from their referents, he cannot enform them into organic constructs without regard for their symbolic significance and he must perforce mould his recollected or imagined experiences into organic unities by selective vision. If he does not do this, what he writes cannot become a work of art by any accession of verbal felicity. But having done this, he must then find language appropriate to express the organized experience he has achieved. For until it is verbalized experience is not literature but the material of literature only. It is in verbalization that literary art is born. It is not infrequent indeed that confirmed literary artists are afflicted by a sensation of discomfort before any unverbalized experience, as though the experience itself contained some hidden and recondite significance which could only be grasped when it had been clothed in language. Marcel Proust records this sensation very clearly when in Part I of *Swann's Way* he is describing his hyperaesthesia as an adolescent. 'Without definite attachment to anything, suddenly a roof, a gleam of sunlight reflected from a stone, the smell of a road would make me stop still, to enjoy the special pleasure which each of them gave me and also because they appeared to be concealing, beneath what my eyes could see, something which they invited me to approach and seize from them, but which, despite my efforts, I never managed to discover. As I felt that the mysterious object was to be found in them, I would stand there in front of them, motionless, gazing, breathing, endeavouring to penetrate with my mind beyond the thing seen or smelt.' He then goes on to tell how on one occasion an accident of circumstances induced him to write a description on the spot of the sight of three church steeples which had caused him this sensation. 'In ascertaining and noting the shape of their spires, the changes of aspect, the sunny warmth of their surfaces, I felt that I was not penetrating to the full depth of my impression, that something more lay behind that mobility, that luminosity, something which they seemed at once to contain and conceal.' But having composed a verbal equivalent of the occasion, he says: 'I found such a sense of happiness, I felt that it had so entirely relieved my mind of the obsession of the steeples, and of the mystery which they concealed, that, as though I myself were a hen and had just laid an egg, I began to sing at the top of my voice.'[1] The verbal description need not, it would appear, be artistically of very high calibre in order to bring relief to the writer—Proust's adolescent description, which he gives, was no more than competent. But when on such occasions the verbal expression is adequate, is itself a work of art enformed in organic unity of expression, it would seem to convey to the reader that 'special thrill' which is of the essence of poetry and

[1] From the translation of Mr. C. K. Scott-Moncrieff.

which, in the words of Mr. C. M. Bowra, is 'something powerful and overwhelming which gives not intellectual light but a sense of more abundant life'.[1] In the field of intellectual experience the same sort of thrill may be conveyed by verbal constructs which have what Gracián called *agudeza* or what was later called *wit*.

Experience, it is clear, may be aesthetically organized in either of two ways. On the one hand massive segments of experience may be unified by being selected and arranged in accordance with consistent and interacting attitudes of mind taken up towards it. Thus Gibbon's *Decline and Fall of the Roman Empire* is, as Professor Lascelles Abercrombie says of it, 'a magnificent pomp of events presented to the imagination'. It is unified in accordance with the outlook adopted and the attitudes taken up by the author, and it may be appreciated as a work of art without any thought of its historical accuracy. So, too, massive sections of recollected experience may be unified as in such autobiographical works as Goethe's *Wahrheit und Dichtung*, Casanova's *Memoires* or T. E. Shaw's *Seven Pillars of Wisdom*. Imagined experience may be unified in novels so diverse as *The Egoist* or *Sense and Sensibility*, or historical and imagined experience may be combined as in *Orlando*. In all such cases the unification is related to attitude and outlook, and if the achievement is literary art, the attitudes which unify the presented experience are inherent in the language in which the experience is presented, inseparable from it and not imposed externally upon it from without. But experience may also be organized more intimately when the elements of one moment of experience are so fused that they interpenetrate and intellect, sensation, feeling and impulse become as it were interchangeable. This is peculiarly the mode of lyrical poetry and is a mode of organization which has become the deliberate aspiration of much poetry in our own time. Thus Mr. Bowra says: 'The senses and the mind work so closely together and their interactions are so intricate that the poet cannot distinguish between them and must show how united they are in the moment of creative illumination. We might think that on such occasions the poet's thoughts merely take on a metaphorical dress, but that is to misunderstand him. The truth is rather that his sensations so penetrate his thoughts that the two constitute a single state.' It is partly because of this fusion of the elements of experience that Mr. T. S. Eliot can say: 'The poet who "thinks" is merely the poet who can express the emotional equivalent of thought.'

If it is necessary to draw a distinction between poetry and prose—that is between poetic art and prose art, not between prose and verse—I

[1] *The Creative Experiment* (1949).

believe that the most fruitful mode of discrimination would be to follow these two modes of the organization of experience and the appropriate verbalization of each. The verbalization of a 'fused' moment of experience is the culmination of literary art. But it is probably incapable of being sustained over large sweeps and massive ranges of experience. And when it is most sustained—as, for example, in the writing of Lautréamont and some of the writing of Blake—the unification of the whole range of presented experience often seems to lag behind the fused unity of the individual moments.

BIBLIOGRAPHY

Abercrombie, Lascelles. *An Essay towards a Theory of Art* (1922).
   The Theory of Poetry (1924).
   The Idea of Great Poetry (1925).
Alexander, S. *Beauty and Other Forms of Value* (1933).
Allen, Walter. *Writers on Writing* (1948).
Apollinaire, Guillaume. *The Cubist Painters* (1949).
Aristotle. *Poetics*.
   Rhetoric.
Arnold, Matthew. *Essays in Criticism* (First Series, 1865).
   Essays in Criticism (Second Series, 1888).
Atkins, J. W. H. *English Literary Criticism: The Medieval Phase* (1943).
   English Literary Criticism: The Renascence (1947).
   English Literary Criticism: 17th and 18th Centuries (1951).
Auerbach, Eric. *Mimesis. Dargestellte Wirklichkeit in der abendlandischen Literatur*
   (1946; Eng. Trans. 1953).

Bach, Carl Philipp Emanuel. *Essay on the True Art of Playing Keyboard Instruments*
   (1753. Eng. Trans. 1949).
Bahle, J. *Eingebung und Ton im musikalischen Schaffen* (1939).
Baldwin, Charles Sears. *Medieval Rhetoric and Poetic* (1928).
   The Renaissance Literary Theory and Practice (1939).
Barea, Arturo. *Lorca, The Poet and his People* (Eng. Trans. 1944).
Barnes, A. C. *The Art of Painting* (1937).
Barnes, A. C., and De Mazia, Violette. *The Art of Henri Matisse* (1933).
   The Art of Renoir (1935).
   The Art of Cézanne (1939).
Baudelaire, Charles. *L'Art romantique* (1899).
Bell, Clive. *Art* (1914).
   Since Cézanne (1922).
   Enjoying Pictures (1934).
Benda, Julien. *Du Poétique* (1946).
Berenson, Bernhard. *The Italian Painters of the Renaissance* (1930).
   Aesthetics and History (1950).
Binyon, Laurence. *The Flight of the Dragon. An Essay on the Theory and Practice*
   of Art in China and Japan (1911).
Birkhoff, George D. *Aesthetic Measure* (1933).
Blackmur, Richard P. *The Double Agent* (1935).
Blom, Eric. *The Limitations of Music* (1928).
Blunt, Anthony. *England and the Mediterranean Tradition* (1945).
Borodin, George. *Invitation to the Ballet* (1950).

BIBLIOGRAPHY

Bosanquet, Bernard. *The History of Aesthetic* (1892).
Three Lectures on Aesthetics (1915).
Bowra, C. M. *The Heritage of Symbolism* (1943).
The Creative Experiment (1949).
Bradley, A. C. *Oxford Lectures on Poetry* (1901).
Breton, André. *Manifeste du Surréalisme* (1924).
Le Surréalisme et la peinture (1945).
Broad, C. D. *Examination of McTaggart's Philosophy* (1933).
Brooks, Cleanth. *The Well Wrought Urn* (1949).
Brooks, Cleanth, and Warren, Robert Penn. *Fundamentals of Good Writing* (1952).
Brunetière, Ferdinand, *Évolution des genres dans l'histoire de la littérature* (1890).
Buermeyer, L. *The Aesthetic Experience* (1924).
Bukofzer, Manfred. *Music in the Baroque Era* (1948).
Studies in Medieval and Renaissance Music (1951).
Bunim, Mariam Schild. *Space in Medieval Painting and the Forerunners of Perspective* (1940).
Burke, Edmund. *A Philosophical Enquiry into the Origin of our Ideas of the Sublime and the Beautiful* (1756).
Burke, Kenneth. *Counter-Statement* (1931).

Carritt, E. F. *The Theory of Beauty* (1914).
Philosophies of Beauty (1930).
Centeno, Augusto (ed.). *The Intent of the Artist* (1941).
Chambers, F. P. *The History of Taste* (1932).
Cheney, Sheldon. *A World History of Art* (1938).
Expressionism in Art (1948).
Chevreul, Michel-Eugène. *The Principles of Harmony and Contrast in Colours* (1890).
Church, R. W. *An Essay on Critical Appreciation* (1938).
Cicero. *De Oratore.*
Clausen, Sir George. *Aims and Ideals in Art* (1906).
Closs, Hannah Priebsch. *Art and Life* (1930).
Cocteau, Jean. *Essai de critique indirecte* (1932).
Coleridge, Samuel Taylor. *Biographia Literaria* (1817).
Collingwood, R. G. *Outline of a Philosophy of Art* (1925).
The Principles of Art (1938).
Combarieu, Jules. *Music, its Laws and Evolution* (1938).
Constable, W. G. *Art History and Connoisseurship* (1938).
Cook, Theodore. *The Curves of Life* (1900).
Coomaraswamy, A. K. *The Dance of Siwa* (1918).
The Transformation of Nature in Art (1934).
Figures of Speech (1946).
Cortissoz, Royal. *Personalities in Art* (1925).

Craven, Thomas. *Modern Art* (1934).
Croce, Benedetto. *Aesthetic* (Eng. Trans. 1909).
 Breviario (Eng. Trans. 1921).
 The Essence of Aesthetic (Eng. Trans. 1921).
 Goethe (Eng. Trans. 1923).
Cruse, Amy. *The Victorians and their Books* (1930).
 After the Victorians (1938).

Davies, Hugh Sykes. *The Poets and their Critics* (1943).
Delacroix, Eugène. *Journal* (1823-63).
Delacroix, Henri. *Psychologie de l'Art* (1927).
Denis, Maurice. *Théories* (1913).
Denniston, J. D. *Greek Literary Criticism* (1924).
Dewey, John. *Art as Experience* (1934).
Dingle, Herbert. *Science and Literary Criticism* (1949).
Dobrée, Bonamy. *Modern Prose Style* (1934).
Doran, Madelaine. *Endeavours of Art* (1954).
Downey, June E. *Creative Imagination* (1928).
Drew, Elizabeth. *The Modern Novel* (1926).
Dryden, John. *Essay of Dramatic Poesy* (1668).
Ducasse, C. J. *The Philosophy of Art* (1929).
Dukas, Paul. *Sur la Musique* (1948).
Dyson, George. *The Progress of Music* (1932).

Eastman, Max. *The Literary Mind: Its Place in an Age of Science* (1931).
Edwards, A. Trystan. *Good and Bad Manners in Architecture* (1924).
Eliot, T. S. *Selected Essays* (1932).
 The Sacred Wood (1932).
 The Use of Poetry and the Use of Criticism (1933).
Empson, William. *Seven Types of Ambiguity* (1930).
 The Structure of Complex Words (1951).
Evans, J. *Taste and Temperament* (1939).
Evans, R. M. *An Introduction to Color* (1948).

Faure, Élie. *Histoire de l'Art* (1921).
 L'Esprit des Formes (1927).
Fechner, Gustav Theodor. *Vorschule der Aesthetik* (1876).
Feibleman, James K. *Aesthetics* (1950).
Fenellosa, Ernest F. *Epochs of Chinese and Japanese Art* (1912).
Ferguson, Donald N. *A History of Musical Thought* (1948).
Focillon, Henri. *La Peinture aux xixe et xxe siècles* (1927).
 Vie des Formes (1947).
Fontaine, A. *Les Doctrines d'art en France* (1909).
Forster, E. M. *Aspects of the Novel* (1927).

BIBLIOGRAPHY

Fowlie, Wallace. *Mallarmé* (1953).
Friedlander, Max J. *Landscape: Portrait: Still Life* (1949).
Fromentin, E. *Maîtres d'autrefois* (1876).
Fry, Sir Roger. *Vision and Design* (1924).
   Transformations (1926).
   Characteristics of French Art (1932).
   Last Lectures (1939).

Gascoyne, David. *Surrealism* (1935).
Gauss, Charles E. *Aesthetic Theories of French Artists* (1949).
Gentile, Giovanni. *La Filosofia dell' Arte* (1931).
Gerard, Alexander. *An Essay on Genius* (1774).
Ghiselin, Brewster (ed.). *The Creative Process* (1952).
Ghyka, M. C. *Esthétique des proportions dans la nature et dans les arts* (1929).
Gilbert, Allan (ed.). *Literary Criticism: Plato to Dryden* (1940).
Gilbert, Katherine, and Kuhn, Helmut. *A History of Aesthetics* (1939).
Gilby, Thomas. *Poetic Experience* (1935).
Gill, Eric. *Art-Nonsense and other Essays* (1929).
   Art (1934).
Glasgow, Edwin. *The Painter's Eye* (1936).
Gleizes, Albert, and Metzinger, Jean. *Du Cubisme* (1912).
Goethe, Johann Wolfgang von. *Poetry and Truth* (Eng. Trans. 1911).
Goldwater, Robert, and Treves, Marco (eds.). *Artists on Art* (1945).
Goodhart-Rendel, H. S. *Fine Art* (1934).
Gracián y Morales, Baltasar. *Agudeza y Arte de Ingenio* (1641).
Greene, Theodore Meyer. *The Arts and the Art of Criticism* (1943).
Groenewegen-Frankfort, H. A. *Arrest and Movement* (1951).
Guillaume, Paul. *La Psychologie de la Forme* (1932).
Gurney, Edmund. *The Power of Sound* (1880).

Hall, Vernon. *Renaissance Literary Criticism* (1945).
Hambidge, Jay. *Dynamic Symmetry* (1920).
Hanslick, E. *The Beautiful in Music* (Eng. Trans. 1891).
Harding, Rosamund E. M. *An Anatomy of Inspiration* (1948).
Hartridge, H. *Colours and How We See Them* (1949).
Hauser, A. *The Social History of Art* (1951).
Havell, E. B. *Ideals of Indian Art* (1911).
Hegel, Georg Wilhelm Friedrich. *The Philosophy of Fine Art* (Eng. Trans. 1920).
Hendy, Philip. *Spanish Painting* (1946).
Henn, T. R. *The Lonely Tower* (1950).
Heye, Bernard C. *New Bearings in Aesthetics and Art Criticism* (1943).
Hildebrand, A. *The Problem of Form in Painting and Sculpture* (1907).
Hirn, Yrjö. *The Origin of Art* (1900).
Hogarth, W. *Analysis of Beauty* (1753).

Holloway, John.   *The Victorian Sage* (1953).

Hopkinson, Vivian C.   *Spires of Form: A Study of Emerson's Aesthetic Theory* (1951).

Horace.   *De Arte Poetica.*

Hospers, John.   *Meaning and Truth in the Arts* (1946).

Housman, A. E.   *The Name and Nature of Poetry* (1933).

Howes, Frank.   *The Borderline of Music and Psychology* (1926).
  Man, Mind and Music (1948).

Hughes, A. M. D.   *The Nascent Mind of Shelley* (1947).

Hughes, E. R.   *The Art of Letters, Lu Chi's 'Wen Fu',* A.D. 302 (1951).

Hulme, T. E.   *Speculations* (1924).

Hussey, C.   *The Picturesque* (1927).

Hutcheson, Francis.   *An Enquiry into the Original of our Ideas of Beauty and Virtue* (1725.)

Jaeger, F. M.   *Principles of Symmetry* (1917).

James, Henry.   *The Art of the Novel* (1935).

Jeans, J. H.   *Science and Music* (1937).

Johnson, Martin.   *Art and Scientific Thought* (1944).

Johnson, Philip.   *Machine Art* (1934).

Jonson, Benjamin.   *Timber* (1640).

Jordan, E.   *The Aesthetic Object* (1937).

Kandinsky, Wassily.   *The Art of Spiritual Harmony* (Eng. Trans. 1914).

Kant, Immanuel.   *Critique of the Aesthetic Judgement* (Eng. Trans., Meredith, 1911).

Katz, D.   *The World of Colour* (1935).

Klee, Paul.   *On Modern Art* (1948).

Koehler, W.   *Gestalt Psychology* (1929).

Koffka, K.   *Principles of Gestalt Psychology* (1935).

Lalo, Charles.   *L'Esthétique experimentale contemporaine* (1906).
  Esquisse d'une esthétique musicale scientifique (1908).
  L'Art loin de la Vie (1939).

Lambert, Constant.   *Music Ho!* (1934).

Langer, Susanne K.   *Philosophy in a New Key* (1941).

Langfeld, S. S.   *The Aesthetic Attitude* (1920).

Leavis, F. R.   *Revaluation* (1936).
  The Common Pursuit (1952).

Leavis, Q. D.   *Fiction and the Reading Public* (1932).

Lee, Vernon.   *The Beautiful* (1913).
  The Handling of Words (1923).

Lemaitre, Georges.   *From Cubism to Surrealism in French Literature* (1941).

Lessing, Gotthold Ephraim.   *Laocoon* (1766).

Lewis, C. Day. *The Poetic Image* (1947).
Lewis, Wyndham. *Time and the Western Man* (1927).
  Wyndham Lewis the Artist (1939).
  The Writer and the Absolute (1952).
Lifar, Serge. *Ballet Traditional to Modern* (1938).
Lipps, Theodor. *Aesthetic* (1906).
Longinus. *On the Sublime.*
Luckiesh, M. *Color and its Appreciation* (1915).
Lukacs, George. *Studies in European Realism* (Eng. Trans. 1950).
Lund, F. M. *Ad Quadratum* (1921).

McAlpin, Colin. *Hermaia: A Study in Comparative Esthetics* (1915).
Mack, Ernst. *Symmetry* (Eng. Trans. 1895).
Mack, Gerstle. *Paul Cézanne* (1935).
Mackail, J. W. *Lectures on Poetry* (1911).
McTaggart, J. M. E. *Nature of Existence* (1921-27).
Mâle, Émile. *L'Art religieux du xiiie siècle en France* (1910).
  L'Art religieux de la fin du Moyen Âge en France (1908).
  L'Art allemand et l'Art français du Moyen Âge (1917).
Mansell, James L. *The Psychology of Music* (1937).
Marangoni, Matteo. *The Art of Seeing Art* (Eng. Trans. 1951).
Maritain, J. *Art and Scholasticism* (Eng. Trans. 1930).
  Redeeming the Time (Eng. Trans. 1943).
Marshall, H. R. *The Beautiful* (1934).
Mathiesen, F. O. *The Achievement of T. S. Eliot* (1947).
Matisse, Henri. *Notes d'un peintre* (1908).
Matsumoto, Matataro. *Psychology of Aesthetic Appreciation of Pictorial Arts* (1926).
Mauclaire, Camille. *L'Impressionisme* (1904).
Mauron, Charles. *Aesthetics and Psychology* (Eng. Trans. 1935).
Mendilow, A. A. *Time and the Novel* (1952).
Merrifield, M. P. *Original Treatises from the xii to the xviii Centuries on the Arts of Painting* (1849).
Mondrian, Piet. *Néo-Plasticisme* (1920).
  Plastic Art and Pure Plastic Art (1928).
Moos, Paul. *Die Philosophie der Musik* (1922).
More, Paul Elmer. *Shelburne Essays* (1904).
Morice, Charles. *La Littérature de tout à l'heure* (1899).
Moulton, R. G. *Shakespeare as a Dramatic Artist* (1885).
Murray, G. Gilbert A. *Essays and Addresses* (1921).
Murry, John Middleton. *Countries of the Mind* (1922).
  The Problem of Style (1922).
  Discoveries (1924).
Mursell, James L. *The Psychology of Music* (1937).

BIBLIOGRAPHY

Newman, Ernest. *Musical Studies* (1910).
Newman, John Henry. *Essays Critical and Historical* (1871).

Ogden, C. K., and Richards, I. A. *The Meaning of Meaning* (1923).
Ogden, C. K., Richards, I. A., and Wood, James. *Foundations of Aesthetics* (1925).
Okakura-Kakuzo. *The Ideals of the East* (1904).
O'Neill, F. R. *The Social Value of Art* (1939).
Osborne, H. *Foundations of the Philosophy of Value* (1933).
  A Mirror of Charactery (1935).
  Theory of Beauty (1952).
Ozenfant, A. *Foundations of Modern Art* (Eng. Trans. 1931).

Parker, DeWitt. *The Principles of Aesthetics* (1920).
  The Analysis of Art (1926).
Parry, C. H. H. *The Art of Music* (1893).
Pascal, Roy. *The German Sturm und Drang* (1953).
Pater, Walter H. *Studies in the History of the Renaissance* (1873).
  Appreciations (1889).
Pepper, Stephen C. *The Basis of Criticism in the Arts* (1946).
Perry, R. B. *General Theory of Value* (1926).
  Realms of Value (1954).
Pevsner, Nikolaus. *Pioneers of the Modern Movement* (1936).
Peyre, Henri. *Writers and their Critics* (1944).
Piper, John. *British Romantic Artists* (1942).
Plekhanov, G. V. *Art and Social Life* (1953).
Pole, William. *The Philosophy of Music* (1924).
Pollock, Thomas Clark. *The Nature of Literature* (1942).
Pope, A. *Introduction to Drawing and Painting* (1931).
  The Language of Drawing and Painting (1949).
Pottle, Frederick A. *The Idiom of Poetry* (1941).
Pound, Ezra. *A.B.C. of Reading* (1934).
  Make it New (1934).
  Guide to Kulchur (1952).
  The Spirit of Romance (1952).
  Literary Essays (1954).
Power, J. W. *Éléments de la Construction Picturale* (1932).
Prall, D. W. *Esthetic Analysis* (1936).
Price, Uvedale. *Essays on the Picturesque* (1810).
Proudhon, P. J. *Du principe de l'Art* (1865).
Prout, Ebenezer. *Musical Form* (1893).
Purser, J. W. R. *Art and Truth* (1937).
Puttenham, Richard. *Arte of English Poesie* (1589).

Quintilian. *Institutio Oratoria.*

Rader, Melvin. *A Modern Book of Aesthetics* (1933).
Raphael, Max. *Proudhon, Marx, Picasso* (1933).
Read, Sir Herbert. *Reason and Romanticism* (1926).
  Art Now (1933).
  Unit One (ed.) (1934).
  Art and Industry (1934).
  Surrealism (ed.) (1936).
  Collected Essays in Literary Criticism (1951).
  The Philosophy of Modern Art (1952).
Redfield, John. *Music: A Science and an Art* (1930).
Reid, L. A. *A Study in Aesthetics* (1931).
Révész, G. *Introduction to the Psychology of Music* (Eng. Trans. 1953).
Reyes, Alfonso. *El Deslinde: Prolegómenos a la Teoría Literaria* (1944).
Reynolds, Sir Joshua. *Fifteen Discourses* (1769-91).
Ribot, T. A. *Essay on the Creative Imagination* (1906).
Richards, I. A. *The Principles of Literary Criticism* (1925).
  Practical Criticism (1929).
  The Philosophy of Rhetoric (1936).
Richardson, A. E., and Corfiato, H. O. *The Art of Architecture* (1938).
Robertson, J. G. *Genesis of Romantic Theory* (1923).
Rodin, A. *Art* (1912).
Rood, O. N. *Modern Chromatics with Applications to Art and Industry* (1879).
Ross, D. W. *A Theory of Pure Design* (1907).
Ross, W. D. *Aristotle* (1923).
Rufer, Josef. *Composition with Twelve Notes* (Eng. Trans. 1954).
Ruskin, John. *Modern Painters* (1843-60).
  Seven Lamps of Architecture (1849).
  Lectures on Art (1870).

Sackville-West, Edward. *Inclinations* (1949).
Saintsbury, G. E. B. *A History of Criticism* (1900).
Santayana, George. *The Sense of Beauty* (1896).
  Reason in Art (1905).
Sartre, Jean-Paul. *The Psychology of Imagination* (Eng. Trans. 1948).
  Baudelaire (Eng. Trans. 1949).
  What is Literature? (Eng. Trans. 1950).
Scarfe, Francis. *The Art of Paul Valéry* (1954).
Schelling, F. W. J. *Relation of the Plastic Arts to Nature* (Eng. Trans. 1809).
Schneider, Elizabeth. *The Aesthetics of William Hazlitt* (1933).
Schoen, Max. *The Effects of Music* (1927).
  The Beautiful in Music (1928).
Schoenberg, A. *Theory of Harmony* (1948).
  Style and Idea (1950).
Schücking, Levin L. *The Sociology of Literary Taste* (Eng. Trans. 1944).

Schumann, Robert. *Music and Musicians* (1877).

Scott-James, R. A. *The Making of Literature* (1928).

Seashore, Carl E. *Psychology of Music* (1938).

Selincourt, O. de. *Art and Morality* (1935).

Sencourt, Robert. *Consecration of Genius* (1947).

Sessions, Roger. *The Musical Experience* (1950).

Severini, Gino. *Du Cubisme au Classicisme* (1921).

Sewell, A. *Physiology of Beauty* (1931).

Shelley, Percy Bysshe. *Defence of Poetry* (1821).

Shumaker, Wayne. *Elements of Critical Theory* (1952).

Sickert, W. R. *A Free House!* (1947).

Sidney, Sir Philip. *Apologie for Poetrie* (1595).

Smith, G. Gregory (ed.). *Elizabethan Critical Essays* (1904).

Smith, Logan Pearsall. *Reperusals and Re-Collections* (1936).

Souriau, Paul. *Le beauté rationnelle* (1904).

Spearman, C. *Creative Mind* (1930).

Spender, Stephen. *The Destructive Element* (1935).
  The Creative Element (1953).

Stace, W. T. *The Meaning of Beauty* (1929).

Stauffer, Donald A. (ed.). *The Intent of the Critic* (1941).
  The Theory of Poetry (1946).

Steegman, John. *The Rule of Taste* (1936).
  The Consort of Taste (1950).

Stein, Leo. *A.B.C. of Aesthetics* (1935).

Sterling, Charles. *Les Primitifs* (1938).
  La Nature Morte (1950).

Stokes, Adrian. *Colour and Form* (1937).
  Art and Science (1949).

Stravinsky, Igor. *An Autobiography* (1936).
  Poétique musicale (1942).

Symons, Arthur. *Studies in Seven Arts* (1906).
  From Toulouse-Lautrec to Rodin (1929).

Taine, Hippolyte. *Philosophy of Art* (1875).

Tamayo, Franz. *Horacio y el Arte Lírico* (1915).

Thaler, Alwin. *Shakespeare and Sir Philip Sidney* (1947).

Thompson, Francis. *Shelley* (1889).

Thorpe, Clarence DeWitt. *The Aesthetic Theory of Thomas Hobbes* (1940).

Tillotson, Geoffrey. *Essays in Criticism and Research* (1942).
  Criticism and the Nineteenth Century (1951).

Tolstoi, Leo. *What is Art?* (1898).

Tovey, D. F. *Essays and Lectures on Music* (1949).

Trilling, Lionel. *The Liberal Imagination* (1948).

Tuve, Rosemond. *Elizabethan and Metaphysical Imagery* (1947).
A Reading of George Herbert (1952).

Underwood, Eric. *A Short History of English Painting* (1933).
Underwood, Leon. *Art for Heaven's Sake* (1934).

Valverde, J. M. *Estudios sobre la Palabra Poética* (1952).
Vasari, Giorgio. *Lives of the Most Eminent Painters, Sculptors and Architects* (1568.
Eng. Trans., 1912).
Vega, Lope de. *El arte nuevo de hacer comedias* (1609).
Venturi, Lionello. *Cézanne* (1936).
History of Art Criticism (Eng. Trans. 1936).
Modern Painters (Eng. Trans. 1947).
Impressionists and Symbolists (Eng. Trans. 1950).
Véron, Eugène. *L'Esthétique* (1882).
Vitruvius. *De Architectura.*
Vivante, Leone. *English Poetry* (Eng. Trans. 1950).

Watkin, E. I. *A Philosophy of Form* (1935).
Webbe, Wm. *A Discourse of English Poetry* (1586).
Wellek, René, and Warren, Austin. *Theory of Literature* (1949).
Weyl, Hermann. *Symmetry* (1952).
Whistler, J. A. M. *The Gentle Art of Making Enemies* (1890).
Wilenski, R. H. *The Modern Movement in Art* (1927).
The Meaning of Modern Sculpture (1932).
The Study of Art (1934).
Ruskin (1937).
Modern French Painting (1940).
Williams, Orlo. *Contemporary Criticism of Literature* (1924).
Wilson, Edmund. *Axel's Castle* (1932).
The Wound and the Bow (1942).
The Triple Thinkers (1952).
Woelfflin, H. *Principles of Art History* (Eng. Trans. 1932).
Gedanken zur Kunstgeschichte (1940).
Wolff, Georg Ernst. *Grundlagen einer autonomen Musikästhetik* (1927).
Worringer, Wilhelm. *Form in Gothic* (Eng. Trans. 1927).
Abstraction and Empathy (Eng. Trans. 1953).

Yeats, W. B. *Autobiography* (1926).

Zehring, A. *The Basis of Musical Pleasure* (1910).
Ziegenfuss, W. *Die phaenomenologische Aesthetik* (1927).
Zola, Émile. *The Experimental Novel* (1894).

INDEX OF NAMES